SMALL BUSINESS IN AMERICAN LIFE

SMALL BUSINESS
IN
AMERICAN LIFE

EDITED BY
STUART W. BRUCHEY

1980
Columbia University Press
New York

Stuart W. Bruchey is Allan Nevins Professor of
American Economic History, Columbia University

Library of Congress Cataloging in Publication Data

Main entry under title:
Small business in American life.

1. Small business—United States—History—Case
studies. 2. Industry—Social aspects—United States—
History—Case studies. 3. United States—Industries—
History—Case studies. 4. United States—Social condi-
tions—Case studies. I. Bruchey, Stuart Weems.
HD2346.U5S58   338.6'42'0973   80-10994
ISBN 0-231-04872-6

Columbia University Press
New York   Guildford, Surrey

To
THOMAS C. COCHRAN
for showing the way

CONTENTS

ACKNOWLEDGMENTS

The seventeen essays in this volume were written at the editor's invitation for the specific purpose of enabling him to compose the "American Report" to the 1980 convention in Bucharest, Romania of the International Commission on the History of Social Movements and Social Structures. The editor's Introduction is that Report. It is one of twenty-eight national reports written by scholars in twenty-eight countries in response to the Commission's inquiry into the impact of industrialization on small business from the late eighteenth century to the present. The entire enterprise was supported by the financial and other resources of the Centre Nationale de la Recherche Scientifique in Paris. The present editor wishes to express his warm appreciation not only to the C.N.R.S. but also to the Secretary General of the International Commission, Mme. Denise Fauvel-Rouif, for her generous and unfailing support. He also acknowledges with warm thanks the financial aid of Columbia University and the interest, cooperation, and support of the project by Dr. Joel Colton, American representative of the International Commission and Director of Humanities for the Rockefeller Foundation. Last, but not least, he wishes to thank Bernard Gronert, Executive Editor of the Columbia University Press, for his understanding aid on this, as well as many other scholarly projects, over the years.

SMALL BUSINESS IN AMERICAN LIFE

INTRODUCTION

A SUMMARY VIEW OF SMALL
BUSINESS AND AMERICAN LIFE

Stuart Bruchey

THESE essays on the history of small business in the United States have been written by scholars possessing specialized knowledge of one aspect or another of the subject. Varying in length and chronology, they make no pretense at complete coverage. Some readers may regret the decision to exclude farmers from formal presentation. Surely tillers of the soil have been small businessmen throughout much of the American past! They have indeed; but they have also been more than that. In many ways, they have formed special groups with special problems. No book, no limited number of essays, can do everything. The emphasis here is upon artisans, mechanics, small manufacturers, small bankers, and retail storekeepers. And upon the reciprocal influence of small business on other areas of economic, social, and cultural life.

For small business not only belonged to every sector of the economy, it also reached out to affect the degree of social mobility, urban power structures, the legal system, and the formation of important values shared by Americans (to say nothing of its effects on labor relations, technological innovation, and big business itself). In a word, small business has formed an integral part of American life. In early times, before the onset of rapid industrial change, it dominated the economy. While its economic position is far less prominent in most sectors today, it retains a surprising degree of importance in the growing service sector and also serves as an adjunct to large manufacturing enterprises. Its place among American values seems scarcely eroded by economic and technological change. As Richard Sylla observes in one of the essays in this collection, "A small-business ideology has been present throughout American history."

Perhaps this ideological persistence owes much to the way in which the status of businessman, as Rowland Berthoff suggests, seems to "keep in balance what would otherwise be two incongruous ideals: stable, self-reliant personal independence on the one hand and upward-mobile, dynamic entrepreneurship on the other." In his essay "Small Business in the American Dream," Berthoff traces the origins of the ideology to sources deep in the European past. From the behavior of English peasant villagers during and after the High Middle Ages may be inferred a "practical balance between the social values of personal independence and communal equality"—especially equality of opportunity to rise in the social and economic scale. When these values were threatened by the great enclosure movement that took place between 1540 and 1640, villagers often resisted that movement and sought to preserve the commons and open fields. It was different though in the New World colonized by the English in the seventeenth and eighteenth centuries: since the distance in wealth and status between self-sufficient, independent farmers and artisans on the one hand, and gentry and merchants on the other, was not great by European standards, the former came to look upon the countinghouse and plantation as "only a larger and not unattainable version of their own farm or shop." Undoubtedly frontiers of opportunity that only slowly receded did much to shore up these confident expectations.

The American Revolution "turned peasant self-sufficiency into an explicitly republican ideal of personal independence." Tracing the sources of this ideal in the writings of Machiavelli and Harrington and in the formulations of English party politics in the eighteenth century, Berthoff shows how the real business interests of farmers, both English and American, together with the exigencies of Revolutionary polemics, created a national ideology that was not simply agrarian but broadly republican in its origins.

This ideology served to rationalize vast inequalities in wealth in the nineteenth century, so long as the latter resulted from entrepreneurial response to the developing economy. Success was attributed to "exemplary devotion to the common civic virtues of 'sobriety, prudence, economy, and industry.' " Special privilege, however, especially when embedded in the legal system, was hotly opposed in the name of equality of rights, duties, and responsibilities. Not to be outdone, defenders of the business corporation sought to identify it with the independent citizen of the republican ideal. Passage of general incorporation laws helped reassure doubters that the business corporation represented "not privilege but equal freedom." That "comfortable consensus," Berthoff writes, blunted the impact of the rapid economic development that took place between the 1840s and 1880s. Even political conservatives now accepted the view that the independent farmer and the businessman "belonged to one single, universal category."

In the remaining pages of his skillful analysis, Berthoff shows the utility of the national ideology to one group after another engaged in a continuing struggle for the support of public opinion. When farmers felt oppressed by banks and railroads, for example, they pictured themselves as "simple yeomen defending their traditional independence." For petroleum producers and refiners bested by Standard Oil the cause was "republican institutions." Not till the end of the nineteenth century, however, did a distinctive "small-business ethic" begin to be defined. The enemy, it then became increasingly clear, was not mere size. Rather, it was the use of secret and unfair business tactics, or legal privilege (in the form of protective tariffs, for example). Once again, as in the years of the Jacksonian Democracy, equality of opportunity emerged as the touchstone of commitment to the ancient ideology. Small business wanted an equal chance to become big business.

And so it has continued. The urge to be an entrepreneur, to be one's own boss, is still virtually universal. Voices continue today to trumpet the nineteenth century "medley of stable independence and dynamic entrepreneurship." Even huge conglomerates "regularly advertise their similarity to small business: tiny beginnings, sometime in the past; ownership 'by the people,' that is, by individual stockholders; and the increased autonomy permitted, in recent years, to managers of their decentralized units." Yet corporate executives seem genuinely convinced that they are practicing "the traditional 'American way.' " They prefer the old ideology of self-respect and fulfillment, the lonely struggle in which initiative and hard work pay off, to organized group effort, especially on the part of government. Big business itself is said to recognize the value of such views: "The current prescription for corporate managers and workingmen alike is 'individuation' . . . . as a practical application of the old ideal." Small businessmen are folk heroes in America. But this is "not surprising in a republic founded on the civic virtue of the ideally self-reliant citizen. . . . ."

Berthoff's splendidly panoramic pursuit of ideology requires little in the way of definitional specificity. Numerous other essays in this collection, however, can hardly avoid confrontation with the question of what one means by "small." The problem is not an easy one and authors approach it differently. Some choose such familiar criteria as volume of output or sales, number of employees, or size of investment. Others adopt a functional approach and define small businesses as those "small enough to be operated with no more than one layer of supervision between owners and workers." Still others confine the category to nonincorporated enterprises that do not do business across state lines and are "under the control of a single family, or a group of associates who are in personal contact day by day." Clearly, some definitions suit the purposes of particular kinds of investigation better than do others. These varied ends would not be well served by definitional rigidity.

Nevertheless, one common understanding appears essential to any discussion of the subject: "small" is a relative concept, not an absolute one. Ideally, "small" enterprise would be examined industry by industry in each sector during a particular period of time, for in a competitive economy, given a similar political and legal environment for all businesses, a firm's investment, output, and other business decisions are influenced primarily by the behavior of firms producing similar goods and services. The dimension of time must be held constant, of course, for the reason that the small businesses of today sometimes emerge as the medium-sized or even large businesses of tomorrow. Finally, there is some justification for denoting an entire industry as "small" in relation to other contemporary industries, despite differences in the size of firms within that small industry. Irene Tichenor's discussion of the larger book and job houses in the printing industry of New York City, 1865–1906, is a case in point. While some printers enjoyed a considerable volume of business, all of them fit one acceptable pattern for smallness: their owners participated in management, their business was confined to local markets, and the relationships between proprietor and customer were personal.

When we turn to look at actual businesses in operation on the eve of industrialization, it is clear that the great majority, by any defining criteria, were small. Throughout the entire colonial period, fewer than half-a-dozen business corporations have been traced. It is true that in the later years of the eighteenth century, unincorporated joint-stock companies sometimes reached surprising size in mining and land speculation, and it is true that shipbuilding enterprises were often large ones, too. And, of course, some merchants in each of the major port cities along the Atlantic coast engaged in foreign trade on a larger scale than did others. Wholesalers and retailers, moneylenders and dealers in bills of exchange, investors in real estate and in vessels, shipowners and builders: acting sometimes as commission agents and at other times on their own accounts, these larger jacks-of-all-trades dispatched cargoes of American farm products to the West Indies, other coastal cities, Mediterranean ports, or the British Isles. But most functioned on a far more modest level, constrained by lesser cash and credit resources, and poorer sources of commercial information, to confine their operations to a schooner or two trading languidly along the coast or in Caribbean ports.

The manufacturing sector was very small; most clothing, foodstuffs, furniture, and utensils were produced in households for use rather than sale. Not everything could be made in the home or on the farm, however. A number of industries, mainly light ones producing consumer goods, engaged in the commercial manufacturing of ironwork, flour, paper, potash, beer, bricks, and other articles. Nearly every village had a sawmill and flour mill, and every port city its contingent of master craftsmen.

Richard Walsh's portrait of the "Revolutionary Charleston Mechanic" makes it clear that not all masters were business proprietors. Such groups as carpenters, bricklayers, carvers, joiners, and tinsmiths were "essentially laborers." Saddlers, cabinetmakers, and shoemakers, on the other hand, are examples of "manufacturing shopkeepers," craftsmen "who fashioned wares and placed them directly on sale at the shop." Most of their sales were by retail to townspeople, for as a rule they did not sell to merchants for export, or themselves enter the coastal or export trade. Sole proprietorships, occasionally partnerships, these mechanic businesses did not always remain small. Prosperous artisans diversified their investments by buying town lots or purchasing shares of vessels plying the West Indian rice trade; they also increased their output by acquiring additional numbers of apprentices, indentured servants, or journeymen. In Charleston, as elsewhere in the South, they also bought slaves. Indeed, of 194 artisans in Charleston between 1760 and 1785 who could be identified in the Census of 1790, 159, or 80 percent of the total, were slaveholders.

Urban growth, population increase, and gradually rising per capita incomes combined to raise the pressure of demand upon these artisanal shops in the early decades of the nineteenth century. Widening foreign markets added to the pressure, and the shops responded by enlarging and adding still more workers to their labor force. However, their proprietors tended increasingly to lose their independence to wholesale merchants, who supplied the necessary capital, organized production under a putting-out system, and shipped off the finished goods. Rural homes, as well as urban craft shops, were part of the network of production and distribution, and goods that were more and more standardized, made to specifications provided by exporters with knowledge of varying tastes abroad, replaced the custom-made goods of earlier days.

The factory system emerged out of the expanded production of shop or handicraft industries. Under the latter regime, workers had been dispersed in numerous small shops or rural homes, and such raw materials as leather and yarn put out to them to work up into finished goods. The essential features of the factory system were the gathering of these dispersed workers into a central workshop, and the equipping of that shop with machinery. Thus defined, the factory system appeared gradually before the 1850s, at different times in different industries. As it did in England, it emerged first in the cotton-textile industry. In the 1820s the factory system grew rapidly in carpet manufacturing. By the 1840s one can speak confidently of factory operations in the iron industry of eastern Pennsylvania and western New Jersey. But in the boot and shoe industry, where workers were gathered into central workshops, power-driven machinery was still lacking on the eve of the Civil War.

The process of industrialization was thus an uneven one in terms of its conquest of economic sectors and geographical areas. Yet, undoubtedly, that process picked up momentum in the final two antebellum decades. Between 1840 and 1860 workers in agriculture fell from 63.4 percent to 53.2 percent of the labor force, whereas their counterparts in factory manufacturing and construction increased from 13.9 percent to 18.5 percent. In 1839, agriculture's contribution to commodity output represented 72 percent of the total, but by 1859, it had fallen to 56 percent. In the same interval, the manufacturing share rose from 17 percent to 32 percent. Rates of urban growth bespeak the same phenomenon of more rapid industrialization. Between 1839 and 1859, the urban proportion of the population nearly doubled, rising from 10.8 percent to 19.8 percent. Finally, more corporate charters were issued during the single decade of the 1850s than in all the previous years of American history.

In this process of industrialization, "the small producer as well as the big capitalist, played an important role." In her examination of the contribution made to industrialization by artisans in many of the traditional crafts of Newark, New Jersey, between 1830 and 1860, Susan E. Hirsch breaks new ground. These crafts did not follow the dramatic model of the textile industry, where "large capitalists—merchants and financiers—revolutionized production and built huge, mechanized mills before 1820 by amassing large blocks of capital through incorporation, introducing costly machines modeled after British design, and tapping a new source of cheaper wage labor in native-born women and children."

In many trades, industrialization was a diffuse process, mechanization came slowly, and artisans themselves revolutionized production methods. This they could do because of their familiarity with technical processes, and because of the limited capital requirements of those early deviations from tradition which marked the first stages of industrialization. The very first stage was that of task differentiation—task breakdown—and as in the manufacturing of shoes in Lynn, Massachusetts, mass production was achieved by workers each doing one task, using hand tools. Workers often owned their own tools and employers had only to supply materials. But artisans who could save a few hundred dollars could start their own firms by joining with several others in the same position. In Newark, such firms "could expand the volume of production per worker by teaching tasks to semiskilled workers and pouring their funds into materials. Master craftsmen in the related fields of shoemaking, saddle making, and leather making all followed this path." In Paterson, New Jersey, "the typical manufacturer in the new locomotive, machinery, and tool industries had been a skilled craftsman or had served an apprenticeship and had founded his business as a small individual firm or as a partnership."

In a word, industrialization was not alien to the artisans of preindustrial America; rather, it often emanated from them. The inventiveness, entrepreneurship, and capital of small producers was a vital force in transforming manufacturing processes. Artisans such as Linus Yale, Jr., made "crucial technological advances in locksmithing." The Newark mechanic Seth Boyden developed a machine for splitting leather, produced the first patent leather in America, and made inventions in many other lines as well—castings for malleable iron, improvements in steam-engine design, and hat-making machinery, for example. Henry Blynn's invention of the first machine for stiffening hats made possible the industrialization of that craft. Possessing "a positive self-image and a common set of values," skilled, educated, proudly individualistic, and the beneficiaries of a cultural unity originating in the close personal relationships fostered by small shops, the mechanics of preindustrial America furthered rather than hindered the process of industrializing the crafts.

By the eve of the Civil War, however, the artisan's role in industrialization was in jeopardy in Newark. Firms started by artisans in the 1830s "were beginning to fall into the hands of their children or partners who were untrained in the old technology and who lacked respect for the old values." Improved transportation and marketing techniques brought cheap machine-made goods into competition with craftsmen using traditional production methods. The use of steam-powered machinery inflated capital requirements greatly—the average capital invested in firms utilizing steam power in the manufacture of hats, saddles, jewelry, trunks, and leather nearly doubled between 1850 and 1860—and only shoemaking was still open to the small producer. And the latter found himself increasingly unable to challenge the New England manufacturers in the wholesale trade. In sum, Hirsch concludes, "The very success of some artisans in expanding their small firms destroyed the viability of small business in the crafts."

What, then, happened to these artisan-entrepreneurs? The question lies on the frontiers of research into census records and into the directories, business advertisements, and other sources of information on occupational change in particular cities. Essays by Stuart M. Blumin and by Clyde and Sally Griffen make excellent use of such sources to suggest some of the contours of change, the former in the antebellum era and the latter in the period 1850–80. The necessary beginning point, however, is stressed in the essay by Stanley C. Hollander: industrialization created both an enormous supply of goods requiring to be moved through marketing channels, and large metropolitan clusters of people almost totally dependent upon stores for their consumption goods. The mounting demand that lay behind this increase in supply made it possible for people to specialize on single occupations, with the result that the general merchant of colonial days, the jack-of-all-trades, tended to give way to businessmen concentrating all their energies on retailing, wholesaling, banking, or other specialties. And within retailing itself, a remarkably clear pattern of product specialization appeared.

Stuart Blumin's examination of newspaper advertisements by businesses in Philadelphia, New York, Charleston, and Hartford reveals these trends unmistakably. As percentages of all commercial advertisers in each of the cities, respectively, general merchants declined from 64.9 percent, 23.5 percent, 37.6 percent and 46.9 percent in 1772, to 1.3 percent, 0.4 percent, 15.2 percent and 5.5 percent in 1855. The percentages for specialized merchants do just the opposite, rising from 13.5 percent, 24.3 percent, 20.5 percent and 15.5 percent in 1772, to 78.8 percent, 87.1 percent, 65.9 percent and 54 percent in 1855. Product specialization on the part of specialized merchants is no less clear.

In Philadelphia, these most specialized of merchants—hat stores, shoe stores, piano stores, and even pet shops—increased from 14 percent of all commercial advertisers in 1772 to 79 percent in 1855. In New York they increased from 24 percent to 87 percent, in Charleston from 21 percent to 66 percent, and in Hartford from 16 percent to 54 percent.

In sum, in all four cities "there occurred a dramatic reversal in the relative proportions of the general and specialized merchants among commercial advertisers, with the latter becoming the dominant figure during the early industrial era."

Changes of the kind depicted by Blumin point suggestively in the direction of an evolving social structure and value system. The demise of the colonial artisan-entrepreneur of the preindustrial era and the emergence of a nonmanual sector of retail and wholesale storekeepers, salesmen, managers, and other nonmanual proprietors and workers brought into being what C. Wright Mills was later to call the "old middle class"—as distinct from the "new middle class" associated with the rise in the late nineteenth and early twentieth centuries of a large, salaried corps of office workers. The old middle class first made clear a distinction between those who worked with their hands and those who worked with their heads—between blue-collar and white-collar workers. The artisan-shopkeeper of colonial days, who produced the goods he sold, had been an esteemed member of the middling orders of society. Selling goods at retail which one neither made oneself nor imported "was not one of the ordinary ambitions of young men of middling rank." By the mid-nineteenth century, however, "retailing had become respectable, and many men were able to fulfill in the retail sector ambitions that formerly would have been fulfilled only in the crafts and in some form of extra-local commerce."

The Griffens document the continuing decline of the artisan-shopkeeper in their rich analysis of census records and credit ratings of business proprietors in Poughkeepsie, New York, between 1850 and 1880. Increasingly, after 1850, men trained as retailers rather than as craftsmen emerged as proprietors of the city's largest hardware, furniture, boot and shoe, clothing, and other craft-related stores. "Skill in business rather than in the craft was now the key to prosperity." Even where artisan-owned shops remained the rule, as in the manufacture of machines, carriages, and barrels, future prospects were not bright. The explanation for this is provided by an admittedly "extreme case," that of furniture making, which registered a decline from 45 cabinetmakers in 1850 to only 7 in 1880: "The competition of factory work in other cities brought sharp contraction in local manufacture." If an artisan-owned shop remained prosperous in 1880, the master worker who combined manufacturing and retailing had "long since . . . adapted to selling more ready-made goods from other shops or factories." Small shops, much more numerous than large ones, were anything but prosperous. Their proprietors "barely earned a living and depended increasingly upon repairing."

As the scale and mechanization of manufacturing increased, as the railroad made it more and more possible for regional and national manufacturers to invade local markets, small shops were pushed to the edge of marginality. They lacked capital to compete, and perhaps even more importantly, they lacked entrepreneurial ability to adapt to technological change, especially to innovation in merchandising methods and aggressive advertising on the part of rising multipurpose department stores in the 1870s and 1880s. Although in Poughkeepsie, and undoubtedly other cities as well, the number of businesses tended to increase or contract with the rise and fall of population, "only a minority became stable, long-lived enterprises."

Of the 1,530 firms in Poughkeepsie evaluated for credit by R. G. Dun and Company and its predecessor between 1845 and 1880, 32 percent lasted three years or less, and only 14 percent lasted twenty years or more. Most businesses faded rapidly; only a few were very promising ventures at the outset. Of the 1,317 firms whose worth was estimated by credit reporters, 42 percent were worth less than $1,000, 38 percent were worth between $1,001 and $10,000, and only 20 percent were rated above $10,000.

In a word, for the more marginal businesses, "self-employment meant almost constant precariousness, and many were forced to return to employment by others."

In urban communities, generally the numbers of small businesses tended to keep pace with growth in real incomes per capita, that is, with economic growth, but the problems of many small businesses tended to mount with the intensifying processes of industrialization and structural change in business firms, which accompanied that growth and, indeed, helped make it possible. Industrialization and growth had been under way since at least the early years of the nineteenth century but the post–Civil War decades witnessed an increase in the rate of change. Even before the war a substantial proportion of the gross national product, from 14 percent to 16 percent, had been devoted to capital formation, but the postwar shares were higher. By the 1870s the shares amounted to 24 percent, and by the 1880s to 28 percent, reflecting increasing capital formation in the form of factories and their equipment and in transportation (especially railroads) and nonfarm construction (especially urban housing). Clearly, it is during these closing years of the nineteenth century that one can first speak of the mass demand of a national urban market, a market brought into being by the railroads and by legal change, and sustained in effectiveness by rising per capita incomes. The latter had averaged an increase of only 1.45 percent per year between 1840 and 1860, but between 1870 and 1900 the rate rose to 2.1 percent, a level at which, roughly speaking, the economy has continued to grow on average throughout the last one hundred years.

Mass production held out the promise of economies of scale or reduce costs per unit of output over a wide range of output. To achieve production in high volume, however, required enlarged plant and equipment. The latter, in turn, required technological knowledge and capital resources generally beyond the capacities of small business firms. Incorporation enabled enterprisers to pool the modest investments of large numbers of people and thus raise the necessary capital. This was an era sometimes known as the age of the Corporate Revolution, and the mark of that age was growth in the size and number of corporations, especially in manufacturing. Between 1880 and 1907, incorporation for the manufacture of food and kindred products, textile-mill products, and other consumer goods bulked large among total incorporations. But while the consumer goods industries were the first to become dominated by great business enterprises, a swelling number of companies were engaged in the manufacture of machinery for the use of producers by the beginning of the twentieth century. Merger of previously independent firms was the chosen way to bigness during the Corporate Revolution. Made permissible by legal change in the form of New Jersey's

Holding Company Act of 1888, holding companies were used as the mechanism for fully 86 percent of the consolidations effected during the great merger movement of 1895 to 1904. Mergers took place in all major manufacturing and mining industries, but most were concentrated in primary metals, food products, petroleum products, chemicals, transportation equipment, fabricated metal products, machinery, and bituminous coal. A number of these industries soon became oligopolistic in their structure, with large proportions of their total output being produced by a handful of large firms.

Despite the occurrence of vast structural changes this era of the "rise of big business" also witnessed a notable rise of little business. In his painstaking pioneer essay "The Position of Small Business in the Structure of American Manufacturing, 1870–1970" Harold G. Vatter estimates that small business establishments (plants) increased by a substantial 37 percent between 1870 and 1900, with rapid growth concentrated in the 1890s, the very decade of the largest merger wave in American history. This positive correlation, Vatter believes, is typical: Small firms "proliferate when the economy and the sector are strongly expanding during an intermediate period; the numbers decelerate when intermediate period general expansion slows." The same generalization also holds for shorter periods of expansion and contraction during the business cycle. During the long depression of the 1870s, for example, an absolute fall in the number of small establishments took place, reflecting "the precarious existence, high turnover rates, and short average life span abidingly typical of small manufacturing enterprise." Then, between 1879 and 1899, the number increased by more than half, a greater rate of increase than in any subsequent twenty-year period.

Apparently, the large manufacturing plants rising out of the merger wave at the turn of the century were not of optimum size. For when growth in optimum size occurs, the entry of small firms into manufacturing tends to be inhibited. The result is that the entrepreneurial activity of small businessmen flows into more open channels in such sectors as construction, retail trade, and services, where the average plant and firm size are typically smaller— and, indeed, have been smaller throughout the century from 1870 to 1970. As we have seen, small business growth was not inhibited despite the rise of big business between 1889 and 1909. Their numbers "were probably minimally affected by the first great merger movement." Vatter also believes it possible that when the rate of growth of manufacturing output is greater than the rate of growth in the size of manufacturing plants, the former tends to "swamp" the retardative influence of increasing plant size, presumably whether optimum or not, on the formation of small businesses in the manufacturing sector.

At any rate, the small firm abided. Thousands of small businesses appeared in such industries as apparel, lumber and wood products, furniture and fixtures, publishing and printing—as the essay by Irene Tichenor on New York printers organized in a trade association known as the Typothetae attests—and in stone, clay, and glass products, fabricated metal products, and instruments. These firms failed to follow the petroleum-refining pattern in which the independent refiner all but disappeared. They manufactured both nonstandardized and standardized products; items tailored to specialized consumer tastes; goods intended for small, local markets, the production of which entailed use of widely dispersed materials, high transport costs, and a large skilled-labor component. The latter, together with the sharing of a craft-specific value system by both journeymen and their employers, goes far to explain why American hat manufacturers in seven eastern cities studied by David Bensman continued to thrive in the late nineteenth century. They did so until improvements in machinery made it possible to displace highly skilled union labor.

James H. Soltow's fine essay on the origins of small business in the metal fabricating and machinery-making firms of New England, 1890–1957, also illustrates the importance of some of the factors cited by Vatter. Some small firms, Soltow notes, have elected to operate on the fringes of an industry dominated by an oligopolistic "leading core," while others have "functioned as 'satellites,' serving as a distributor of the products of one large corporation or as a supplier to a single large customer in a modern version of the putting-out system." At best, however, owner-managers have found "little sense of independent entrepreneurship in these situations because of low incomes, instability of operations, and/or sharing with a large firm some of the decision-making functions with respect to pricing and even investment." More promising than these alternatives was the strategy of acquiring "a strong market position as a small firm by adapting to a niche in the market which afforded some degree of isolation from complete and direct competition with other firms, both large and small."

Some of the eighty New England firms studied by Soltow specialized in the manufacture of products, for example, ships' clocks or miners' cap lamps, the total demand for which was so limited as not to tempt entry into the field on the part of large corporations oriented to mass production and distribution. Others specialized in a specific process, for example, metal stamping, electroplating, or sheet-metal fabrication. To protect themselves from the competition of other small producers, the firms sought to differentiate their product by rendering special services to customers, including personal sales representation, and by seeking to earn a reputation for dependability.

Soltow notes that although many aspects of modern economic life have encouraged a trend toward bigness and rationalization, an "increase in the diversification of intermediate and final products associated with economic growth has favored industrial differentiation. Within the intricate nexus of economic activities reflecting a complex division of labor among firms of varying size, entrepreneurs sought to adapt to niches in which small enterprises could carry on efficient and profitable operations." Yet the structure of the division of labor by firm may vary considerably even among advanced economies. There is today, and indeed has been since at least the 1890s, a significantly higher degree of specialization by firm in the United States than in Europe. Metal-fabricating firms in Belgium in the 1960s, another of Soltow's studies reveals, were more vertically integrated than similar companies in the United States.

Small enterprises specializing in particular final products normally produced most of the components which they required, in contrast to American product specialists of this size which concentrated on final assembly and contracted the manufacture of parts to process specialists, many of which were themselves small firms. Maintenance by product specialists of their own facilities to make components discouraged the organization of firms specializing on specific processes, which might have achieved some measure of success, as in the United States, by applying their functional skills to the solution of problems common to the manufacturers—both large and small—of a wide range of finished products.

In the United States "the existence of a network of process specialists made it possible for product specialists to concentrate their resources on developing facilities for final assembly and marketing, at the same time having access to the services of experts in the machining, stamping, cutting, and shaping of metals. Similarly, the existence of such a body of product specialists constituted an encouragement for process specialists in many narrowly defined lines in an industry like metal working." While the extent of the market is the principal economic force determining the division of labor—so that the large size of the American economy is the "most obvious explanation of the more extensive specialization found in the United States"—Soltow also emphasizes the importance of social and cultural factors. "Since the nineteenth century, American industrialists have assigned a higher value to efficiency than have their European counterparts, who have continued to emphasize 'prowess,' or pride in the process of manufacturing an article from start to finish."

Most of the founders of the small firms analyzed by Soltow entered independent business "in the same, or closely related, field to that in which they had previous experience as employees." Having acquired both technical and business knowledge in the highly specialized lines of metal working, they could recognize the niches in the business world which small firms could profitably occupy. To be sure, by the mid-twentieth century the increasing complexity of both technology and business rendered the limited education and bench skills that had been sufficient before World War I no longer adequate. However, rising educational levels in the population as a whole and multiplication of management positions in large corporations provided a growing proportion of working people with skills and experience. Indeed, Soltow concludes, "it would not be an exaggeration to regard Big Business as an increasingly important training school for potential small entrepreneurs."

In another essay in this collection Roland I. Robinson notes a similar phenomenon, viz., the existence of small businesses that are "based on competence in sophisticated technology." Temperamentally impatient with the bureaucracy of large organizations and possessed of an independence of mind and action better suited to the atmosphere of small enterprise, persons involved in experimental science as employees of corporations, universities, and government "have burst out of their jobs and started small businesses" of their own.

Because of their ability to occupy special niches more to the economic advantage of large firms to utilize than to carve out via their own investments, we find 165,083 small manufacturing businesses, defined roughly as unincorporated establishments, accounting for 76.4 percent of the total business population of the United States in 1904. Vatter believes they were "probably almost all single-plant, single-product enterprises averaging about 10 wage earners per establishment," in contrast with large plants under the corporate form employing over 75 persons per establishment. Between 1904 and 1919, the number of small businesses in manufacturing grew by nearly one-third. In the 1920s, though, small-business growth appears to have been inhibited by a failure of output to grow much greater than plant size, the two ratios being 64 percent and 62 percent, respectively. Opportunities for additional new plants were slowed. Smaller unincorporated enterprise appears to have suffered a high mortality rate, in view of a rise in the number of manufacturing corporations by more than one-third. While the capital/output ratio was beginning to decline, the capital requirements of big business per unit of output always exceeded by far those of small enterprise. Accordingly, small manufacturing firms were necessarily relegated to those branches of industry that were more labor intensive than capital intensive. Thus, their share of the manufacturing labor force has been typically larger than their share of output. Unfortunately, "low capital investment has historically gone hand in hand with high mortality and short life span." And since the Griffens note the same relationship in retail trade, the generalization is probably widely applicable to small-business enterprise in the United States.

Not surprisingly, the "depression decade" was also a time of high mortality for small manufacturing firms, but in the post–World War II years from 1947 through 1954, small enterprises in that sector entered upon a period of considerable growth. It was to be short-lived. After 1954, the small manufacturer "apparently experienced almost two decades of constriction and severe relative decline," the apparent victim of competition from multi-plant companies that were to an increasing extent also becoming multi-industry conglomerates. Thus the long-run (secular) rate of growth in the number of small businesses in manufacturing "has definitely declined," and so too has their profitability and economic significance. Although it remains a fact of economic life that smaller units continue to survive in certain subsectors of manufacturing, competition between firms of different size has sifted out small enterprises of lesser efficiency. In consequence, the small entrepreneur has been "pushed" into nonmanufacturing areas.

Two of these areas, retail trade and banking, are worthy of particular note, in view of the growing importance of the service sector in the American economy. "Approximately three-quarters of the way through the twentieth century," writes Stanley C. Hollander, "the retail trade remains a haven for small business." Indeed, the fifty largest retailing firms accounted for slightly less than 19 percent of all United States retail trade in 1972. The three major forms of large-scale enterprise, the mail-order house, the department store, and the chain store, emerged in the second half of the nineteenth century. Yet neither then, nor later, has industrialization, in the sense of mechanization, exerted a significant effect on retailing. "Reductions in labor-intensity came primarily through transfer of functions to consumers (self-service). Increases in capital investment came largely from the use of larger and more elaborate buildings (supermarkets, enclosed shopping malls), concomitant larger merchandise inventories, and perhaps from locational competition." While big retailing gained from mechanization during the first fifty years of the century, "it did not obtain an overpowering advantage" over small retailing. As recently as 1975–76, estimates of initial capital requirements for gift, shoe, apparel, sporting goods, toy, hobby and craft, automotive supply, and camera shops ranged from $30,000 to $130,000 and "seemed to center around $65,000 to $75,000." Small retailers could—and can—obtain capital "from numerous sources, including personal savings, friends, supplier credits, bank loans, and from some governmental programs." Larger firms have greater access to the capital market, and they also seem able to outbid small stores for desirable employees, but the differences are far more easily bridgeable than in the manufacturing sector.

At any rate, as of 1972, large enterprise had "gained less market share more slowly in retailing than in many other sectors." Even in the face of competition from large firms or groups, some small retailers, like their counterparts in manufacturing, survive and even prosper "by finding niches in the marketing system that can provide adequate business and yet are too small to be tempting to larger firms." These retailers may locate in small towns, serve distinct clienteles in larger communities, feature personal service and advice, or offer unique lines of merchandise, for example, gourmet foods or arts and crafts shops. "Some may survive by being willing to work harder, longer and/or more cheaply than paid employees would require."

The role of small business in the history of American banking, Richard Sylla tells us in his essay on that subject, "is perhaps greater than what obtains in any other nation." Certainly the United States was unique among the industrializing nations of the nineteenth century, for only in this country were there to be found vast numbers of small, independent banks occupying central places in the monetary and fiscal system. For the most part, these were commercial banks, institutions which make loans by creating deposits in the form of credits on their account books, against which their borrowers may draw checks. There were more than 30,000 such banks in the United

States in 1920, the great majority of them operating out of a single office staffed by a handful of employees in a small town. Small-business banking was then at the peak of its development and influence. The number of small, independent banks has since greatly declined as a result of disappearances, mergers, and the expansion of branch banking. Nevertheless, small-business influence still remains important in American banking, for even today more than 10,000 independent banks continue to function in the United States.

What explains America's uniqueness in this respect? Why did American experience differ so markedly from that of England, for example, where the number of independent banks reached a high point of some 700 units in the first quarter of the nineteenth century, only to yield to a development of large joint-stock banks with branches, a mere dozen of which dominated the English banking scene by the end of the century? (In less extreme form other industrializing economies also exhibited "this same pattern of increasing dominance by large, consolidated banking organizations.") The answer is supplied in large measure by differences in legal systems, by "the laws and regulations, or lack thereof, under which American banks were organized and operated." These laws were products of a political power in nineteenth-century America that was not concentrated but diffused among different levels of government, a diffusion which reflected in part the federal structure of the republic, and in part an ethos of individual opportunity and enterprise, an ideology of small business. Perhaps even more importantly, however, independent small banks were economically efficient. What made them so were the "personal nature of many banking services, the costs of gathering information in an economy of continental dimensions with millions of small producers who were bank clients, and the well-documented reluctance of capital to migrate from surplus to deficit saving sectors during the great expansion of the American economy in the last century." In a word, "real economic forces operated along with ideology and legal arrangements to promote small-business banking."

During roughly the first half century of American commercial banking, from 1782, when the first bank received a charter of incorporation, to the 1830s, banks were typically not small businesses. Whether compared with later years or with other contemporary enterprises, their average size was large. State charters authorized them, on average, to gather capitals of about a half-million dollars; furthermore, from 1803 to 1837 available data on paid-in capital show that the banks operated with from one-half to two-thirds of their authorized capital. Thus, they belong among the major private institutions of the early republic.

A trend toward smaller average bank sizes, as measured by capital stock, began to take shape around the middle of the nineteenth century. From then till the early twentieth century, the 830 state banks of 1850 increased by thousands, while their average capital stock fell to less than a third of what it had been. What initiated the trend was the passage of free banking laws, first by Michigan and New York in the late 1830s, and then by more than half the states by 1861. Such laws contrast with the "special" laws under which each state bank had previously received its charter, the enactment of free or general laws being responsive to a developing public opposition to special and sometimes monopolistic privileges granted a favored institution under the regime of special legislation.

This legislative stimulus to growth received a setback from the passage of the National Bank Act of 1863, especially from a companion law of 1865 which placed a prohibitive tax on banknotes issued by state banks. The purpose of the tax was to compel state banks to take out federal charters, and in this the law achieved a notable initial success; only 261 state banks remained out of the system by 1870. National banking, however, was subject to severe restrictions—among them relatively high minimum capital requirements and a prohibition on real-estate loans. State legislatures gradually responded to these limitations by enacting laws much less restrictive to small business than the National Banking legislation. Minimum capital requirements typically ranged from $10,000 to $25,000, in contrast with a federal minimum of $50,000 before 1900. Furthermore, almost all states permitted their chartered banks to make loans on the security of real estate. These and other less restrictive conditions served to stimulate a mushroom growth in small-business banking. Before the automobile and other forces in the 1920s began to dismantle the advantages enjoyed by these small institutions, their success probably reflected "their superior information about local conditions and the quickness with which they could act in a fluid and rapidly developing economy." Perhaps, Sylla suggests, they were creatures of the extraordinary geographic expansion of the nineteenth century. If so, small banks deserve a place among the frontier institutions celebrated by Frederick Jackson Turner.

It is no easy task to summarize the long and changeful involvement of small business in the economy and society of the United States. Perhaps the most defensible generalization is this: it has endured in those sectors where its costs per unit of output are lower than those of larger enterprises. Surely one of the sources of lower cost has been the willingness of managerial labor to work excruciatingly long hours for the noneconomic reward of personal independence, especially in retail trade. On the other hand, capital requirements, although relatively small, have been costly to meet because of the high risk of failure. Lower labor costs, however, have tended to offset this.

In his thoughtful essay "Labor and Small-Scale Enterprise During Industrialization," David Brody points to an advantage on the part of the small producer that has proved of enduring significance. When output rose in the nineteenth century, the manufacturer was no longer able to supervise his work force directly. Instead, he broke it up into units small enough to be controlled by contractors, craftsmen, and foremen. The supervision of labor was thus decentralized, and despite the efforts of "scientific management" to reduce labor to systematic control, it has "proved much more intractable a subject for rationalization than any other phase of plant administration." Above all, the problem of motivating the worker remained, of providing incentives to maximize his productivity. Even today, a prime objective of rationalized labor relations is "to recover for the large-scale enterprise human dimensions of work that were inherent in the small business."

In those industries, especially in the manufacturing sector, in which mechanization has permitted economies of scale, small business has declined to relatively small significance overall, while continuing to hold its place in "niches" affording shelter from the competition of both big and little business. In other sectors, so long as there continue to exist demands for services of an individual and personal nature—splintered, differential demands that are difficult to aggregate, standardize, and hence mechanize—so long as there exist thousands of small local markets too costly to organize and service by techniques of mass production and distribution, small business is likely to be economically viable. There are tens of thousands of these neighborhood markets in the contemporary American economy and it is therefore not surprising that the overwhelming majority of businesses are small. According to the Chairman of the Senate Small Business Committee, 97 percent of all businesses in the United States were small businesses in 1976. Of the 14 million enterprises, nearly 2 million were corporations, about 1 million were partnerships, and almost 11 million sole proprietorships.

A numerical preponderance of small firms has characterized the entire course of American history. But the relative stability of these overall proportions has concealed restless motion beneath the surface as small enterprises have come to life, all too quickly died, and been replaced by others. Today, as yesterday, failure rates are relatively high, especially in the early years of life. And, as Roland I. Robinson observes, "A rather large fraction of small businesses, even though they survive, provide their proprietors with only a skimpy living." Their contribution to aggregate output has probably been in secular decline since the rise and dissemination of mass-production techniques a century ago. And gross private investment by small business has shrunk as well, from 15 percent of the total in 1953, for example, to 7.5 percent by 1973.

Still, the desire "to be one's own boss" has not faded from the American value system, nor has the widespread conviction, present in this country since its beginnings, that roots of either national or personal political independence are best sunk in the ground of economic independence. The continuing vitality of this "small business ideology" helps explain the enactment of antitrust legislation by Congress during the period of the "rise of big business," as well as the passage of other laws in the interests of small enterprise. In the last forty years or so, an organized, active pressure group has sought to induce Congress to extend additional aids to small business and one of the apparent fruits of its efforts was the establishment of the Small Business Administration (SBA) in 1953.

At the beginning the SBA itself made direct loans to small enterprises but its policy soon switched to that of providing government guarantees of private loans. Sources of the latter, Roland I. Robinson indicates in his essay "The Financing of Small Business in the United States," are numerous and include both large and small commercial banks—institutions which have long been "major suppliers of credit to small business"—other businessmen with greater capital accumulations than they can profitably reinvest in their own businesses, partners and wealthy clients of investment-banking firms on the lookout for risky but promising business ventures, private venture-capital institutions, for example, American Research and Development Corporation (whose best known success stories are High Energy and Polaroid), and the federal government. Loans to small businesses by commercial banks and other private sources guaranteed by the SBA have totaled between $1 and $2 billion in each of the last several fiscal years, with emphasis being placed on the availability of credit for minority-owned businesses. The SBA has found that "although a fairly large proportion of its loans are not repaid according to the original terms, ultimately collections appear to be about 95 percent of the loans made." In addition, the SBA has authorized the organization of private investment companies specializing in supplying equity capital to small business. Surveys of the latter generally place finance as "one of its leading problems, if not the most important one." Robinson disagrees: "It can be said that at the present time the facilities for small-business finance in the United States are remarkably good."

Interest on the part of the federal government in the problems of small business is a relatively recent development. In our earlier history, Lawrence Friedman points out in his essay on law and small business, both political and legal power were diffuse and decentralized, converging at local rather than national levels. And it was precisely at local levels that small business had most of its leverage: "It dilutes the political strength of small business when power flows from the towns to state capitals . . . to the federal government." In many communities in the late nineteenth century, merchants were able to protect their local markets from outside competitors by getting their towns to impose heavy license fees on peddlers.

Big-business outsiders were a tougher nut to crack. Friedman reviews the judicial controversies involved in the efforts of small retailers to protect themselves against price cutting on the part of mail-order houses, chain stores and department stores. They did so by entering resale price agreements. Not surprisingly, state courts tended to uphold these price-maintenance schemes—until the Supreme Court of the United States disallowed them (in 1911) as illegal restraints of trade. In the twentieth century, however, and against the backdrop of the Great Depression, national legislation responded favorably—in the Miller-Tydings Act (1937) and Robinson-Patman Act (1936)—to renewed efforts to preserve small business from extinction.

As these instances show, the pendulum of national power has swung back and forth between the interests of big and little business. The Sherman Antitrust Act illustrates the same tendency. Enacted (1890) in the interests of small shippers, merchants and farmers, it first lay fallow for years—a "largely symbolic" victory—before being gutted with ruthless interpretation. On the other hand, occupational licensing laws passed by the states— laws which protected many small businesses (pharmacists, plumbers, owners of barbershops)—were upheld by the courts. Other state legislation, together with the establishment of small-claims courts, aided small business-men in their credit and collection problems.

In general, Friedman concludes, the place of small business in the legal system is ambiguous. Despite the establishment of the Small Business Ad-ministration, despite "rhetoric, in Congress and in government, about the virtues of small business," it "has little power in Washington." Many gov-ernment programs—for example urban renewal, which "bulldozed hundreds of small businesses to death"—are quite destructive of small business. The "modern state tends to criminalize some small businesses"—slum land-lords and loan sharks, for example—and to "squeeze others out of the mar-ket." Those that survive do so by finding niches and crevices in the market. The "protection of the law is, as it has been, less decisive than appears at first glance."

Lawrence Friedman is undoubtedly correct in his belief that local levels of government and law were more responsive than federal levels to the pres-sures exerted on behalf of small business during the long years of nineteenth century laissez-faire. Yet we are insufficiently well informed about the makers and beneficiaries of municipal policies at that time. David C. Ham-mack's scholarly survey of the literature, "Small Business and Urban Power," proposes three periods of municipal economic policy stretching be-tween the colonial era and the opening decades of the twentieth century. The first of these—running from late colonial times into the early nineteenth cen-tury—was, outside of New England, "the era of the closed, corporate, com-mercial municipality: an era which afforded special protections and advan-tages to many small businesses." "By granting freeman status sparingly, . . . for example, and otherwise limiting entry into trades, colonial cities could limit competition and protect established tradesmen." Yet, although in this and numerous other instances the "legal record" seems to suggest advantages enjoyed by small enterprises, "we lack an analysis of the impact of changing municipal economic policies on the fortunes of economic in-terest groups of all kinds, including small businesses in their diverse vari-ety."

Much the same has to be said about the second period, in which munici-palities moved from the regulation of business to its promotion via direct in-vestment in canals, railroads, bridges, wharves, and other public utilities. Numerous studies have been made of municipal economic policies during this period of the so-called American System, which lasted till the 1870s or 1880s, yet it is "not clear" how those policies "affected small business." Hammack believes the impact was "incidental" and that policy was more dominated by the "bigger business interests, particularly those of the whole-sale merchants, than the first had been."

The last decade of the nineteenth century saw the start of a third period in urban economic policy, which Hammack designates as one of "municipal progressivism." Between 1890 and 1900 state and local expenditures per capita to initiate new services and facilities, particularly in fields relating to public health (improved water and sewer systems, for example), and to ex-pand such established services as public education and police, rose 66 per-cent in real terms. Yet none of these "directly helped small businesses" and "it is increasingly clear that the effective demand for them came from those who owned and managed the larger businesses, from the leading profes-sional groups, and from settlement-house workers and others involved in the social welfare and the social gospel movements." Perhaps most impor-tantly, since most of our knowledge of these nineteenth-century develop-ments rests upon studies of just two or three cities, "it is impossible even to begin to suggest how municipal economic policy, and its effects on various economic interest groups, may have varied according to a city's size, range of economic functions, geographic location, age, population composition, or other relevant variables."

Given the state of our present knowledge, it would appear that the histori-cal impact of municipal policies on small business is unclear, while that of the federal government in more recent days is both ambiguous and inade-quate. The latter, in particular, is to be regretted. Federal policies in aid of small enterprise mount an offensive on a vital front in the war against mo-nopoly; antitrust enforcement constitutes a second front. What is fundamen-tally at stake in that war are the liberties of the people.

The nation's more narrow economic interests are also clear. A complex economy increasingly dependent upon science-based sources of technolog-ical advance can ill afford to neglect the significant source of invention and innovation represented by a small business. In his broad survey of small business in the late nineteenth century, Harold Livesay cites many technical contributions originating in that sector—among them being those of Thomas Edison, who "gave the world the electric light, the phonograph, motion pic-tures, the mimeograph, an improved telephone, . . . the vacuum tube, wireless telegraphy, radio, and television, and made scores of other discoveries ultimately woven into the intricate web of modern industrial technology.''

In his wake came many other individualists—Thomas Watson at IBM, Sol Linowitz at Xerox, Edwin Land at Polaroid—who proved that Edison's performance was a precedent, not a fluke. In the hands of these and similar men, small business has continued to be a source of technological pioneering. So much so, in fact, that some observers believe that small business has made a more dynamic contribution to research and development than its giant counterparts.

Finally, one must consider, as Eli Ginzberg does in his widely ranging essay, the role of business among the multiple institutional and other sources of skill acquisition in American society. That role was preeminent in the world of small and medium-sized businesses that characterized most of the nineteenth century. Given the shortage of labor and skills required by the developing economy, not only manufacturing firms but the American farmer as well "became an avid customer for farm machinery.''

This made each family farm a vocational school, where youngsters—especially young men but also young women—had an early exposure to coping with mechanical devices. When the flow away from the farms accelerated during the second half of the nineteenth century, this native labor force was well positioned to move into industry with little or no difficulty; this was quite unlike the pattern of most rural-urban movements, in which the newcomers required a considerable period of orientation before they could be fitted into the industrial structure and could perform effectively.

In the cities, "the ease with which individuals with modest capital could start a business created a powerful magnet for workers, most of whom were at least quasi-skilled, to try to make the transition to entrepreneurship''—including immigrants with skills in the needle trades, shopkeeping, and bookkeeping. While temporary loss ensued from the pool of scarce skills, the successful plumber, drayman, or painter himself generated training and employment opportunities for other workers. "In the long run, his metamorphosis contributed to swelling the total pool of skill and competence.''

In Ginzberg's judgment:

The major challenges that the United States confronts in the area of skill-acquisition are to improve the rate of job expansion so that all who are able and willing to work, the trained as well as the untrained, have an opportunity to do so; to improve the linkages between schools and training institutions, and the world of work; and to use

more efficiently the large sums that it invests in education and training to assure that
these investments are more responsive to the needs of the individuals and the economy.

"In meeting these three challenges," Ginzberg concludes, "small and medium-sized businesses have a significant role to play in the future—as they
have played in the past."

This, then, is the gist of 17 essays by leading American scholars on small
enterprise in varied relationships to the economy, society, and culture of the
United States over two centuries. Incomplete as they necessarily are, it may
well be doubted whether any comparably broad view of the subject over so
long a period has ever before been presented.

Selected Bibliography

Ames, Edward and Nathan Rosenberg. "The Progressive Division and Specialization of Industries." Lance Davis and J. R. T. Hughes, eds., *Purdue Papers in Economic History,
1956–1966.* Homewood, Ill.: R. D. Irwin, 1967.

Averitt, Robert T. *The Dual Economy.* New York: W. W. Norton, 1971.

Blumin, Stuart M. "Mobility and Change in Ante-Bellum Philadelphia." In Stephan Thernstrom and Richard Sennett, eds., *Nineteenth-Century Cities: Essays in the New Urban History,* pp. 165–208. New Haven: Yale University Press, 1969.

Brody, David. "The Rise and Decline of Welfare Capitalism." In Braeman, et al, eds.,
Change and Continuity in Twentieth Century America: The 1920's, pp. 152–57. Columbus,
Ohio: Ohio State University Press, 1968.

Bruchey, Stuart. *The Roots of American Economic Growth.* New York: Harper & Row, 1965.
———. *The Growth of the Modern American Economy.* New York: Harper & Row, 1975.

Duncan, J. Delbert and Stanley C. Hollander. *Modern Retailing Management.* 9th ed. Homewood, Ill.: R. D. Irwin, 1977.

Friedman, Lawrence M. *The Legal System: A Social Science Perspective.* New York: Russell
Sage Foundation, 1975.

Griffen, Clyde and Sally Griffen. *Natives and Newcomers: The Ordering of Opportunity in
Mid-Nineteenth-Century Poughkeepsie.* Cambridge: Harvard University Press, 1978.

Gutman, Herbert G. "The Reality of the Rags-to-Riches 'Myth'." In Stephan Thernstrom and
Richard Sennett, eds., *Nineteenth-Century Cities: Essays in the New Urban History,* pp.
98–124. New Haven: Yale University Press, 1969.

Hammack, David C. "Problems in the Historical Study of Power in the Cities and Towns of the
United States, 1800–1960." *American Historical Review* (1978), 83:323–49.

Hirsch, Susan E. *The Roots of the American Working Class.* Philadelphia, Pa.: University of
Pennsylvania Press, 1978.

Mayer, Kurt. "Small Business as a Social Institution." *Social Research* (1947), 14:332–49.

Mayer, Kurt and Sidney Goldstein. *The First Two Years: Problems of Small Firm Growth and
Survival.* Washington, D.C.: Small Business Administration, 1961.

Nelson, Daniel. *Workers and Managers*. Madison, Wis.: University of Wisconsin Press, 1975.

Phillips, Joseph D. *Little Business in the American Economy*. Urbana, Ill.: University of Illinois Press, 1958.

Porter, Glenn. *The Rise of Big Business, 1860–1910*. New York: Crowell, 1973.

Porter, Glenn and Harold C. Livesay. *Merchants and Manufacturers*. Baltimore: Johns Hopkins Press, 1971.

Robinson, Roland I. *Financing the Dynamic Small Firm*. Belmont, Calif.: Wadsworth Publishing Co., 1966.

Small Business and Society. Hearings before the Select Committee on Small Business of the U.S. Senate, 94th Cong., 1st Sess., Dec. 2–4, 1975.

Soltow, James H. *Origins of Small Business: Metal Fabricators and Machinery Makers in New England, 1890–1957*. Philadelphia: American Philosophical Society, 1965.

——. "Entrepreneurial Strategy in Small Industry: Belgian Metal Fabricators." *Proceedings of the American Philosophical Society* (1971), 115:32–64.

Sylla, Richard. *The American Capital Market, 1846–1914*. New York: Arno Press, 1975.

——. "American Banking and Growth in the Nineteenth-Century: A Partial View of the Terrain." *Explorations in Economic History* (Winter 1971–72), 9:197–227.

Vatter, Harold G. *Small Enterprise and Oligopoly: A Study of the Butter, Flour, Automobile, and Glass Container Industries*. Corvallis, Ore.: Oregon State University Press, 1955.

——. *Some Aspects of the Problem of Small Enterprise As Seen in Four Selected Industries*. New York: Arno Press, 1978.

Walsh, Richard. *Charleston's Sons of Liberty*. Columbia, S.C.: University of South Carolina Press, 1959.

1

INDEPENDENCE AND ENTERPRISE:
SMALL BUSINESS IN
THE AMERICAN DREAM

Rowland Berthoff

"THE best society," so an antitrust lawyer recently assured a congressional committee, "is one composed of the largest feasible number of independent entrepreneurs, free men who bend the knee only to Divine Providence, who personally own the tools of their trades, who work in accordance with rules of their own making and thus take no orders from any other mortal man." Unfortunately, he conceded, this "Jeffersonian ideal," manifestly inherited from a simpler age, now seems a hopeless anachronism. For whatever reasons (he blamed governmental policy), the economy is dominated by great bureaucratic business corporations, whose managers neither own nor even handle the tools of any trade, and whose wage-earning workers are hardly free of orders from a good many mortals.[1]

As early as the 1920s, indeed, the independent proprietor seemed obsolete. The typical shopkeeper, as one journalistic purveyor of breezy advice to housewives described him, was "a dirty, illiterate, short-sighted, half-Americanized foreigner, or a sleepy, narrow-minded, dead-from-the-neck-up American."[2] It was all very well for the national folklore to enshrine the memory of "Uncle Henry's store," with the "idlers around the stove," the head of the J. C. Penney chain observed, but the inefficiency of the surviving examples levied a "tax on all the goods [the] family buys."[3]

Research for this chapter was supported by a grant from the Penrose Fund of the American Philosophical Society.

Folklore may nevertheless be more persuasive than economics. The regularity with which, year by year, hundreds of thousands of Americans launch small businesses of their own, defying a notoriously high rate of failure, can only be explained, according to one recent student, by something "inherent in the nature of United States society, . . . an 'autonomous demand' for the status of 'businessman' in certain segments of the labor force."[4] That status may be the more attractive for seeming to keep in balance what would otherwise be two incongruous ideals: stable, self-reliant personal independence on the one hand and upward-mobile, dynamic entrepreneurship on the other.

An aspiration so widespread that it has been calculated to vary only with "the size of the economically active population" must spring from sources deep in the American past.[5] They antedate by several hundred years, indeed, the English colonization of North America. From the behavior of English peasant villagers of the High Middle Ages there may be inferred, at least, a practical balance between the social values of personal independence and communal equality. Medieval villagers were not, of course, egalitarian in any modern sense, but they evidently valued the middling status, lower than gentry but above the mere laborer, of the self-sufficient holder of some fifteen to thirty acres of ploughland and grazing rights on the common pastures.[6] Roughly equal among themselves and substantially independent, apart from the limited obligations of their manorial tenure, yeomen with property of that sort—perhaps half the village—made up the community of neighbors, which, under the forms of the manorial court, regulated their own agriculture, grazing, and related local affairs.[7]

Since a fairly free local market in land was a perennial feature of the independence they prized, the practical equality among them was always in jeopardy as the prosperous grasped opportunities to engross the land of the less fortunate.[8] As a few, from time to time, became large farmers or even gentry and many others slipped down into the ranks of laboring cottagers, the liberty of the peasant-entrepreneur upset the old middling equality. That both personal independence and communal equality remained peasant ideals is shown by the vigor with which the speeding up of these changes, in the classic era of enclosure of open fields and commons between 1540 and 1640, was resisted in villages where circumstances made that possible.[9]

It was in the same century that English colonization of North America began. To the ordinary Englishman, the limitless expanse of the New

World, even though monopolized at the start by chartered trading companies and proprietors of royal grants, offered new scope to realize popular ideals. The rural society that grew up there was, to varying degrees in different regions, a "peasant utopia" of self-sufficient, independent farmers and artisans.[10] To be sure, wherever opportunity presented to exceed mere static independence—notably in the tobacco and rice districts of the South and in the commercial ports from Boston to Charleston—there soon arose a colonial gentry of planters and merchants. But since by European standards the distance in wealth and status between them and ordinary men was not great, as late as the onset of the Revolution in the 1760s, the countinghouse of the merchant or the plantation of the owner of dozens of slaves seemed only a larger and not unattainable version of their own farm or shop.[11]

The American Revolution turned peasant self-sufficiency into an explicitly republican ideal of personal independence. If it had peasant roots, it also drew on an even older set of political ideas that enabled citizens of the new republic to spurn thereafter the very name of peasant. This classical doctrine was derived from the civic humanism of Machiavelli's *Discourses* on Livy's history of republican Rome (c. 1516), by way of James Harrington's *Oceana* (1656). It had been further adapted to eighteenth-century English circumstances by the minuscule but eloquent "Country" party in opposition to the novel executive government of Sir Robert Walpole (1721–1742). The theoretically mixed and balanced powers of king, lords, and commons they accused Walpole of having corruptly usurped through manipulation of the whole modern nexus of commercial speculation, the national debt and the Bank of England—and, in particular, high land taxes for a standing army and the current series of imperial wars. Country writers idealized the once-independent landholders of the realm, yeomen as well as gentry, their property now sapped by taxation and their civic virtue subverted by the web of official patronage and "influence."[12]

The Country ideal, which invoked not only the classic virtue of the Roman republic but also a Merry England reaching back beyond medieval peasants to half-mythical Saxon warrior-farmers, seemed to Americans, in the crisis of 1776, to distinguish their own character from the corruption into which the mother country had fallen. It was of course enormously heartening to the Revolutionary cause to be able to explain recent British colonial policy as an unconstitutional conspiracy, and, in due course, the Country doctrine, adjusted to a society lacking either king or aristocracy, was embodied in the federal Constitution of 1787.[13]

Since the most literal exemplar of the independent citizen was the landowning farmer or planter, the concept has usually been labeled—even by students of the businessman—as an "agrarian" myth and associated with Thomas Jefferson's well-known strictures against the corruptions of cities.[14] The English Country theorists had, indeed, believed bankers, merchants, and manufacturers, employers and employees alike, to be unduly vulnerable to the uncertainty or "caprice" of trade and therefore apt to resort to the easily corrupted and corrupting favors of government. Actually, since English landed gentlemen of the eighteenth century were also heavy investors and speculators in trade, the distinction was false. In America too, farmers and planters strove like other entrepreneurs to wring what profit they could from commercial markets. In any case, Revolutionary polemicists muted the point. It would have been folly to discriminate against the notable merchant adherents to the cause; long afterward the name of "JOHN HANCOCK, an American merchant," could be invoked in defense of the civic virtue of the businessman.[15] The national ideology of the United States was thus originally republican, not simply agrarian.

As the states extended the suffrage, by the 1820s, to almost all white men, this democratization was justified on the grounds that their general industriousness, frugality, and ambition to *acquire* the property associated with personal independence, and their devotion to local and national development, adequately demonstrated the classical republican virtues.[16] And, in fact, something like the old ideal remained the practical goal of most men, not least the millions of immigrants from northwestern Europe after 1815 and southern and eastern Europe after 1880 who clung to peasant or artisan social values. If for most of them the outcome was not literally the old self-sufficiency, they were usually satisfied with such symbols of independence as ownership of a house and lot, small farm, or shop.[17] Not streets paved with gold but streets lined with owner-occupied buildings was the most common "American dream."

The neorepublican ethic of work, saving, and reinvestment rapidly diluted, however, the old ideal of self-reliant but static independence by conflating it with the dynamic entrepreneurship of the nineteenth century. Thus, the enormous wealth that certain businessmen were acquiring was generally attributed to their exemplary devotion to the common civic virtues of "sobriety, prudence, economy, and industry" (said of Stephen Girard in 1831) and "untiring industry and fidelity" (John Jacob Astor, 1848).[18] "Your wealthy men of to-day," one of their admirers said in 1837, without contradiction,

"were your poor men of yesterday, . . . the working men of the country
. . . the honest and enterprising, and hard working mechanics."[19] The
plain fact that many of the new commercial and industrial elite had actually
started with at least some capital and inherited social status was usually ignored, along with the devious business methods of some of them.

Here and there, an old-fashioned warning of the corruption of republicanism into a "system . . . based on avarice, . . . the most incurable vice of
the human heart," could be heard in the 1830s.[20] Jacksonian Democrats virtually repeated the English Country "quarrel with modernity" of a hundred
years before.[21] One of them lamented "the gradually increasing desire to
amass wealth, independently of industry," whereby "all classes, of all political complexions, . . . from Maine to Louisiana, from the Atlantic to the
Mississippi, . . . have been beguiled."[22] In condemning an "aristocracy of
wealth," however, Jacksonians meant only the "speculating party" of
"bank officers, stockholders, stockdealers," and others who, "prompted to
reckless speculation by bank facilities," were led to "despise the slow accumulations of honest labor."[23] The "industrious, producing and unprivi-
leged," on the other hand, encompassed everyone who could be said to live
"by honest industry," broadly defined as "the commercial classes, . . . the
agricultural and mechanical classes, and the manufacturing class, . . . who
ask for nothing but liberty, equality, and a government of just law, as the elements of a common prosperity."[24]

The basic distinction in the 1830s was not between small business and
large but between "equality of rights, equality of duties, and equality of responsibilities" on the one hand and special privilege on the other.[25] Banks,
the central Bank of the United States in particular, provoked the loudest
outcry, because of their special charters of incorporation. Although the Bank
of the United States now seems to have been distinctive as the only modern
big business of its time (in the sense of a nationwide corporation with a bureaucratic hierarchy of branch managers), the main ground on which its
rechartering was vetoed in 1832 by Andrew Jackson—an imperious president of unshakably republican views—was the monopoly, inherent in any
central bank, which made other banks less than equal competitors.[26] Some
critics also feared other "corporations for money making purposes," such as
the early coal-mining and iron-smelting companies.[27]

Defenders of the business corporation in the 1830s, usually Whigs, sought
to identify it with the independent citizen of the republican ideal. Legal in-

corporation, from that point of view, was simply a "system of joint association" whereby "every man may become a capitalist and . . . a stockholder":

In this way, too, a number of journeymen mechanics of any kind, shoemakers for instance, might unite together and put into the general stock, twenty or fifty dollars a piece, and keep themselves in employment, when they could not get good wages from their former employers, or they might carry on a permanent business advantageously by themselves.[28]

Supposedly the same principle explained the recent proliferation of banks, which one weaver of neorepublican fustian described as

generally composed of men of little wealth, and they united together upon the joint stock principle, with a view to render more useful and available, their small individual means. . . . These corporations, sir, sprung [sic] from the people. . . . The whole argument against the banks, is an argument against the right of the people to govern themselves, and to direct and manage their own concerns.[29]

Far from endangering civic virtue, "commerce and credit" were "the last hope of republicanism" and "the best chance of stability," a Whig lawyer of Pittsburgh said in 1838; "if you deny the poor man the means to better his condition, . . . you have destroyed republican principles in their very germ."[30] By the 1850s, the passage of state laws for granting general charters, purporting to make incorporation equally available to all, helped reassure any remaining doubters that the business corporation represented not privilege but equal freedom.

That comfortable consensus blunted the impact, between the 1840s and 1880s, of rapid economic development: full commercialization of agriculture; industrialized manufacturing; near-completion of the continental railway network. Even political conservatives now assumed that "the independent yeomanry and men of business" belonged to one single, universal category.[31] It was true enough that farmers were coming to resemble businessmen, although when they plunged into borrowing for capital improvement many of them got mired in permanent tenancy. They continued, however, especially when feeling oppressed by banks and railroads, to picture themselves as simple yeomen defending their traditional independence.[32] Skilled artisans were also reluctant to concede, as one craft after another was displaced by factory labor, that the journeyman's hope of independent proprietorship was finally passing. Even the early trade unions held to the faith, as late as the 1860s, that capital and labor shared a common interest in "free contract," which, without resort to state regulation, might still bring about "the good time coming [when] every man will be a capitalist."[33]

Immigrant artisans from Europe typically clung to the independent status of the small proprietor long after most native American craftsmen had succumbed to factory competition. The foreign shoemaker resorted first to cobbling and then to keeping a "small Dutch grocery" or other retail or service shop of some kind.[34] Unskilled immigrants had only the latter alternative to industrial wage labor. In either case, their purpose was typically limited to supporting the family on its peasant holding back home or, in time, to transplanting it to a subsistence farm, perhaps one abandoned by more ambitious native Americans, near Lowell or Scranton or Cleveland. (Ultimately many of their American-born children would also be dissatisfied with the small comforts of peasant self-sufficiency.)[35]

Not until the end of the nineteenth century did a distinctive "small-business ethic" begin to be defined.[36] The popular demand in the 1880s for state and federal regulation of railroads—culminating in the first federal regulatory agency, the Interstate Commerce Commission—inveighed less against their size than against their secret freight-rate agreements with large shippers, especially the Standard Oil "trust." The antitrust movement, in turn, usually laid the blame for the new combinations "in restraint of trade"—the phrase taken over from the common law by the Sherman Antitrust Act of 1890—on some official privilege, the protective tariff in particular, that supposedly enabled them to set the price of oil, steel, sugar, whisky, or cotton bagging. The businessman who held out against trust control was generally admired, no matter how big he himself might be. "I came to this country from Germany for liberty," the California sugar refiner Claus Spreckels, who was resisting takeover by the "Sugar Trust," announced in 1888 to the applause of a congressional committee, "and liberty I shall maintain."[37] Petroleum producers and refiners who were unable to compete with Standard Oil likewise pictured themselves as defenders of "republican institutions," which one of them vividly defined as "an even chance, and the devil take the hindmost in the race."[38]

Here and there, an antitrust reformer singled out the small businessman as a still uncorrupted repository of republican values. In 1899, the progressive politician Hazen S. Pingree, a New England farm boy and factory hand who had become a shoe manufacturer and Governor of Michigan, warned a conference on the trust problem that such combinations were objectionable mainly for their effect "upon our national life, upon our citizenship, and upon the lives and characters of the men and women who are the real strength of our republic." That strength, he said, "has always been in what is called our middle class, . . . manufacturers, jobbers, middle men, retail and wholesale merchants, commercial travelers and business men generally. . . . Close to them . . . are the skilled mechanics and artisans . . . the sinew and strength of the nation." All of these, "the independent, individual business man" and "his trusted foreman and his employees" alike, when deprived by trust control of "the stimulus and ambition which goes with equality of opportunity," lose "their personal identity" and "sense of independence," Pingree complained, in "a vast industrial army with no hopes and no aspirations. . . . I care more," he concluded to thunderous applause, "for the independence and manliness of the American citizen than for . . . control [of] the commerce of the globe."[39]

A more up-to-date but less popular commentator, the economist George Gunton, attempted to refute Pingree's fears. Gunton, although born into a farm laborer's family in England, had led a New England textile workers' union in the 1870s and then educated himself as a practical authority on business and labor. "The laborer's freedom and individuality depend," he asserted, "upon two things—permanence of employment and good wages," not the "precariousness" of small business. "The laborer," Gunton lectured his unreceptive audience, "has not a single interest, social, economic or political, in the existence of employers with small capital." What society needed now was not "individuality as producers but individuality as citizens."[40] Recent assessments of the antitrust opinion of the time indicate that, despite itself, the usual concern was closer in some ways to Gunton than to Pingree—less a concern for the independent proprietor than for the consumer, the solvency of whose household was endangered by monopoly prices.[41]

The casual nineteenth-century conflation of dynamic entrepreneurship with stable independence persisted into the twentieth, even among those most disposed toward social stability and order. "The steadying and quieting of the temper" with which an assured salary endowed the "lifelong clerk or employee," a clergyman wrote in 1904, was "unquestionably a notable social contribution." He could only deplore, however, the growing practice of choosing corporate executives from men who, having come up their company's bureaucratic ladder, had never known "that independence of action and that breadth of view which only the responsibility of directing their own affairs can produce."[42] At the culmination of the antitrust movement, the Clayton and Federal Trade Commission acts (1914) sought to keep equal opportunity open for the independent entrepreneur not only to compete but to grow into a big businessman himself. As long as a large company appeared to have stayed within such laws of "fair competition," public opinion remained reluctant to see it as anything but a onetime small business grown commendably successful.[43] By the 1920s, indeed, the public benefits apparently flowing from holding companies and other amalgamations submerged almost the last of the classical republican fears.

One exception was the clamor of the 1920s against chain stores—the corporation-owned syndicates of grocery, drug, or five-and-ten-cent variety retail shops that had been proliferating since the mid-nineteenth century. At first the chains provoked only the displaced wholesalers, jobbers, and commercial travelers to demand state taxation to restrict their growth.[44] Some small grocers also reacted by joining "cooperative chains" in order to obtain the advantages of mass purchasing while retaining ownership of their stores—and the honorific name of "independent." The Federal Trade Commission's investigation of the chains in the early 1930s dwelt not on social value but rather on possible violations of the antitrust laws.[45]

For their part, the chains now argued that their "multiple" stores, and not the "unit" stores (as they preferred to call them), represented true republican values. Restrictive taxes, the future head of the Kroger grocery chain complained in 1929, were "economically unsound, unjust, discriminatory and have for their purpose the benefiting of a few at the expense of the many." The unit store stood only for the inertia of "traditional obsolete methods," certainly not for initiative or individualism. Since "every great chain," so he asserted, "has had its beginnings in one small store," its success must be due to "the determination, the industry, the vision or service of one man"—or, he added, one "group of men."[46] The president of the J. C. Penney variety stores defined "the chain principle" as "designed to strengthen and maintain every individual member and associate in the chain" by linking them together like mountain climbers.[47] One self-styled "home merchant" of the 1920s, who assumed the mantle of "competitive individual initiative, with equality of opportunity and co-operative working and living," was actually an officer of the great John Wanamaker department store of Philadelphia; to him those old virtues were "the foundation of all progress . . . of the community, the state, the country and all mankind."[48]

In the 1930s, chains encouraged their branch managers to join civic associations and otherwise to identify with the local community. They also found merit in their policy of not selling on credit, as independent storekeepers, whose prices generally were higher, often had to do, especially in working-class neighborhoods. The boast that the chains had "put some people on a cash-paying basis" resembled at least superficially the hard-money republicanism of the eighteenth century.[49] During the Great Depression, at all events, their customers made little complaint of that sort of big business. In 1933, not one person interviewed in some thirty towns criticized chain stores for suppressing personal independence or equal opportunity. Instead satisfaction seemed general that "the day of the dirty, ill-kept grocery and food store is past." If perhaps "the bulk of the people sympathize with the independents," a local editor observed, "they buy where they can get the most for their money."[50]

Between the mid-1930s and mid-1950s, the republican critique of one or two hundred years before was turned completely upside down. Now it was the small retailer, though still posing as the independent citizen of old, who sought special legal privileges. The first federal legislation to protect small business, the Robinson-Patman Act of 1936 against "price discrimination" and the Miller-Tydings "Fair Trade" Act of 1937, echoed the old concern for economic stability, less from preference, however, than from depression-era doubt about further growth. A New Deal economist, conventionally blaming the "passing of the frontier [of] free land," warned that the loss of the old "vigor of competition" now curtailed "the ability of individuals, in free association, to design affirmatively the main forms and directions of life."[51] If the small businessman could no longer hope to grow, he would have to be content with opportunity simply to continue in business at all. "He has hopes," as a senator put it, "that the government will enact laws which will enable him to live an honest life himself and make the other fellows do the same."[52]

The Robinson-Patman Act attempted to reduce the advantages that chain stores derived from their ability to purchase directly from manufacturers, and the Fair Trade Act permitted manufacturers, especially of proprietary drugs, liquor, and books, to set minimum retail prices for chains and in-

dependents alike.[53] Even in the gloom of the mid-1930s, this retreat from
the expansiveness of the past century had to be presented as a battle for individualism. Representative Wright Patman, known as a populist throughout a
long congressional career, denied that his bill, even after a series of confus-
ing amendments, would "shelter the independent merchants . . . or reward
the inefficient." It would, instead, simply "give equal rights, equal privileges, and equal benefits to all alike," thereby maintaining "opportunity for
all young people" and protecting local communities from monopoly control.[54] A western colleague delivered the definitive version of American history from this point of view:

Every village, every town, every city, large and small, in the United States, was
founded by a pioneer independent merchant. The first building in every one of the
thousands of villages, towns, and cities which dot the land, was a rude little store.
Then more stores. Then from among these merchants came the men who founded the
little banks. They built the mills and the slaughterhouses and the little industries.
They built the school systems and the water systems and the sewer systems and the
light systems and the streetcar systems. They became the mayors of the towns and
the civic leaders. They built the fine homes and the fine business blocks. The man
who built that first little store built the fine home on the hill and the fine business
block downtown, and every town and city in America is a living monument to him;
and all without outside help or capital. He hewed and builded his town out of the
earth. He was the foundation of the commercial structure of America. Shall he be
preserved or shall he be destroyed? That is the issue.[55]

Twenty years after passage of the " 'Magna Carta' of small business," Patman recalled it as "the independence day for the independents."[56]

    In 1938, the Roosevelt administration, in order to show due concern for
small businessmen, invited a thousand of them to Washington for a "White
House conference." Tumultuous to the point of anarchy, the assemblage
united only in condemning the economic controls of its New Deal hosts: the
National Labor Relations Act; wage and hour laws; the social security
payroll tax; taxes on undistributed profits and capital gains; and, in general,
"government competing with private enterprise." They proclaimed their
common identity with big business, excepting only their direct competitors,
the chain stores and "manufacturer-controlled consumer outlets," and also
trusts. ("Holding companies formed for legitimate purposes" were, however, acceptable.)[57] Jesse Jones, the Texas banker and chairman of the federal Reconstruction Finance Corporation, addressed the conference "as a
little business man myself." Only "organizations like General Motors, big
Steel, and so forth," he said, "are big business—the rest of us are little

business."[58] Most of the half-dozen national small-business associations that were organized soon after the conference were dedicated to that same view of "The Business Twins—Big and Little," as one of them put it; "we have no quarrel with big business . . . all we want is the opportunity to grow." To some students it seems clear, accordingly, that "there is no small business interest," as such.[59]

During the economic boom induced by the Second World War, the concept of the independent proprietor as entrepreneur of progress enjoyed an Indian Summer revival. By 1943, the cry once more was for "opportunities for self-employment, self-direction and self-realization" for "the man with ideas, ambition and small capital." (It was noted that discontent among shopkeepers in Germany had contributed to the rise of Hitler.)[60] Congressional committees sought to ensure that relatively small manufacturers got a share in government contracts for war materiel—an odd concern, perhaps, for heirs of eighteenth-century classical republicans.[61] The practical problem of inadequate capital, which made really great success highly infrequent for new firms—though the hope of it was believed to be still of "strong influence upon the character of our society"—called for more positive governmental support for small business than the restrictions of the 1930s on their large competitors.[62]

Amid the clamor for easier credit to help the small proprietor become a big one, the classical idea of his noneconomic virtue was asserted once more. "Perhaps," an economist mused in 1944, "a nation of artisans, of farmers, of shopkeepers is the happiest."[63] At the end of the war, the sociologist C. Wright Mills—better known thereafter for sardonic studies of the "power elite" and their impotent white-collar employees—produced a paean to the "civic spirit" of the "independent middle class," true enterprisers rather than corporate "business careerists." The "small business cities" where they predominated were distinguished, Mills found, for diversified industry, stable employment, and equality of incomes and, consequently, for home-ownership, social services, schools, literacy, and modern conveniences generally. A businessman of the approved sort agreed that he was a model of independence: "I own this whole outfit. As a matter of fact, my father did before me. It's all paid for. In addition, I have a little stock (a major United States corporation) and a little farm my grandfather bought up. So when the plants slacken up or close down I can coast for a while."[64]

The fact that his independence was inherited may, however, have been the significant point. One postwar sceptic, who doubted that business opportunity had ever been equal, concluded that now, certainly, independent proprietorship was "a status devoid of opportunities for self-fulfillment," a merely psychological struggle for outward symbols of success.[65]

Although a series of federal agencies were established to assist small business with loans, contracts, and advice, from the Smaller War Plants Corporation (SWPC) of 1942–46 and the Small Defense Plants Administration during the Korean War to the Small Business Administration (SBA), created in 1953, they found it difficult to comprehend, within a single definition of smallness, both the economic dynamism of the true entrepreneur and the classical stability of the artisan or shopkeeper. The SWPC's arbitrary standard of companies with fewer than 500 employees (which received, however, only about a third of its contracts and loans) admitted some fairly large firms as well as, theoretically at least, the very small ones.[66] The SBA, in turn, has refined the problem without resolving it.

Significantly, the SBA was conceived as a partial replacement for the big-business-oriented Reconstruction Finance Corporation (1932–53). Most of the arguments advanced for it, and for its subsequent extension, have stressed economic benefits, especially the technical innovations to which the independent entrepreneur—meaning the small manufacturer rather than the retail shopkeeper—is presumably more open than the long-established large corporation.[67] Congressional critics of the bill objected, moreover, that the proposed $100,000 limit on loans had nothing to do with relatively small competitors of General Motors but only with "little bitty business" like "the corner drugstore, the ice-cream stand, and the gas station"[68] As amended (with a slightly higher loan limit), the act declared, grandly but vaguely, that "free competition is the essence of private enterprise. Only thus can free markets, entry into business, and chance for growth of personal initiative and judgment be assured." Its definition of a small business—"one independently owned and operated, not dominant in its field"—might conceivably include Kaiser Steel or Reynolds Aluminum, small only by comparison with U.S. Steel or Alcoa.[69]

The ceilings that the SBA adopted for various categories of small business eligible for its assistance admitted companies with as much as $2 million annual volume in mercantile and service trades and $5 million in construction and, for different kinds of manufacturers, as many as 250, 500, or 1,000 employees.[70] Clearly the emphasis has been to encourage small but dynamic firms to compete to the point where they might begin to be serious rivals of the established giants. On the other hand, the SBA has also had within its province the unenterprising, unincorporated shopkeeper who himself performs the basic work with few if any employees and whose goal is his family's subsistence rather than growth of the business. Perhaps it would be better, some suggested, to call him a "little" businessman.[71]

The rationale for the existence of the latter figure, in his own mind as well as that of lobbyists for governmental assistance for him, has necessarily been more social than economic and more nostalgic than progressive. The hundreds of thousands of men and women who every year start businesses of their own have the hope, however illusory, of personal autonomy of the sort once valued by European peasant immigrants and by the classical republicans of the American Revolution. Study after study since 1930 has warned that failure within a few years is almost certain for many of them in the absence of relevant experience and adequate capital. Many of the would-be businessmen have been ludicrously unbusinesslike: stocking a variety store with $20 or $30 worth of canned goods; setting up a greeting-card shop without noticing that the drugstore next door carried the same merchandise; situating a fancy cooky shop in a poor working-class neighborhood. If the main object of such a venture had been entrepreneurial growth, a larger income than in a previous job, or even merely an alternative to unemployment, the proprietor might have planned more rationally and, in many cases, decided against going ahead.[72] Evidently a deeper drive was at work—"the urge," as an economist noted in Buffalo in 1930, "to become independent of the job." He found that, in the twentieth century as in the nineteenth, recent immigrants in particular "look upon a job as a workman as lower in the social scale" than any sort of independent proprietorship.[73]

The most minimal results of such a venture, other than outright failure, were found preferable to working for someone else. "I didn't expect to get rich," a former taxi driver operating a pizza restaurant in Providence, about 1960, observed, "but I always wanted to be my own boss." A mechanic had opened a gas station of his own "to make money," he said, "and so I don't have to take no guff from anyone." Others said much the same. A cook started his own restaurant because after twenty-eight years he was "sick and tired of working for someone else." Although "being in business for yourself means more work," as a meatcutter now running his own meat-delivery service explained, "the freedom is worth it." (All of these soon failed and went out of business.)[74] For every man who actually launched such a venture, there were many others, a study of automobile workers in the late 1940s discovered, who cherished the dream of independence, some of a subsistence farm but most of a small business. "The main thing," one machine operator said, "is to be independent and give your own orders and not have to take them from anybody else."[75]

Independence of that sort has often remained only a dream for the manager of one of the "franchises" that proliferated during the 1960s and 1970s—a fast-food restaurant, a gasoline station, an automobile dealership. The corporate promoters play on an almost irresistible attraction when, as a gas-station operator long in the business has described it, they "take the new victim uptown and show him colored motion pictures and tell him about the free enterprise system."[76] As the publisher of a trade journal expatiated in 1973, becoming "an independent businessman . . . is what franchising [is] all about." Even he conceded, however, that the aspirant "has to give up certain innovative ideas and a certain amount of his freedom, so to speak, in order to get into the franchising business."[77] To one critic of the system, which might require a hundred-thousand dollar investment and a large non-interest-bearing security deposit, the franchisee seemed "roasted and toasted five times" over.[78]

In the 1970s, however, when small business was touted as "a singular opportunity" for blacks, Chicanos, or Indians "to achieve a greater minority participation in our free enterprise system," federal lending policy was loosened in the hope of making independence, or at any rate the availability of franchises, more nearly equal.[79] That might contribute, in turn, to restoring to cities like New York what a small-town editor called, in 1975, a "middle people"—"the merchant, the community printer, the independent grocer, the small plant operator, the tailor, and the carpenter"—to whose disappearance from the ghettos he attributed the violence endemic there. Although, unlike the progressive Pingree three generations earlier, he did not equate the middle class with the republic itself, he saw it as at least "a buffer between the have-nots and the have-a-lots."[80] Experience would seem, however, to indicate that a basic economic security, including that of would-be proprietors of small businesses, is more likely to continue to be built upon minimum-wage laws, collective bargaining, unemployment compensation, old-age pensions, and other twentieth-century arrangements.

Voices still trumpeting the nineteenth-century medley of stable independence and dynamic entrepreneurship have a patently disingenuous ring. The largest conglomerates regularly advertise their similarity to small business: tiny beginnings, sometime in the past; ownership "by the people," that is, by individual stockholders; and the increased autonomy permitted, in recent years, to managers of their decentralized units.[81] But corporate executives themselves seem genuinely convinced that they are practicing "the traditional 'American way.' " Three out of four who were polled in 1975 claimed to prefer that old ideology of "self-respect and fulfillment . . . from an essentially lonely struggle in which initiative and hard work pay off" to the contrary system of organized group effort with which, they feared, government—and not their own kind of business—was rapidly replacing it.[82] Undaunted by specters of socialism, the ritual invocations go on of what Winthrop Rockefeller called, in 1972, "this nation's promise to its citizens [of] a high degree of personal control by the individual over his personal environment, life circumstances and destiny."[83] Inevitably, attempts to explain how that ideal relates to the actual small businessman end in "floundering about somewhere in between individualism and collectivism," as a law professor frankly confessed to a congressional committee in 1975.[84] To some sceptics, the ordinary men and women who try to put the small-business ideal into practice no longer appear even seekers after symbols so much as victims of a harmful psychological quirk.[85]

And yet, two hundred years after the American Revolution, successful executives as well as "Mom and Pop" corner grocers keep kicking against both state and corporate collectivism. Around the country in recent years there have been many relatively small but thriving companies whose owner-managers gave up substantial big-business positions out of "a strong desire for autonomy."[86] Big business itself is said to recognize the utility of such individuals, "yearning for independence and ideals," in recovering the dynamism lost by "servile functionaries or self-protective bureaucrats," the overly static "organization men" of the past generation.[87] The current prescription for corporate managers and workingmen alike is "individuation"—or, at least, "control by people who are relatively visible"—as a practical application of the old ideal.[88] Hope has even been expressed that the anarchic youth of the "counterculture" of the late 1960s, reborn as small businessmen, may yet transform the rebelliousness of "doing your own thing" into a "marvelous new value system," purged of greed and envy and dedicated to producing and selling only the useful and nonpolluting.[89] The ever renewed faith charms the sceptic, whether economist or moralist, notwithstanding the air of the habitual sleepwalker that hangs about the neorepublican dream of virtuous stability in a dynamic economy. Congress and the Small Business Administration continue, at any rate, to wrestle with the still "virtually universal . . . urge to be an entrepreneur . . . to start," however unfavorable the odds, "a business of one's own."[90] That the desire for "autonomy, usually ranked with security," has been found to cut across all categories of economic class and social status is not surprising in a republic founded on the civic virtue of the ideally self-reliant citizen and among a people most of whose forebears were European peasants.[91] As a recent official report observes, small businessmen remain "folk heroes" in America. Chained heroes thus far, perhaps: the report goes on to seek ways in which they might be freed from the constraints of modern government and big business and realize, after all, the American dream.[92] Folk heroes have a way of outlasting sceptics and changed circumstances.

Notes

1. *The Future of Small Business in America,* Hearings before the Subcommittee on Antitrust, Consumers, and Employment of the Committee on Small Business, House of Reps., 95 Cong., 2 sess., 1978, pt. 2, p. 7.

2. Christine Frederick, "Listen to This Sophisticated Shopper!" *Chain Store Age* (June 1925), 1:36.

3. E. C. Sams, in E. C. Buehler, *Debate Handbook: The Chain Store Question* (Lawrence: University of Kansas, 1932), p. 100.

4. Edward D. Hollander et al, *The Future of Small Business* (New York: Praeger, 1967), p. 98. Cf. Kurt Mayer, "Small Business as a Social Institution," *Social Research* (1947) 14:340.

5. Hollander, *Future of Small Business,* p. 100.

6. Edward Miller and John Hatcher, *Medieval England: Rural Society and Economic Change, 1086–1348* (London: Longman, 1978), pp. 143–45.

7. Warren O. Ault, *Open Field Husbandry and the Village Community: A Study of Agrarian By-Laws in Medieval England* (Philadelphia: American Philosophical Society, 1955).

8. Alan Macfarlane, *The Origins of English Individualism: The Family, Property and Social Transition* (Oxford: Blackwell, 1978), passim.

9. Margaret Spufford, *Contrasting Communities: English Villagers in the Sixteenth and Seventeenth Centuries* (Cambridge: Cambridge University Press, 1974), chap. 5.

10. Kenneth Lockwood, *A New England Town: The First Hundred Years, Dedham, Massachusetts, 1636–1736* (New York: Norton, 1970), p. 19.

11. Rowland Berthoff, *An Unsettled People: Social Order and Disorder in American History* (New York: Harper and Row, 1971), chaps. 2–6.

12. J. G. A. Pocock, *The Machiavellian Moment: Florentine Political Thought and the Atlantic Republican Tradition* (Princeton: Princeton University Press, 1975).

13. Gordon S. Wood, *The Creation of the American Republic, 1776–1787* (Chapel Hill: University of North Carolina Press, 1969).

14. E.g., Mayer, "Small Business as a Social Institution," p. 340; Elmo Roper, "The Public Looks at Business," *Harvard Business Review* (1949), 27:170; John H. Bunzel, *The American Small Businessman* (New York: Knopf, 1962), chaps. 3, 5.

15. *Proceedings and Debates of the Convention of the Commonwealth of Pennsylvania, to Propose Amendments to the Constitution* (Harrisburg, 1837–1838), 2:520 (James C. Biddle).

16. Rowland Berthoff, "Independence and Attachment, Virtue and Interest: From Republican Citizen to Free Enterpriser, 1787–1837," in Richard L. Bushman et al, eds., *Uprooted Americans: Essays in Honor of Oscar Handlin* (Boston: Little, Brown, 1979), pp. 97–124.

17. Stephan Thernstrom, *Poverty and Progress: Social Mobility in a Nineteenth-Century City* (Cambridge: Harvard University Press, 1964), chaps. 4–6; Charlotte Erickson, *Invisible Immigrants: The Adaptation of English and Scottish Immigrants in Nineteenth-Century America* (Coral Gables: University of Miami Press, 1972), pp. 27–28.

18. Sigmund Diamond, *The Reputation of the American Businessman* (Cambridge: Harvard University Press, 1955), pp. 15, 28.

19. *Proceedings of Convention of Pennsylvania*, 6:211 (John M. Scott).

20. Ibid., 6:82 (James Clarke).

21. Pocock, *Machiavellian Moment*, p. 546.

22. *Proceedings of Convention of Pennsylvania*, 5:437–38 (Almon H. Read).

23. Ibid., 6:89 (Clarke).

24. Ibid., 1:362 (Charles Ingersoll).

25. Ibid., 1:366.

26. Alfred D. Chandler, *The Visible Hand: The Managerial Revolution in American Business* (Cambridge: Harvard University Press, 1977), chaps. 1–2; Marvin Meyers, *The Jacksonian Persuasion: Politics and Belief* (Stanford: Stanford University Press, 1957), chap. 2.

27. *Proceedings of Convention of Pennsylvania*, 6:84 (Clarke); 7:159 (George W. Woodward). Cf. Louis Hartz, *Economic Policy and Democratic Thought: Pennsylvania, 1776–1860* (Cambridge: Harvard University Press, 1948), pp. 69–79; C. K. Yearley, Jr., *Enterprise and Anthracite: Economics and Democracy in Schuylkill County, 1820–1875* (Baltimore: Johns Hopkins University Press, 1961), pp. 84–90.

28. *Proceedings of Convention of Pennsylvania*, 6:382 (Thomas Earle). Cf. 7:157 (Thaddeus Stevens).

29. Ibid., 7:107–8 (William M. Meredith).

30. Ibid., 7:304 (Walter Forward).

31. Samuel Jones, *A Treatise on the Right of Suffrage* (Boston, 1842), p. 27.

32. Richard Hofstadter, *The Age of Reform: From Bryan to F.D.R.* (New York: Knopf, 1955), chap. 1.

33. Ira Steward, quoted in David Montgomery, *Beyond Equality: Labor and the Radical Republicans, 1862–1872* (New York: Knopf, 1967), p. 259. Cf. Norman Ware, *The Industrial Worker, 1840–1860: The Reaction of American Industrial Society to the Advance of the Industrial Revolution* (Boston: Houghton Mifflin, 1924), chap. 4.

34. Clyde Griffen and Sally Griffen, *Natives and Newcomers: The Ordering of Opportunity in Mid-Nineteenth Century Poughkeepsie* (Cambridge: Harvard University Press, 1978), pp. 119, 130, 147–48.

35. William Hoglund, "Finnish Immigrant Farmers in New York, 1910–1960," in O. Fritiof Ander, ed., *In the Trek of the Immigrants: Essays Presented to Carl Wittke* (Rock Island, Ill.: Augustana College Library, 1964), pp. 141–55.

36. Ross M. Robertson, "The Small Business Ethic in America," in Deane Carson, ed., *The Vital Majority: Small Business in the American Economy* (Washington, D.C.: Small Business Administration, 1973), pp. 29–30.

37. "Proceedings of the Committee on Manufactures in Relation to Trusts," *House Report* 3112, 50 Cong., 1 sess. (July 30, 1888), p. 184.

38. Ibid., pp. 89, 216.

39. *Chicago Conference on Trusts* (Chicago: Civic Federation of Chicago, 1900), pp. 263–67.

40. Ibid., pp. 281–82.

41. E.g., Hans B. Thorelli, *The Federal Antitrust Policy: Origination of an American Tradition* (Baltimore: Johns Hopkins University Press, 1955), p. 227.

42. Henry A. Stimson, "The Small Business as a School of Manhood," *Atlantic Monthly* (1904), 93:339–40.

43. Thorelli, *Federal Antitrust Policy*, p. 520.

44. Maurice W. Lee, *Anti-Chain Store Tax Legislation* (Chicago: University of Chicago Press, 1939), p. 5; Godfrey M. Lebhar, *Chain Stores in America, 1859–1962* (New York: Lebhar Friedman, 1963), pp. 117–24.

45. *Chain Stores: Cooperative Grocery Chains* (Washington, D.C.: Federal Trade Commission, 1932), pp. xvi–xvii, 18–19, 34.

46. Albert H. Morrell, in Buehler, *Debate Handbook*, p. 151.

47. E. C. Sams, in ibid., p. 101.

48. Joseph H. Appel, in ibid., pp. 130–31.

49. Federal Trade Commission, "Chain Stores: The Chain Store in the Small Town," *Sen. Doc.* 93, 73 Cong., 2 sess. (November 22, 1933), pp. 30, 60–64, 68.

50. Ibid., pp. 72, 73.

51. Temporary National Economic Committee, *Verbatim Record* (Washington, D.C.: Bureau of National Affairs, 1939), 1:98, 100 (Leon Henderson).

52. Ibid., 1:53.

53. Ellis W. Hawley, *The New Deal and the Problem of Monopoly: A Study in Economic Ambivalence* (Princeton: Princeton University Press, 1966), chap. 13.

54. *Congressional Record*, 80, pt. 3, 74 Cong., 2 sess., p. 3447 (March 9, 1936); pt. 7, p. 8111 (May 27, 1936). Cf. Lebhar, *Chain Stores in America*, p. 270.

55. *Congressional Record*, 80, pt. 7, 74 Cong., 2 sess., p. 8131 (May 27, 1936; John A. Martin).

56. *Price Discrimination: The Robinson-Patman Act and Related Matters*, Hearings before the Select Committee on Small Business, House of Reps., 84 Cong., 1 sess. (1955), pp. 204, 214.

57. *New York Times*, February 4–5, 1938. Cf. Bunzel, *American Small Businessman*, pp. 3–9. Small business opinion ten years later was much the same. Henry C. Link, "What Little Business Thinks of Big Business," *Nation's Business* (October 1949), 37:31–32, 70–71.

58. *New York Times*, February 3, 1938.

59. Harmon Zeigler, *The Politics of Small Business* (Washington, D.C.: Public Affairs Press, 1961), pp. 45, 66.

60. Emerson P. Schmidt, *Small Business: Its Place and Problems* (Chamber of Commerce of the U. S. A., Post War Readjustment Bulletin No. 7, 1943), pp. 20–21.

61. Zeigler, *Politics of Small Business*, chap. 7.

62. Alfred R. Oxenfeldt, *New Firms and Free Enterprise: Pre-War and Post-War Aspects* (Washington, D.C.: American Council on Public Affairs, 1943), pp. 179–80, 187.

63. Marshall D. Ketchum, "The Financial Problems of Small Business," *Journal of Business* (April 1944), 17:172.

64. C. Wright Mills and Melville J. Ulmer, "Small Business and Civic Welfare," *Sen. Doc.* 135, 79 Cong., 2 sess. (February 13, 1946), pp. 5–12, 14–15, 22–23, 26.

65. Mayer, "Social Institution," pp. 348–49.

66. Zeigler, *Politics of Small Business*, p. 99.

67. E.g., statement by Commissioner Stephen J. Spingarn, in *Monopolistic Practices and Small Business*, Staff Report to the Federal Trade Commission for the Subcommittee on Monopoly of the Select Committee on Small Business, Senate, 1952, pp. 1–9; *Small Business and the Quality of American Life: A Compilation of Source Material, 1946–1976*, Select Committee on Small Business, Senate, 1977.

68. *Congressional Record*, 99, pt. 5, 83 Cong., 1 sess., pp. 6128, 6149 (June 5, 1953).

69. Ibid., p. 6128; "Establishment of Small Business Administration and Liquidation of Reconstruction Finance Corporation," *Sen. Report* 604, 83 Cong., 1 sess. (1953), pp. 2, 9, 10.

70. *Definition of "Small Business" Within Meaning of Small Business Act of 1953, As Amended*, Hearings before Subcommittee No. 2 of the Select Committee on Small Business, House of Reps., 1958, pp. 2-3, 15ff., 280.

71. Joseph D. Phillips, *Little Business in the American Economy* (Urbana: University of Illinois Press, 1958), pp. 17–18. Cf. Hollander, *Future of Small Business*, pp. 4–7.

72. Kurt B. Mayer and Sidney Goldstein, *The First Two Years: Problems of Small Firm Growth and Survival* (Washington, D.C.: Small Business Administration, 1961), pp. 163–66, 172–76.

73. Edmund D. McGarry, *Mortality in Retail Trade* (Buffalo: University of Buffalo Bureau of Business and Social Research, 1930), pp. 71–80.

74. Mayer and Goldstein, *First Two Years,* pp. 30, 31.

75. Ely Chinoy, *Automobile Workers and the American Dream* (New York: Doubleday, 1955), p. xvi.

76. *FTC Industry Conference on Marketing of Automotive Gasoline,* Hearings before Subcommittee No. 4 on Distribution Problems of the Select Committee on Small Business, House of Reps., 89 Cong., 1 sess., 1965, 1:63.

77. *The Role of Small Business in Franchising,* Hearings before the Subcommittee on Minority Small Business Enterprise and Franchising of the Permanent Select Committee on Small Business, House of Reps., 93 Cong., 1 sess., 1973, pp. 148, 149.

78. Ibid., p. 87.

79. Ibid., p. 49.

80. *Small Business and Society,* Hearings before the Select Committee on Small Business, Senate, 94 Cong., 1 sess., 1975, p. 23.

81. Francis X. Sutton et al., *The American Business Creed* (Cambridge: Harvard University Press, 1956), pp. 58–61.

82. William F. Martin and George Cabot Lodge, "On Society in 1985—Businessmen May Not Like It," *Harvard Business Review* (Nov.–Dec. 1975), 53:143–52.

83. *The Future of Smalltown and Rural America: The Impact on Small Business,* Hearings before the Subcommittee on Small Business Problems in Smaller Towns and Urban Areas of the Select Committee on Small Business, House of Reps., 92 Cong., 2 sess., 1972, 1:9.

84. *Small Business and Society,* p. 123.

85. Albert Shapero, "The Displaced, Uncomfortable Entrepreneur," *Psychology Today* (November 1975), 9:83–88.

86. *Small Business Success: Operating and Executive Characteristics (Metal-Working Plants)* (Cleveland: Western Reserve University Bureau of Business Research, 1963), pp. 156, 166.

87. Michael Maccoby, *The Gamesman: The New Corporate Leader* (New York: Simon and Schuster, 1976), p. 107; *Small Business and Society,* pp. 49–50.

88. *Small Business and Society,* pp. 11, 51.

89. *Future of Small Business in America,* p. 239 (Carter Henderson, Princeton Center for Alternative Futures).

90. Ibid., p. 4.

91. Richard P. Coleman and Lee Rainwater, *Social Standing in America: New Dimensions of Class* (New York: Basic Books, 1978), p. 50.

92. *The Study of Small Business* (Washington, D.C.: Small Business Administration, 1977), pp. 11, 14.

2

THE REVOLUTIONARY
CHARLESTON MECHANIC

Richard Walsh

AMONG the three influential classes in Charleston during the Colonial and Revolutionary periods were the mechanics. The artisans were the first to move in the direction of revolution in 1765. Here were the men who with their retinue of apprentices, journeymen, and slaves formed the advanced guard of rebellion. Why? This essay intends to investigate that question. The simple question, however, requires a complex answer. Thus the totality of the Charleston mechanic's affairs, his life, the conduct of his business, his place in the class structure of British-American society, the uniqueness of his position in plantation society, his uncomfortable commitment to slavery, his relationship with his free black counterpart, all must be viewed before coming to grips with the leading role these workers, shopkeepers, and small businessmen played in Revolutionary politics.[1]

1. THE MECHANIC INDUSTRIALIST
OF CHARLESTON

Of the many profitable mechanic industries on the eve of the Revolution, shipbuilding headed the list. During the period, shipwrights of Carolina, most of whom worked in or near Charleston, built vessels totaling over 6,141 tons—schooners, brigantines, sloops, and heavier craft. Great numbers of pettiaugers and small crafts were also constructed for floating the provincial staples, rice and indigo, down river to market.[2]

The work of the Carolina shipbuilders was considered to be of high quality. Carolina-wrought vessels, while not as numerous as those made in Massachusetts, were noted for their durability and strength; but they were also expensive, perhaps because of the shortage of labor. In 1751, the Assembly had encouraged the development of the industry, passing legislation inviting artisans to the province and extending a bounty as an incentive to shipbuilding. The act was repealed later, allegedly because few came, since no one applied for the grant. Yet by 1760, shipbuilding accounted for the employment of hundreds of men. Besides construction of new vessels, there were endless repairs and alterations to be made in the very active commercial town where, during the busy season, it was customary to see 200 to 300 vessels in the harbor awaiting cargoes of rice for Portugal, the Indies, and England. Carpenters were employed; painters, glaziers, ironwrights, sail and ropemakers, even cabinetmakers, found encouragement for their arts at the bustling port. Toward the close of the century, the trade declined, probably because the builders of eastern Massachusetts and Philadelphia greatly undersold the Carolina shipwrights.[3]

Another important industry was barrelmaking. The entire countryside must have abounded in coopers. From Charleston were sent millions of staves, hoops, and barrels for rice, pitch, tar, turpentine, indigo, beef, and pork. Much of the coopering was probably done on the plantations by slave artisans; there is no way of knowing what proportion of the work was Charleston's, for records are scanty. But one Charleston cooper, David Saylor, became very wealthy and maintained what amounted to a cooperage factory on the city wharves, employing as many as 30 persons. Another, Gabriel Guignard, amassed a small fortune at the craft. Newspaper advertisements and the Charleston Inventories attest to a large number of these tradesmen working in the city.[4]

Between 1760 and 1785, 21 chandlers supplied candles and soap for the provincials, and exchanged quantities of these items for the rare woods and sugar of the West Indies—a commerce which brought much needed specie into the province. However valuable, the chandler was constantly the target of Grand Juries who "presented" the craft as dangerous to the health and safety of the town. To the chandler was attributed many a city fire, and the stink of the boiling tallow sent many Charlestonians holding their noses and gasping for pure air. Complaints accompanied demands that chandlers be moved into the country. Later, they were merely licensed, not removed.

With the bakers, they continued to be the unintentional incendiaries of the town, to the rage and frustration of residents.[5]

In tanning, the city had another industrial prize. For example, 41,701 sides of leather left Charleston for the Indies and England during the Revolutionary period. Some 21 tanners operated yards during the time. Men who labored at this "art" were apparently among the more substantial mechanics, as the wills of such tanners as James Darby and Samuel Jones evidence. Tanning required large outlays of capital for land and tools and a mill to grind bark. From workers in this industry were to come some of the most prominent South Carolina families. Consider the case of the humble saddler John Laurens; his son, Henry, became one of the merchant princes of the American colonies.[6]

Because they were indispensable, tailors were numerous and powerful tradesmen. Tailors outfitted the provincial dandies with their scarlet coats with gold buttons and their velvet capes, and provided the livery for their servant men. Their cloth was imported from England, and, dependent upon English trade, many became Loyalists during the war. Not all did so, evidently, for a tailors' society which was formed as early as 1760 was still operating during the Revolution and complaining in the newspapers about the American economy. Typically, critics of early labor organizations accused their society and others like them of attempted monopoly and setting of high prices.[7]

The shoemakers were also important. Quantities of "Negro shoes" as well as fine shoes and boots for men and ladies' and children's pumps were made by cordwainers like John and Simon Berewick, Patrick Hinds, and John Potter. The former partners kept a tanyard which supplied them with leather for their shop in town, where were placed on sale at one time more than a thousand pairs of shoes that they had fashioned. Patrick Hinds and John Potter boasted ownership of a town warehouse from which they could serve the inhabitants of the low country. Patrick Hinds, who served during the whole era, died a wealthy man.[8]

Saddlers often worked with the cordwainers and tanners. There were many in town, judging from the newspaper advertisements, and their services were greatly in demand. The saddler manufactured his own riding equipment but frequently imported and sold fine saddlery from England.[9]

The town also contained a number of coachmakers, among whom were the political cohorts of Christopher Gadsden, the radical revolutionary.

H. Y. Bookless, John Laughton, Benjamin Hawes, and Richard Hart were chaisemakers who participated in a meeting at the Liberty Tree in 1766. At that critical time they and other mechanics listened to a "harrangue" by Gadsden against the Declaratory Act. These coachmakers, who built coaches and riding chairs "in the most complete and elegant manner," often found themselves reconditioning old models from England. As wheelwrights, they made spinning wheels for self-sufficient townsmen and planters, and gave force to the anti-British boycotts of the Revolutionary period by selling them to potentially practical provincials.[10]

There were numerous gunsmiths on whom the military forces especially depended to repair arms. Almost every colonist owned a weapon of some kind, from blunderbuss to finely wrought pistol. From the first settlement of the province, most able-bodied men were enrolled in the militia. The white-smiths seem to have made few weapons, though during the war they were useful in manufacturing some for the army, and in service to the rebel ordinance corps. In the years of peace, however, like any mechanics, they found themselves repairing imported English guns. Like the watchmakers, they were adept at making scales and other objects requiring a high degree of mechanical skill and the mind of the inveterate tinkerer.[11]

A listing of such craftsmen is nearly endless. There were barbers and hair-dressers who provided the imposing eighteenth-century styles of London and Paris for the provincial ladies. Perukemakers enabled this generation to change the color of its hair at the slightest whim. Powdermakers manufac-tured powder for the wigs of townsmen, and provided the whiteness of aris-tocratic ladies' complexions as proof they had never worked in the fields or the open air. Staymakers stuffed the ladies' excessive fullness into stylish ballroom figures. Weavers made cottons, woolens, and "threadcloth." Dyers worked silk as well as homespun and scoured gentlemen's garments. Seamstresses, embroiderers, mantuamakers fashioned clothing for women and taught their skills to young girls. Confectioners concocted sweets. To-bacconists prepared delicate mixtures and kept "smoaking shops" after the style of England. Brewers made ale and beer with "double brewed Spruce Beer." Mr. Speaker, Peter Manigault, praised highly one of the brewers, Edmund Egan, for keeping "above £20,000 per year in the province." There were also upholsterers who hung drapery, repaired worn furniture, worked with the cabinetmakers, and made umbrellas and parasols after the best European fashion. Tinsmiths made "fire-buckets," covered roofs, and lighted the streetlamps of the city. Bakers prepared fancy pastry, bread, and "shipbread" or hardtack for seamen. And lowly butchers rose to wealth by purchasing meat from farmers and reselling it to townsmen, to the militia, and to ship captains. Indeed, it seems that at no time was eighteenth-century Charleston without the benefits of multiple tradesmen. They were an integral and colorful part of the scene; some shipped their wares overseas and in a small way helped to balance the economy of the province. They made of Charleston a busy, bustling, hawking little London in America.[12]

2. THE MECHANIC AS ARTIST

Foremost among the industrial artists of Charleston were the cabinetmakers. There were approximately 28 in 1760, 35 in 1790, and 81 by 1810. There were about 250 plying their trade between 1700 and 1825. Despite their numbers, almost no record of their production exists. But the account book of Thomas Elfe, apparently one of the leading cabinetmakers of Charleston, gives some insight into their productivity. Between 1768 and 1776, this artisan alone produced 1,500 pieces of furniture: bedsteads, chests, desks, clothes presses, all sorts of chairs, card tables, tea tables, sofas, clock cases, bookcases, and so on.[13]

Among the cabinetmakers, there was keen competition, as the following statement of Richard Magrath suggests. He wrote in the *South Carolina Gazette* that he had "lately been so fortunate as to discover the wretch, who for some time past has been mean enough to attempt injuring him in his Business, and whose ill nature and prejudice have extended so far as to enduce him to go to several Gentlemen's Houses and find Fault with his Work," but he hoped "that his Customers for the future will pay no Regard to the words of such a low groveling fellow, pregnant with impudence, Ignorance and Falsehoods, and who is too insigificant a Creature to have his Name mentioned in a public paper, notwithstanding he has the assurance to call him The Ladies Cabinet Maker." He is "destitute of both Truth and Abilities."[14]

The cabinetmakers worked in the same styles as the English masters— Sheraton, Hepplewhite, Chippendale, and Adams. In some particulars, however, there were American peculiarities evolving. Elfe, who used the customary mahogany—and for his secondary woods the local cypress, cedar, and poplar—developed singularly graceful frets on his furniture, by which his work can be accurately identified. Bedsteads of other craftsmen had removable headboards so that a sleeper might be cooled by the infrequent breezes of hot Charleston nights. On other pieces were carved rice ears and leaves after the staple of the lower country.[15]

The silversmiths of Revolutionary Charleston were also noteworthy artisans. Thomas You, Jonathan Sarrazin, James Askew, and Alexander Petrie sold imported trinkets and other baubles, but they also turned out many tankards, coffee and tea pots, punch bowls, ladles, strainers, and other handiwork, which graced the great planters' tables and matched for their beauty the products of English smiths. They copied the rococo but executed it with more restraint, and later went over to the plain or republican style, when ornateness smacked of kings and courts and undemocratic things.[16]

Engravers worked frequently with the silversmiths, but performed on their own as well, producing coats of arms, ornaments, nameplates, and so on. Often they made plates for the provincial currency. One of these men in the hire of the province, Thomas Coram, was apparently quite talented. He announced in 1776, thereby manifesting his political interests, that he had for sale a view of the engagement at Sullivan's Island on a copperplate 10½ by 15 inches. Coram, like others in his trade, tried his hand at painting. A picture, which he did on wood, now in the Cherokee Place Methodist Church in Charleston, indicates that he had marked technical skill in the classical mode.[17]

Another important metal worker was the blacksmith. He was undoubtedly the most versatile craftsman of all. Of course, he shod horses and repaired wagons; he also erected lightning rods. In fact, one, William Johnson, came to Charleston from the province of New York as a lecturer on electricity, and was well received. Apparently, he was a popularizer of Franklin's findings. He became one of the town's leading radicals, and John Rutledge called him the first mover of the "ball of revolution." He was the father of the historian Joseph Johnson and of the federal justice William Johnson, another opponent of centralized power.

Blacksmiths were noted for their artistry in iron. They emulated English masters and apparently copied their style from worked iron imported from England, provided these imports were simply done and within the Charleston smith's experience. The design of the imported altar rail of St. Michael's, for instance, set a standard which local smiths imitated in the countless grills, balconies, and gates for which the city is still famous. The influence of the ironwright of the West Indies was also evident.[18] Another aid was the folios of engravings published by Robert Adam, the Scottish architect. Thus such smiths as Johnson, Tunis Tebout, James Lingard, and John Cleator advertised that they performed scroll or plain work on railings for staircases, lamp-irons, "and many other branches that are manufactured in Iron too tedious to enumerate."[19]

House painters were also men of artistic abilities. They advertised that they rendered coats of arms on coaches and other objects of family pride. Among the painters were several artists and teachers of art. George Flagg and Benjamin Hawes taught drawing to the youth of the city for many years. One wonders if politics did not find a place in their lectures. Both were leading radicals of the Revolution and supporters of Christopher Gadsden.

Two other busy artists were John and Hamilton Stevenson, who maintained a painting academy where they offered the study of art, and of painting and drawing in the manner of the Roman school. Evenings they instructed mechanics with a bent for self-improvement in planning and architecture. This pair also gave lessons without charge each year to two young men recommended by the South Carolina Society, a benevolent organization. The paintings of the masters themselves comprised such works as landscapes, historical scenes, and portraits.[20]

Of the many limners, painters, and gilders who labored in Revolutionary Charleston, Jeremiah Theus was perhaps the finest of all—at least the one most preferred by low-country planters and merchants. Examples of his art are the prized possessions of many a present-day, low-country family which traces its forebears to the colonial and Revolutionary periods. He came from Switzerland about 1739 and commenced practicing his craft in Charleston a year later. From then on, he illuminated books, parchment, and script. In his portraits, the coloring is considered excellent; but, typical of the colonial artists, his work is primitive and his figures stiff, though he was trained in the early Northern school. It is said that his portraits of women demonstrate his best style. He excelled in depicting their fine laces and draperies. On the other hand, it is to be hoped that Charleston's upper crust ladies were in life less homely and one dimensional than the artist saw them![21]

The last group of industrial artists were the builders—carvers, plasterers, carpenters, bricklayers, and similar tradesmen. House carpenters and bricklayers often worked as architects—a profession not so well developed and organized then as now. Samuel Cardy, architect of famous St. Michael's Church, had as contemporary housewrights John and Peter Horlbeck, Timothy Crosby, and Daniel Cannon (all of whom were, incidentally, decided rebels). Carpenters were very numerous and, like the tailors, united in 1782 to form the Carpenters Society. They were also accused of raising the prices of their labor and materials to take advantage of the postwar boom in the reconstruction of plantation and town houses. They probably did. Everyone of the above died a wealthy man in the 1790s and 1800s.[22]

Such men built the Exchange, an excellent example of colonial architecture, the Miles Brewton House (the Heyward Washington House), several churches, and various other landmarks of Charleston past and present. For example, in the case of the State House—undergoing construction on the eve of the Revolution and a source of great artistic pride to Revolutionary Charlestonians—after the ordinary bricklayers, carpenters, joiners, and plasterers were dismissed, the artists went to work. The gilder, one Thomas Bernard, executed the King's arms, while Thomas Wooten carefully carved sixteen Corinthian columns in the Council chamber. Similarly, some unknown artist planned and constructed the home of the rich merchant Miles Brewton. Here, Ezra Waite, contracted as a carver but advertised as a joiner, civil architect, and general housewright, worked the Ionic entablature, the carvings in front and around the eaves, the decorations in the principal rooms, and all the tabernacle frames except those in the dining room. A true artist, he guarded his reputation jealously, for when a rival claimed that Waite had not done the work, the latter exploded in his advertisement in the *Gazette* with an offer of one hundred guineas to anyone who could verify the statement of his competitor, for he knew certainly no one could.[23]

The architectural styles of public buildings were Georgian, and their woodwork displayed the Chippendale mode of carving with skillfully blended Chinese and rococo motifs. For customers' dwellings, the builders generally adopted the house plan of northern Europe, but made it more suitable to the semitropical climate. In imitation of those of the old country, Charleston homes had thick walls of brick (manufactured locally); but piazzas were added for relief from torrid weather. Often town houses were characterized by wrought-iron balconies, after those of the West Indies. The relatively low price of town property permitted another alteration, in the shape of rambling servants' quarters, kitchens, and stables. Not infrequently, nature added to the general effect, as flower and vegetable gardens were planted, even in the middle of town.[24]

Thus did the mechanic enrich the life of Charleston and its environs. To say that the arts were undeveloped is patently absurd. Had such a claim been made of the Charleston mechanic of this era, it would surely have produced a denouncement such as an Ezra Waite or a Richard Magrath could handily deliver. The mechanic-artist even showed tendencies toward founding a Charleston style; such was the case with the builders, some cabinet-makers—Elfe, for example—ironwrights such as Johnson, the painters and silversmiths—Theus, Petrie, or Sarrazin. They performed in the same styles as Englishmen generally, but their American environment was evolving innovations.

3. THE MECHANICS IN BUSINESS

As the small businessmen of the colonial and Revolutionary periods, the mechanics may be divided into two classifications. One was the manufacturing shopkeepers, such as the saddlers, cabinetmakers, and shoemakers, who fashioned wares and placed them directly on sale at the shop. Rarely did they sell to merchants of the town who, as in England, then resold elsewhere. Charleston makers of goods, with the exception of tanners, chandlers, and coopers, did not usually export nor—like Philadelphia or New York artisans—enter the coastal trade. The other mechanics, though masters, were essentially laborers. These included such groups as carpenters, bricklayers, carvers, joiners, and tinsmiths. They did not keep shop, except as headquarters for an extensive establishment—for example, a master housewright or shipbuilder.

Two business forms were employed, the sole proprietorship and the partnership. Almost invariably the former was used, but it was not uncommon for the mechanic to take in a partner, by which means additional capital, a good name, or skill was gained, or perhaps a competitor eliminated. Such must have been the case in the partnership of John Fisher and Thomas Elfe. Elfe was one of the opulent mechanics of Charleston who loaned money at interest. Some of the most prominent inhabitants, including artisans, were indebted to him. Another partnership combining skills was that of Edward Weyman, a glazier and upholsterer, and John Carne, who advertised himself as a cabinet- and chairmaker. An advertisement of the painter Hawes, the wheelwright Laughton, and the coachmaker Bookless, refers to a "Company of Coachmakers.'' But this was not a company in the modern sense. The three were merely partners, the establishment unincorporated, and probably the chief offering of the trio was skill. By means of the newly joined company, they wrote:

> They can now advertise the publick, that they have brought all branches of the coach making business to such perfection, as not to exceed in quality the materials, goodness of the work, or neatness, by any importation; so that they can make and finish, without any assistance, out of their own shop all sorts of Coaches, Chariots, Phaeton, Post Chaises, Landau, Currices, Sedans, Sleighs, in the most complete and elegant manner, and afford them at more reasonable rates than can be imported.[25]

There were no business corporations in Charleston. However, mechanics in the same trade and with similar economic interests united. The tailors combined in 1760, and the Grand Jury complained that Negro apprentice chimney sweeps had joined together to raise their wages. The latter probably represents one of America's oldest labor unions, but unfortunately nothing more is known about it than the Jury's grievance. After the Revolution, the Carpenters', the Barbers', and the Master Coopers' societies were formed, and in 1794 various tradesmen began the Mechanics' Society, which admitted ''any number of free white Mechanics, Manufacturers, and Handicraftsmen.'' These organizations tried to increase their wages or the prices of their wares, for which the legislature was reluctant to incorporate them. Only when it was convinced that they were not combinations for ''forestalling and monopoly'' and were benevolent and charitable societies were charters granted. Thus were the Master Tailors' and Mechanics' societies finally incorporated, the first in 1784, the other at its inception.[26]

The mechanic of this day was ambitious, ever watchful of his interests, and always ready to improve and extend them. Sometimes his shop was the center of several activities which had nothing whatever to do with his trade but gave additional income. Thomas Nightingale, advertised as a saddler, serves as a case in point. He augmented his earnings by keeping a racetrack, at which was run the ''Mechanicks Purse,'' and prizes were also awarded for the fastest mounts owned by planters and merchants. Besides this, Nightingale also conducted cock fights, loaned money at interest, auctioneered, rented wagons for carting, ''entertained Indians'' for the province. A shop was also a family concern.

As proof that not all of the mechanic businesses remained small, there were from time to time notices in the gazettes offering to bring to date and balance the books of tradesmen as well as merchants.[27]

As with all colonists, land was a main investment. If the artisan was only fairly prosperous, he speculated in town lots—often to a fault during the Revolution, when property changed hands repeatedly because of inflation. But if the mechanic were more cautious, he built on his land and rented the buildings. Buying plantations was also common among the artisans. Such a purchase was sound not only monetarily but also socially, affording entrance into the planter class, the pinnacle of Southern society.[28]

Shipowning was another avenue of investment. To illustrate, Benjamin Hawes and George Flagg, the painters, bought a 15-ton vessel in 1763, with which to enter the West Indian trade in rice. Another of several shipowners was Walter Mansell, who with George Sheed, a plumber, acquired a 65-ton vessel. They operated with such success that they rose to the rank of merchants. When the economy became rocky during the war, Jonathan Sarrazin quit silversmithing and with his son, Edward, used his ship to eke out a living. The examples of ship buying were by no means few.[29]

In his shop, the artisan employed apprentices. These supplied him with cheap labor for at least four years, and each apprentice brought a fee of £20 sterling, in payment for which he was faithfully taught the craft. Apprenticeship had its disadvantages, however. As a worker, the apprentice was but an irresponsible learner, usually beginning training at the age of twelve to fourteen years. He found the town gaming houses more intriguing than the shop, and so pressing was this problem that in 1762 the legislature acted to prevent "excessive gaming" of servants, apprentices, and journeymen. By the frequency of such notices in the gazettes, runaways also plagued masters. Weyman, a glazier, once advertised in disgust for the return of a persistent perambulator: "Whoever shall deliver him to the master, shall receive a reward of Two Large Hand Fulls of Pine Shavings for their trouble."[30]

Use was made of indentured servants. Evidently these repeated all the woes of apprentices—running away, idleness, stealing, and whatnot. But often the "servant man" was as skilled as his master, and having availed himself of one or more, the master might advertise that he had added another "branch" to his shop. For example, Alexander Learmouth, a tanner, boasted that since he had supplied himself with tanners and curriers from England, he could sell leather cheaper than any yet done. The servant, like the apprentice, was impermanent and after his period of service, about five to seven years, departed. He then could and frequently did, become his master's competitor.[31]

Journeymen and masters lacking tools or wealth to enter trade on their own account were also hired. One master often employed another, for there existed no agency, such as a guild, to set standards of workmanship or the rank of artisans. The customer determined quality and capital, rank. As soon as the free laborer saved sufficient funds, he began his own enterprise, making free labor so scarce that the newspapers record tradesmen sending as far as England to engage an experienced workman.[32]

Because of this apparent scarcity of labor, and its instability, the artisan resorted to slavery. He gained from this system permanent workers whose wages and skill belonged to the owner. Among the numerous slaveholding artisans was Thomas Elfe, whose account book illustrates the system. Elfe kept six slaves valued at £2,250 sterling. They were trained as house painters, cabinetmakers, and carpenters for use in the shop and for hire by town and countrymen. Elfe's income from the latter employment amounted to £632:16:2 in 1768, £405:19:00 in 1769, and £279, in 1770.

His is not the only example. A court record indicates that Nathanial Scott, a carpenter and housewright, used himself, some white carpenters, and his Negroes Ben, Cudgoe, and Harry in building for one of the townsmen. David Saylor, a cooper, worked as many as thirty slaves in his packing-house. At one time Hawes entered a typical advertisement in the *Gazette*, saying that he could undertake any job of house painting by the use of his white apprentices and Negroes.[33] In 1785 a visitor to the city commented, in somewhat exaggerated terms, that he had seen tradesmen go through the city followed by a Negro carrying their tools. He added the accusation that barbers were supported in idleness and ease by Negroes who did the work; indeed, "many of the mechanics bear nothing more of their trade than the name."

The census of 1790 listed 1,933 heads of families in Charleston, of whom 1,247 owned one or more slaves. Of the 79 mechanics who left wills between 1760 and 1785, 37 specifically mentioned ownership of slaves. Of the 194 artisans who worked during these years and who could be identified in the census of 1790 there were 159 slaveholders. In other words, the percentage of slaveholders stood at 80 percent of the total number.[34] The many manuscript volumes of the *Inventories of Estates,* 1763–1810, also confirmed that of mechanics who died with property appraised at £400 or more, as much as 80 percent of such property had been invested in slaves. Slaves were trained for sale to the planters or townsmen at great profit. Sometimes the slave was a chattel kept as a legacy for the family. In case of the death of the master, the Negro became the wage earner or maintained the shop, while some member of the family supervised the business, as was very probably the case with the blacksmith Sarah Bricken. It was not unusual that the judicious purchase of a black craftsmen made a carpenter of a white jeweler or a bricklayer of a baker.[35]

Thus were the tradesmen of Charleston saddled with slavery. They were not happy with it and found that "jobbing Negroes" worked at low rates for some nonartisan townsman, merchant, or planter, at times making employment scarce for whites. They had fashioned their own dilemma, however. Journeymen and poor masters hated the system more than the shopkeeping tradesmen. It meant for labor only ruinous competition and low wages. In 1796, after the incorporation of the city, free labor secured a law to force masters to employ at least one white apprentice or journeyman for every four Negroes; yet the have-nots displayed human inconsistency. Upon acquiring enough capital to set up for themselves, they joined the slaveholders with a purchase or two. Such was the condition of Southern society.[36]

4. THE FREE NEGRO ARTISAN

A very important addition to the industrial and social life of the city were the free black craftsmen. By 1790 the free blacks numbered 586 and many were practicing every branch of trade, keeping their own shops or working for others. They were 5.14 percent of the total population of 11,389.[37]

Despite their numbers the freemen were shadowy figures. Unlike the white artisans they did not advertise in the city's several gazettes. Nor were they listed in the *Directories* of 1782, 1785, 1790, and 1800. Apparently they got their jobs by the reputation of their good workmanship. Their names were seen occasionally in the newspapers after a death when property was up for auction. They were identified in the *Probate Court Records,* the wills and inventories. In many of the inventories white mechanics served as appraisers of their remains. Sometimes a free black served in this capacity and the document spoke plaintively when a daughter or wife signed as administratrix with a mark. Among these black mechanics, literacy was ascertained, perhaps some considerable learning as well, as is evidenced by the "parcel of books" which sometimes appeared in the evaluation of an estate.[38]

Early evidence exists of the white mechanics' suspicion of, and discrimination against, their black counterparts. There were no black members of the mechanics' societies. Their names do not show up as members of the Carpenters', the Coopers', and the Tailors', nor any of the other white artisans benevolent fraternal and political organizations. They were excluded from the Mechanics' Society of 1794.

Although there is a myth that the free blacks were generally prosperous, their inventories of estates show just the opposite to be true. They were not as well off as their white counterparts. A few owned some property. For example, John Fenwicke, a bricklayer, was enabled through his lifelong labors to gain a house and shop. In his interesting will, he left small bequests to his friends and his sons and daughters—£10 currency, equivalent at the time to about £2 sterling. Several of his children were still slaves, showing the highly complicated nature of lives under the system of slavery, whether the industry involved was planting or craftsmanship.[39]

One of the most prominent of freemen was George Bedon, carpenter. At the time of his death in 1794, he left only £47:4.6 in sterling and $20 in cash (not quite £5 in sterling). Typically, he possessed few luxuries in his household. He owned no slaves, although this was unusual among the free black artisans. They apparently also practiced "hiring out" for the slaves' wages.[40]

That there was a separation of the black and white craftsmen, even in Revolutionary times, in which brotherhood and fraternity were common words, was evidenced by the formation of exclusive societies. George Bedon was one of the founders of the first of these and president of the long-lived Brown Fellowship Society, begun in 1790.[41]

The organization was racially conscious and discriminatory. None but mulattoes were accepted as members, and membership was limited. The society seemed to be closely imitative of the white organization, the Fellowship Society, founded by mechanics on the eve of the Revolution. The Brown Fellowship Society ruled against arguing or discussing politics or any matters of a controversial nature. They were carefully scrutinized by the white city government. The city magistrates thoroughly investigated them during the Denmark Vesey troubles of later years, and their conduct was thought to be exemplary. In the meantime, free Negroes, irritated at the racist behavior of the Browns, formed their own exclusively "black" societies, such as the Society of Free Blacks in 1791.[42]

But neither brown nor black was docile. Men shouted, talked, and wrote about liberty during the Revolutionary era. The black artisan would have to be dead not to have heard the Declaration of Independence read in the public squares in 1776. And he witnessed, and sometimes joined in, the struggle for independence. The freeman worked in the bastions; like his white counterpart his skills were badly needed. Some slaves would join the ranks of freemen because of their war services. Unquestionably, Denmark Vesey—who bought his freedom from Captain Joe Vesey, a chandler, in 1800 by winning a lottery ticket—walked the streets of Charleston in the mid-1780s when debates and rioting over the nature of the new freedom was rampant. The youthful slave-artisan was executed for inciting an insurrection in 1822. The evidence, however, only proved that he was outspoken, and he was probably innocent. The free Negro kept to a narrow line.[43] When a free Negro pilot named Jerry publicly asserted that he would guide the British across the bar, he was hanged on August 18, 1775; his only hearing was before the Committee of Safety.[44] For these reasons, enslaved blacks in Carolina, perhaps as many as five thousand, chose to go with the British, who had promised them freedom. Carolinians alleged that they were carried off and stolen by the enemy.[45]

The free artisans, having a stake and deep roots in American society, probably stayed on. Their numbers doubled by 1800. Their lives, however, were hard.

As late as 1790, Matthew Webb, a butcher, Thomas Cole, a bricklayer and builder, and Peter B. Mathews, a butcher, pointed out that at a time when the federal and the new state constitution of 1790 provided Bills of Rights, they, as free citizens, were excluded. They petitioned the South Carolina Senate. At least that body had refused a white mechanic's petition to prevent any Negro from working for himself except under the direction of a white man.[46]

These butchers and the bricklayer asserted that Negro artisans could not give testimony on oath in prosecutions on behalf of the state. They could not testify to recover debts owed them. They were denied trial by jury and subjected to the unsworn testimony of slaves. They reminded the Senators that they were citizens and taxpayers, and that they were peaceful and constructive South Carolinians. The Negro Act of 1740 still prevailed against them. This harsh act against blacks had been the result of the Stono Rebellion and massacre of Negroes back in 1739. The Senate refused redress of their grievances. Their petition was rejected. Thus the free black artisans—the

carpenter Matthew Webb, the builder Caesar Benoist, the carpenter George
Bedon, the artisan George Gardiner, and those who kept only their first
names: Joe the shoemaker, and Quash, the African-named carpenter, and
Friday the painter—endured.[47]

5. SOCIAL STRUCTURE

In the white social structure of the times, the mechanics as a class were
regarded as beneath the merchants, while at the very top of society were the
planters. It was chiefly the British and aristocrats who constantly reminded
the mechanics of their status. The implication seems to have been that since
they worked with their hands, they were the unwashed, vulgar herd. "Stick
to your lasts," or "Stay out of matters of state," they were warned by their
Revolutionary-period antagonists. Before the Revolution the mechanics were
rarely addressed as mister, never as esquire. They were not a proletariat in
the eighteenth-century definition of the word, however deeply the British
seemed to believe this.

American status depended upon economic position, not on socially im-
mobile and artificial notions of society. To be sure, studies of the *Charleston
Inventories* to estates during the era indicate that about 24 percent of the
mechanics were relatively poor, renting their places and leaving less than
£100 at the end of their days. Some left absolutely nothing. This number
would have been greatly swelled had "mariners" been included. Incredible
are the number of inventories in which the mariners left not a shilling. Many
were artisans—sailmakers, ship carpenters, ropemakers and the like, but few
were permanent members of the community.

Sixty-six percent of the mechanics were in good, while 10 percent were in
excellent, financial condition.[48] At the top, the carpenter and political
leader, Daniel Cannon, was one of those whose fortune rivaled that of any
of the great planters. Cannon, who died in 1802, held household items of
£19,055, including Negroes. He owned a large tract of land in the city from
which he sold lots. For purchase of lands on Edisoto River, various individuals owed him $11,622.74. He held many in debt to him; that which was
collectible amounted to £2,098:18.3 in sterling. Half the debtors were de-
faulters. Another rich mechanic was the ship carpenter and politician Nathanial Lebby, who died in May 1802, with an estate of £7,171.60, including
a town house with a shop, and a plantation at Hobcaw. Thomas Elfe, the

famous cabinetmaker, whose inventory was dated September 14, 1776, left over £33,734. He apparently also kept a stock farm, containing 35 head of cattle, 26 sheep, 60 horses, and 19 hogs. Independence gave such men as these higher social standing and recognition.[49]

Their living conditions were unpretentious. Except for the wealthy artisans, they were strictly townsmen. Inventories and newspaper advertisements describe their undistinguished residences. Newspapers called them "neat" or "commodious." In general, their houses contained either four or six rooms, with the front lower room being a shop, or with an outbuilding on the premises which served that purpose. Sometimes business was carried on in the rooms downstairs while the upstairs rooms were the living quarters. If an inventory mentioned no outbuildings on the lot, yet contained several working black people, then the slaves must have lived in the house with the master's family. Bedsteads were the most numerous and common pieces of furniture listed in the valuations of estates. The skilled "jobbing" Negro's condition was better than the field hand's on a plantation who slept on a straw tick on the ground, in unheated and crowded quarters. However, since the average number of a household was between five and six persons, the six-room townhouse with shop hardly precluded crowding for any mechanic's family.[50]

Their residences lined King Street (now the main road out of town), Meeting Street, and the streets and alleys near the wharves. Some tradesmen, such as ship carpenters and coopers, located the businesses on the wharves. As we have noted, chandlers, bakers, and tanners, the city fathers tried to keep at some distance from the community, because of the danger from fire or the stinking nature of their work. Air pollution is not solely a twentieth-century problem. Consider also that wood burning was the only source of heat or industrial fuel in crowded Charleston.

Their residences were close to each other and conversation rather than letter writing was their main form of communication. But they were not entirely a nonwriting group, as their newspaper advertisements and the political essays of their leaders prove. Although half of their leadership were members of the Anglican Church, they were well aware of the natural and deistic leanings of the times. Evidently the rank and file of the mechanics could read and write. About 96 percent of their wills were signed, and they appear literate from other court records. In these same records, women more often than men affixed a mark to a document.

Their inventories indicated that many of the well-to-do mechanics owned books. What they read, however, cannot be ascertained. The appraisers of property listed merely "a parcel of books," or a "shelf of books," without further description.

Women numbered among the mechanics. Their occupations generally were milliners, tailors, pastry, or general cooks. They formed a small part of the working force. Of more than 1,400 mechanics listed in my files, they made up about 1 percent. The *Directory of 1790*, containing 190 names, shows 59 working women, however, which is 31 percent of the total. There were a few "Spinsters" among them, who were their own proprietors. Most of the ladies married and helped in their husband's shop. The wife of the politician-upholsterer Rebecca Weyman, for example, seems to have carried on Edward's trade through most of his lifetime. He was too busy with the Committee of Safety and other offices of the Revolution, and for nearly two years he was imprisoned by the British during the fall and occupation of Charleston. In any case, there were no ladies of leisure among the mechanics class.

Their inventories run the gamut from poverty to middling circumstances. For instance, Elizabeth Ross, a tailor, left an estate of $5,071.15 in 1804. Another, Mary Darling, a seamstress, left £78:10 in 1783. She had made "flags for the forts," according to the Commons House of Assembly records for 1765. But another milliner, Mary King, died in near poverty, leaving £26:17.10 after her belongings were auctioned, while over £12,460 in inflated currency was owed her estate.[51]

6. MERCANTILISM AND THE MECHANIC

Mercantilism aided many groups of mechanics. Hemp makers were given British bounties, and coopers were subsidized. Manufactories of potash were assisted by the removal of duties on the product upon its importation into Great Britain. The London Society of Arts also aided the fertilizer makers. Shipbuilders and those who produced naval stores were encouraged by the Empire with grants of money.[52]

On the other hand, the spirit of mercantilism was an absolute discouragement to all the artisans who competed with their counterparts in England. Artisans of Charleston daily saw English-made furniture, silver, guns, iron, coaches, saddles, and shoes unloaded at their port for sale to the provincials. English merchants, offering long-term credit, consistently flooded the market with wares, thereby depriving Charleston artisans of customers and profits. Indeed, at times, they were the forgotten men of the colony as their manufactures were passed over for English importations. Not slavery, but imperial notions of society and economics largely discouraged Charleston artisans.

There were no laws passed by Parliament directly curtailing their manufacturing. The Hat Act did not, for example, immediately affect them, nor did the Iron Act. There is no record of a hatter in Charleston, and there was only one manufactory of iron, in York County, which was in a very poor condition. But the attitude which brought about such acts, the favoritism shown for Englishmen over Americans by the Parliament, did not sit well with the mechanics.[53]

The Charleston artisan, mainly interested in the invasion of the local market by English mechanics, was very favorably disposed toward the boycotts and embargoes erected on the eve of the Revolution. Such antimercantilistic weapons brought the mechanic new and willing customers. The phrases in so many Charleston newspaper advertisements—"As good as imported," "As cheap as imported"—were not written idly; these were aimed at England.

Monetary difficulties were also the result of the imperial system, affecting every mechanic industry. In general, acting in the role of creditor to the colonies, the British consistently tried to keep the value of money at a high level, forbidding or only grudgingly assenting to issues of Carolina paper money. The province employed the subterfuge of issuing certificates, or bills of credit, to be used for the payment of taxes only, but which circulated readily. When the province spent heavily, as during the war with France, money was plentiful and times were good. Correspondingly when less was spent and a large number of certificates were retired, times were exceedingly bad. Debtors and creditors were at one another's throats.[54]

The mechanics and the planters were in agreement over the merits of cheap money, which they wanted for buying tools, materials, and labor, and for expansion and payment of debts. On the other side, the merchants, being creditors, naturally leaned toward the hard-money policies of the British and were for this reason very hesitant to move against the Crown on the eve of the war. They carried on little or no clandestine trade, unlike their brothers in New England, and were only mildly annoyed at the political harpies, the customs collectors, who descended on their port as a result of the acts of trade of the 1760s.[55]

But there were occasions when the mechanics could sympathize with the advocates of hard money, for they too were sellers of wares and services. During difficult times, unable to collect sums due from the planters, they were in turn squeezed by the merchants from whom they had purchased materials or borrowed money. At such times a mechanic might call "to those who have open accounts with him, to discharge the same immediately, else, when the courts open, their neglect may prove fatal to him," or as Sarrazin the silversmith warned his debtors, not to "take it amiss if I call often upon them, as I must keep up my credit." He added: "My worthy friends must also consider that the sun is very hot to walk in . . . I spend more time in collecting . . . money than earning it."[56]

7. THE MECHANICS IN
REVOLUTIONARY POLITICS

Before the Revolution, the mechanics were apparently contented with their political situation in provincial society. To translate economic and social desires into legislative action, they employed the petition or the ballot. Most of them were property owners, and the suffrage act of 1721 required merely the ownership of 50 acres of land, or the payment of 20 shillings taxes in currency, in order to vote. They also used the Grand Juries of the two parishes which made up the town, St. Philip's and St. Michael's, to make their sentiments more directly known to the Commons House of the Assembly.

They also played a minor role in parochial affairs. As elected Anglican vestrymen, together with two wardens—always planters and merchants—they oversaw the orphanage, pest house, the parish schools, and the securing of clergymen. Artisans served in the fire department, such as it was, and frequently performed as constables. Sometimes one was appointed by the Commons House as a wood and coal measurer of the market.[57]

But no mechanic ever sat in the Commons House of Assembly representing the town and their interests, even though many could meet the necessary property qualifications. Before the Revolution, in aristocratic British and

Charleston society, they were regarded as socially inferior to merchants and planters and unfit to manage affairs of state. The attitude of William Drayton was typical: mechanics were a "useful and essential part of society . . . but every man to his trade: a carpenter would find himself put in an awkward situation on a cobbler's bench. When a man acts in his own sphere, he is useful in the community, but when he steps out of it, and sets up for a statesmen [sic], believe me he is in a fair way to expose himself to ridicule."[58]

And on the very eve of the Revolution, the assistant rector of St. Michael's Church declared from the pulpit that "every silly Clown, and illiterate Mechanic [takes it upon himself] to censure the conduct of his Prince and Governor, and contribute, as much as in him lies, to create and foment those misunderstandings which . . . come at last to end in Schisms in the Church, and sedition and rebellion in the State. . . . There is no greater Instrument or Ornament of Peace then for every man to keep his own rank, and to do his own duty in his own station"—all of which created an uproar leading to the minister's dismissal.[59]

Lower class though they were thought to be, the mechanics became very articulate during the years of revolution. In 1762, the upholsterer Edward Weyman founded the Fellowship Society, a benevolent organization chiefly composed of mechanics and concerned with building a hospital and other charitable works. Although the founders were the very same group who supported Gadsden at the time of the Stamp Act, no political pronouncements emanated from the society—at least, nothing like this is contained in the earliest records of the organization. Yet to conclude that not a word of politics was uttered in their meetings would be unwise. The founder was one of the leading radical townsmen. Later in the 1760s, merchants of more conservative temperament gained admittance, but by then the mechanics appear prominently in such Revolutionary societies as the John Wilkes Club or the Palmetto Society.[60]

The mechanics vigorously opposed the Stamp Act. It was at this time that they cemented an alliance with Christopher Gadsden (the first man in the province to advocate independence), which lasted until 1778, when he broke with them for their continued rioting and other disturbances.[61]

That they were enthusiastic followers of the program of the radicals of New England was reflected by Gadsden when he wrote Sam Adams that during the early days of the revolt many Charlestonians looked upon the

"New England States with a kind of Horror, as artful designing Men altogether pursuing selfish purposes." "How often," he related, "I stood up in their Defence and only wish'd we would imitate instead of abusing them. . . . I thank'd God we had such a Systematical Body of men as an Assylum that honest men might resort to in the Time of their last Distress, supposing them driven out of their own States. I bless'd God there was such a People in America. That for my part I never look upon any danger from them."[62]

In 1768, the mechanics supported John Wilkes for his *North Britain* No. 45 and the 92 antirescinders of Massachusetts Bay for their resistance to Royal authority. At a meeting which has been described as America's earliest political convention, they chose their candidates for the Commons House, Gadsden among those selected, and then, in the words of Peter Timothy, the rebel editor of the *South Carolina Gazette:*

the company partook of plain and hearty entertainment, that had been provided by some upon whom this assembly will reflect lasting honour. About 5 O'clock they all removed to a most noble LIVE OAK, in Mr. Mazyck's pasture, which they formally dedicated to LIBERTY, where many loyal patriotic, and constitutional toasts were drank, beginning with the glorious NINETY-TWO Anti-Rescinders of Massachusetts Bay and ending with, unanimity among the members of our ensuing Assembly not to rescind from the said resolutions [to boycott England], each succeeded by three huzzas. In the evening, the tree was decorated with 45 lights, and 45 skyrockets were fired. About 8 O'Clock, the whole company preceeded by 45 of their number, marched in regular procession to town, down King-street and Broad-street, to Mr. Robert Dillon's tavern; where the 45 lights being placed upon the table, with 45 bowls of punch and 45 bottles of wine and 92 glasses, they spent a few hours in a new round of toasts, among which, scarce a celebrated Patriot of Britain or America was omitted; and preserving the same good order, and regularity as had been observed throughout the day, at 10 they retired.[63]

As indicated in the above, they were the first party to take steps against the Townshend Acts. Their influence grew as America and Britain moved toward war. So great had their power grown in 1769 that they were given equal representation with the planters and merchants when the thirteen mechanics were elected to the Committee of Enforcement of the boycott. During this struggle, they were adamant proponents of action prohibiting importation of British manufactures. When the merchants offered a program of nonimportation which did not contain this prohibition, it drew the prompt response of: "A Mechanic": "How can it be expected that any Planter, Mechanic, or other inhabitant . . . will subscribe to their Resolution . . .

when THEY do not contain a single syllable *Encouraging American Manufactures."* The mechanics, with Gadsden's assistance, finally won their point at a meeting of the inhabitants under "Liberty Tree" and a nonimportation program was accepted which satisfied them.[64]

In 1775, with the colonies on the brink of war, and a British task force lying off Charleston harbor, the provincial radicals hoped to provoke attack. Two Tories were tarred and feathered by a mob turned loose by the rebellious aristocrat William Henry Drayton and upholsterer Edward Weyman. Gunner Walker of the British army received a "suit of Cloathes . . . without the assistance of a single Taylor," and as the mob carted its victim through the streets of the city, as a warning to everyone of royalist leaning, it passed by the Governor's house and threw a bag of feathers on his balcony; the mob "desired he would take care of it till his turn came." The unfortunate Gunner was forced to drink "Damnation to Lord North" with grog demanded of the chief magistrate. Walker was afterwards deposited at the door of His Majesty's surgeon general to Carolina forces, one Dr. Johnston-Milligan, who had been pressed to declare his loyalty to the Americans by Weyman, Cannon, Johnson, and the carpenter Fullerton.[65] Artisans were also prominent in attacking the royal arsenals.[66]

Why were the mechanics so enthusiastic in the cause of independence? In 1769, Gadsden answered this question:

There are not wanting wealthy men amongst the . . . mechanics; yet in common their circumstances are but low; and oppression, when at its height, generally falls heaviest upon men, who have little before-hand, but depend, almost altogether upon their daily labor and industry, for the maintenance of themselves and families; it is no wonder, that throughout America, we find these men extremely anxious and attentive to the cause of liberty.

He continued that there was in America no great danger of starvation and that the mechanic here finds himself in a more comfortable situation than his European counterpart. "The distinctions . . . between the farmer and the rich planter, the mechanic and the rich merchant, being abundantly *more* here in imagination, than reality," but

When oppression stalks abroad, then the case is widely different: For in arbitrary governments, tyranny generally descends, as it were, from rank to rank, through the people, til' almost the whole weight of it, at last, falls upon the honest, laborious farmer, mechanic, and day laborer. When this happens, it must make them poor indeed. And the very apprehension thereof, can not but cause extreme uneasiness.

This, therefore, naturally accounts for these people, in particular, being united and steady, everywhere to prevent, if possible, being reduced to so dismal a situation: Which should it be unhappily the case, they can not but know, they must then see it out, and feel it out too, be it what may.[67]

It was not entirely a question of forestalling poverty that motivated the ambitious Revolutionary mechanic, particularly the master. He wanted his man in the Assembly; this he won. When the first Provincial Congress convened, George Flagg, William Johnson, Edward Weyman, and Daniel Cannon were therein seated, active in guiding the rebellion with radical planters and merchants. He desired "encouragement" for his manufactures. This he achieved in the form of a tax exemption on his profits in trade.[68] The Revolution, it seemed to him, eliminated his overseas rival in London, Glasgow, Manchester, and other British cities. In later years, he found himself again forgotten, as cotton tied the South to the factories of England. But during the Confederation, the Charleston mechanic identified himself with fellow artisans in Boston, Philadelphia, and New York in their intensive program for the support of manufactures, just as he had agreed with the associations emanating from those cities on the eve of the war.[69] In 1788, at the ratifying convention for the Constitution, the delegates Johnson, Cannon, and Sarrazin voted for the Constitution. One suspects they were as favorably disposed toward tariffs as Hamilton himself.[70]

The Charleston mechanics were thus a very important element. To the economy and to society in general, they were essential, and in the history of the period they are significant.

Notes

1. *The Charleston Directory*, 1790; E. Milbury Burton, *Charleston Furniture 1700–1825* (Charleston, S.C.: 1955); *South Carolina Silversmiths 1690–1860* (Charleston, S.C.: Charleston Museum, 1942). Leila Sellers, *Charleston Business on the Eve of the American Revolution* (Chapel Hill, N.C.: University of North Carolina Press, 1934), pp. 102–3; also Carl Bridenbaugh, *The Colonial Craftsman* (New York: New York University Press, 1950), pp. 30–32, which fails to note that Charleston was an exception to the dubious statement that by the time of the Revolution no " 'class of Mechanicks' emerged to meet the South's wants except the crude artisans of the backcountry."

Other very creditable scholarship on the mechanics of other cities are Charles S. Olton, *Artisans for Independence: Philadelphia Mechanics and the American Revolution* (Syracuse, New

York: Syracuse University Press, 1975). Howard B. Rock, ''The American Revolution and the Mechanics of New York City: One Generation Later,'' *New York History*, July 1976, pp. 367–94. Rock's first note cites further work on the New York City artisans.

This essay is a major revision of my article in the *South Carolina Historical Magazine* of 1959, beginning page 123. Parts of the original are published by permission of the South Carolina Historical Society.

2. Ship Registers, 1730–65; 1765–74; Journals of the House of Representatives, 1784, p. 31, February 2, 1784; MSS, South Carolina Archives Dept., hereafter cited S.C.A.D.; Sellers, *Charleston Business*, pp. 62–64.

3. Ship Registers, 1730–65; Victor S. Clark, *History of Manufactures in the United States, 1607–1928*, 3 vols. (New York: Peter Smith, 1949), 1:138, 3:367; Richard Champion, *Considerations of the Present Situation of Great Britain and the United States* (London, 1784), pp. 73–74. Thomas Cooper and David J. McCord, *Statutes at Large of South Carolina*, 10 vols. (Columbia, S.C.: A. S. Johnston, 1836–1841), 3:742, 4:10–11.

4. Charles Joseph Gayle, ''The Nature and Volume of Exports from Charleston, 1724–1774,'' *Proceedings of the South Carolina Historical Association* (1937), p. 31; David Saylor Receipt Book, 1784–87, Ms, South Carolina Historical Society, Charleston. *Records of the Court of Chancery of South Carolina: 1671–1779*, Anne King Gregorie, ed. (Washington: American Historical Association, 1950), p. 570. Saylor's workmen were apparently slaves; see *Heads of Families, 1790*.

5. Gayle, ''Nature and Volume of Exports,'' p. 33; *South Carolina Gazette*, June 8, 1765; February 22, 1773; hereafter cited *S. C. G.*; Alexander Edwards, *Ordinances of the City Council of Charleston* (Charleston, S.C.: W. P. Young, 1802), p. 83.

6. Gayle, ''Nature and Volume of Exports,'' p. 33; Charleston Wills, MSS, transcripts, S.C.A.D., Book A, 20:74–75; Book A, 16:257–64; David Duncan Wallace, *The Life of Henry Laurens* (New York: Putnam, 1915), pp. 7–9; *South Carolina and American General Gazette*, May 25, 1778, hereafter cited as *G.G.; South Carolina Gazette and Daily Advertiser*, March 7, 1785.

7. Petition, accounts, and other papers of Charles Atkins, petition of the Master Tailors' Society, MSS, S.C.A.D.; *Charleston Gazette*, January 18, 1780. Also included in the clothing industry were milliners and mantua-makers, of whom there were many; see, for example, *South Carolina Gazette and Country Journal*, December 27, 1768, hereafter cited, *C.J.; S.C.G.*, May 2, 1761, June 28, 1760.

8. *C.J.*, September 23, 1766, November 20, 1770; *S.C.G.*, January 21, 1773; petitions, accounts, and other papers of Patrick Hinds, Ms, S.C.A.D.

9. Charleston County, Clerk of the Court of Chancery, Judgement Book Records from February 1767—August 1768, Book DD, Ms, typewritten copies, South Caroliniana Library, Columbia, S.C., pp. 130, 301, 302, 383, 384; also Judgement Book, 1770–1771, pp. 8–10.

10. *G.G.*, November 14, 1766; *S.C.G.*, July 6, 1769; R. W. Gibbes, ed., *Documentary History of the American Revolution*, 1767–76 (New York: Banner Press, 1855), pp. 10–11.

11. *G.G.*, December 30, 1774, January 6, 1775; *S.C.G.*, July 30, 1753, October 4, 1760.

12. See the Charleston newspapers, which are the best source for the artisans of the period; also, more available but not complete, is Alfred Coxe Prime, *The Arts and Crafts in Philadelphia, Maryland, and South Carolina* (Philadelphia: Walpole Society, 1929). However, some

examples of the above are the following: Richard Bell, wigmaker and hairdresser, *S.C.G.*, September 7, 1755; powder and starch manufacturer, Robert Stringer, *ibid.*, October 8, 1773; weaver, Anthony Parasteau, *Gazette of the State of South Carolina*, June 9, 1777, hereafter cited *G.S.S.C.*; dyers, John and William Brown, *S.C.G.*; June 19, 21, 1773; *C.J.*, March 18, 1766; seamstresses, mantua-makers, staymakers, milliners, John Burchett, *S.C.G.*, December 7, 1767, Eleanor Chapman, *ibid.*, July 23, 1772; Sarah Damon, *ibid.*, September 28, 1765, John Duvall, *ibid.*, March 2, 1765; confectioner, William Sandys, Charleston Wills, Book B 1774–79, 17:467–69; tobacconists, Stewart and Barre, *South Carolina Gazette and Public Advertiser*, September 1, 1784; brewer, Edmund Egan, W. Richard Walsh, "Edmund Egan, Charleston's Rebel Brewer," *South Carolina Historical Magazine* (October 1955), 56:200–204, hereafter cited *S.C.H.M.*; upholsterer, Richard Bird, *S.C.G.*, September 11, 1762; bakers, Francesco Morrelli, *ibid.*, October 11, 1773; butcher, John Baker, *C.J.*, June 3, 1766; tinsmith, George Ross, *South Carolina Gazette and Public Advertiser*, April 7, 1785.

13. E. Milby Burton, "The Furniture of Charleston," *Antiques* (Jan. 1952), 21:53–55; Jennie Haskell Rose, "Pre-Revolutionary Cabinet Makers of Charleston," *Antiques*, 2:184–85. E. Milby Burton, "Thomas Elfe, Charleston Cabinet Maker," *The Charleston Museum Leaflets* (Charleston, S.C.: Charleston Museum, 1952), pp. 14–15. Burton, *Charleston Furniture*, p. 6.

14. *S.C.G.*, July 9, 1772.

15. Burton, *Charleston Furniture*, pp. 13–15; "Thomas Elfe," pp. 13, 16–33; Rose, "Cabinet Makers," Part I, 128, Part II, 185.

16. Burton, *South Carolina Silversmiths*, pp. 14–16, 73–76, 146–49, 163–69, 203, 206. Some works of these smiths are in the Charleston Museum.

17. Prime, *Arts and Crafts*, pp. 17–18. The "Battle of Sullivan's Island" engraving or prints could not be found.

18. *G.G.*, May 11, 1770; Alston Deas, *The Early Ironwork of Charleston* (Columbia, S.C.: Bostwick & Thornley, 1941), pp. 15–18; 27–30, fig. 8; William Johnson, *A Course of Experiments in that Curious and Interesting Branch of Natural Philosophy Called Electricity, Accompanied With Lectures on the Nature and Properties of Electric Fire* (New York, 1765); Donald G. Morgan, *Justice William Johnson, The First Dissenter* (Columbia, S.C.: University of South Carolina Press, 1954), pp. 3–23.

19. *G.G.*, December 12, 1768, January 2, 1769.

20. Prime, *Arts and Crafts*, pp. 8–10.

21. *The Charleston Yearbook for 1899* (Charleston, S.C.: News and Courier Press, 1899), appendix, pp. 141–42, 145–46; Margaret Simons Middleton, *Jeremiah Theus, Colonial Artist of Charleston* (Columbia, S.C.: University of South Carolina Press, 1953).

22. *C.J.*, October 20, 1767; *S.C.G.*, February 7, 1765; Rose, "Cabinet Makers" Part II, 128; Prime, *Arts and Crafts*, pp. 221–22; House Journal, 1765–1768, p. 257, February 23, 1768, p. 656, April 7, 1768; Albert Simons and Charles Lapham, Jr., *The Octagon Library of Early American Architecture, Charleston, South Carolina* (New York: American Institute of Architects, 1927), p. 19; *South Carolina Gazette and General Advertiser*, October 18, 25, November 4, 22, 1763; February 24, 1784; Rules of the Charleston Carpenters' Society . . . (Charleston, S.C.: [in South Carolina Archives], 1805); *G.S.S.C.*, May 12, 1777, October 8, 23, 1783.

23. *C.J.*, August 22, 1789.

24. *S.C.G.*, July 12, 1773; Simons and Lapham, *Octagon Library*, pp. 19–23; Julia Cherry Spruill, "Southern Houses Before the Revolution," *North Carolina Historical Review* (October 1935), 12:329.

25. Rose, "Cabinet Makers," Part II, 184; Burton, "Thomas Elfe," pp. 11–12; *S.C.G.*, August 25, 1764, August 17, 1765; Thomas Elfe Account Book, Ms., South Carolina Historical Society, Charleston, A brief description of a partnership, Kensie Burden and Richard Muncrief, joiners and carpenters, in Gregorie, *Court of Chancery*, pp. 608, 613, 616, 617; *G.G.*, November 14, 1766.

26. *S.C.G.*, November 5, 1763; Rules of the Carpenters' Society; petitions of the Master Tailors; of the Barbers', of the Coopers', of the Mechanics' Societies, MSS, S.C.A.D.; *Constitution of the Mechanics Society* (Charleston, S.C., 1811); Cooper and McCord, *Statutes at Large*, 7:247, 7:336, 7:364.

27. *S.C.G.*, April 12, October 15, 1763; January 28, February 25, 1764; House Journal 1764, p. 40, May 25, 1764; *C.J.*, December 15, 1767; March 22, April 5, 1768; *G.G.*, April 26, October 28, 1774; Cooper and McCord, *Statutes at Large*, 4:142, *G.S.S.C.*, May 6, 1784.

28. Sellers, *Charleston Business*, p. 58; *South Carolina Gazette and General Advertiser*, July 27, 1784; Burton, "Thomas Elfe," p. 10; Charleston Willis; Burton, *South Carolina Silversmiths*, pp. 12–210; *C.J.* September 1, 1767; *G.G.*, December 5, 1768; (no editor), "Letters to General Greene and Others," *S.C.H.M.*, (Jan. 1916), 16:10.

29. Ship Register, 1765–74.

30. See numerous advertisements concerning apprentices in the Charleston newspapers of the period; also, Burton, "Thomas Elfe," p. 11; Cooper and McCord, *Statutes at Large*, 3:544–46, 4:158–61; *S.C.G.*, September 27, 1768; Will of Robert Cripps, tailor, Ms, South Caroliniana Library.

31. For advertisements of indentured servants, see *C.J.*, October 24, September 30, 1766; *G.G.*, January 8, February 13, March 18, 1768.

32. See, for example, Thomas Elfe Account Book; see also S. McKee, Jr., *Labor in Colonial New York* (New York: Columbia University Press, 1935), p. 22.

33. Charleston newspapers *passim*. (Thomas Elfe Account Book.)

34. Judgement Book, 1767–68; pp. 224–26; David Saylor Receipt Book; *Heads of Families*, 1790; *S.C.G.*, December 3, 1764; Joseph W. Barnwell, "Diary of Timothy Ford, 1785–1786," *S.C.H.M.* (July 1912), 13:142. See also Marcus W. Jernegan, "Slavery and the Beginnings of Industrialism in the American Colonies," *American Historical Review* (Jan. 1920), 25:220–40.

35. *Heads of Families, 1790*, pp. 38–44. Copies of Charleston Wills, 1760–1800, *S.C.A.D.*, originals in the Charleston County Court House. Inventories to Estates 1760–1810, copies in the Genealogical Library, Church of the Latter Day Saints, Salt Lake City, Utah, micro. nos., 194635–194638.

36. Yates Snowden, "Labor Organizations in South Carolina," *Bulletin of the University of South Carolina*, No. 38, Part IV (July 1914), pp. 5–9, Senate Journal, 1783, Ms, *S.C.A.D.*, p. 189, February 22, 1783. Alexander Edwards, *Ordinances of the City Council*, p. 164; Jernegan, *Beginnings of Industrialism*, pp. 220–40.

37. In the *Census of 1790* the Heads of Households lists 42 males and 59 females. Of these 20 appeared to be mulatto, 11 men and 9 women listed as free and using family and surnames,

which seems to indicate the difference. C. Horace Fitchett, "The Traditions of the Free Negro in Charleston, South Carolina," *Journal of Negro History* (Apr. 1940), 25:14, hereafter *JNH*.

38. In the *Director of 1800,* or *Nelson's Charleston Directory and Strangers Guide for the Year . . . 1801* (Charleston: John Dixon Nelson, 1801) lists one Jehu Jones, then a tailor and later to become a famous hostler in Charleston. None of the Negro clubs are listed in any of the directories.

39. Will of John Fenwicke, Will Books, 1767–71, Vol. 12, W.P.A., p. 543. He signs with his mark. One of his daughters was owned by Rawlins Lowndes, later president of the state.

40. George Bedon's Inventory is in documentary Book C, 1793–1800, fol. 86 Charleston County Court House. He owned a "small box of books," thus he was apparently literate. Also *JNH*, 25:148. My mechanics file contains a George Bedon who died in 1762 and was a cooper and a carpenter. George Bedon's Will, 1794 desired that his sons be educated to age fifteen and then bound to a handicraftsman for six years. He wished his daughter to be educated to age fourteen and then apprenticed to a mantua-maker.

41. *JNH*, 25:144–47. The club became known as the Century Club. According to H. Fitchett, its records are still in existence, carefully kept: i.e., as of 1940, this author has traced these down. Fitchett says the club was located on Pitt Street in Charleston. At my last inquiry the Brown Fellowship Society records are in the College of Charleston Library. John Lofton, *Insurrection in South Carolina: The Turbulent World of Denmark Vesey* (Yellow Springs, Ohio: Antioch Press, 1964), pp. 54–210. Justice William Johnson, son and namesake of the revolutionary blacksmith, harbored grave doubts about there being a plot at all and that panic had seized the city based on lies, fear, and injustice compounded. Robert S. Starabin, ed., *Denmark Vesey: The Slave Conspiracy of 1822* (Englewood Cliffs, N.J.: Prentice-Hall, 1970), part 2, December 3; also Richard Wade, December 17, pp. 166ff.

42. Lofton, *Insurrection,* pp. 84–85.

43. Wallace, *Life of Henry Laurens,* p. 214.

44. Benjamin Quarles, *The Negro in the American Revolution* (Chapel Hill, N.C.: Published for the Institute of Early American History and Culture by the University of North Carolina Press, 1961), pp. x, 164–67. Wallace, *Life of Henry Laurens,* p. 214.

45. R. Walsh, *Charleston's Sons of Liberty* (Columbia: University of South Carolina Press, 1959, reprinted 1968), p. 125.

46. Memorial of Thomas Cole, Peter Bassinet Mathews, and Matthew Webb to the Senate. S.C.A.D., General Assembly petitions, 1791 #181. They addressed the Senate President Dr. David Ramsay, the physician and historian reputed to lean towards abolition. Inventory of Matthew Webb microfilm 194638, Charleston: Inventories of Estates fol. 364, Book C. October 4, 1798; February 20, 1799. Among his personal effects were books but few luxuries. He had several slaves, who from their conditions, women, children and an "old Negro Fellow Sambo," seemed to have been kept for benevolent rather than commercial reasons. His administratrix, Elizabeth Webb, signed with her mark. He married one Susanna Cane, a free black woman, earlier. *Register of St. Philip's Parish, 1754–1810,* p. 197. He apparently worked for the Parish from whom he had £159:6:2 in his estate, but the rest of his account books were in a "deranged situation." Thomas Cole Inventory, the father of the petitioner December 3, 1771; vol. 1772–76 fol. 7. micro. 194636. His estate: £2,327:1:3, a lot of land under seven-year lease worth £500, all in currency at about 5 to 1 sterling.

47. Quash was earlier apprehended as a runaway. He was described as short and stocky, and very insistent to his captors that he was free: *S.C.G.* July 6, 1765. He shows up in *Census of 1790* as free, p. 40. Friday's Inventory Book 1776–78, fol. 231–32, micro. 194637. George Flagg, painter and a white leader of the mechanics appraised the estate.

48. Inventories to Estates, 1763–1810. Microfilm nos. 194635-194638. Genealogical Library, Church of Latter-Day Saints, Salt Lake City, Utah. Originals in the Charleston County Court House. Total number counted was 96, £0–99 = 23; £100–499 = 29; £500–999 = 22; £1,000–1,999 = 21; £2,000–4,999 = 5; £5,000 + = 5, converted to pounds sterling. The Inventories also gave real estate holdings in the period after 1783. Comparison with Wills, however, indicates that sometimes holdings in a probated will differed from that in the Inventory. My conclusion, the inventories amassed give some good evidence of conditions of wealth but are by no means conclusive. They are more accurately reliable to picture life styles in furnishings, etc.

49. Daniel Cannon, Inventory 1800–10 Book D, October 4, 1802, micro. 194638. fol. 197. Nathanial Lebby Book D, May 17, 1802 fol. 194. Thomas Elfe, 1776–78, September 14, 1776, fol. 77–79, micro 194637. For examples of poor mechanics, James Zealey, shoemaker, *C* 1794 Book C, 1793–1800, fol. 70, micro. 194638. Thomas Brooks, carpenter, Book A, 1783–87, September 7, 1785, fol. 365, micro. 194638. James Tourme, house carpenter, Book D, 1787–93, micro. no. 194638.

50. Several houses for sale or for rent are described in the *S.C.G.,* April 13, September 14, 1765; December 29, 1776, etc. The inner description of a town house and shop are detailed in Inventory of Robert Beard, tinsmith no. 88 Broad Street, Book D, 1800–10, June 6–8, 1797, fol. 23–24, micro. 194638. Thomas Murray, Cooper Book C, 1793–1800, micro. 194638. Edward Weyman, Book B, fol. 519, 1787–93, micro. 194638. George Norris, saddler, May 15, 1801, fol. 46, Book D, micro. 194638. John Reid, tinworker, Book D, fol. 391–2, May 8, 1805, micro. 194638.

51. E. Ross, tailor, Inventory Book D, 1800-10, *C,* December 1804, f. 308, micro. 194638. Mary Darling, seamstress, H.J. 1765–68, fol. 577, Book A, fol. 165, Inventory micro. 194638; Mary King, milliner, Book A, fol. 125, October 1, 1783, micro. 194638. The Inventories and the newspapers are dotted with women who worked alone, were widowed, or worked the husband's shop. A few names are Anne Fowler, Inventory is dated February 26–27, 1783, fol. 21–22. Book A, micro. 194638; in the same is Mary Simpson Baker, Book C, 1793–1800, fol. 274. Inventory B, Jane Daves, staymaker, 1793–1800, fol. 373–74, micro. 194638. Inventory Elizabeth Harvey, staymaker, *C* May 1777, fol. 48–49, micro. 194637. Eleanor Chapman, nurse and seamstress, *S.C.G.,* July 23, 1772. Rebecca Weyman, *C.J.,* December 15, 1767.

52. House Journal, 1765–68, p. 348; April 8, 1767; 1772–75, p. 204; February 14, 1775. See, for example, the tax act of 1764 in Cooper and McCord, *Statutes at Large,* 4:200–206; Clark, *History of Manufactures,* 1:24, 25, 33, 36.

53. *Ibid.,* 1:14–24; *S.C.G.,* January 21, 28, May 17, 1778. Burton thinks that the cabinetmakers were not hindered by English incorporations, since these goods took up too much space aboard the small vessels of the day: "The Furniture of Charleston," pp. 44–45.

54. See tax acts in Cooper and McCord, *Statutes at Large,* III, IV.

55. Edward McCrady, *The History of South Carolina: The Royal Government, 1719–76* (New York: Macmillan Company, 1899), pp. 409–12.

56. *C.J.,* January 21, April 1, 1766.

57. Cooper and McCord, *Statutes at Large*, 3:135–140; *S.C.G.*, February 7, April 18, 1771, May 17, October 31, 1774.

58. *S.C.G.*, April 11, 1774; Edson L. Whitney, "Government of the Colony of South Carolina," *Johns Hopkins University Studies in Historical and Political Science* (Baltimore, Md.: John Hopkins University Press, 1895), pp. 69–73, 73–74, 80–81; Cooper and McCord, *Statutes at Large*, 3:544; William Henry Drayton, *Letters of Freeman* (London, 1771), p. 61.

59. Frederick Dalcho, *An Historical Account of the Protestant Episcopal Church in South Carolina* (Charleston, S.C.: A. E. Miller, 1820), pp. 200–203; George W. Williams, *St. Michael's Charleston* (Columbia, S.C.: University of South Carolina Press, 1951), pp. 29, 33–38, 312.

60. Rules of the Fellowship Society, 1762; Minute Book of the Fellowship Society, 1769–79; Treasurers Account Book, 1774–1815, MSS, Fellowship Society Building, Charleston. Edward McCrady, *Education in South Carolina Prior to and During the Revolution* (Charleston, S.C.: News and Courier Book Presses, 1883), p. 33; Wallace, *Life of Henry Laurens*, pp. 154–55; *South Carolina Weekly Gazette*, May 10, June 28, July 5, September 20, 1783; *South Carolina Gazette and Public Advertiser*, June 2, 1784; *G.S.S.C.*, May 12, June 30, 1777.

61. *DAB*, 7:82–3. Richard Walsh, "Christopher Gadsden: Radical of Conservative Revolutionary," *S.C.H.M* (Oct. 1962), 68:195–203. William Moultrie, *Memoirs of the American Revolution*, 2 vols. (New York: David Longworth, 1802), 1:14; J. Almon, ed., *Journal of the Provincial Congress of South Carolina, 1776* (London, 1776). Other artisans seated in the Provincial Congress were Peter Timothy, printer of the *South Carolina Gazette*, Cato Ash, carpenter, Theodore Trezavant, tailor, Mark Morriss, housepainter, John and Simon Berwick, shoemakers, Joshue Lockwood, jeweler and watchmaker, Anthony Toomer, carpenter, Joseph Veree, carpenter, James Brown, carpenter.

62. Christopher Gadsden to Sam Adams, April 4, 1779, Ms, Bancroft Collection, New York Public Library. Also Richard Walsh, *The Writings of Christopher Gadsden* (Columbia: University of South Carolina Press, 1966), pp. 161–65. *S.C.G.*, October 3, 1768.

63. *S.C.G.*, October 3, 1768.

64. *Ibid.*, July 6, 13, 27, 1769.

65. John Drayton, *Memoirs of the American Revolution*, 2 vol. (Charleston, S.C.: A. E. Miller, 1821), 1:273–74, 1:285–86, 1:300–302. Joseph W. Barnwell, "Correspondence of Arthur Middleton," *S.C.H.M.*, (July, 1926) 27:126–27, 129; Chapman J. Milling, ed., *Colonial South Carolina*, R. L. Meriwether, gen. ed., *South Caroliniana No. 1* (Columbia, S.C.: University of South Carolina Press, 1951), pp. xix–xxi.

66. J. Drayton, *Memoirs of the American Revolution*, 1:221–25; Joseph Johnson, *Traditions and Reminiscences . . .* (Charleston, S.C.: Walker and James, 1851), p. 44.

67. *S.C.G.*, November 9, 1769.

68. Cooper and McCord, *Statutes at Large*, 4:729, 5:25, 58, 130, 150, et passim.

69. In 1783, Ann Timothy, her husband now dead, reprinted an article from the *Pennsylvania Journal* stating that manufacturing should be encouraged by the passage of the general duty law, *G.S.S.C.*, November 6, 1783; other articles in *South Carolina Gazette and Advertiser*,

August 23, September 8, 1785; *Columbia Herald and Patriotic Courier of North America*, September 19, 1785; *Charleston Evening Gazette*, August 15, 1785.

70. *Debates . . . in the House of Representatives of South Carolina on the Constitution of the United States . . . Notices of the Convention* (Charleston, S.C.: A. E. Miller, 1831), pp. 380, 398.

3

FROM ARTISAN TO MANUFACTURER: INDUSTRIALIZATION AND THE SMALL PRODUCER IN NEWARK, 1830–60

Susan E. Hirsch

ACCORDING to most accounts, the active agent in American industrialization was the capitalist entrepreneur, who introduced the corporate form to manufacturing, and who undermined traditional artisans and their hand techniques by employing the latest, often imported, machinery and new workers, usually women, children, or immigrants. In this view, American artisans, if not backward and hostile to change, were significant only for inventing some of the machines that capitalists profitably employed. American artisans, however, were neither averse to change nor were they mere assistants in the process of industrialization: artisans themselves revolutionized production in many traditional crafts. The agents of change, the pace and timing of change, and the content of change varied from one branch of manufacturing to another; there was no single path of industrialization that all industries followed. The small producer, as well as the big capitalist, played an important role in American industrialization.

The common view of American industrialization derives from the much-studied example of the New England textile industry, in which American industrialization began. In this field, large capitalists—merchants and financiers—revolutionized production and built huge, mechanized mills before 1820 by amassing large blocks of capital through incorporation, introducing costly machines modeled after British design, and tapping a new source of cheaper wage labor in native-born women and children. Skilled workers made many of the important innovations in textile machinery, but the expense of equipment excluded them from becoming industralists themselves. Big capitalists played a similarly crucial role in the iron industry, beginning in the 1850s. American artisans in the iron industry had done little innovating, perhaps because capital requirements were relatively high even for traditional methods of production. Only imported technology and concerted scientific experimentation by engineers and chemists backed by corporate funds produced advance in iron making. And the manufacturers in iron and steel introduced new techniques only by substantially replacing native-born craftsmen with unskilled or semiskilled immigrants.[1]

In some cases, small capitalists, not large ones, were the innovators, especially in fields where the leap from craft to factory production was not as dramatic as in the case of textiles.[2] In Lynn, Massachusetts, for instance, a long period of task differentiation—mass production achieved by workers each doing one task using hand tools—separated traditional craft production of shoes from the factory system. After 1800, Lynn shopkeepers, small capitalists who controlled the marketing of locally produced shoes, began to undermine the master shoemakers and rearrange production by hiring cutters and packers and ''putting-out'' piecework to local families. Shopkeepers became manufacturers, and mechanized factories replaced domestic labor only slowly, beginning in the late 1850s.

Industrialization in the nineteenth century was not always the product of outsiders to the work process, however. Artisans themselves revolutionized production in many traditional crafts by expanding markets, developing new techniques, and becoming partners with others who had small amounts of capital. In Paterson, New Jersey, for intance, the typical manufacturer in the new locomotive, machinery, and tool industries had been a skilled craftsman, or had served an apprenticeship, and had founded his business as a small individual firm or as a partnership. Artisans such as Linus Yale, Jr., who made crucial technological advances in locksmithing, laid the foundation for mass production in their field.[3] Industrialization was not alien to, but often emanated from, the preindustrial American artisan class, and the inventiveness, entrepreneurship, and capital of small producers was a vital force in early-nineteenth-century industrialization.

In Newark, New Jersey, the country's leading industrial city in 1860, artisans similarly had been the architects of change and growth by searching out new markets, developing new processes, amassing the necessary capital, and finding a new labor force in male immigrants from Northern Europe. Newark was the nation's eleventh largest city in 1860 with a population of 71,941, and the value of its manufactures, $28 million, was the sixth largest in the country.[4] The output of six crafts—shoemaking, hatting, saddle making, jewelry making, trunk making, and leather making—accounted for 42 percent of that value. All six crafts had been practiced in Newark in their traditional form, and artisans had guided their evolution into major industries by 1860. The role of Newark artisans in the development of these industries illuminates another path in the complex process of industrialization in the United States.

Unlike the mill towns that grew up overnight about the textile factories, Newark had a long history as a manufacturing town, where artisans had employed traditional methods of production. New modes of production were not simply imported whole but emanated from, or were introduced within the context of, artisan traditions. In Newark's crafts, each artisan could create a finished product, using only hand tools and the skills that he had acquired in a long apprenticeship spent in the home of a master craftsman. By 1826, over 80 percent of Newark's labor force was engaged in some form of manufacturing; thirty-four distinct crafts were practiced in the town, and there were printing offices, distilleries, breweries, grist mills, and a few factories and foundries as well.[5] Relatively few men worked at each craft except shoemaking, and most men labored alone or in small shops; the average workshop contained only eight men (table 3.1). Traditional craft production in Newark, and throughout America, differed from that in Europe in one crucial aspect, however—the absence of guilds. American artisans were individualists, who could join or leave their craft at will, and who could try new methods without hindrance.

Despite the absence of formalized unity in guild structures, artisans in Newark, and elsewhere in preindustrial America, possessed a positive self-image and a common set of values. Craftsmen—masters, journeymen, and apprentices—were all "mechanics," whose skill gave them pride and independence. The cultural unity of mechanics originated in the close personal relationships fostered by small shops, and in the expectation of apprentices and journeymen that with age, experience, and hard work, they could become self-employed master craftsmen. The mechanics' self-image and their values furthered rather than hindered American industrialization, because they encouraged new experiences.

Table 3.1 Total Workers Employed, Newark

Craft	1826[a]	1836[b]	1845[c]	1850[d]	1860[e]
Shoemaking	685	734	689	1,135	1,198
Saddle making	57	527	494	488	1,044
Jewelry making	22	100	234	547	777
Trunk making	7	35	107	308	740
Leather making	81	169	319	568	957
Hatting	70	610	894	1,324	1,677
All industries	1,980				18,851[f]

[a]*The First Jubilee of American Independence, Newark* (Newark: M. Lyon & Co., 1826).

[b]*Journal of the American Institute of the City of New York* (New York: T. B. Wakeman, 1836), 1:475–79; *Newark Daily Advertiser*, September 15, 1836.

[c]*Newark Daily Advertiser*, January 6, 1846.

[d]Manuscripts of the U.S. Census of Population, 1850, and of the U.S. Census of Manufactures, 1850.

[e]Manuscripts of the U.S. Census of Population, 1860, and of the U.S. Census of Manufactures, 1860.

[f]United States Census Office, *Statistics of the United States in 1860* (Washington, D.C., 1866), p. xviii.

The mechanic's pride in his intelligence was one basis for his positive self-image, and for his receptivity to the new; the artisan possessed both manual and mental skills, and his extensive education laid a basis for technological change. Newark masters provided apprentices with night schooling in basic subjects like grammar and mathematics, as well as teaching them the secrets of their trade, and townsmen set up an Apprentices Library, open in the evenings, for the moral and secular edification of the young men.[6] In the 1820s, artisans pressed for systems of public education for the young, and in many cities they formed educational associations to further develop their own skills too. Having confidence in their abilities, artisans sought greater exposure to the latest scientific theories, in order to apply that knowledge to make improvements in their crafts. The Newark Mechanics Association for Mutual Improvement in the Arts and Sciences, which was formed in 1828 by 114 craftsmen, was one of many which held regular meetings and provided a series of lectures each year. While only one of these associations, the Franklin Institute of Philadelphia, endured more than a few years and fostered extensive technological advance, the artisan's drive for self-improvement contributed to the favorable climate for invention.[7]

The mechanic's high evaluation of his worth to the community also bolstered industrialization by encouraging men to devote themselves to manufacturing. In tones heard in many other towns, a Newarker declared in 1829 that crafts were "the life blood, bone and sinew of the land—may pursuits *so* honorable and useful, result in individual prosperity and happiness."[8] The ethic which shaped the artisan's self-image identified the "useful" with the "good." Mechanics believed that they glorified God by their useful endeavors as they helped themselves and their neighbors to prosper. The honest "callings" were those which demanded skill and were pursued with diligence but without greed.[9] Providing necessary goods and following honest callings, Newark artisans viewed themselves as the natural leaders of the community. In towns like Newark, which lacked the wealthy commercial class of the seaports, artisans dominated the social order, and local celebrations confirmed their high status in the community.[10] The first observance of American independence in Newark, in 1788, had been celebrated by an industrial procession, with various crafts represented by masters and their journeymen, and these constituted the festivities in later years as well. In 1826, the town declared the beneficence of national independence was proved by the numerical increase of the population, and by the variety of crafts and businesses carried on in the township.

Mechanics perceived a mutually reinforcing bond between their work and America's political heritage. During the 1760s, American artisans had first viewed their work, home manufactures, as vital to American freedom and had supported the nonimportation agreements; in the 1820s, mechanics were still reiterating the connection between democracy and production.[11] Under English tyranny, human faculties had been cramped, and the mechanical arts had advanced but slowly. Since the Revolution, artisans believed, democracy had enabled the mechanic to do both God's work and man's to the benefit of the entire community. Conversely, they saw technological advance as proof of the superiority of democracy. By the 1820s, the association of technology and democracy was complete, as Americans defined the notion of the "greatest good" largely in material terms, as a matter of living standards and "goods," and artisans perceived a moral basis for mass production. Even the hesitant Jefferson, ideologue of agrarianism, praised the application of steam engines to small consumer goods' production as help for the "many."[12]

Believing in the worthiness of their endeavors, Newark's mechanics used their talents to expand their own and the town's prosperity. In the 1790s, Moses Combs, a master shoemaker and tanner, introduced mass production to Newark by organzing local farmers to make shoes on a putting-out basis as a winter occupation.[13] He created the market for his product by making contacts with prospective buyers in the South and by shipping his goods through New York City. Other master shoemakers—not shopkeepers, as in Lynn—followed his lead. The masters provided the materials, paid the farmers piece rates, and marketed the finished product. The farmers, who were each taught only a part of the process, worked in three-person teams (one to sew uppers, one to sole, and another to finish) to produce relatively cheap goods for the wholesale market. As Newark developed as a shoe center, goods of all grades were produced. By 1826, one-third of Newark's labor force was employed in shoemaking, some skilled craftsmen making custom-order, quality products, most semiskilled workers producing cheap, wholesale goods (table 3.1). Although he began the industrialization of shoemaking in Newark, Moses Combs was no traducer of traditional artisan values. He continued to train apprentices, many of whom became leaders of Newark's shoe and leather industries, and he established a night school and a church for them. Combs's industry, piety, and disdain for luxury were an example to many, and he was much admired by fellow Newarkers.

Artisans contributed to mass production not simply by introducing task differentiation, but also by making many innovations in technology. In the first half of the nineteenth century, Newark's foremost inventor was Seth Boyden, a mechanic as were his forebears.[14] After studying in his father's shop, Boyden came to Newark to interest local leather makers in a machine he developed for splitting leather. Newarkers quickly accepted him and, in 1818, he produced the first patent leather in America, providing the foundation for the expansion of Newark's leather industry. In later years he made inventions in many lines—castings for malleable iron, improvements in steam-engine design, and hat-making machinery, among others. Boyden was a local hero during his lifetime, and grateful citizens honored him after his death by erecting a statue of him in a city park. Most artisans who made inventions lacked Boyden's scope and were confined to their own field, but these, like Newark hatter Henry Blynn, who invented the first machine for stiffening hat bodies in 1835, made the industrialization of crafts possible.[15]

Besides introducing new modes of production, master craftsmen who fostered industrialization used their entrepreneurial skills to expand capital supplies and extend markets. Moses Combs himself helped to found Newark's first bank and a fire insurance company, became treasurer of a turnpike company, and aided the reopening of a ferry.[16] Newark's craftsmen reached wholesale markets on a large scale in the 1830s, because they aggressively publicized their goods at Mechanics Fairs throughout the East, supported transportation improvements, and helped to develop financial institutions.[17] In 1832, the Morris Canal opened, connecting Newark with the Delaware Valley; it provided new easy access to natural resources, like coal, ore, hides, and wood bark, that were necessary for the iron and leather industries. The opening of the railroad to Jersey City, in 1834, reduced the travel time between Newark and New York to approximately one hour, improving access to that important marketplace and banking center. Artisans also supported local financial institutions in the 1830s—many of the directors of the new Mechanics Bank of Newark were master craftsmen or manufacturers, as were many of the directors of the local fire-insurance companies.[18]

Artisans raised the capital to start their firms by using their small savings to join in partnerships with others. A craftsman who could save a few hundred dollars could become self-employed by joining with several others in the same position. "Outside" sources of capital became available for manufacturing when a merchant with money, but no craft skill, became a partner with a craftsman who had little money. Corporations were not prevalent in manufacturing before the Civil War, and opposition to them as monopolies was widespread in the 1830s.[19] Many of Newark's leading firms began as partnerships of artisans with small savings. In 1841, for instance, Newarker Aaron Carter, who had served an apprenticeship to a local jeweler, formed a partnership with two others: he contributed $524.61 to the capital of the new enterprise, and his partners, Pennington and Doremus, put up $400.18. Despite such humble beginnings, the firm grew rapidly and added several new partners.[20] By 1860, it was one of Newark's leaders, with a capital investment of $85,000 and 115 employees.[21]

With improved transportation and more capital, Newark's artisans were able to expand wholesale production in the early 1830s in many crafts. In 1835 Dr. Jabez Goble, a local physician and town booster, estimated that the annual exports of Newark to the South, South America, and the West Indies exceeded $8 million—a total composed of such items as saddles, carriages, shoes, hats, springs, lamps, plated ware, cabinet ware, patent leather, and malleable iron. The shoe industry continued to predominate in wholesale manufacture; there were fourteen large shoe firms in Newark in the mid-1830s, with an average of 52 employees each (table 3.1). The largest shoe company—Shipman, Crane, and Company—sold shoes worth $400,000 to $500,000 to southern customers in 1836.[22]

In order to produce for the wholesale trade, artisans in many crafts began to emulate Newark's shoemakers and institute mass production. Although mechanization came slowly in many trades, industrialization was a diffuse process in the crafts. In most cases, the reorganization of tasks and mechanization proceeded in small steps, often initiated by different firms over a period of years. Artisans were especially influential in the first stages of industrialization because of their familiarity with technical processes and the limited capital requirements of these first deviations from tradition. In the first stage of industrialization—task breakdown—workers often still owned their tools, and employers had only to supply materials. Artisans with limited capital could expand the volume of production per worker by teaching tasks to semiskilled workers and pouring their funds into materials. Master craftsmen in the related fields of shoemaking, saddle making, and leather making all followed this path.

Newark's master saddlers began task differentiation in the early 1830s, and by mid-decade there were eleven saddle-making firms with an average of 48 employees each (table 3.1).[23] Elements of a domestic system existed, as craftsmen even in the largest firm took work home for female relatives to sew. Peter Jacobus, a master saddler since the early 1820s, was one of those who took a partner and began producing for the wholesale market.[24] He and Stephen Condict expanded their business throughout the 1840s and, by the end of the decade, they employed 75 hands and had $50,000 invested in their firms. Like many master craftsmen who became manufacturers, Jacobus' search for more capital involved him in ancillary financial institutions: he was a director of the New Jersey Fire Insurance Company. Owen McFarland was another artisan who welcomed growth and change; he set up a harnessmaking shop in Newark in the 1830s, and, by 1860, he employed 144 hands to produce wholesale goods. Mechanization came to the saddle-making industry only in the 1850s, when masters-become-manufacturers, like McFarland and Condict, introduced sewing machines, and the largest saddlery experimented with some steam-powered machinery (table 3.2).

Large factories did not develop in leather making prior to the 1840s, but new processes and increased demand led to task differentiation between

Table 3.2 Percentage of Employees Working in Firms Using New
Technology, Newark[a]

	1850	1860	
Craft	Steam-Powered Machinery	Sewing Machines, No Steam	Steam-Powered Machinery
Shoemaking	0	48	0
Saddle making	0	56	18
Jewelry making	48	n.a.	79
Trunk making	4	9	68
Leather making	38	n.a.	78
Hatting	69	15	66

[a] Computed from data in the manuscripts of the U.S. Censuses of Manufactures, 1850 and 1860.

firms, so that some specialized in tanning, currying, morocco dressing, or patent-leather making, and men specialized in less-complicated operations within these subdivisions (table 3.1). James Halsey and James Tucker, curriers, became partners in Newark in the 1830s, and by 1846 they were shipping leather as far as the Philippines.[25] Mechanization came much more quickly in leather making than in saddle making, but artisans were often the source of this innovation too: by 1850 firms like Halsey and Tucker were using steam-powered machinery (table 3.2). Skilled tanners and curriers could use their knowledge to enter even rapidly mechanizing fields like patent-leather making. T. P. Howell came to Newark to learn tanning from his uncle, and they formed a partnership in 1840, and began making patent leather with two journeymen and one apprentice.[26] By 1860, T. P. Howell and Company was one of the largest leather-making firms in the city, with the most advanced steam-powered machinery, a capital investment of $220,000, and 167 workers.

In the 1840s, industrialization entered a new stage in Newark with the application of steam power to machines used in the crafts. In 1840, not a factory in Newark used steam power, but by 1846 more than one hundred did.[27] Artisans who utilized their scientific and craft skills to invent new processes or machines to simplify production in their own or allied fields made a major contribution to this new stage of industrialization. The patent laws of the time were favorable to craftsmen such as William Scarlett, who labored as a journeyman shoemaker in Newark during the 1830s and 1840s.[28] In 1847, when he was employed by the Newark India Rubber

Company, Scarlett invented a machine for making suspender buckles, an item used by the company in making one of its products. With merchants as partners, he opened his own factory, using steam-powered machinery and child labor, and he found his former employer to be a good customer.

Hatting was one of the few crafts in Newark that was highly mechanized before the 1840s, and that converted to steam power quickly. Using steam-powered machinery, a silk hat could be made from a rough hat body in two hours and five minutes in 1850, and two-thirds of all hat makers worked in factories using steam-powered machinery (tables 3.1 and 3.2). Newark's hatters, like William and Andrew Rankin, had introduced mechanization in the form of simple, human-powered machines by the early 1830s. The Rankin brothers had come to Newark in 1811, and had been producing fine articles by traditional methods, but although both still trained apprentices in the 1830s, each had a mechanized factory for wholesale production. To acquire the necessary capital, they had taken partners, and William became a director of two fire-insurance companies, while Andrew was a director of the Mechanics Bank and the New Jersey Fire Insurance Company. Other hatters followed their lead, and there were eight hat factories in Newark in 1836, with an average of 76 employees each. William's firm, Rankin, Duryee, and Company, continued to lead the field in the 1840s, and by 1850 it was the largest in the nation with over 600 employees and modern factory buildings equipped with steam heat and gaslight. Rankin's scale and success did not eliminate all opportunities for other artisans in hatting, however. George Booth and his five sons, for instance, began hatting on a small scale in Newark in 1849. By 1860 they had acquired steam-driven machinery and had 80 employees.[29]

The introduction of steam power, with the concomitant increase in capital requirements, did not signal the end of the artisan as an agent of industrialization, because many crafts were either just beginning to change or still in the first stage of industrialization. Small businesses flourished, many started by artisans on meager amounts of capital. Of the 108 firms in the six crafts that supplied information to the 1850 U.S. Census of Manufactures, 32 had a capital investment of $1,000 or less. The availability of rental factory space aided those with few resources to become manufacturers; in Newark, private speculators built entire structures of undifferentiated industrial space for lease by small firms. One such venture was the Phoenix Buildings, which housed 10 companies employing a total of 200 workmen in 1847. In

Table 3.3 Percentage of Employees
Who Were Female, Newark[a]

Craft	1850	1860
Shoemaking	34	14
Saddle making	8	3
Jewelry making	8	10
Trunk making	19	13
Leather making	1	1
Hatting	49	28

[a] Compiled from data in the manuscripts
of the U.S. Censuses of Manufactures,
1850 and 1860.

the Clinton Works, a central steam engine in the basement drove all sorts of small machines for the twenty small firms that rented space.[30]

Newark's jewelers first began to industrialize their craft in the 1840s by introducing task differentiation, just as saddlers, shoemakers, and leather makers had earlier (table 3.1). The partners, John Taylor and Horace Baldwin, were among the first to produce for the wholesale market, and by 1845 many of their 50 employees were specializing in tasks like chain making, watchcase making, and engraving. Jewelers who were breaking down tasks also began to hire women to do polishing (table 3.3). The market for quality jewelry was strong, however, and the best products were made by artists who executed the complete process. Although few jewelry apprentices boarded with their masters, many served terms of at least five years to learn to make quality products.[31] In the 1850s, some jewelers, like Aaron Carter, introduced steam-powered machinery to take over such simplified tasks as chain making and watchcase making (table 3.2). At the same time, they differentiated more tasks—diamond mounting, diamond cutting, and ring making—while introducing a host of small machines, such as circular saws, lathes, and the like. Artisans who first opened their own shops in these years also embraced the new technologies; Moses Field, who had worked for another Newark jewelry firm, started his own business in 1848 with about 20 journeymen using only hand tools. But in the 1850s Field acquired more capital, introduced steam-powered machinery, and expanded his work force. As large factories became common in jewelry making, employers separated production and sales functions, often hiring superintendents and foremen to supervise the workers while they concentrated on distribution (table 3.4).

Table 3.4 Average Number of Workers Per Firm,
Newark

Craft	1845 [a]	1850 [b]	1860 [c]
Shoemaking	24	23	14
Saddle making	55	49	52
Jewelry making	12	39	36
Trunk making	18	77	82
Leather making	14	24	37
Hatting	39	63	76

[a] Computed from statistics in Newark Daily Advertiser,
January 6, 1846.

[b] Computed from data in the manuscript U.S. Census of
Manufactures, 1850.

[c] Computed from data in the manuscript U.S. Census of
Manufactures, 1860.

The wholesale jewelry market was centered in New York and Philadelphia, and one-third of Newark firms had moved their showrooms to these cities by the late 1850s.[32] Artisans had both revolutionized the technology of production and transformed themselves from mechanics into absentee employers.

Similarly, beginning in the mid-1840s, Newark's trunk makers overturned the old methods of production in their craft. Thomas B. Peddie, who came to Newark from Scotland in 1833 and went to work for a saddle-making firm, began making trunks in a basement in 1835. A decade later he took a partner, John Morrison, and with 10 journeymen, they began wholesale production—although Peddie still trained apprentices. By 1850, Peddie and Morrison had 150 employees and had instituted task differentiation, so that boys would remain apprentices only a few years and then leave to get journeymen's wages. Firms like Peddie and Morrison had introduced a line of trunks of lower quality, simplified design, and cheaper price for the wholesale trade, in addition to filling custom orders for ornate baggage. While the latter employed skilled workers, the cheaper products were made by semi-skilled personnel, and the larger employers instituted the putting-out system and hired women to make carpetbags (tables 3.1 and 3.3).[33] Through 1850, almost all work was done by hand, but in the next decade, Newark's trunk makers pushed mechanization quickly, introducing steam-powered machinery for many tasks (table 3.2). Although smaller establishments did not use steam, they did follow the larger ones in using sewing machines. Like

Newark's jewelers, local trunk makers opened offices in wholesaling centers as their factories grew, and Newark retained only the production facilities (table 3.4). Peddie and Morrison had stores in New York and New Orleans by 1850, and Horatio Peters, who had four employees in 1840 and 150 ten years later, had stores in New York, Philadelphia, and Cincinnati.

The artisans who revolutionized Newark's crafts also transformed their own work. The master craftsman had used both mental and manual skills; the manufacturer used only the mental, concentrating on management, finance, distribution, and new technology. The manual work was consigned to a machine operator, and an important facet of the manufacturer's role in industrialization was to find a relatively cheap labor force from which to recruit these machine operators. In part because of their grounding in the mechanic's tradition, in part because of pressure by the community and by journeymen, Newark's manufacturers did not take the same path as the New England textile manufacturers and hire women and children.[34] The crafts had been a male preserve, with children consigned to the role of apprentice, and women limited to helping out by doing hand sewing if it was required. Newark's manufacturers, like other Victorians, believed that woman's place was in the home, and as former mechanics, they believed women should be confined to their traditional tasks. In Newark, manufacturers failed to expand woman's sphere in their factories: hundreds of women worked in the six crafts, but overwhelmingly they trimmed hats, bound shoes, or sewed carpetbags (table 3.3). Manufacturers gave women only a few ancillary non-sewing tasks, like jewelry polishing. Moreover, when the sewing machine came into use in the 1850s, women felt the full force of technological displacement, and their percentage in the crafts declined significantly. Statistics for child labor are not available, but it is doubtful that it was common in these crafts. Journeymen, who were quick to unionize and protest replacement by less-skilled adults, never charged their employers with this practice. Furthermore, the percentage of teenage boys employed in the crafts even decreased as industrialization proceeded (table 3.5). Newark's manufacturers found the new workers they needed among the adult male immigrants from Ireland and Germany, who swelled the city's population in the 1840s and 1850s. By 1850, over two-fifths of the craftsmen were foreign-born, and a decade later, all the crafts except jewelry making had absorbed more immigrants (table 3.5). The manufacturers' choice of a new labor force allowed Newark's immigrants necessary job opportunities as it conserved traditional sex roles and family patterns.

Table 3.5 Characteristics of Male Workers, Newark[a]

	Percentage Aged 15–20		Percentage U.S. Born	
Craft	1850	1860	1850	1860
Shoemaking	10.2	5.3	54.2	36.2
Saddle making	30.7	26.9	59.2	39.9
Jewelry making	36.1	22.1	58.5	60.5
Trunk making	43.7	17.0	62.5	40.1
Leather making	16.6	11.0	36.0	28.0
Hatting	25.5	17.2	51.4	38.2

[a] Compiled from data in the manuscripts of the U.S. Censuses of Population, 1850 and 1860.

Despite the spread of industrial techniques, the use of immigrant workmen, and the profits some former mechanics were making, few artisans became open opponents of change. The growing number of wealthy urbanites created a demand for luxury goods, and in crafts like jewelry making and trunk making, artisans continued to do custom work both in small shops and in some large firms. They were not displaced by women, children, or immigrants. In 1855, for instance, Baldwin and Company, one of the largest jewelry firms in Newark, made an $1,800 diamond-studded watchcase to order. No unions arose among trunk makers in Newark, and journeymen jewelers did not organize until 1859, perhaps because of the alternative available for the older skilled journeymen to do custom-order work in both small and large firms if they could not found their own companies.[35] Moreover, although workers in hatting, leather making, and saddle making had unionized as early as the 1830s, they did not inhibit technological change or expansion in their crafts.[36]

Newark's journeymen shoemakers did not impede technological change in their craft, but they did halt the expansion of local firms. To obtain higher wages, they formed five unions in the 1830s—four of men making different grades of boots and shoes, and one of women binders.[37] At the same time, Newark's shoe manufacturers experienced severe competition in the wholesale market from cheap New England goods: in 1837, Lynn manufacturers sold one pair of shoes for every 2.5 white females in the country.[38] Newark's manufacturers lost their southern market, and the large wholesale firms collapsed in the late 1830s. Journeymen shoemakers' unions continued to exist in Newark in the following decades, and shoemakers' wages remained higher there than in New England.[39] Newark manufacturers were never able to counter competition in the national market with new techniques or lower wage levels, and in the 1840s and 1850s, Newark shoemakers produced mainly for the remaining local market. The three-task system instituted in the beginning of the century remained, shops became smaller, and by 1860 less than half of all shoemakers worked in establishments using sewing machines, the first step in mechanization in this trade (tables 3.2 and 3.4).

Although shoe manufacturers suffered severe reversals in Newark, artisans who fostered industrialization in other trades transformed them into major industries dominated by large firms. In 1860, 22 firms in the six crafts were big businesses by the standards of the day, having at least $50,000 in capital and/or 100 employees. Three-fifths of these firms had originated as artisans' workshops.[40] While the roots of the others are obscure, especially those firms established by migrants to Newark, none is known to have begun as a corporation or without artisan sponsorship. By 1860, however, the artisan origins of these industries were becoming obscure as manufacturers became divorced from production processes, devoting their energies to marketing and finance, and large, heavily capitalized firms captured the wholesale market.

The artisans who accomplished this transformation had of necessity converted themselves from mechanics into businessmen, concentrating their attention on managerial, marketing, and financial functions. Newark leather manufacturer Noah Farewell Blanchard is an example of the mechanic turned businessman.[41] Blanchard had served an apprenticeship in leather making and had opened his own small shop in New England, but his first attempt at business failed. He came to Newark in 1847 as an employee of T. P. Howell, and his knowledge of the trade served him well. As the number of Howell's employees grew, new managerial positions were created, and Blanchard became the superintendent. He then joined the firm as a partner and, in 1860, he once again began his own business—but this was a well-capitalized, mechanized leather firm. As a manufacturer, Blanchard's interests widened, especially in the financial realm, and in the 1870s he became one of the founders of the Prudential Insurance Company, today one of Newark's most important economic institutions.

Although they concentrated their energies in new directions, artisans-become-manufacturers did not necessarily relinquish all mechanic's values or greatly alter their world view. Rather they stressed certain aspects of their mechanic's heritage and ignored others. Manufacturers ceased to value their own manual skill and that of others, judging achievement in terms of profit alone.[42] They still honored some of the mechanic's virtues, however, such as hard work, thrift, inventiveness, and independence. Moreover, they continued to define their work in terms of "the useful and the good"—they made money because God intended them to be useful to society, and their work produced good through their philanthropies. These mechanic's values had always overlapped substantially with those of the merchant, and the new manufacturers shared much with their associates in marketing and finance.[43]

Artisans played a crucial role in the industrialization of Newark's crafts, because they were as interested in expanding production and markets as any merchant, and because they had both entrepreneurial skills and technological expertise. By 1860, however, the artisan's role in industrialization was in jeopardy. The firms started by artisans in the 1830s were beginning to fall into the hands of their children or partners, who were untrained in the old technology, and who lacked respect for the old values. Because of improved transportation and marketing capabilities, craftsmen using traditional production methods found it ever more difficult to escape the competition of cheap machine-made goods. Those who hoped to join the competition no doubt had more difficulty becoming self-employed, since steam-powered machinery inflated capital requirements greatly. By 1860 the average capital invested in firms in the five crafts utilizing steam power was $40,579; only a decade earlier, when more human power was employed, the average was but $22,467. Only shoemaking still was open to the small producer in Newark, but he could not challenge the New England manufacturers in the wholesale trade. The very success of some artisans in expanding their small firms destroyed the viability of small business in the crafts.

The artisan's role in industrialization in the United States has been obscure, because one result of his success was to destroy the vestiges of his world. Furthermore, American industrialization was a regional experience, confined primarily to the Northeast in the early nineteenth century, but far from universally felt nor equally experienced even there. Development proceeded along different lines in various areas: shopkeepers instituted task differentiation in shoemaking in Lynn, but artisans did it in Newark. Only further research into a wide range of industries in different locales will reveal the magnitude of the artisan's contribution to American industrialization, but the experience of crafts in one of America's leading industrial cities suggests that it is much larger than previously estimated.

Notes

1. W. Paul Strassman, *Risk and Technological Innovation* (Ithaca, N.Y.: Cornell University Press, 1959); Katherine Stone, "The Origins of Job Structures in the Steel Industry," *Radical America* (1973), 7(6):19–66; David Brody, *Steelworkers in America* (New York: Harper & Row, 1960); Hanna Josephson, *The Golden Threads* (New York: Duell, Sloane, & Pearce, 1949).

2. Alan Dawley, *Class and Community: The Industrial Revolution in Lynn* (Cambridge, Mass.: Harvard University Press, 1976), pp. 25–29.

3. Herbert Gutman, "The Reality of the Rags-to-Riches 'Myth': The Case of Paterson, New Jersey, Locomotive, Iron, and Machinery Manufacturers, 1830–1880," in Stephen Thernstrom and Richard Sennett, eds., *Nineteenth-Century Cities,* (New Haven: Yale University Press, 1969), pp. 108–112; Siegfried Giedion, *Mechanization Takes Command* (New York: Oxford University Press, 1948), pp. 52–71.

4. U.S. Census Office, *Compendium of the Eleventh Census: 1890,* Part I (Washington, D.C., 1897), p. 437; *Manufactures of the United States in 1860* (Washington, D.C., 1865), pp. 348–52.

5. All figures for population and industries in 1826 are derived from the town census of 1826 printed in *The First Jubilee of American Independence, Newark* (Newark: M. Lyon & Co., 1826).

6. Indenture of James Brady . . . to Ambrose Tomkins, MG 1, document I 107, New Jersey Historical Society; *Sentinel of Freedom,* Newark, December 19, 1820, April 16, 1822, and August 30, 1825.

7. Bruce Sinclair, *Philadelphia's Philosopher Mechanics* (Baltimore: Johns Hopkins University Press, 1974); Milton J. Nadworny, "New Jersey Workingmen and the Jacksonians," *New Jersey Historical Society Proceedings* (1949), 67:185–98; Committee of the Newark Mechanics Association, *Address of Samuel L. Southard to the Association, April 5, 1830* (Newark: W. Tuttle & Co., 1830); Newark Mechanics Association, *Constitution and Bylaws of the Newark Mechanics Association for Mutual Improvement in the Arts and Sciences, 1828,* New Jersey Historical Society.

8. *Sentinel of Freedom,* July 7, 1829.

9. Howard Mumford Jones, *O Strange New World* (New York: Viking Press, 1964), pp. 212–14.

10. Frank J. Urquhart, *History of Newark, New Jersey,* 3 vols. (New York: Lewis Publishing Co., 1913), 1:466–88; *Sentinel of Freedom,* June 20, 1826, and July 11, 1826.

11. Charles S. Olton, *Artisans for Independence* (Syracuse: Syracuse University Press, 1975), pp. 32, 93; *First Jubilee,* pp. 28–30.

12. Hugo Meier, "The Ideology of Technology," in Edwin Layton, ed., *Technology and Social Change in America,* (New York: Harper & Row, 1973), p. 85.

13. William H. Shaw, *History of Essex and Hudson Counties, New Jersey,* 2 vols. (Philadelphia: Everts & Peck, 1884), 1:560; John T. Cunningham, *Newark* (Newark: New Jersey Histor-

ical Society, 1966), pp. 83–84; "A Cobbler's 'Ten Footer,' " *Newarker,* April 15, 1936, p. 34.

14. Cunningham, *Newark,* pp. 95–108; *Dictionary of American Biography,* 20 vols. (New York: Scribners, 1929), 2:528–29.

15. *Manufactures of the United States in 1860,* p. clxii.

16. Urquhart, *History of Newark,* 1:519.

17. Wheaton J. Lane, *From Indian Trail to Iron Horse* (Princeton: Princeton University Press, 1939), p. 249; Shaw, *History of Essex,* 1:561.

18. All information on directors of Newark banks and fire insurance companies comes from B. T. Pierson, *Directories of the City of Newark, 1835–1860* (Newark Daily Advertiser, 1835; Daily and Sentinel Office, 1836, 1837; Scott and Co., 1838, 1839; Aaron Guest, 1840–60).

19. Glenn Porter and Harold C. Livesay, *Merchants and Manufacturers* (Baltimore: Johns Hopkins University Press, 1971), pp. 58–63.

20. "Newark, The City of Gold and Platinum and Precious Stones," *Keystone,* Newark, May 1925, p. 175; photostat of Account Book of Carter, Pennington, and Doremus, New Jersey Historical Society.

21. All information cited in this paper on capital invested, number of employees, and types of technology for Newark firms in 1850 and 1860 comes from the manuscripts of the U. S. Censuses of Manufactures for those years. Coverage in the censuses was not complete—many firms failed to respond, and the census takers did not attempt an enumeration of those firms with less than $500 in capital invested. There was no strict definition of capital invested either, so that no great faith should be put in fine-grained comparisons of firms, and none is attempted. For illustrative purposes, however, the magnitude of these figures has value.

22. Shaw, *History of Essex,* 1:561; *Newark Daily Advertiser,* May 5, 1836.

23. Cunningham, *Newark,* p. 98; Shaw, *History of Essex,* 1:561; *Newark Daily Advertiser,* October 11, 1834, August 22, 1836, February 23, 1837, March 8, 1837, August 11, 1840.

24. The histories of all partnerships cited in this paper were reconstructed from Pierson, *Directories of City of Newark,* 1835–60.

25. *Newark Daily Advertiser,* December 17, 1846.

26. *Commerce, Manufactures and Resources, Newark, New Jersey* (n.p.: National Publishing Company, 1881), pp. 14–15.

27. B. T. Pierson, *Directory of the City of Newark. 1846–47* (Newark: Aaron Guest, 1846), p. 251.

28. *Newark Daily Advertiser,* November 13, 1847.

29. Cunningham, *Newark,* p. 94; Shaw, *History of Essex,* 1:561; *Newark Daily Advertiser,* June 9, 1838, March 16, 1850, September 26, 1850.

30. *Newark Daily Advertiser,* August 10, 1847; September 1, 1847; April 1, 1850.

31. "Newark, The City of Gold," p. 163; *Newark Daily Advertiser,* January 27, 1858.

32. The sites of offices outside of Newark were reported in advertisements in Pierson, *Directories of the City of Newark, 1835–60.*

98   SUSAN E. HIRSCH

33. Cunningham, *Newark,* p. 121; *Newark Daily Advertiser,* March 10, 1846 and April 5, 1850.

34. See Susan E. Hirsch, *Roots of the American Working Class* (Philadelphia: University of Pennsylvania Press, 1978), chap. 3, for a fuller discussion of the transformation of the labor force in the crafts.

35. *Newark Daily Advertiser,* February 10, 1855 and March 25, 1859.

36. See Hirsch, *Roots of the Working Class,* chap. 6, for a more detailed discussion of the nature of the labor movement in Newark.

37. *Newark Daily Advertiser,* May 25, 1835.

38. Dawley, *Class and Community,* p. 26.

39. Dawley, *Class and Community,* p. 53; *Newark Daily Advertiser,* October 11, 1850, June 22, 1854, April 2, 1859. Lynn shoemakers averaged $20 per month according to the 1850 U. S. Census of Manufactures, while Newark shoemakers averaged $22 per month, or 10 percent more.

40. Information on the craft background of founders of the 22 firms was collected from the sources listed above, *Newark and Its Leading Business Men* (Newark: Mercantile Publishing Co., 1891), and William Ford, *The Industrial Interests of Newark* (New York: Van Arsdale & Co., 1874).

41. Cunningham, *Newark,* pp. 186–88; "The Wider Use of Leather Restoring Tanning Prestige of this City," *The Call,* Newark, December 13, 1936.

42. Gary J. Kornblith, "From Artisans to Businessmen: Master Mechanics in New England, 1789–1850," presented at the annual meeting of the Organization of American Historians, April 1978, pp. 10–17. Kornblith suggests that the pursuit of profit and the shift in values caused emotional distress for the artisan who made the transition to "successful" manufacturer.

43. Jones, *O Strange New World,* pp. 221–26.

Selected Bibliography

Cochran, Thomas C. "The Entrepreneur in Economic Change." *Explorations in Entrepreneurial History,* 2d series, 3 (1965), pp. 25–38.
Dawley, Alan. *Class and Community: The Industrial Revolution in Lynn.* Cambridge, Mass.: Harvard University Press, 1976.
Giedion, Siegfried. *Mechanization Takes Command.* New York: Oxford University Press, 1948.
Gutman, Herbert. "The Reality of the Rags-to-Riches 'Myth.' " In *Nineteenth-Century Cities,* Stephan Thernstrom and Richard Sennett, eds., pp. 98–124. New Haven: Yale University Press, 1969.
Hirsch, Susan E. *Roots of the American Working Class.* Philadelphia: University of Pennsylvania Press, 1978.
Jones, Howard Mumford. *O Strange New World.* New York: Viking Press, 1964, chapter 6.
Kornblith, Gary J. "From Artisans to Businessmen: Master Mechanics in New England,

1789–1850." Presented at the annual meeting of the Organization of American Historians, April 1978.

Meier, Hugo. "The Ideology of Technology." In *Technology and Social Change in America*, Edwin Layton, ed., pp. 79–97. New York: Harper & Row, 1973.

Porter, Glenn, and Harold Livesay. *Merchants and Manufacturers*. Baltimore: Johns Hopkins University Press, 1971.

Sinclair, Bruce. *Philadelphia's Philosopher Mechanics*. Baltimore: Johns Hopkins University Press, 1974.

Strassman, W. Paul. *Risk and Technological Innovation*. Ithaca, N.Y.: Cornell University Press, 1959.

4

BLACK COATS TO WHITE COLLARS: ECONOMIC CHANGE, NONMANUAL WORK, AND THE SOCIAL STRUCTURE OF INDUSTRIALIZING AMERICA

Stuart M. Blumin

IT is increasingly evident that the white collar–blue collar dichotomy that has served so long as the primary symbolic distillation of this culture's concept of its class structure (and particularly that point in the structure where the "middle class" is distinguished from the "working class") is today breaking down under the force of economic change. Several decades of successful wage negotiations by large and fully institutionalized labor unions, combined with the emergence of a huge tertiary sector of clerical and service workers, have produced a broad belt of middle income earners who confound the old categories by weakening the connection between type of work and income. Today it will no longer do to assume that a person who wears a "white collar" at his nonmanual desk job enjoys a higher income, better life-style, more respect within his community, more rewarding work experience, or greater opportunity for advancement than does his "blue collar" counterpart on the assembly line or behind the wheel of a television repair truck. To be sure, nearly all of those who are above or below this broad belt of moderate incomes conform quite well to the old categories. But within it there are too many, ever-more-numerous exceptions. "Postindustrial society," whatever that may come to be, will require its own short-hand vocabulary to describe class.

But if the "industrial" vocabulary and its attendant perceptions and values are destined to have an end, we may presume that they also had a beginning (a prehistory) and even an evolving life (a history). Clearly, the industrial age dawned in a world that could have made little use of a white collar–blue collar dichotomy, even in the little urban economies that were mere islands in a sea of rural life and work, and even if we translate our anachronistic sartorial imagery into that of the black coat of the clerical worker and the leather apron of the urban artisan. For in the immediate preindustrial era (as, increasingly, in our own day), the difference between manual and nonmanual work did not correspond even remotely to that critical disjuncture between the "middling sorts" and "meaner sorts" within the urban class structure. The figure most responsible for this disjuncture of disjunctures was, of course, the master craftsman, the artisan-shopkeeper, who was both the producer and the retailer (and sometimes the wholesaler) of his goods, and a solid member of the city's middle orders. As long as all, or even most, of the consumer and capital goods made in the city were produced in the small shops of the independent artisan, by the master himself working alongside his journeymen and apprentices, and as long as the master's citizenship was that of the city or nation as a whole and not just its "producing classes," there could be no social stigma attached to the leather apron—certainly not, at least, by those who wore the black coat.

Industrialization, as we know very well, changed all this, first by eroding the independent craftsman's economic position, and then by eliminating him entirely from most lines of production. And as production was transferred from the small shop to the large shop, the "manufactory," and ultimately the mechanized factory, the distinctions between nonmanual and manual work, and between middle-class and working-class status, came increasingly into alignment. Those who "worked with their hands" were socially demoted into, or confirmed within, the "working class." Those who "worked with their heads" were promoted into, or confirmed within, the "middle class." Eventually, the evolution of a salaried, office-bound component of the latter group would bring to life the symbolic shorthand of the industrial era—"blue collar" and "white collar."[1]

If this sketch seems too simple and too abstract, it is probably because it joins two lines of historical inquiry that have too seldom converged—the evolution of status distinctions in industrializing societies, and the *specific* economic events that underlay this evolving concept of social position and worth. What it suggests, therefore, is the need for a social and cultural his-

tory of industrializing societies (focused, in the current instance, on changing concepts of social class) that pays far closer attention to the relevant details of economic history. What specific structural, or merely quantitative,
changes in economic life (in economic *relationships*) provoked men and
women into altering their view of the social order? When did these changes
occur? How should they affect our understanding of both the character and
the timing of the effects of industrialization on society?

I do not mean to suggest that nothing of this sort has even been attempted.
On the contrary, historians of the working class in America have been pro-
ceeding in something of this fashion ever since John R. Commons (be-
leaguered prophet!) provided the model in his long article on American
shoemakers in 1909—though one might have hoped for more progress in industries other than boots and shoes since that date.[2] But historians of the
working class, even at their best, can be expected to do only part of the job.
What about the experiences of those who were not in the working class? Retailers, wholesalers, brokers, bankers, managers, clerks, salesmen, and
many others were affected by the economic changes of the industrial era;
and these changes in turn affected both their position within, and their concept of, the class structure. Yet we have no history of the nonmanual work
force (no *Making of the American Middle Class*) that we may place alongside those histories that follow the laborers, journeymen, and degraded master craftsmen into the factories and the new working class. Until we do,
even a fully developed history of the industrial working class will tell us
only half of the story of the changing economic foundations of social class
in the industrial era.

Actually, the contribution of the labor historians is more than "half," for
the history of the nonmanual work force in the nineteenth century is in many
respects the reciprocal of the history of the emerging working class, and the
historian of the middle class must call upon many of the same events already
detailed by the historians of labor—if only to look at "the other side."
Thus, the increasing association of nonmanual work with middle-class status
may be said to be a product of the social degradation of manual work that
accompanied the transfer of production from the artisan's shop to the factory. The nonmanual middle-class was formed, according to this line of
reasoning, by the evaporation of the manual component—the gradual disappearance of the artisan-entrepreneur from the economy and class structure.
And since the labor historian has already described this phenomenon from

the artisan's point of view, the middle-class historian is left with what appears to be the simple and humble task of deducing its consequences to those who were *not* demoted to the working class.

On the other hand, it is not clear that the middle class was entirely "made" by "the making of the working class," or that the middle-class historian's role is necessarily a residual one. Events occurring within the world of nonmanual work—events parallel to, but different from, those already catalogued by the labor historians—may have helped shape and give consciousness to the emerging "white collar" middle class. What might these events have been? How shall we write their history? These are difficult questions, made still more difficult by the historical neglect of the small-scale, nonmanual entrepreneur and worker. As Arno Mayer has recently pointed out, the lower middle class (to use his phrase), unlike either the working class or the large-scale merchants and industrialists, has never been an appealing subject to historians.[3] And in the American setting, at least, it has been particularly unappealing from just that point in history when it lost its artisan component! Thus, there are studies of colonial craftsmen as middle-class entrepreneurs and even as middle-class revolutionaries,[4] but there is no analogous study of middle-class entrepreneurialism or political activity for the retail shopkeepers, dealers, agents, and salesmen of the industrial era.[5] Studies of commercial life in both eras do exist, but they are confined to the large-scale merchants, whose wealth and standing placed them among the urban elite—or at least at the upper levels of the middle class—and are quite unrevealing about the nature of work and life in the smaller shops.[6] Clearly the kind of analysis that I am proposing—one that isolates those economic changes in nonmanual work that contributed to the development of the white collar–blue collar dichotomy—must be built largely on its own foundation of ideas, evidence, and actual research. In this article, I shall attempt to lay a part of that foundation by proposing several ideas, discussing a body of evidence that seems especially pertinent to the subject, and analyzing selections from that evidence in a way that I hope will suggest what might be accomplished by further research on these particularly anonymous Americans.

I shall begin in the most basic way possible—with numbers. In some dichotomous distillations of the social structure—those which focus on the inequalities of wealth and power between such groups as lords and peasants, or capitalists and industrial workers—the size of the two classes is significant, because it emphasizes the inequity of the domination of a very large class by a very small one. It is the imbalance that is important, and it may be said that the dominant group is visible as a class, not because it is large, but precisely because it is small. The white collar–blue collar dichotomy that has generally prevailed in modern American perceptions, however, is quite different in this respect. The dichotomy itself, though hierarchical, does not purport to explain the mechanisms of domination and exploitation in society: indeed, it implicitly denies their importance by leaving room for the existence of elites within, or even beyond, the white-collar class, by simultaneously denying the fundamental importance of these elites, and by substituting a large, amorphous (if uniformly attired) middle class for Marx's capitalists in the historical *pas de deux* with the working class. Where Marxism in effect posits a small upper class and a large proletariat, the white collar–blue collar dichotomy allows for a small but essentially insignificant upper class, and posits large middle and lower classes, between which there lies a rather more narrow chasm of power and wealth. The point that needs emphasis here is the *size* of the class on the upper side of the basic dichotomy. Not accorded any inherent structural significance, the white-collar middle class acquires visibility and importance by growing in size, to a point where sheer numbers allow it to be placed in apposition to the blue-collar working class.

How large, then, was the nonmanual work force at various points in the industrial era? Did the growth of this work force, or particular components of it, help establish in people's minds the significance of the apposition of nonmanual and manual work? Certainly, the growth of the salaried, office-working component in the latter-nineteenth and early-twentieth centuries was crucial, as is revealed by the very imagery of the dichotomy as it finally evolved. But what of earlier changes that may have laid the foundation by suggesting the significance of the difference between working with one's "head" or one's "hands," well before the collective eye was redirected to one's shirt collar?

In the aggregate, the nonmanual work force seems to have changed very little in the decades before the proliferation of salaried office workers. My own study of the Philadelphia work force, for example, indicates that the proportion of merchants, storekeepers, professionals, clerks, and others who "worked with their heads" rose slightly between 1820 and 1860, from about 27 percent to just under 30 percent, while Thernstrom's study of Boston places the nonmanual work force at 32 percent in 1880 and 38 percent in

1900 (all of these figures refer only to males).[7] What these calculations suggest is a steady but very gradual growth of the nonmanual sector of the urban work force through the nineteenth century—a trend so gradual that it was probably not even noticed by those who lived through it, much less perceived as a change of consequence to the class structure. But these calculations of aggregate change may be misleading. The more rapid growth of certain segments of the nonmanual sector during the early phases of industrialization may have provided the foundation for just the sort of alteration of perspective as occurred later, during the "white collar" era. In particular, the expansion of *retailing* as a distinct activity of distinct persons and firms, and the proliferation of *services* not before offered within the urban economy, would seem to have had a large potential impact on the perceptions of the city dweller. It is clear that both the retailing of consumer goods and the provision of such services as banking, insurance, local and nonlocal transportation, advertising, organized entertainment, and formal instruction of various kinds, changed rapidly in character during the early industrial era. How were these changes related to changing perceptions of the class structure?

Let us look first at retailing in the preindustrial American city. According to most accounts, there was but a small "retail sector" in the American towns of the eighteenth century. Most goods were sold to the public by the artisans who made them, by the farmers who grew them and carted them to town, and by the importers who imported them, sold them wholesale to country merchants, and only incidentally retailed them to individuals. Other goods were sold not in stores but by peddlers who carted or carried them through the streets. Such retail stores as did exist, moreover, were often very small, and yielded small incomes to their proprietors, many of whom were spinsters, widows, and seafarers' wives—the Aunt Hepzibahs of the colonial era.[8] By the middle of the nineteenth century, this picture had altered greatly. American-made goods had largely supplanted the imports that had given the large-scale merchants and their cluttered wharves such an important role in the urban economies of the colonial period,[9] and the men and women who made these goods engaged far less often in their sale to the public.[10] Retailers—of hats and shoes, dry goods and hardware, pianos and paintings—filled the vacuum. Farmers' markets continued to exist, as they do in our own day, but were gradually losing custom to the full-time grocers. Perhaps, too, storekeepers of various kinds were forcing the peddlers into such lines as oysters and pepper-pot soup, and the collecting of rags and bones. Not all of these changes would have produced an increase in the overall proportions of nonmanual workers in the urban work force. The separation of sales from production may have increased the numbers of retail stores, but the numbers of storekeepers and sales clerks who worked in these stores were easily offset by the enlarged numbers of manual wage earners in the growing industrial sector. Nor did the transfer of retail activity from the importers to nonimporting storekeepers require a massive increase in nonmanual personnel. Yet, both changes were highly significant, for they enlarged that portion of the nonmanual work force—the retail storekeepers and their store clerks—who begged comparison, as the importers never did, with the increasingly dependent (i.e., wage-earning) working class. The retailers were becoming what the skilled workers once were—small-scale, independent businessmen. And the increasing *numbers* of these small businessmen, who sold goods they neither manufactured nor imported, made the comparison with the dependent manual workers that much more compelling.

The growth of the service sector contributed to the manual–nonmanual dichotomy too, though its major impact was reserved for a much later period. The number of nonmanual jobs in the "tertiary sector" of the nineteenth-century urban economy was still small, but it was larger than it had been in the eighteenth century. Institutional innovations introduced bankers, insurance salesmen, and credit investigators into the urban economy, while the general maturation of the city provided new opportunities for lawyers, real-estate agents, employment bureaus, Italian dancing teachers, and others outside the flow of tangible commerce. To the more radical workers and intellectuals, these men, even more than the industrialists and merchants, were the "accumulators" who produced nothing, but gained comfortable livings from other people's labor.[11] To those of a more conservative hue, they were simply additions to the nonmanual middle class. From either perspective, the increase in the numbers of such nonmanual positions in the service sector strengthened, however modestly, the emerging manual–nonmanual dichotomy.

But how shall we examine and specify these quantitative shifts in the nonmanual work force through the course of the industrial era? The question is not as easily answered as might first appear, largely because the city directories and census manuscripts that constitute the basic sources for historical studies of the occupational structure are usually insufficiently precise, partic-

ularly in the early stages of industrialization. Seldom do they distinguish between owners of large and small enterprises, or between wholesalers and retailers (or artisans and manufacturers), and they often fail even to distinguish
between employers and employees. The opportunities for combining these
sources with others that help resolve these ambiguities, as Clyde and Sally
Griffen have recently done with such effectiveness in Poughkeepsie, seem
confined to the period after 1850.[12] How shall we contend with the crucial
period that precedes that date? One possibility is to treat the business advertisements appearing in a particular city's newspaper as a kind of business directory for that city, a method that has the advantage of being applicable to a
period stretching as far back as the mid-eighteenth century for several American cities. The disadvantages and pitfalls inherent in this method, however,
are all too obvious. First, the advertisements are not a complete directory, or
a representative one, and the degree and direction of bias in their inclu-
siveness of a city's economic units may well have changed over time. Second, the advertisements, though usually far more informative than the simple labels one finds in an occupational list, often to not reveal enough about
the character of the businesses that placed them—whether they are large or
small, wholesalers or retailers, or even whether they are regular businesses
or just private parties placing what we would now call a classified ad. For
some purposes, as I shall argue shortly, the newspaper ads constitute a valuable source, but for calculating the changing proportions of different kinds
of businesses in the urban economy (much less different kinds of workers)
they are suspect at best, and are probably worthless. There may, in fact, be
no way of reliably reconstructing the urban economies of the early industrial
era in a way that will reveal the timing of the emergence and complete development of the retail and service sectors. (The New York state census tab-
ulates 9,617 retail stores in New York County in 1855.[13] How many stores
were there in New York in 1800?) But there should be little doubt that such
a phenomenon accompanied, and gave further significance to, the more familiar events that shaped the careers of the industrial workers.

Perhaps, though, this point is better expressed not in terms of numbers,
but in terms of the changing character of the nonmanual sector. As I have already noted, most retail goods were sold in the colonial city by men whose
main activity lay in their production or importation, by other men—the
peddlers—whose modest scale of operations placed them below the artisans
in the social and economic scale, and by women, who found in shopkeeping

a substitute for, or supplement to, a husband's wage.[14] Keeping a retail store was not one of the ordinary ambitions of young men of middling rank, and the term "merchant" was reserved for the large-scale import-exporters. By the mid-nineteenth century, retailing had become respectable, and many men were able to fulfill in the retail sector ambitions that formerly would have been fulfilled only in the crafts or in some form of extra-local commerce. Undoubtedly, this enhancement of the respectability of retail trade was underpinned by a significant increase in the incomes that were earned in the retail sector. There were a few spectacular examples of this, such as A. T. Stewart of New York, who opened a dry goods store in 1823 and went on to become one of the wealthiest men in America, and in every city there were less spectacular but still very visible examples of retail merchants (as they could now be called) whose stores brought them not merely comfort but prosperity. The changing fortunes of more ordinary retailers, however, are difficult, if not impossible, to determine. As is the case with the changing size of the retail sector, the evidence is as elusive as the argument is compelling.

Fortunately, one aspect of retailing in the industrializing American city—one that bears on the changing character of retail institutions, and the work performed in them, if not on the incomes earned in selling—may be examined with more confidence, and it is here that the greatest opportunities for research in this area probably lie. I refer to a specialization and regularization of retail activity that may be regarded, in my view, as a form of institutional development analogous to the new forms of production that were transforming the industrial sector. During the colonial era, product specialization—and the close knowledge of particular products that specialization implies—belonged mainly to the artisans. Commerce, whether wholesale or retail, was a highly diversified and episodic affair, in which individual firms offered for sale whatever goods happened to be arriving in the town from foreign parts, the coastal trade, or the back country. For the larger firms in the larger towns, and for most of the firms in smaller towns, it was also a two-way affair, involving the purchase of hinterland produce at the same time as, and often in exchange for, imported goods. The evolution of a far different system, in which the sellers of goods offered specialized product lines from regularly replenished inventories, while leaving the purchase of hinterland produce to other specialized dealers, was a phenomenon of the early industrial era. And it was a phenomenon that may be traced with some reliability through the very newspaper advertisements that proved unreliable in estimating the changing sizes of the various sectors of the local economy. The newspapers still provide a biased "sample" of local firms, of course, but for the purpose of inferring structural changes in commercial activity (as opposed to inferring the changing numbers of different types of businesses) the bias is probably quite constant. In all eras, it is the more prosperous, more fully rationalized, and more cosmopolitan firms of each type (wholesaler, retailer, and so on) that we expect to find making regular use of existing channels of advertising. For this segment of the urban economy at least, therefore, we can reliably compare the merchandising practices of commercial firms of the preindustrial and industrial eras, to the extent that these practices are revealed in the newspaper ads.

To accomplish such a comparison, I selected four cities of differing regions, sizes, and character, whose surviving newspapers stretch back to at least the late eighteenth century. I then selected eight relatively normal economic years spanning the preindustrial and early industrial era, and specified which newspaper from each city and each year was to be used for the analysis. A coding scheme for products and certain other aspects of each ad was developed, and, according to this scheme, information was recorded from every advertisement appearing in four issues (one issue each from January, April, July, and October) of each specified newspaper in each year. The cities are Philadelphia, New York, Charleston, and Hartford, and the years are 1772, 1792, 1805, 1815, 1825, 1835, 1845, and 1855. The product codes and the list of newspapers are detailed in the appendixes to this essay. The newspapers utilized were those available at Olin Library, Cornell University, and because of the incompleteness of this collection, there are a number of gaps, but for each city it was possible to construct a time series covering much of the period.

The most interesting and telling results from this analysis are those pertaining to the specificity of the products offered for sale in the four cities' commercial firms. In each city there is a remarkably clear pattern, visible at several levels, of increasing product specialization. Table 4.1 divides the retailers and wholesalers of each city into four categories representing various levels of specialization: (1) general merchants, who offered goods from three or more of the product categories defined in the coding scheme; (2) slightly less general merchants, who offered goods from two different categories (but not including those who clearly specialized in one type of

product while tacking on a few articles of another type); (3) merchants offering a variety of goods within a single product category; and (4) highly specialized merchants, offering for sale a restricted and specific product line. In
all four cities, the proportion of advertisers in the first category declined dramatically over the period, with the exception that in Charleston it leveled off
at 10 to 15 percent after declining from 38 percent in 1772. In Philadelphia,
where the pattern is most clear, the general merchants declined continu-
ously, from 65 percent in 1772, to 12 percent in 1805, and to a mere 1 percent in 1855. Clearly, the general merchant, that central figure of the colonial urban economy, was on the way out. Nor was he replaced by those at
the next level of specialization. Advertisers offering goods from two product
categories also declined between 1772 and 1855, although the decline was
more gradual and seems to have begun somewhat later in the period. In all
probability, this second category of table 4.1 represents a transitional stage
of specialization and includes a number of once-general merchants who were
in the process of shedding certain product lines while gradually coming to
focus on others. Ultimately, these firms too were shaken out of the urban
economy—in the three seaport cities, they constituted only 2 percent of the
commercial advertisers in 1855.

The third level of specialization in table 4.1—firms offering two or more
types of products within a single product category—reveals no consistent
pattern of change. In Philadelphia, this type of firm increased relative to
other advertisers between 1772 and 1792, and then maintained a fairly stable
proportion through the rest of the period. In New York (where gaps in the
data make the timing of change most difficult to observe) there was a significant decline between 1772 and 1855. In Charleston the proportion remained
fairly stable through 1835, then rose in 1845, then fell drastically in 1855.
In Hartford, it rose between 1792 and 1805, and then remained stable thereafter. Only at the fourth and final level of specialization, therefore, do we
find a pattern reciprocal to that of the general merchants. In Philadelphia,
these most specialized of merchants—hat stores, shoe stores, piano stores,
and even pet shops—increased from 14 percent of all commercial advertisers
in 1772 to 79 percent in 1855. In New York, they increased from 24 percent
to 87 percent, in Charleston from 21 percent to 66 percent, and in Hartford
from 16 percent to 54 percent. In all four cities, in short, there occurred a
dramatic reversal in the relative proportions of the general and specialized
merchants among commercial advertisers, with the latter becoming the dom-

Table 4.1 Product Specialization, All Commercial Advertisers[a]

Philadelphia	1772	1792	1805	1815	1845	1855
General merchants	64.9%	28.6%	11.7%	9.0%	2.1%	1.3%
Merchants offering goods in two product categories	10.8	9.5	9.1	10.3	3.6	1.7
Merchants offering a variety of goods in one product category	10.8	24.9	19.5	20.5	21.6	18.2
Specialized merchants	13.5	37.0	59.8	60.3	72.7	78.8
Total[b]	100.0%	100.0%	100.1%	100.1%	100.0%	100.0%
n	37	189	77	78	473	527

New York						
General merchants	23.5%				0.0%	0.4%
Merchants offering goods in two product categories	12.6				7.8	2.1
Merchants offering a variety of goods in one product category	39.5				12.6	10.4
Specialized merchants	24.3				79.5	87.1
Total[b]	99.9%				99.9%	100.0%
n	119				301	241

Charleston	1772		1825	1835	1845	1855
General merchants	37.6%		15.2%	10.6%	13.3%	15.2%
Merchants offering goods in two product categories	6.5		6.1	8.3	3.5	2.3
Merchants offering a variety of goods in one product category	35.5		30.3	28.0	39.8	16.7
Specialized merchants	20.5		48.5	53.1	43.4	65.9
Total[b]	100.1%		100.1%	100.0%	100.0%	100.1%
n	93		66	132	113	132

Hartford	1792	1805	1815	1825	1835	1845
General merchants	46.9%	49.0%	25.5%	13.8%	8.1%	5.5%
Merchants offering goods in two product categories	18.8	14.0	7.3	11.3	11.5	13.1
Merchants offering a variety of goods in one product category	18.8	29.0	30.9	34.4	27.7	27.4
Specialized merchants	15.5	8.0	36.4	40.4	52.8	54.0
Total[b]	100.0%	100.0%	100.1%	99.9%	100.1%	100.0%
n	32	100	110	247	235	274

[a] Excludes those deemed to be artisans, factories, providers of services, and private parties.

[b] Rounded off.

Table 4.2 Product Categories of Specialized Merchants (percent of all commercial advertisers)

Philadelphia	1772	1792	1805	1815	1845	1855
Dry goods and clothing	8.1	12.7	1.3	11.5	14.6	16.3
Home furnishings	2.7	2.1	0.0	3.9	7.4	12.0
Food products	0.0	12.2	10.4	9.0	6.1	7.6
Buildings and construction products	0.0	2.1	1.3	1.3	2.3	4.2
Equipment, hardware, and tools	2.7	3.2	5.2	6.4	5.9	7.0
Printing, publishing, paper	0.0	4.2	39.0	16.7	8.5	2.9
Drugs	0.0	0.0	0.0	6.4	9.9	3.4
Other goods	0.0	0.5	2.6	5.1	18.0	25.4
Total	13.5	37.0	59.8	60.3	72.7	78.8
New York						
Dry goods and clothing	5.0				22.3	23.2
Home furnishings	0.8				10.3	24.5
Food products	8.4				6.0	2.9
Buildings and construction products	0.0				4.3	10.0
Equipment, hardware, and tools	0.8				11.6	5.8
Printing, publishing, paper	4.2				9.0	11.6
Drugs	3.4				3.0	2.5
Other goods	1.7				13.0	6.6
Total	24.3				79.5	87.1

Charleston	1772		1825	1835	1845	1855
Dry goods and clothing	2.2		6.1	9.9	8.9	12.1
Home furnishings	0.0		0.0	1.5	2.7	6.1
Food products	7.5		16.7	10.6	4.4	6.8
Buildings and construction products	0.0		1.5	0.8	0.0	2.3
Equipment, hardware, and tools	1.1		1.5	0.8	3.5	3.0
Printing, publishing, paper	1.1		10.6	6.8	5.3	9.1
Drugs	1.1		9.1	7.6	7.1	17.4
Other goods	7.5		3.0	15.1	11.5	9.1
Total	20.5		48.5	53.1	43.4	65.9

Hartford	1792	1805	1815	1825	1835	1845
Dry goods and clothing	3.1	0.0	6.4	2.0	2.6	6.9
Home furnishings	0.0	0.0	0.9	0.0	3.8	6.2
Food products	6.2	2.0	8.2	14.6	11.5	4.4
Buildings and construction products	3.1	1.0	2.7	4.9	3.8	3.3
Equipment, hardware, and tools	3.1	2.0	4.6	2.8	6.8	4.0
Printing, publishing, paper	0.0	0.0	1.8	2.8	4.3	2.9
Drugs	0.0	1.0	0.9	1.6	3.4	13.5
Other goods	0.0	2.0	10.9	11.7	16.6	12.8
Total	15.5	8.0	36.4	40.4	52.8	54.0

inant figure during the early industrial era. And as table 4.2 reveals, the emergence of the specialist was not restricted to one or two lines of goods. In each city, specialized sellers of dry goods, clothing, home furnishings, and many other consumer goods took up increasing amounts of newspaper advertising space, and so did firms selling particular types of equipment, construction materials, and other capital goods. The increasing specialization of wholesale and retail sales was a general and pervasive fact in the economies of the industrializing city.[15]

Specialization took other forms, moreover, than the increasing focus on particular goods. For example, firms that formerly engaged in a two-way exchange of goods, and that thereby served two often radically different markets, gave way to firms that facilitated the flow of goods in only one direction, and therefore may be said to have specialized in a particular market. More tangibly, storekeepers who sold dry goods or hardware did not also become grain or cattle dealers as a secondary pursuit, because they dealt increasingly with cash or credit customers and not with exchanges of consumer goods for country produce. Requiring no knowledge of how to move grain or livestock to mills, slaughterhouses, or foreign ports, they could focus their attention on the market for dry goods or hardware, and become specialists in that sense as well.

Table 4.3 attempts to assess the magnitude of this change by recording the proportion of each city's commercial advertisements that specifically mention the advertisers' willingness to purchase or exchange goods. This method, I contend, greatly understates the increasing specialization in a single market, for many firms in the earlier period (but few, I believe, in the later period) engaged in two-way commerce without specifically mentioning that fact in their advertisements. Still, a pattern is evident in all the cities, and is quite pronounced in the inland city of Hartford, where a large number of advertisers did specify two-way exchanges in the earlier years. In Phila-

Table 4.3 Percentage of Commercial Advertisements Offering to Purchase or Exchange Goods

	1772	1792	1805	1815	1825	1835	1845	1855
Philadelphia	6.4	2.0	0.0	0.0			1.0	0.7
New York	1.3						0.0	0.3
Charleston	6.1				1.3	0.0	2.6	0.0
Hartford		34.1	12.4	4.4	2.6	5.4	4.2	

delphia, New York, and Charleston, the decline is from a small proportion in 1772 to a negligible proportion or nil in 1855. In Hartford, the decline (and hence increasing specialization) is from 34 percent in 1792 to only 4 percent in 1845.

The newspaper advertisements include at least one other datum suggestive of a significant change in the character of urban commerce in the early industrial era. In the colonial period, many commercial ads prominently mention the arrival of a specific shipment. Many, indeed, are in effect *announcements* of the arrival of a particular ship, with particular goods offered for sale. During subsequent decades, however, advertisements of the form "Just Arrived on the Sloop Elizabeth" gave way to those which make no mention of particular shipments, and which imply the regular replenishment of inventories by means that are of no intrinsic interest to the consumer. What this in turn implies is a more general regularization of commercial activity, a phenomenon that should be expected of an age that was turning to regularly scheduled railroads, steamboats, and packet lines as the carriers of its goods. Of course, the "just arrived" form of advertising is based on other things besides the actual regularity of supply, so we should not expect to find that it completely disappeared in the railroad age. Indeed, it is still with us. But as table 4.4 indicates, it did decline markedly between 1772 and 1855—most markedly in Philadelphia and Charleston (actually disappearing from the latter city's ads), rather less so in the smaller city of Hartford. The newspaper advertisements of all four cities, in sum, imply the development of a commercial life that was a good deal less episodic than the one that prevailed in the colonial era.

But how did these various changes in the process of merchandising promote the association between nonmanual work and respectable social status? It is reasonable to suggest that the specialization and regularization of commerce created a new *physical and institutional setting* in which nonmanual

Table 4.4 Percentage of Commercial Advertisements Announcing a Particular Shipment of Goods

	1772	1792	1805	1815	1825	1835	1845	1855
Philadelphia	72.2	57.7	23.1	25.6			1.5	0.8
New York	70.0						11.6	32.2
Charleston	53.8				23.4	11.4	9.7	0.0
Hartford		46.9	57.0	45.5	41.2	30.2	28.5	

work was both more distinct, and more professional, than it had been before. It was certainly more distinct from manual work, for even the physical locus of the job of selling had become increasingly separated from the locus of production. Retail and wholesale firms that had no workshops provided both an institutional and physical boundary between the environments of manual and nonmanual work, but the separation of these environments was no less significant within the producing firms themselves. An interesting glimpse of this is provided by fig. 4.1, an 1850s lithograph of the Chestnut Street hat store of Charles Oakford of Philadelphia.[16] The view is that of an elegant retail sales area, a store with marble floors, ornate counters topped by still more ornate gaslight fixtures, and, along each wall, glass-doored display cases filled with long rows of silk and beaver hats. Oakford's firm seems to have made the hats it offered for sale, but the workshop, and its journeymen hatters, are nowhere in sight. The lithograph suggests nothing of the process of hat making, of the existence of the men who made the endless rows of hats, or of the possibility that these men might ever communicate with the men who sold the hats from the glass display cases. There are several of the latter depicted in the lithograph, and each wears the fine suit (and white collar) that clearly tells the store's customers that these are

Figure 4.1.
Charles Oakford's Model Hat Store, Occupied by Oakford 1854–60.
Courtesy Library Company of Philadelphia.

men who do not "work with their hands." Yet, the fact that the display cases hold hats and nothing but hats tells them also that these men are specialists, who can advise them in an expert way about the quality of this or that beaver skin, about the superior way in which Oakford's hats are constructed, about fit, and about the proper time and place to wear a silk hat. These men are not sea captains' widows, or peddlers, or black-coated clerks, but specialists of a new kind—nonartisanal experts in a particular product line. As such, they are the inheritors of the respect that formerly accrued to the master craftsmen themselves, even while they escape the stigma that now increasingly attached to the workshop, the leather apron, and manual labor.

In end analysis, it is the latter phenomenon—the demise of the artisan-entrepreneur—that must remain central to our understanding of the way in which the manual–nonmanual dichotomy came to dominate our view of the class structure. But, as I hope these pages have suggested, events occurring in the world of nonmanual work made their own, independent contribution to the increasing alignment of work-type and social status. Decades before the emergence of a large, salaried corps of office workers gave rise to the "new middle class" of the late nineteenth and early twentieth centuries, other economic events affecting the nonmanual sector helped produce what C. Wright Mills later called the "old middle class" of retail and wholesale storekeepers, salesmen, managers, and other nonmanual proprietors and workers of various types.[17] The term suggests a static residual category, no more than a baseline from which interesting history can begin. But Mills's "old middle class" was itself once "new," and the events that created it may tell us more than we previously imagined about the evolution of the social structure of industrializing America.

APPENDIX A

Product Codes

100 = general *

200 = dry goods and clothing, general
201 = cloth

* If ad lists products from two of the following major categories, list the first digit of each category as the second and third digits of the general code (e.g., an ad for dry goods and china should be coded as 123.)

202 = clothing (except as below)
203 = hats or caps
204 = wigs, perukes
205 = gloves
206 = boots or shoes
207 = other specific clothing
208 = table or bed linens
299 = other specific dry goods

300 = home furnishings, general
301 = furniture (cabinets, chairs, upholstery, etc.)
302 = carpets
303 = wallpaper
304 = pianos, organs (incl. pianofortes)
305 = mirrors
306 = stoves
307 = china or pewter
308 = silver or gold ware
399 = other specific housewares

400 = food products, general (excluding restaurants, etc.)
401 = meat
402 = baked goods
403 = groceries
404 = fish
405 = grain, rice, flour
406 = sugar, molasses, rum
407 = wine
408 = whiskey, beer, or ale (excl. taverns, etc.)
409 = fruit
410 = confectionary (candy, etc.)
411 = tea, coffee
499 = other specific foods

500 = buildings & construction products & services, general
501 = transfer of completed buildings and land
502 = construction of buildings, general
503 = lumber
504 = carpentry
505 = bricks
506 = bricklaying
507 = marble, stone, slate or tile, lime

508 = masonry, roofing, or tiling
509 = glass
510 = glazing
511 = paint or plaster (incl. paint & chemicals)
512 = painting, plastering, or paper hanging
513 = plumbing
514 = gas
515 = gas fitting, stove fitting
516 = locks
599 = other specific construction products or services

600 = equipment, transportation equipment, hardware, tools & repairs, general
601 = stationary machinery, boilers, & other heavy equipment
602 = plows and other agricultural equipment
603 = artisans' tools, other small equipment
604 = iron, steel, other heavy metal
605 = blacksmithing, coppersmithing, etc.
606 = guns, gunsmithing
607 = carriages, coaches, wagons, carts
608 = RR locomotives, cars, axles, wheels, etc.
609 = ships, boats
610 = sails, blocks, pumps, rope, nets, masts, etc.
699 = other specific equipment, tools, etc.

700 = printing, publishing, paper, general
701 = books
702 = periodicals (incl. newspapers)
703 = engravings, lithographs
704 = printing, engraving, lithography, bookbinding
705 = printed forms
706 = paper
799 = other specific printed or paper goods

800 = drugs, general
801 = patent medicines
899 = other specific drugs

900 = specialty items, other items, general
901 = watches, jewelry
902 = instruments (musical, scientific)
903 = brushes, combs, spectacles, etc.

904 = barbering, hair dressing
905 = cigars, tobacco
906 = paintings, sculpture
907 = photographs, daguerrotypes
908 = other specific specialties
909 = slaves
910 = trees, seeds
911 = whale products
912 = indigo, dyes, resin, sandlewood, gum
913 = cotton, wool
914 = hay, animal feed, fertilizer
915 = horses, other animals (excl. pets)
916 = linseed oil, flaxseed
917 = pets
918 = coal, firewood, other fuel
919 = pearlash, potash
920 = hides, leather
999 = other specific items

APPENDIX B

Newspaper List for Selected Cities

	Philadelphia	New York	Charleston	Hartford
1772	*Pennsylvania Gazette*	*Gazette & Weekly Mercury*	*South Carolina Gazette*	
1792	*Dunlop's American Daily Advertiser*			*American Mercury*
1805	*United States Gazette*			*American Mercury*
1815	*United States Gazette*			*American Mercury*
1825			*Mercury*	*Connecticut Courant*
1835			*Mercury*	*Connecticut Courant*
1845	*Public Ledger*	*Herald Tribune*	*Mercury*	*Connecticut Courant*
1855	*Public Ledger*	*Herald Tribune*	*Mercury*	

120 STUART M. BLUMIN

Notes

1. It should be emphasized that the alignment between work type and status was never complete and could be modified considerably in the individual instance. My argument here is that it had proceeded far enough by the second half of the nineteenth century to affect general perceptions of the class structure, and to produce the white collar–blue collar dichotomy as an expression of those perceptions.

2. John R. Commons, "American Shoemakers, 1648–1895," *Quarterly Journal of Economics* (1909), 24:39–84. See also Paul Faler, "Cultural Aspects of the Industrial Revolution: Lynn, Massachusetts Shoemakers and Industrial Morality, 1826–1860," *Labor History* (1974), 15:367–94, and Alan Dawley, *Class and Community: The Industrial Revolution in Lynn* (Cambridge, Mass.: Harvard University Press, 1976).

3. Arno J. Mayer, "The Lower Middle Class as Historical Problem," *Journal of Modern History* (1975), 47:409.

4. For example: Carl Bridenbaugh, *The Colonial Craftsman* (New York: NYU Press, 1950); Richard Walsh, *Charleston's Sons of Liberty: A Study of the Artisans, 1763–1789,* (Columbia, S.C.: University of South Carolina Press, 1959); Staughton Lynd, "The Mechanics in New York Politics, 1774–1788," *Labor History* (1964), 5:215–46; Charles S. Olton, "Philadelphia's Mechanics in the First Decade of Revolution, 1765–1775," *Journal of American History* (1972), 59:311–26; Eric Foner, *Tom Paine and Revolutionary America* (New York: Oxford University Press, 1976).

5. A modest exception is C. Wright Mills, *White Collar: The American Middle Classes* (New York: Oxford University Press, 1951), pp. 3–59.

6. For example: William T. Baxter, *The House of Hancock* (Cambridge, Mass.: Harvard University Press, 1945); Virginia D. Harrington, *The New York Merchant on the Eve of the Revolution* (New York: Columbia University Press, 1935); Leila Sellers, *Charleston Business on the Eve of the American Revolution* (Chapel Hill, N.C.: University of North Carolina Press, 1934); Frederick B. Tolles, *Meeting House and Counting House: The Quaker Merchants of Colonial Philadelphia, 1682–1763* (Chapel Hill, N.C.: University of North Carolina Press, 1948); Robert Greenhalgh Albion, *The Rise of New York Port [1815–1860]* (New York: Scribner's, 1939); Ralph M. Hower, *History of Macy's of New York, 1858–1919: Chapters in the Evolution of the Department Store* (Cambridge, Mass.: Harvard University Press, 1943).

7. Stuart M. Blumin, "Mobility and Change in Ante-Bellum Philadelphia," in Stephan Thernstrom and Richard Sennett, eds., *Nineteenth-Century Cities: Essays in the New Urban History* (New Haven: Yale University Press, 1969); p. 198; Stephan Thernstrom, *The Other Bostonians: Poverty and Progress in the American Metropolis, 1880–1970* (Cambridge, Mass.: Harvard University Press, 1973), p. 50.

8. The best account is still Carl Bridenbaugh, *Cities in the Wilderness: Urban Life in America, 1625–1742* (New York: Ronald Press, 1938), pp. 188–98, 341–54; and Bridenbaugh, *Cities in Revolt: Urban Life in America, 1743–1776* (New York: Ronald Press, 1955), pp. 274–81.

9. See Diane Lindstrom, *Economic Development in the Philadelphia Region, 1810–1850* (New York: Columbia University Press, 1978).

10. Once again, I refer to the transfer of production from the craftsman's shop to larger industrial units that divorced production from sales.

11. See Edward Pessen, *Most Uncommon Jacksonians: Radical Leaders of the Early Labor Movement* (Albany: SUNY Press, 1967); Bruce Laurie, " 'Nothing on Compulsion': Life Styles of Philadelphia Artisans, 1820–1850," *Labor History* (1974), 15:337–66.

12. Clyde Griffen and Sally Griffen, *Natives and Newcomers: The Ordering of Opportunity in Mid-Nineteenth-Century Poughkeepsie* (Cambridge, Mass.: Harvard University Press, 1978).

13. *Census of the State of New York for 1855* . . . (Albany, 1857), p. 479. Also listed for New York County are 4,289 wholesale stores, 3,426 groceries, and 1,742 hotels and inns.

14. There were also a number of women import-export merchants. See Jean P. Jordan, "Women Merchants in Colonial New York," *New York History* (1977), 58:412–39.

15. The above analysis includes wholesalers as well as retailers, mainly because it is so difficult to distinguish between the two groups on the basis of their advertisements. If we do attempt to isolate and focus on the retailers, the results are much the same. In Philadelphia, among those deemed to be retailers, specialists in a single product line increased from 37 percent to 81 percent between 1792 and 1855. In New York the increase was from 36 percent to 90 percent between 1772 and 1855. In Charleston it was from 29 percent to 79 percent over the same period, and in Hartford it was from 24 percent to 60 percent between 1792 and 1845. For a rare discussion of increasing specialization among retailers in this era see Hower, *History of Macy's*, pp. 82–88, 92–97.

16. This lithograph may be found in George B. Tatum, *Penn's Great Town: 250 Years of Philadelphia Illustrated in Prints and Drawings* (Philadelphia: University of Pennsylvania Press, 1961), plate 101. It is described on pages 188–89.

17. Mills, *White Collar*, pp. 3–12.

5

SMALL BUSINESS AND OCCUPATIONAL MOBILITY IN MID-NINETEENTH-CENTURY POUGHKEEPSIE

Clyde and Sally Griffen

FEW Americans ever rose from rags to riches, but many have started their own businesses, whether in hopes of riches, modest prosperity, or independence from bosses. Before the twentieth century, the achievement of self-employment was the most common first step toward success. Outside of agriculture, proprietorships usually took the form of small shops for retailing or manufacturing or a combination of both. The most dramatic change in occupational structure between 1800 and the present has been the decline of self-employment, reflecting the increased scale of manufacturing and commercial firms as well as the attrition of farm proprietors.[1]

Perhaps because the future lay with large-scale marketing and industrial firms, historians have not studied very closely the varying rewards offered by different types of small businesses.[2] Nor have they paid much attention to the consequences of the erosion of local opportunities for self-employment, especially in the crafts.[3] Historical mobility studies have tended to aggregate their data in very broad categories, concentrating on movement from blue-collar to white-collar employments, rather than distin-

This essay draws heavily upon the research published in our book, *Natives and Newcomers: The Ordering of Opportunity in Mid-Nineteenth-Century Poughkeepsie* (Cambridge, Mass.: Harvard University Press, 1978). Since the local materials we used would not help other scholars, we have not provided citations to them for this essay. Those interested in our sources should consult *Natives and Newcomers*, especially chapters 3, 5–8 and their footnotes.

guishing within the latter between the patterns for proprietors and those for professionals, managers, and clerical and sales workers.[4] They have not described how the avenues to self-employment varied for different groups of workers. They have not shown how the avenues changed over time as increased scale and capitalization affected entry into business and survival in different lines of commerce and manufacturing. They have not discovered, therefore, the consequences for differences in opportunity between American communities.

The investigation of local variation in mobility through self-employment in business is important for our general understanding of social and economic history, especially in showing the limitations of linear views of the progress of industrialization based upon knowledge of nationwide trends in different industries. Alfred Chandler's propositions in *The Visible Hand,* for example, help explain why modern large-business enterprise "began when it did, where it did, in the way it did" for whole industries in the nation, but do not predict the condition of any given industry in a given locality at a given time.[5] The progress of an industry in some localities often was accompanied by regression in organization and contraction in work force in other localities. Moreover, the new labor history for the nineteenth century has been showing how groups of workers from immigrant and artisan subcultures helped limit, in the short run, the rationalizing tendencies in economic development.[6]

This uneven progress of industrialization meant that the frequency and significance of business opportunities could vary widely between communities. Thomas Kessner has found, for example, very high rates of upward mobility among Jewish and Italian immigrants in New York City at the end of the nineteenth century. Occurring during the very period of the rise of big business, these high rates call attention to the special importance of small-shop industries in New York City's economy.[7] Even where the frequencies of mobility are very similar, as they are somewhat earlier for Poughkeepsie, New York—a city with 20,000 inhabitants in 1880—and for the much larger and more dynamic city of Boston, we must presume differences in the relative importance of particular paths of mobility between the two cities.[8]

The present essay on occupational mobility through small business in Poughkeepsie between 1850 and 1880 is intended to show the importance of closer examination of local variations. Through an examination of the census records of individual businessmen as well as of the credit reports

compiled by R. G. Dun and Company on 1,530 firms, we have assessed the
meaning of different kinds of self-employment in Poughkeepsie during these
thirty years. Not surprisingly we have found that while mobility studies
usually categorize all small businessmen as "white collar" on a vertical
scale, many proprietors eked out marginal livings. More important for an
historical sense of industrialization during the nineteenth century, it became
more difficult during our period for artisans to become prosperous proprietors. Increasingly, journeymen who achieved self-employment were confined to a repairing business, as men trained to retailing rather than a craft
came to own the more successful businesses, even in craft-related lines.

Our discussion of small business will follow the example of Theodore
Hershberg and his associates in the Philadelphia Social History Project in
treating firms with less than 50 workers as small and medium-sized.[9] Any
definition of scale is historically relative and debatable; this one agrees with
our own sense that, as late as 1880, firms of more than 50 workers were
regarded as large by contemporaries in most localities. Although establishments with several hundred workers became increasingly numerous in many
industrial centers during the 1870s, a very large minority or even a majority
of the manufacturing workers in most cities continued to be employed in
shops with less than 50 workers. Furthermore, from the 1870s until at least
the 1960s, more than 80 percent of all manufacturing firms in the United
States remained small or medium-sized by this definition.[10]

Size of work force is the most convenient definition of scale, but it does
discriminate against firms which are capital intensive and tells us nothing
about the traits by which Alfred Chandler and others have defined modern
enterprise. Suffice it to say for the purposes of this essay that almost all of
Poughkeepsie's factories before 1880 remained single business units run as
partnerships, with the most minimal managerial hierarchy. With a few partial exceptions like the Vassar brewery and the iron furnaces, they were neither capital- and energy-intensive nor continuous process. In retailing, the
movement toward the modern department store appeared in Poughkeepsie
during the 1870s but had not been completed by 1880. In short, this small
city, in the three decades after 1850, seems a particularly useful place to see
the changing economic significance of occupational mobility through small,
less modern enterprise during a period when larger, more modern businesses
became increasingly important nationally in many industries.

Although Poughkeepsie early in its history became important for its hinterland as a commercial and transshipment center, its economy also depended upon manufacturing. The city never developed a successful manufacturing specialization such as upstate Troy did in stoves, with numerous firms and auxiliary enterprises providing external economies. Nor did any closely knit group of entrepreneurs with similar interests emerge. In 1850, the largest employers included a blast furnace, dyewood mill, brewery, and cotton, carpet, and chair factories.

The fortunes of particular industries shifted during the next three decades. The city's cooperages, carriage shops, and foundries, which had depended heavily upon the southern trade, declined in relative importance after 1860. The sixties and seventies saw expansion of iron manufacture, a temporary decline in garment making, followed by a depression-born revival in factories, and the emergence of factories in new lines, notably agricultural implements, shoes, and glassware.

Most of Poughkeepsie's varied enterprises fit our definition of small and medium-sized business. In 1880, about 60 percent of the workers reported in the manufacturing census labored for firms employing fewer than 50 hands. The city had no factories with more than 100 workers on the eve of the Civil War; it did have six with more than 50 employees and twenty-four with between 20 and 49. In 1880, the new shoe factory employed nearly 300 hands and six other factories reported 100 or more, but the proportion of workers in firms of 20 to 49 hands and of 50 or more hands had not changed much between 1860 and 1880.

Judged by average number of workers per firm, Poughkeepsie's shops remained small when compared with industrial cities like Paterson and Troy, which show averages in 1880 of 57 and 44. Most cities in New Jersey, Connecticut, and New York State that year show averages of between 15 and 26 workers, with Poughkeepsie at 18. It seems probable that cities in this latter range of averages, and especially those toward the higher end of it, resemble Philadelphia, where three-fifths of the workers in the fourteen industries described by Theodore Hershberg and his associates labored in firms employing more than 50 hands, but where the median work force remained less than 8 workers in all but one industry.

In some lines of manufacturing in Poughkeepsie, especially where custom work and hand methods continued to prevail, the median size of firms decreased during the middle decades. One- or two-man shops were especially frequent among immigrants, but, regardless of the nativity of proprietors, large tailoring, shoe, cabinet, carriage, and harness-making shops became less common in Poughkeepsie as national and regional competition increased. The invasion of goods manufactured elsewhere limited many firms to local customers and, increasingly in some lines, to a repairing business.

Retailers also were affected by changes in the distribution and marketing of goods. Even before 1880, local firms in some lines began to face competition from branches of national chains like the Atlantic and Pacific Tea Company or branches of firms in other cities. Agencies of national manufacturers—at first primarily of agricultural implements and sewing machines—became more common by 1880. And just as small-shop manufacture was being replaced in some lines by large-factory production, local retailing began to show an increase in scale and complexity of organization, notably the evolution of its two largest dry-goods firms toward the modern department store.

The willingness of Poughkeepsians to start businesses corresponded closely to the city's growth. Using the listings of firms in the classified section of the city directories, in most lines the number of firms increased more rapidly than the proportionate increase in population between 1859 and 1870. Between 1870 and 1900, a period of much slower population growth, there was a decrease, or slower growth, in the number of firms in many lines. Only businesses catering primarily to a local, often a neighborhood, clientele, such as saloons, groceries, confectioneries, bakeries, and barbershops, increased at a rate faster than the population as a whole.

A large influx of new proprietors during the sixties indicates that a community which was prospering and expanding readily attracted outside businessmen. Similarly, proprietors persisted in the city as long as times were good but left more frequently when the expansion slowed. In 1870, 58 percent of the proprietors in the 1860 census remained in Poughkeepsie but, by 1880, only 48 percent of the 1870 proprietors remained.

Although periods of rapid growth stimulated the founding of businesses, only a minority became stable, long-lived enterprises. Of the 1,530 firms in Poughkeepsie evaluated for credit by R. G. Dun and Company and its predecessor between 1845 and 1880, 32 percent lasted three years or less, and only 14 percent lasted twenty years or more. Most businesses faded rapidly; only a few were very promising ventures at the outset. Of the 1,317 firms whose worth was estimated by credit reporters, 42 percent were worth less than $1,000, 38 percent were worth between $1,001 and $10,000, and only 20 percent were rated above $10,000.

Community studies which rely only upon census returns will give a picture of greater stability in business. Proprietors in Poughkeepsie, for example, persisted in the city at a higher rate than any other group in the census. What the census does not capture is businessmen who moved in and out of the city in the years between enumerations. For example, the census missed entirely a German who sold his shoe store in Poughkeepsie in 1864, subsequently opened one in Philadelphia, returned to Poughkeepsie in 1866 to start another shoe store, and by 1868 had disappeared from the city again.

Moreover, the census designations omit the varied business careers of some proprietors. They do not record the many cases where men carried on several businesses simultaneously or shifted businesses several times during the course of a decade. Listing in two censuses as a stove merchant did not record one Quaker's ventures into dry goods, a country-store proprietorship, and a confectionery. An Irish Catholic's listings as a merchant and lumber merchant fail utterly to convey the multiplicity of his ventures; credit reporters described him variously as "a trading kind of man" and "in too many kinds of business," including ice, grain, liquor, groceries, a steam sawmill, a drydock, and a lime kiln, together with extensive real-estate speculation.

One result from the census on stability among proprietors does find confirmation in tracing through annual directories; the larger proprietors, distinguished by amount of property, more often remained in the same business. And credit reports confirm that, in general, the richer a firm, the longer its life. Thus, 50 percent of the firms that received reports for twenty years or more had a maximum worth during their lifetime of $10,000 or more, but only 4 percent of the firms lasting three years or less, and 22 percent of the firms lasting between 10 and 19 years, ever achieved a worth of $10,000. Conversely, a majority of businesses with an estimated worth of $1,000 or less lasted three years or less, while a near majority of those who at any time had an estimated worth of over $25,000 continued for more than twenty years.

On the other hand, longevity did not guarantee prosperity. A large minority of firms reported on for more than twenty years ended up in serious trouble, one-third slipping into a C.O.D. rating and another one-tenth experiencing fluctuations and reversals during their existence. Firms lasting between ten and nineteen years had a greater tendency to decline, 40 percent ending up with a C.O.D. rating. The record of prosperity for firms is paralleled by that for individuals. An examination of the property mobility of those proprietors who owned real estate in the city in 1870, and remained as proprietors in 1880, reveals that 40 percent increased their real-estate holdings significantly, 35 percent owned approximately the same amount, and 25 percent experienced loss.

Proprietors of the richest firms suffered less from reversals. They often had the capital resources to recoup or to make new investments elsewhere. Nevertheless, fires, changing conditions in the national market, and overextension in real-estate investments temporarily injured even the most affluent and long-lived proprietors in Poughkeepsie. For the more marginal businessmen, self-employment meant almost constant precariousness, and many were forced to return to employment by others. The more fortunate remained on the fringes of the commercial world by shifting to clerical and sales occupations.

Well-established businessmen who fell on hard times usually did not take manual jobs, but younger shopkeepers proved somewhat more vulnerable to this form of downward mobility. In the sixties and seventies, only 10 percent of Poughkeepsie's proprietors who were in their twenties at the start of a decade, compared to 5 percent of men over 50, suffered that change by the next census. Saloonkeepers, grocers, and other small shops, especially ventures run at home in residential neighborhoods, comprised almost all those who reported manual work late in life; almost invariably they had pursued it previously.

For manual workers, self-employment at the least offered the possibility of economic security in old age. That motive remained potent long after hopes of achieving any prominence in Poughkeepsie diminished. Among skilled manual workers, the frequency of becoming proprietors declined with age, but not sharply. In the first two decades after 1850, 16 and 20 percent of all journeymen in their forties at the start of the decade, and only a slightly lesser proportion of those in their fifties, had opened their own businesses by the next census. This compares with 22 and 26 percent of journeymen in their thirties and slightly more of those in their twenties.

The relative importance of different avenues to proprietorship changed between 1850 and 1880, with profound consequences for the forms of mobility readily available to manual workers, especially immigrants. A major change which sharpened stratification between manual and nonmanual workers was the decline of the artisan shop owners, who had formed an important part of the city's substantial middle class. If he remained prosperous in 1880, the master worker who combined manufacturing and retailing in his shop long since had adapted to selling more ready-made goods from other shops or factories.

Increasingly, after 1850, men trained to retailing, not to the craft, emerged as proprietors of the city's largest hardware, furniture, boot and shoe, clothing, and other craft-related stores. This change varied between industries. It did not characterize baking and confectionery and was less rapid in merchant tailoring in Poughkeepsie than in shoes and furniture. In the extreme case of the last two lines, however, most of the owners of the larger shops in 1850 had apprenticed in the craft, whereas by 1880 the leading merchants either had begun in retailing or in unrelated forms of manual work.

The organization of manufacturing in Poughkeepsie also shifted visibly. Men who had begun as merchants launched Poughkeepsie's new shoe and garment factories in the seventies. Even where artisan-owned shops remained the rule, as in the manufacturing of machines, carriages, and barrels, there were clear signs by 1880 that few of these businesses would prosper in the future as their predecessors had in the past. The bigger firms both in retailing and in manufacturing in craft-related lines did continue to coexist with a much larger number of small shops, most of them run by artisans, but the majority of the proprietors of these small shops barely earned a livelihood and depended increasingly upon repairing.

The recruitment of the city's proprietors reflected the decline of the artisan businessman. The proportion of proprietors who started out as skilled workers had decreased by 1880. A slight and temporary increase in the proportion of proprietors drawn from the ranks of the skilled during the sixties reflected the attempts of immigrant artisans to set up shops, as well as the tendency of rapid population growth to stimulate the founding of new businesses, many of which faded quickly. The drop during the seventies in the proportion of proprietors who previously had been artisans was too dramatic to attribute solely to the depression, since the proportion who previously had been unskilled workers continued to rise in that same decade.

Clerical and sales workers became an increasingly important source of new proprietors. Among men already in the city who became proprietors during the fifties, those who held clerical and sales jobs at the start of the decade were only one-fifth as numerous as those who had been at skilled work; the ratio changed to one-third in the sixties and one-half in the seventies. At the end of the period, the business class still drew more of its new members from skilled than from clerical and sales workers, but the differences had narrowed dramatically. First- and second-generation immigrant businessmen were still twice as likely to be drawn from skilled work, but in the recruitment of new businessmen of native parentage, the skilled no longer had any superiority during the seventies.

Furniture making provides the extreme case in Poughkeepsie of the decline of artisan shop owners. The competition of factory work in other cities brought sharp contraction in local manufacture. There were 45 cabinetmakers at the 1850 census, and two firms accounted for 22 workers. By 1880, only 19 craftsmen remained, divided among seven firms. The businesses of the two largest employers of the sixties had passed into the hands of men untrained in the craft. One of these new men had been a dry goods merchant, merchant tailor, and mowing-machine manufacturer previously; another, the city's most versatile and peripatetic businessman, had been in half a dozen kinds of business in the previous ten years. A third shop owner—a newcomer to furniture dealing, who would have the city's biggest store in that line by the turn of the century—had been a craftsman but in a different industry. Apprenticed as a carriage trimmer, he had had his own shop in that trade, but by the mid-seventies had shifted into auctioneering and commission selling before entering the furniture business.

The triumph of dealers trained in retailing is emphasized by contrast with the later careers of some of the city's older and reputable self-employed cabinetmakers. One, who had received accolades from credit reporters as an "expert workman," was reported by 1871 as having "no store, simply runs a little repair shop, one-house affair." Actually this craftsman continued to make desks and bookcases to order, but so marginal a business did not belie the reporters' judgment that the subject was a "very old-fashioned man, scarcely up to the times . . . no calculation." The second largest employer in 1865 with the "best custom in the city" had already been pegged as a good mechanic, industrious and prudent, but not a good businessman; reporters were not surprised by his subsequent failure and resort to a small repairing shop off the main street.

The decline in local opportunities for artisan success through businesses of their own was less obvious in tailoring for several reasons. Merchant adventurers with no training in the craft long had been prominent in partnerships in the larger men's clothing firms. Moreover, cutters remained more highly paid than any other manual workers in the city except locomotive engineers. Cutters often could save enough to start new businesses and they remained attractive as new partners in well-established firms.

The trade also saw one former journeyman become one of Poughkeepsie's self-made success stories. By 1880, a Prussian-born Jew was well on his way to becoming the biggest merchant tailor and clothier not just in Poughkeepsie but in the entire mid-Hudson region. M. Shwartz's methods, however, suggest that he was the exception that proves the rule, in this case the rule that skill in business rather than in the craft was now the key to prosperity. By 1877, he advertised a "One Price Clothing House" with the "largest stock of men's, boys' and children's ready-made in the city."

In his own words, Shwartz "saw that if goods were bought direct from the manufacturers and . . . a sufficient number of garments could be sold to give employment to a regularly organized corps of finishers, there was no good reason why good clothing could not be made here even more cheaply than in the larger cities, where living is more expensive." By 1887, his firm boasted that "seven to eight cutters are employed steadily the year around, and from 100 to 150 hands making garments, while 14 or 15 men are employed as salesmen and stockkeepers." Symptomatically, Shwartz's stepsons began their careers in the family business as clerks, not as apprentice tailors.

Shwartz alone employed more than half of the city's 103 male tailors in 1880. Yet proprietors still comprised one-fourth of the total number of tailors, suggesting how modest most of these businesses were. Journeymen could not hope realistically to save enough to start up with a good stock and a good location; except for the cutters, tailors' wages compared unfavorably with those in other crafts. One immigrant, for example, worked nine years as a journeyman before starting his own business in 1869 for "making, repairing, and cleaning clothing." He "commenced by working at the bench, got in a little stock and now does a fair trade," but he never got much beyond keeping "a few samples of cloth upstairs, not strong enough for credit in New York."

The limited prospects for substantial prosperity in new businesses in most crafts after the early seventies brought reduction in the number of firms in some lines but not in all. The frequency with which journeymen continued to try self-employment reminds us how lively, and not just how precarious, small business remained in the Age of the Trust. At one extreme, the demand for fresh baked goods, including bread, supported twice as many shops in Poughkeepsie in 1900 as in 1870, although the population had increased by only 20 percent. Not until the twentieth century would regional and national manufacturers' invasion of local markets sharply reduce the opportunities for local craftsmen to run small baking and confectionery shops.

At the other extreme, self-employment was uncommon among machinists, with less than one-tenth reporting their own shops at every census but 1860. This minority usually tried manufacturing some specialty, often a patent of their own invention. Frequently they failed or earned not much more than a livelihood for the owners and an assistant or two. Small machine shops doing a more general business did not fare much better.

Carriage making fell between these extremes in Poughkeepsie. Although local manufacture declined in the face of midwestern competition, the carriage-repairing business remained important and could be carried on satisfactorily by self-employed individuals or by contractual business arrangements, in which the participating craftsmen retained substantial interest. Alternatively, because little "factories" of 10 to 15 men still offered a livelihood, a few artisans who had apprenticed locally in the carriage trades continued to start them.

Whatever the variations, the general tendency in the traditional crafts, especially by the seventies, was toward severely limited prospects for reward for the self-employed. As the scale, and increasingly the mechanization, of manufacturing increased, artisans had to adapt their businesses to survive. Few outside the larger firms did so with much success.

In lines like barrel making there was little retailing or repairing to take up as local manufacture lost ground. Even large employers who had insufficient capital, or entrepreneurial talent, to keep up with advances in technology sold out to larger firms elsewhere, becoming their local managers or agents. By 1880, two of the three biggest cooperages in Poughkeepsie no longer were owned locally, and their bosses did not prosper by the change. One of them had employed 80 journeymen on the eve of the Civil War, but now was reduced to acting on behalf of a New York City firm with his work force less than half its former size.

The economic marginality of artisan shop owners who could not adapt to technological change was more visible in an industry like shoemaking, where small shops had been numerous, and where retailing and repairing provided alternatives as the demand for custom manufacture declined. More than a decade before a shoe factory was established in Poughkeepsie, the organization of local shoemaking showed signs of regression in the face of an influx of immigrant craftsmen. Whereas four shoe houses had reported employing 12 or more workers each in 1850, a decade later these firms employed fewer workers and reported a decrease in value of product.

A large increase in the number of very small shops accompanied this reduction of manufacture in medium-sized shops. Of the 22 firms first appearing in the 1860 census, 3 had four or five workers, the rest had fewer, and the owners were overwhelmingly of German and Irish parentage. By the time a wholesale shoe merchant from Brooklyn opened his large factory in Poughkeepsie in 1870, there were still 111 men who identified themselves as shoemakers or boot and shoe dealers and more than one-fifth worked for themselves.

Self-employment increased temporarily in shoemaking, but the reward for it did not. Signs of trouble in artisan shops began to increase in credit reports during the late sixties, and the depression of the seventies wiped out the former prosperity of many others. One native had kept a small store and employed two men in the fifties. But by 1867, credit reporters described him and his son as "mostly custom work, both work at the bench, have very little stock on sale" and by 1874 said that the son, now alone, "depends principally on repairing."

The wiser and more ambitious shoemakers who remained associated with their trade pushed into retailing ready-made goods as quickly as they could. For an artisan with little capital the shift to retailing was hazardous, however. He faced competition throughout the period from merchants who already had invested, or could afford to invest immediately, in a big stock of ready-made goods, well assorted in size, style, and price.

Those who pushed into retailing in Poughkeepsie after the Civil War produced only one big success story. Michael Timmins, the son of an English shoemaker of Irish parentage, expanded from working at the bench into doing a "very good cash business in cheaper grade of goods . . . mainly among the lower classes." He kept his shop on a side street in an immigrant neighborhood until 1882, when he opened a second shop in the central business district to appeal—successfully—to the quality trade. No other shoemaker after the sixties approximated Timmins' achievement, but a minority as late as the eighties did fit this description of one German: "Small custom trade. . . . Has plenty of work to do and seems to be getting along in usual way."

The long-term decline of small-shop craft manufacturing during the last half of the century should not obscure its short-term significance for immigrant adaptation to an industrializing economy. The impressive occupational mobility of immigrant artisans in Poughkeepsie at mid-century reflected primarily the frequency with which they became shop owners in their trades. Especially for those who set up in business before the Civil War, the prospects for achieving at least modest prosperity were more favorable than any general account of the decline of custom manufacture indicates. And the occupational mobility of their sons suggests some benefit from their father's achievements.

In less than a generation, immigrant artisans constituted a majority of shop owners in a number of crafts. The Germans alone accounted for well over half of the total in tailoring, baking, butchering, brewing, and cigar making. They benefited from the longer survival of hand methods in cigar making, baking (except for crackers), and butchering (not reduced to the specialty of meat cutting before the eighties). But the early, if usually modest, success of German shop owners occurred in a greater variety of handicrafts, reflecting the limited progress as yet of specialization and mechanization in them in the United States. By 1880, the limitations of the initial prosperity of German artisans in Poughkeepsie had become evident, pointing up how much their successful adaptation had been a fortuitous result of the right people arriving at the right time.

The organization of crafts in Germany and the competition within them prepared emigrants to capitalize upon the lag in America between the time ready-made goods became common and the time they took to dominate local markets. Especially before the Revolution of 1848, these artisans tended to be masters with their own shops, property, and families, rather than apprentices or unmarried journeymen. These masters often had enough property to pay for their travel and then set up in business for themselves in the New World. At the same time, the surplus of artisans in Germany by the 1840s taught new lessons about the tactics necessary for survival. American artisans could not easily compete with them in habits, standard of living, and expectations; moreover, the Germans proved as flexible as natives in switching trades when opportunity beckoned.

While the most successful Germans in Poughkeepsie made money initially within their trades at a time when older methods of manufacture still prevailed, their increase in fortunes primarily reflected subsequent shrewd investment in real-estate or moneylending. Moreover, local careers in business begun in the fifties and sixties tended to be more successful than those begun later. A comparison of Germans assessed in the tax lists of 1880 and 1890 reveals that fortunes made earlier have grown larger by 1890, but there are hardly any names added to the ranks of those with property assessed at more than $10,000.

In the short run, German artisans had adapted to Poughkeepsie's economy with impressive results, becoming preeminent as shop owners in the food and apparel trades. But in the longer run, this very concentration may have been a disadvantage in the competition for occupational and property mobility. The native-born of German parentage tended to cluster more often than the immigrant generation in the by now relatively poorly paying trades like cigar making, butchering, and barbering, where they found preference in hiring and more chance for self-employment.

Throughout the middle decades, small retail and service businesses—such as groceries, saloons, and variety or fancy-goods stores—provided an alternative means of self-employment for artisans, and one increasingly attractive to men in crafts threatened by factory competition. Of the shoemakers listed in city directories between 1843 and 1880, a little less than 6 percent became shop owners in the trade and slightly more shifted to other kinds of jobs, nearly half of them in retailing and service. Even artisans who already owned shoemaking shops shifted lines, especially after the Civil War. One native who in 1866 had been "doing a safe business, with two or three men hired, himself, mostly small custom work" had opened a meat market by 1870 and sold fruits and vegetables as well.

In the contracting woodworking trades, most journeymen achieving self-employment did so outside their crafts. For example, two German woodcarvers, who first appeared in 1860 when they were in their twenties, abandoned their trade by 1880 for saloonkeeping. Small retail and service ventures had three advantages over craft-related shops, especially for men trying to achieve security for their old age. These ventures did not require the keenness of eye or the strength important in many crafts, they could be run by wives and other relatives if hard times forced owners temporarily to take outside employment, and they required little capital, especially when operated in the proprietor's own home.

The same reasons made these ventures attractive to unskilled workers, who had still less likelihood than artisans of becoming businessmen by 1880. However, the hierarchy in opportunity had become less sharp since 1850. During the decade after 1850, 22 percent of the journeymen of that census became proprietors, compared to only 5 percent of the unskilled workers. For the decade after 1870, this difference had shrunk to 13 and 8 percent, respectively. As artisans less frequently became self-employed in their trades, and as laborers, gardeners, teamsters, and other less skilled workers more often opened small retail and service businesses, Poughkeepsie moved toward that convergence in occupational mobility between the strata of manual workers which Stephan Thernstrom finds in Boston after 1880.

Like craft-related businesses, retail and service shops offered unequal rewards. Success in these businesses varied according to type, location, and the ethnic origin of the proprietor. Immigrants generally owned small retail shops off the main street, while natives owned almost all of the larger, better-financed firms. Businesses run by native proprietors accounted for 85 percent of the firms ever evaluated as worth more than $25,000 by credit reporters.

In lines which required large amounts of capital, such as dry goods or coal and lumber, natives predominated. In lines which could be started up with little capital, such as groceries, the larger firms belonged to natives but immigrants made substantial progress. Only in marginal enterprises such as saloons, small hotels, and peddling did this ethnic stratification disappear and immigrants seem to have a decided advantage.

Native preeminence rested upon easier access to capital and credit and upon familiarity with the local native clientele. Also, since clerking was the customary apprenticeship for many businesses, natives had a decided advantage over immigrants. While the native-born of foreign parentage found clerical and sales jobs in proportion to their numbers in the labor force, whites of native parentage still accounted for 73 percent of the total in 1880.

A comparison of dry-goods and fancy-goods stores points up the native advantage in retailing. Dry-goods merchants had the reputation of being "the safest class of businessmen in the city"; over half of those enumerated in the income tax list for 1866 reported more than $2,500, a very comfortable income that year. Because a complete line of dry goods required a large investment, native sons frequently relied upon family members to give them capital, a support rarely available to immigrants. A publisher loaned his son $4,500 when he entered his first partnership. Moreover, most dry-goods merchants in Poughkeepsie learned the business by clerking for local firms. Not surprisingly, native whites owned two-thirds of the dry-goods businesses.

Immigrants owned a majority of the fancy-goods stores. Such stores did not sell a complete line of dry goods but specialized in combinations of hoop skirts, corsets, ribbons, and other accessories for ladies. Correspondingly, it required little capital to start such a business. Only 8 percent of the fancy-goods stores ever were estimated by credit reporters to be worth more than $10,000, as compared to 41 percent of the dry-goods firms.

Unlike dry-goods merchants, who usually started out as clerks, male proprietors of fancy-goods stores often came from the ranks of skilled workers. In many cases they operated these small stores while carrying on their trades. A German Catholic reported himself as a chairmaker at two censuses and continued to work at that trade while his wife minded the store. A German Jew who conducted a string band also left the running of the store to his wife. If not outright failures, most of these stores remained at best very modest ventures. There were a few exceptions. An iron moulder of Irish parentage opened a fancy-goods store in 1867 with a few hundred dollars; by 1886 his worth was estimated as between $30,000 and $40,000. He succeeded by catering to a special clientele; he concentrated upon "furnishing regalia to the different societies and his regalia pays good profit."

If retailing methods had remained as before, the gradual immigrant progress in fancy goods might eventually have enabled the Irish and Germans to expand into dry goods proprietorships. But by the eighties the rise of the multipurpose department store, exemplified in Poughkeepsie by Luckey, Platt & Co., had diminished opportunities in dry goods for both immigrants and natives. Disparities between larger and smaller firms had increased, and a few large firms received the lion's share of the trade.

Luckey's expansion depended less upon superior capital resources—other native dry-goods merchants had as large stocks and capital—than upon innovation in merchandising methods and aggressive advertising. By 1879, the firm boasted 15 departments, including notions, hosiery, gents' furnishing goods, cloaks, and carpets, and it employed 20 clerks. Its largest competitor had only nine clerks and the more traditional dry-goods firms listed three or four each. In the extreme case, the "wealthiest dry goods firm in Poughkeepsie" of 1872, which did not approve "of the modern style of business," saw its business shrink drastically as it continued to sell a very fine class of goods at high prices.

The department store had a devastating effect on the traditional dry-goods business. Although Poughkeepsie's population continued to grow, the number of firms in this line declined from a high of 23 in 1873 to 13 in 1900. A number of merchants began in the seventies to shift into other lines because of competition from the department stores and the decreased demand for cloth and trimmings caused by the rise of ready-made clothing. Fancy-goods stores also declined, since many of their specialties could be bought at the department stores.

In other retail lines, such as groceries, which remained easier of entry for new firms, immigrants and former manual workers generally made significant progress. The capital needed to start a grocery remained modest. Moreover, since local wholesalers in groceries and flour and feed were more numerous than wholesalers in any other line, it was less often necessary to establish credit in New York City, an advantage for a worker of good local reputation but no business experience.

Because grocers served a neighborhood clientele, immigrant proprietors could attract the patronage of their countrymen. Credit reporters noted this appeal, be it "a small Dutch grocery" or "an Irish trade and similar location." Attesting to their social importance, many immigrant grocers served as aldermen and supervisors. They also benefited disproportionately from reimbursements for outdoor relief, which enabled many customers to patronize their neighborhood groceries during depressed times, albeit at a reduced level of consumption.

Although natives owned the large wholesaling firms and most of the groceries worth over $10,000, the foreign-born owned half of the groceries worth between $5,000 and $10,000. For the Irish in particular, groceries served as an important avenue of mobility. Of the 20 foreign-born proprietors worth more than $5,000, 11 were Irish or sons of Irish parents. John Corcoran's father appeared as a laborer with no property in the 1850 census and died a few years later. John began working in a brass foundry at age 13, then as a gardener. He moved for a time to Norwalk, Connecticut, running a florist business there, then returned to Poughkeepsie in 1869 to open a grocery store. While his store initially was "a small grocery on a cross street" with an estimated worth of $1,000, by 1877 it had a "safe, steady trade." In 1880, when he took as a partner fellow countryman John Nevins, the estimate had climbed to $5,000. By the late eighties, Corcoran and Nevins employed three clerks and engaged also in wholesaling. Eventually Corcoran became an alderman, a vice-president of the Board of Trade, a member of the Retail Merchants' Association, and of the Board of Water Commissioners, as well as a leader in St. Peter's Church and the Catholic Benevolent Society.

None of the Irish grocers, however, could hope to compete seriously with the native-owned W. T. Reynolds and Co., largest commission merchants in the county, who in the eighties expanded their flourishing flour and feed business to include the wholesaling of groceries. Moreover, for smaller immigrant and native firms alike, the constant proliferation of new shops meant rigorous competition. New entrants into the grocery trade did not decline markedly even during the depression decade of the seventies. But, reflecting the marginal character of many of the firms throughout the period, almost half of the groceries traced in annual city directories disappeared within two years and only one-fourth lasted ten years.

The proportion of small ventures, and the rate of disappearance, among groceries were higher than in many lines of business, but they remind us once again of the short lives of the majority of firms in any city. It is not surprising, therefore, to find that few businesses in Poughkeepsie passed from one generation to the next. Of the 1,530 firms reported on by R. G. Dun and Company, 106 at some time included fathers and sons as partners, but in only 45 of these firms did the sons finally succeed to the business. In another 44 cases, sons inherited their fathers' businesses without ever having been partners, making a total of 89 firms that passed from one generation to the next within the same family. Since these firms tended to be among the most prosperous in the city, the sons had an obvious economic inducement to continue the business.

Even among the prosperous, however, sons frequently chose not to stay in the family firm. A fifth of the sons who had been taken into partnerships with their fathers subsequently left the business. Moreover, only about one-third of the grocers' sons listed in the census became grocers themselves, and only a slightly higher proportion of the sons of large merchants in lumber, dry goods, and the like pursued businesses in those lines.

Whether or not the sons of proprietors ever achieved self-employment themselves, the majority of those who remained in Poughkeepsie beyond the age of 30 held nonmanual employment. But the frequency of nonmanual work varied according to the father's type of business. Sons of large merchants and manufacturers, for example, rarely fell back to manual work, 90 and 83 percent respectively remaining at nonmanual occupations past age 30. Grocers' sons experienced more downward mobility, but even among them 75 percent stayed in white-collar jobs. By contrast, only 10 percent of the sons of saloonkeepers sustained nonmanual jobs past age 30.

The evidence on vertical mobility, between as well as within generations, in different lines of commerce and manufacturing points up the increasing stratification within Poughkeepsie's business life between 1850 and 1880. Ethnic stratification, however, was never rigid or absolute. The preeminence of native-born proprietors as a group over immigrant and second-generation businessmen did not prevent precariousness in the situation of many native proprietors. Moreover, the striking success of some businesses launched by men of Irish and German parentage after the Civil War shows the limitation of easy generalizations about group preeminence.

With time, the native advantage in business would lessen, but the erosion of opportunities for self-employment in crafts would have more permanent consequences. The sharper separation between business and working-class worlds, which the Lynds described for Middletown in the 1920s,[11] seems to us the probable result of the tendencies in occupational mobility in Poughkeepsie by the 1870s. The narrowing range of occupational mobility for skilled artisans and other manual workers suggests the gradual emergence of a working-class world, in which most manual workers would have more in common with each other than they would with substantial businessmen in any line. They still might hope to become shop owners, but they no longer could anticipate realistically the substantial prosperity which many artisan proprietors had achieved before the Civil War.

Notes

1. Stanley Legergott, "The Pattern of Employment since 1800," in Seymour Harris, ed., *American Economic History* (New York: McGraw-Hill, 1961), pp. 290–92.

2. The continuing high frequency and vulnerability of new entries in different lines was suggested long ago by R. G. and A. R. Hutchinson and Mabel Newcomer, "A Study in Business Mortality: Length of Life of Business Enterprises in Poughkeepsie, New York, 1843–1936," *American Economic Review* (Sept. 1938), 28:497–514.

3. Studies of a particular industry in one locality often suggest how opportunities for self-employment changed over time; for a good example, see Margaret Walsh, "Industrial Opportunity on the Urban Frontier: Rags to Riches and Milwaukee Clothing Manufacturers, 1840–1880," *Wisconsin Magazine of History* (Spring 1974), 57:175–94. But they do not provide a comparison with other types of business in the same locality. Studies of an entire industry across time rarely have provided more than the most general sense of the variation in rewards and opportunities for self-employment in different localities and regions. Only recently, for example, have Paul Faler and Alan Dawley shown in detail the contraction of employers in one of the shoe industry's major centers, Lynn, Massachusetts. See Dawley's *Class and Community: The Industrial Revolution in Lynn* (Cambridge, Mass.: Harvard University Press, 1976). chaps. 1 and 6. Similarly, Daniel Walkowitz has described the increasing concentration of ownership in the iron foundries of Troy, New York, in his *Worker City, Company Town: Iron and Cotton-Worker Protest in Troy and Cohoes, 1855–84* (Urbana: University of Illinois Press, 1978), especially pp. 22–28, 39–44. But for neither industry do we have for comparison local studies of less important centers of production.

4. A major exception is Peter R. Decker, *Fortunes and Failures: White-Collar Mobility in Nineteenth-Century San Francisco* (Cambridge, Mass.: Harvard University Press, 1978) which presents frequencies of mobility for more specific occupational categories among nonmanual workers as well as describing their occupational worlds in detail. Howard Gitelman's *Workingmen of Waltham: Mobility in American Urban Industrial Development, 1850–1890* (Baltimore, Md.: Johns Hopkins University Press, 1974) is an earlier attempt at refinement in the analysis of occupational mobility, but is not easy to relate to studies of other localities. Herbert Gutman's richly detailed analysis of opportunity for some craftsmen in Paterson's locomotive, iron, and machine manufacturing is limited to the careers of 30-odd successful manufacturers. It does not tell us how frequent upward mobility was for most craftsmen. See Gutman, *Work, Culture and Society in Industrializing America* (New York: Alfred A. Knopf, 1976), chapter 4.

5. Alfred D. Chandler, Jr., *The Visible Hand: The Managerial Revolution in American Business* (Cambridge: Harvard University Press, 1977), pp. 11–14.

6. See especially Herbert Gutman's essays collected in *Work, Culture and Society*. For a sympathetic critique, which argues that these essays overemphasize the extent to which working-class culture in the United States after the Civil War was tradition-bound or "preindustrial," see David Montgomery's review essay, "Gutman's Nineteenth-century America," *Labor History,* (Summer 1978), 19:416–29.

7. Thomas Kessner, *The Golden Door: Italian and Jewish Immigrant Mobility in New York City, 1880–1915* (New York: Oxford University Press, 1977). While Kessner describes some of the variety of kinds of small shops through which his immigrants achieved self-employment, he does not show what proportion of their mobility into "white-collar" jobs was comprised by these petty proprietorships, including the numerous "peddlers."

8. Stephan Thernstrom, *The Other Bostonians: Poverty and Progress in the American Metropolis, 1880–1970* (Cambridge: Harvard University Press, 1973), pp. 236–40.

9. Bruce Laurie, Theodore Hershberg, and George Alter, "Immigrants and Industry: The Philadelphia Experience, 1850–1880," in Richard L. Ehrlich, ed., *Immigrants in Industrial America, 1850–1920* (Charlottesville: University Press of Virginia, 1977), pp. 127–30.

10. Organization for Economic Cooperation and Development, *Problems and Policies Relating to Small and Medium-sized Businesses* (Paris: n.d.), p. 50: Table I.

11. Robert S. and Helen M. Lynd, *Middletown* (New York: Harcourt, 1959).

6

THE POSITION OF SMALL BUSINESS IN THE STRUCTURE OF AMERICAN MANUFACTURING, 1870–1970

Harold G. Vatter

A TREATMENT of the small firm with respect to industrial structure can feasibly imply only an *emphasis* within the usual structure–function or structure–performance dichotomy. Hence, the concept of small as employed here will refer not only to size and other structural matters, but also to various functionally or behaviorally defining characteristics. Besides, it is doubtful that as economic historians we are very interested in exclusively structural changes in abstraction from larger matters pertaining to the role of small enterprise. As for how big is "small," we shall perforce have to be as flexible and arbitrary as time change and the nature of the data require.

In a brief anatomical survey such as this, it will be distressingly necessary to pass over almost all of the enormous variation between officially defined "industries," and to confine ourselves generally to aggregates.[1] Also, the context will be economic, to the neglect of political and social aspects. Only a selected, few, major economic aspects can be treated. Finally, references to details of the maddeningly inappropriate character of the crude census data, upon which I must heavily rely, will be minimized.

Most firms and plants have always been "small" on any reasonable definition. In the last three decades of the nineteenth century, the total number

The author is much indebted to Professor Joseph D. Phillips for critical comments.

of manufacturing establishments (plants) gives us the best and only—albeit imprecise—clue to the growth of the small-business-enterprise population. For 1870–1970 and subsequently, I shall often have to use plants as a proxy for firms and totals as a proxy for "small." Of course, the multi-plant firm was beginning to spread, so the establishment figures should exceed any accurate estimate of the total enterprise population. I shall assume, however, that in the first three decades of this hundred-year survey, all small firms were one-plant organizations.[2]

THE EARLY DECADES

These early establishment estimates, as well as the corresponding output estimates, exclude "hand and neighborhood industries" on the ground that they were typically not business firms with at least one full-time employee, but rather corresponded to what we now call the self-employed. With these and other minor adjustments from the census establishment totals for all manufacturing, we get the following:[3]

1869	194,375
1879	176,991
1889	200,821
1899	267,245

While there is probably some underestimation of the increase in establishment population,[4] the rise was nonetheless a substantial 37 percent, concentrated in the 1890s, for the thirty-year period of very rapid growth in manufacturing output. The hundred-year record shows that this positive correlation is typical: small firm numbers proliferate when the economy and the sector are strongly expanding during an intermediate time period; the numbers decelerate when intermediate-period general expansion slows.

The same generalization holds also for shorter, cyclical expansion and contraction periods.[5] The above estimates indicate an absolute fall in the number of establishments (and by implication, firms) during the so-called long depression of the seventies.[6] This cyclical sensitivity of the number of plants (and firms) reflects the precarious existence, high turnover rates, and short average life span abidingly typical of small manufacturing enterprises. From that 1879 cyclical nadir in plant numbers to the comparatively high level cycle year at the turn of the century, the number of plants (and firms, to an approximately equivalent extent) increased by more than one-half. No subsequent twenty-year period produced an equal percentage increase in total establishments.

Since manufacturing output over this period increased very fast, much faster than the number of establishments (and firms), the average plant size, measured by output, increased 323 percent, according to calculations based on the following:[7]

	Manufacturing Output (Millions of 1879 Dollars)	Output per Establishment (1879 Dollars)
1869	1,078	5,546
1879	1,962	11,085
1889	4,156	20,695
1899	6,262	23,432

The percentage rise in establishment size, as measured, was much greater than the rise in total output in the economy for this whole period, which was about 220 percent.[8] I make this comparison in order to present two empirical postulates that cannot be tested in this somewhat pioneering survey, but which will have to derive their efficacy from their "intuitive reasonableness." These postulates are that typically over the intermediate period, such as about a decade, and aside from secular and short-run influences, when the growth rate of plant or firm size in manufacturing (entry barrier) exceeds that for gross or net private product (nonmanufacturing business opportunities), (1) the total number of new small plants (firms) entering into manufacturing will tend to be inhibited by this relationship,[9] and (2) limited-resource entrepreneurs, insofar as entrepreneurial ability is nonspecific to type of economic activity, will tend to be propelled, as their numbers mount, into nonmanufacturing, "small business" sectors, such as construction, retail trade and services, where the average plant and firm size was typically smaller throughout the hundred-year period under consideration. As the numbers of small manufacturing firms rise over any given time period, they find themselves crawling along an opportunity ceiling that limits their total contingent. In the short-run, cyclical period, the number of manufacturing plants has been positively sensitive, with a lag, to expansion and contraction of industrial output, but not in the longer intermediate period. Furthermore, in the secular long run, the percentage increase in the number of officially defined establishments, always mostly small, has definitely declined. On a decadal basis, the era of large plant-number increases was 1889–1909, with plant increases amounting to one-third over each of the encompassed decades. Thereafter, aside from the post–World War II reconversion years, decadal plant numbers rose substantially less than ten percent. Hence, the long run was wrought ever less favorable prospects for growth of the small-manufacturing business population.

At this juncture, let me intrude into my more or less strictly chronological approach to buttress these postulates with some additional data that are also relevant to the general subject under examination. While manufacturing output historically kept pace with gross national product, the number of manufacturing business organizations did not keep pace with the number of all business organizations, as the very rouch estimates on firms in table 6.1 appear to show. On the basis of any available crude estimates, then, the average manufacturing firm was getting larger, as measured by output, relative to the average nonmanufacturing firm.[10] My hypothesis is that this created a relative entry barrier, operating from the supply side, for the former.[11] Of course, very rapid growth in manufacturing output could, and no doubt did, more than offset this inhibiting influence.

One additional factor probably inhibiting the growth in small-firm numbers and the capacity of the small firm to endure between 1869 and 1899 and indeed up to about 1919, was the rising capital requirements per unit of manufacturing output.[12] Winn properly avers that capital/output ratios serve as a proxy for an absolute capital-requirement barrier to entry.[13] And Mansfield, in an attack upon the empirical validity of Gibrat's law (that the probability of a given proportionate change in size during some period is the same for all firms in a given industry, regardless of their size at the beginning of the period), found that for four industries in the twentieth century the entry rate would decrease by at least 7 percent if its capital requirements doubled.[14] On the other hand, smaller firms were favored by the fact that they were generally less capital intensive than large enterprises.[15] By the same token, small firms were generally relegated to those branches of industry that were more labor intensive. That was one reason why, then and thereafter, small firms' industry share of the manufacturing labor force was typically larger than its share of output,[16] and the ratio of the two shares

Table 6.1 Number of Manufacturing Plants or Firms Relative to All Concerns in Business, Selected Years 1869–1973

Year	Manufacturing Establishments	All Concerns Total Concerns in Business (3-Year Average)	Ratio
1869	194,375	427,000 (1870)	.455
1879	176,991	703,000	.252
1889	200,821	1,070,000	.188
1899	267,245	1,143,000	.234
1904	213,444	1,320,000	.162
1909	264,810	1,483,000	.179
1919	270,231	1,747,000	.155

	Manufacturing Firms (Thousands)	Total Nonfarm Firms (Thousands)	Ratio
1929	257	3,029	.085
1947	302	3,651	.083
1954	331	4,240	.078
1958	329	4,533	.073
1963	313	4,797	.065

	Manufacturing Corporations (Thousands)	All Corporations (Thousands)	Ratio
1916	80.2	341.3	.235
1929	92.2	509.4	.181
1947	112.2	587.7	.191
1958	150.7	1,032.6	.146
1963	181.8	1,381.7	.132
1970	197.8	1,747.6	.113
1973	209.0	1,905.0	.110

Source: *Historical Statistics*, Part 2, pp. 666, 911, 912–913, 914; *Statistical Abstract*, 1976, p. 507, No. 824.

increased notably between 1904 and 1967.[17] The fact that capital/output ratios as well as capital/labor ratios increased with asset size was ironically fortunate in one aspect, if not in others, because no doubt, in those earlier decades, the small enterprise was already viewed by lenders of funds on long term as a high-risk proposition subject to relatively high interest charges, poor credit availability, and inelastic supply. On the other hand, low capital investment has historically gone hand in hand with high mortality and short life span. For example, on the basis of a study of three Minnesota cities in the prosperous 1920s, E. A. Heilman concluded that "investment is the decisive factor in determining the ability of business enterprises to survive. . . . The firms with substantial amounts of capital survive the longest, and . . . have the lowest mortality rates. The lowest rate is that for manufacturing, . . . about 12.4 a year, and the probable life expectancy for the average firm is therefore 8 years."[18]

Nevertheless, the small-firm group abided. While the Twelfth Census of 1900 revealed that 185 large corporations "controlled" 2,040 establishments, employing about 8 percent of the workers and turning out about 14 percent of product value,[19] this left plenty of living space for thousands of small firms in industries such as apparel; lumber and wood products; furniture and fixtures; printing and publishing; stone, clay, and glass products; fabricated metal products; instruments; and miscellaneous activities. These small-firm manufacturing sectors, at that time with relatively few incorporated concerns, failed to follow the petroleum-refining pattern in which the "independent" refiner all but disappeared. They were sectors marked by both nonstandardized and standardized products, items often tailored to specialized consumer tastes, small-market and local-market production, wide spatial dispersion of materials that entailed high transport costs, and a large skilled-labor component.[20] Such aspects of production and marketing[21] already give us a partial but important answer to the question of how small manufacturing continued to survive, numerically at least, in the face of scale disadvantages, lower capacity utilization rates than large firms, and lack of product, plant, and spatial diversification, to say nothing of disadvantages in purchasing, marketing, and the procurement of finance.

The listed areas of small-firm opportunities may be added to the previous point regarding low capital intensity, which buttressed ease of entry. Thus, by 1904, we can find the small-business population crudely represented in the 165,083 unincorporated establishments, 76.4 percent of the total. They were probably almost all single-plant, single-product enterprises, averaging about 10 wage earners per establishment, contrasted with "large" plants (not firms), which were under the corporate form and employed over 75 wage earners per establishment.[22] The numbers were probably minimally affected by the first great merger movement.

THE EARLY TWENTIETH CENTURY

The census sets for us another unit of time, 1899–1919, chiefly because the revised establishment criterion is the same for those two decades: a plant or factory with annual value of shipments (product value) of $500 or more.[23] Certainly, any smaller minimum would be too small to be "small" for our purpose: a business firm should have at least one full-time employee. The number of establishments, thus delineated, grew over this twenty years by almost one-third, the greater portion by far in the first decade: [24]

1899	207,754
1904	213,444
1909	264,810
1914	258,436
1919	270,231

Had this percentage rise in plant numbers persisted, by 1972 there would have been over 550,000 manufacturing establishments in the United States instead of the actual 313,000.[25]

I presume, as usual, that this notable increase in numbers consisted chiefly of small plants and firms, since the overwhelming majority are always "small."[26] According to Thorp's breakdowns, noncorporate establishments, always smaller than corporations, increased 20 percent from 165,083 to 198,588 from 1904 to 1919, but the average number of wage earners per establishment *fell* from 9.73 to 6.15 for this group. Establishments under the corporate form, by way of contrast, increased in number by 79 percent, and the average number of wage earners per establishment for this category *rose* from 75.6 to 86.1. This in indeed a striking duality of performance. While the first category was clearly a small plant and firm group, we of course cannot presume that all the plants under the corporate form were nonsmall. The preference by manufacturing entrepreneurs, including small entrepreneurs, for the corporate form was already clearly evident. But I shall also assume that the unincorporated plant and firm, with some notable exceptions, was even more overwhelmingly small business than the total population, and the secular decline in the absolute numbers of this business form is an index of the passage of the one-man-directed small enterprise. By 1972, there were only 43,000 manufacturing plants under individual proprietorship.[27]

For the twenty years 1899–1919, manufacturing output rose about 4.4 percent a year. From 1879 to 1899 it had risen about 5.9 percent a year. As we have presumed, the number of small plants (and firms) should have increased more slowly in the later period, and the above *total* establishment increase of 30 percent is consistent with that presumption. Output per establishment rose again, as follows:

	Output, Billions of Constant Dollars	Output per Establishment
1899	13.61	$6,647
1904	16.95	7,941
1909	21.52	8,127
1914	25.23	9,399
1919	30.18	11,168

Entry must have been relatively encouraged, despite this rise in average plant size of 68 percent; for manufacturing output increased about 145 percent while real GNP rose only about 99 percent.[28] And the number of small firms must have grown considerably, particularly those under the corporate form (plants under that form rose from 51,097 in 1904 to 91,517 in 1919, according to Thorp).[29] Some idea of the counteracting roles of manufacturing-output growth and plant-size growth with respect to the increase in number of plants (or firms) may be seen by comparing the two twenty-year periods, 1879–99 and 1899–1919. The percentage increases were as follows:

	Manufacturing Output	Plant Size	Number of Plants
1879–1899	219	111	50
1899–1919	122	68	30

It would seem that the influence on plant numbers of manufacturing-output growth in both periods swamped the restraining effect of the interrelated growth of plant size.[30] Note also that the output percentage increases greatly exceed the plant-size percentages increases.

Also, in this period of rapid electrification of manufacturing industries, the shift from plant-produced to purchased electric power helped new entry by small manufacturers.[31] Small-firm entry may have been restrained, however, by the continued rise in manufacturing's capital/output ratio in this period: 29 percent compared to 25 percent, 1880–1900.[32] But this effect would have been relative to trends in that ratio elsewhere, and there the data are uncertain.[33]

PROSPERITY AND DEPRESSION DECADES

I turn now to the next two contrasting decades, the 1920s and the 1930s. After 1919 and until 1947, the census reported only establishments with annual products valued at $5,000 or more. The change in 1919, which brought the plant minimum somewhat more into line with the rising price level, eliminated in that year about 65,000 small plants having an annual product value between $500 and $5,000. As a group, these accounted for less than 1 percent of the value of products of all reporting establishments! Many thousands of these must have continued to exist for some time, and many certainly met the criterion used here of at least one full-time employee at some time during the census year. It is perhaps ironic that the census turned to this latter criterion in 1947.

For the 1920s, I return to the establishment estimates of Everett S. Lee et al.

1919	205,668
1929	207,760

Historical Statistics [34] presents, beginning with a sharp recession year:

1921	192,059
1929	206,663

Neither series shows the kind of increase in plant (and firm) numbers that we would expect during a decadal rise in manufacturing output of 64 percent, a moderately good annual compound rate of 5 percent (the GNP rate of growth was only 3.4 percent, 1919–29).

The net entry of new plants was inhibited drastically. What happened? I think it must have been a poor decade for new, small manufacturing enterprises, but a decade of expansion in the size of both small and other-sized established manufacturing firms. As is well known, that was a decade of mergers, acquisitions, and the very rapid spread of the multi-plant firm. While total plant numbers languished, the estimated number of *corporate* manufacturing *firms,* officially recorded, increased from 67.8 thousand to 92.2 thousand! [35] And average plant size grew greatly: [36]

	Output, Billions of Constant Dollars	Output per Establishment
1919	30.18	$14,670
1929	49.48	23,810

This was a striking 62 percent increase in average plant size in only one decade. The stifling effects on entry of increasing plant size in that decade were self-reinforcing: an increase almost as great as the 64 percent rise in output, slowed down the opportunities for additional new plants.[37] It was fortunate for the potential entrepreneur with limited resources that he could turn to activities other than manufacturing when faced with this barrier to entry. Income generated per firm in manufacturing in 1929 (current dollars) was over nine times that for the average firm in wholesale and retail trade. In 1970, it was almost twelve times as great.[38] Apparently the beginning of the decline in the capital/output ratio was of little help to new entry. With the number of manufacturing *corporations* rising by well over one-third,[39] smaller, *noncorporate* enterprise must have suffered a high mortality rate.

It does not appear that the twenties was any golden age for small firms. Indeed, the general business failure rate in the twenties was notoriously high for a "prosperity decade," over twice that for the mixed economy after World War II.[40] One study found that in three Minnesota cities, while there were 1,974 manufacturing firms in existence in 1930, some 1,225 firms, or 62 percent "closed" between 1926 and 1930, and the lower the net worth of the enterprise, the greater the mortality rate.[41] Even in the sphere of corporate manufacturing, the proportion of total corporate net income reported by the smallest 75 percent of the firms (size measured by net income) declined steadily from 6.33 percent in 1918 to a miniscule 4.49 percent in 1929,[42] a period of falling wholesale industrial commodity prices.

This fact touches upon a characteristic of incorporated small firms: they tend to be less profitable than medium and large firms,[43] even though they pay lower hourly wage rates and are typically less unionized.[44] One of the most recent and careful studies for manufacturing in the 1960s also confirms the hypothesis that smaller firms experience lower long-run rates of return on assets than larger firms.[45] Indeed, in one of the better pieces of profitability evidence I have encountered, data based upon FTC and SEC reports also show that over the years from 1952 to 1965, the share of the total earnings of U.S. manufacturing corporations received by the $10-million-and-under asset category declined almost monotonically from 22.6 percent in 1952 to 15.4 percent in 1965; whereas the share of the over $50-million asset category enjoyed an almost monotonic increase from 61.1 percent in the first year of the period to 75.0 percent at the end.[46] This is one of the few reasonably suggestive pieces of evidence indicating a decline in the small-enterprise economic position over a significant time period. Of course this 32 percent decline in the small-firm share no doubt was due in part to the accompanying price rise, which would tend to reduce that group's asset share also, but by how much we do not know.[47]

THE FIRST SIXTY YEARS

By way of stocktaking, after sixty years of laissez-faire and on the eve of the Great Depression, we note that, ignoring changes in census coverage, there were about 207,000 manufacturing plants in the United States, compared with table 6.1's differently defined (but adjusted to eliminate the very small) 194,000 in 1869. In a world in which the total business population kept approximate pace with the human population, this negligible long-run growth in the adjusted number of manufacturing plants (and firms) was a remarkable distinguishing feature of the manufacturing sector in general and of small manufacturing in particular. The comparative long-run ceiling on the number of manufacturers is found even when taking *incorporated* manufacturing *firms,* which grew from 8 per 1,000 human population in 1916 to only 10 per 1,000 in 1970, whereas all corporations grew from 34 to 86 per 1,000 human population.[48]

DEPRESSION DECADE

If the twenties was no heyday for the growth in either numbers—or, probably, economic importance—of small manufacturers, the depression decade was also, of course, a time of high mortality. Manufacturing establishments, reflecting the customary cyclical sensitivity, fell from 206,663 in 1929 to a nadir of only 139,325 in 1933, and recouped partly to only 173,802 in the "peak" year of the thirties, 1939.[49] Plant size again increased between 1929 and 1939 (22 percent) because, while manufacturing output was about the same in the latter year, the number of plants had decreased. Average plant size therefore rose much faster than both manufacturing output and GNP.

Small manufacturing suffered relatively more than all the other "small business sectors," except, of course, contract construction. Whereas the number of nonfarm firms in all industries rose 6 percent between 1929 and 1939, the number of firms in manufacturing declined absolutely by 14 percent.[50] If we use manufacturing corporations as a very crude proxy for "large," and "active proprietors of unincorporated manufacturing enterprises" for "small," we see a dramatic cyclical contrast and, by implication, a striking testimonial to the small firm's (1) relatively high turnover rates, (2) relatively short life span, and (3) relatively high capacity for new entry in the short run:[51]

	Number of Corporations (Thousands)	Number of Proprietors, Unincorporated Firms (Thousands)
1929	92.2	128
1933	88.6	69
1939	86.2	119

First of all, we note the stability of the "large firm" corporate series in the cyclical contraction. It is almost entirely the "small" firms that cause the fluctuations in the aggregates. Second, we see the 46 percent drop over the cyclical contraction in the number of "small" manufacturers in existence (which decline of 59,000 may be compared with the drop in establishments, shown above, of about 67,000). Third, we observe the 72 percent increase in the number of "small" firms in the cyclical expansion 1933–39, even as the corporate contingent was experiencing almost no change in numbers at all.[52] There was then, and still is, "easy entry" for numerous small manufacturers in the short run; but they generally must stay small and not live very long.

While a discussion of concentration is to be avoided here, reference has frequently been made, or implied, to the multi-plant firm. This gives some clue to the magnitude of the plant–company difference, and also gives some idea on a cross-sectional basis of "how small is small." Walter F. Crowder examined for the TNEC the place of the "central-office group" in 1937, that is, the control or operation of two or more establishments by one ownership interest.[53] Crowder found that of 166,794 establishments, only 25,699 plants, or 15.4 percent, were controlled by these multi-plant organizations, numbering 5,625. We can look at the reverse side of Crowder's coin and presume that "small" manufacturing was single-plant organization. On that presumption, with the reversal procedure, there were 141,095 "small" manufacturing firms in 1937.[54] This was, of course, 85 percent of the establishments, 96 percent of the firms.

While big in numbers, as usual, small business was disproportionately moderate in market importance: 49 percent of the total wage earners, 45 percent of the manufacturing wage bill, only 39 percent of total product value.[55] Actually, small manufacturing was much less important, for the middle-sized firms are included in these figures. Incidentally, the central-office firms must have had bigger establishments: Ralph Nelson, for example, found an important but positive relation between establishment and company size.[56] Also, the large plant, and particularly the multi-plant, central-office firms were likely to be more product diversified. The smaller one-plant firm was, and is, less likely to be product diversified. One study in depth of a small group of successful and unsuccessful little one-plant metal-working firms found lack of product diversification to be a significant factor in failure, "considerable" diversification a factor in success.[57]

WORLD WAR II

For the war period, we have available a special compilation made for the Smaller War Plants Corporation by the Bureau of Old Age and Survivors Insurance of the Social Security Board.[58] This report is by firm rather than by establishment. The number of firms reported in the study for 1939 is 203,900—again notably larger than the number of establishments given by the census, because of the exclusion of plants with annual products of less than $5,000.[59] The number of firms with less than 20 employees, but at least one employee, in 1939 accounted for about 69 percent of all enterprises.[60] By 1944 (October-December average) the number of reported firms had increased by 7 percent to 218,381, which would be a very modest growth for a civilian economy that expanded as much as manufacturing production grew—over 100 percent—in those years. The number of firms with less than 20, but at least one, employee(s) in 1944 accounted for about 66 percent of all firms.[61] This criterion suggests constricted opportunities and a somewhat unfavorable experience for small manufacturing during the war.

In the share of total manufacturing employment accounted for by firms with between 1 and 19 employee(s), and employing that criterion of "small," the small manufacturer appears to have fared very badly, for the share declined between December 1939 and December 1944 from 7.2 percent of all workers to only 5.5 percent.[62] Similar results ensue if we raise the "small" line to up to 99 employees: the decline is then from 25.9 to 18.9 percent. Clearly there was something to the wartime clamor that small enterprise was not getting its share of procurement contracts and would come out of the war with a relatively weakened status.

POST–WORLD WAR II

Another census world begins in 1947, with its new establishment definition of at least one employee. This identical size criterion for the whole post-1947 period is most satisfactory and helpful for present purposes because I treat the post–World War II mixed economy as a fairly homogenous milieu: governmentally underwritten, dampened cycles, fairly sustained growth.

Tables 6.2 and 6.3 provide us with some essential, relevant information on this quarter century. We should immediately note that the redefinition of the minimum-sized plant, together with recovery from the Great Depression and opportunities from wartime expansion of manufacturing, raised the number of plants reported by 67,005 above the 1939 number.

We also see at once from Table 6.2 that the total number of plants, in the context of a percentage output rise more than twice the plant-size increase, rose substantially (19 percent) over the seven years 1947–54, and thereafter

Table 6.2 Census Establishments: Total, Number with under 20 Employees, and Number in Single-Unit and Multi-Unit Firm Establishments, Selected Census Years, 1947–72

Year	Total Number of Manufacturing Establishments (Thousands)	Establishments with Less Than 20 Employees (Thousands)	Establishments in Single-Plant Companies (Thousands)	Establishments in Multi-Plant Companies (Thousands)
1947	241	158	206	35
1954	287	196	255	32
1958	299	203	256	42
1963	307	207	261	46
1967	306	199	254	52
1972	313	203	251	70

Sources: *1958 Census of Manufactures*, v. 1, 2-2; *Statistical Abstract*, 1975, p. 736, No. 1260, and p. 741, No. 1263. The totals listed in column one differ slightly from the totals used in the single-plant/multi-plant classification.

Table 6.3 Percentage of All Manufacturing Employees in
Multi-Plant-Firm Establishments and Single-Plant-Firm Establishments,
And Average Number of Employees per Establishment, Selected Years,
1947–72

Year	Multi-Plant-Firm Establishments	Single-Plant-Firm Establishments	Employees per Establishment, All Manufacturing
1947	56.0	44.0	59.3
1954	60.6	39.4	56.1
1958	65.4	34.6	52.8
1963	67.8	32.2	54.5
1967	72.0	28.0	62.1
1972	75.0	25.0	59.2

Source: *Statistical Abstract,* 1975, p. 741, No. 1263; p. 729, No. 1246.

only slowly crept upwards: 9 percent for the 18 years 1954–72. With dampened cycles, there is little evidence of cyclical fluctuations.

Small plants with less than 20 employees followed a very similar pattern
to that for total establishments. And viewing the single-plant firm as a proxy
for the small manufacturer, the pattern over time is again similar. If we look
elsewhere at the treacherous data on the number of manufacturing firms in
operation, we again get this sharp distinction between 1947 and 1953–54,
when the number rose 10 percent to a postwar peak of 331,000 in 1953–54,
then declined steadily through 1963, when the series terminates.[63] Noncorporate establishments increased 13 percent over that first seven years, but
declined 37 percent from 1954 to 1972.[64]

I conclude that 1947–53, during which time manufacturing output surged
upwards at an annual compound rate of 5.7 percent,[65] was a period of considerable growth of small business in the manufacturing sector as a whole.
This is consistent with turnover data. For example, the average annual
number of new and discontinued manufacturing businesses per 1,000 in
operation was as follows:[66]

	New	Discontinued
1947–52	98	83
1953–59	83	87
1960–62	80	93

We note how the new entry rate declined over this decade-and-a-half, how
the discontinuance rate advanced; how the entry rate exceeded the discontin-

uance rate in the 1947–52 period of notable small-business increase; how the absolute discrepancy between the two rates was greatest of all three sub-periods in 1947–52; and how entry fell short of discontinuances, and by increasing absolute amounts, in the last two subperiods.

One of the reasons for the absolute growth of 46,000 in total establishments between 1947 and 1954 was the inclusion of an additional 13,000 mostly small logging contractors—and "independent" logging camps not operating sawmills—in the 1954 estimates and thereafter, that were not included before, in the lumber and wood products industry.[67] While this explains 85 percent of the rise in establishments in this "small business" industry of over 26,000 plants in 1947, it should be noted that even were they excluded, there would still be a rise in total plant numbers for all manufacturing of about 33,000, and that number exceeds considerably the whole number of establishment augmentation over the ensuing 18 years.

That the years 1947–54 were unusually good ones, during the immediate post–World War II era, for entry of small manufacturing enterprise, is underscored also by the fact that the plant-number increases outside lumber and wood products were noteworthy in several of the other small-business sectors of manufacturing. In these sectors, as I have noted previously, plants (and firms) are traditionally numerous. For example, for this eight-year period we have such increases in establishment numbers as:[68]

	1947	1954
Furniture and fixtures	7,551	10,373
Printing and publishing	29,078	32,530
Fabricated metal products	16,877	22,516
Machinery, except electrical	17,910	25,600
Electrical equipment & supplies	3,970	5,758

Only stone, clay, and glass; food and kindred products; and apparel, among the very important small-business industries, were passed by in this expansion period. It was traditionally in industries like fabricated metal products, machinery parts, and equipment, that small manufacturers were able to find a niche as satellite or dependent enterprise,[69] doing work on contract, not for a general market, but usually for a single large buyer. These adjectives are designed to suggest a kind of subordination and loss of the independent decision-making power that is presumed to obtain where there is atomism on both sides of the market.

After 1953–54, however, the small manufacturer, despite a moderate downward drift in the capital/output ratio, apparently experienced almost two decades of constriction and severe relative decline,[70] in the face of an annual rate of manufacturing output growth of over 4 percent. The probable fall in small manufacturing corporations' share of earnings between 1952 and 1965 has already been noted. The slow rise in establishment numbers, both total and for those with less than 20 employees, after 1954 is a telltale trend. Output-per-establishment growth lagged slightly behind both manufacturing output and GNP rise, but the difference was too close to buoy up the entry rate. Comparison of 1953–72 with the two earlier twenty year periods in these respects is enlightening. Thus we have for 1953–72 the following percentage increases:

Manufacturing output	90
Plant size	75
Number of plants	9

We find a comparatively much slower growth in plant numbers because manufacturing output grows more slowly, and because the discrepancy between the production percentage increase and the plant-size percentage increase is not very great.

Small establishments with less than 20 employees, about two-thirds of all plants, increased only 3.6 percent over the eighteen years (table 6.2) even though the average-sized plant for all manufacturing, measured by employee numbers, was practically unchanging (table 6.3). But the clearest clue to the relative decline was the constancy in numbers and the decline in the proportion of establishments in single-plant companies after 1954 (tables 6.2 and 6.3). By contrast, the proxy for middle and large firms—multi-plant-company establishments—doubled both in number and as a percentage of all manufacturing plants.[71]

These companies, also, to an increasing extent were becoming multi-industry conglomerates. Table 6.3 further shows the drastic shrinkage of over one-third in the share of small, labor-intensive, single-plant-firm establishments in all manufacturing employment from 39.4 percent to 25 percent, even as their customarily predominant share of total establishments dropped but moderately.[72] This seems to be a very exceptional piece of evidence, free from price effects, attesting to a relative decline in the economic significance of small manufacturing. The result appears to be consistent, incidentally, with the slippage of its position in the important area of military procurement over these years.[73]

Table 6.3 should also be considered an excellent illustration of the operation of what George Stigler, building upon an insight of J. S. Mill and an earlier work by Willard Thorp, has called the "survivor principle": the competition between different-sized firms sifts out the least effective enterprises.[74] The survivor technique, when real magnitudes are employed, consists of classifying firms or plants by size and calculating the share of total output, capacity, or employment accounted for by each size class over time. Although it has been used widely to determine the optimum-sized unit, it also serves our purposes here, for all we need say, on the basis of table 6.3, is that the single-unit firms, taken as a whole, were clearly nonoptimal on the criterion of performance, since the declining employment share of that group was very pronounced, beginning even in 1947. This decline amounted to 43.2 percent. Calculation of the value added by manufacture for each group, which of course contains price effects,[75] shows that the share accounted for by firms with one plant dropped from 40.8 percent to 19.2 percent between 1947 and 1972, a decrease of 52.9 percent in the share. In other words, the small firms' share of value added, always less than its share of employment, fell more than its share of employees. Hence, value added per worker, a partial productivity measure, declined in comparison with the middle and large multi-unit firm sector, whose value added proportion rose more than its employee proportion.

Such a relative partial productivity decline on the part of the small-firm sector lends plausibility to the decline in the earnings share of smaller manufacturing enterprises, referred to earlier, from 1952 to 1965.[76] It is doubtful that the productivity of capital in the single-unit-firm sector, while enjoying a higher *level* of output to capital, was superior to the middle-sized and large-firm sector's rise *over time,* so the former's total factor-productivity performance over time was no doubt also the poorer of the two. In other words, taking the small-firm sector as a whole, we are observing what J. S. Bain termed the precariously existing, "inefficient fringe" of small operations, a group disadvantaged chiefly because of "small plant sizes, generally though not always found in single-plant firms.[77]

The 20 employees per establishment in the declining, single-plant group in representative 1963 averaged only one-twelfth the number for the multi-plant category—240 employees per establishment. Here is a bifurcated world. Establishments in other sectors of the small-business world—services, retail and wholesale trade, construction, *averaged* only 6 to 10 employees—less than half the size of even the single-plant manufacturing firm.

The numbers of plants remain large in the single-plant companies only because high entry (and high exit) rates persisted—the more numerous single-plant companies characteristically must have borne the overwhelming impact of high turnover rates.[78] Between 1947 and 1963, manufacturing was the only major small-business sector, outside of farming, in which the number of firms in operation failed to increase.[79] Manufacturing was the only small-business sector between 1947 and 1970 in which the income of unincorporated enterprises failed to grow. And even the number of corporations in manufacturing increased between 1947 and 1970 only 76 percent; whereas, in wholesale trade, the number rose 196 percent; in retail trade, 254 percent; in services, 511 percent; and in contract construction, 584 percent.[80] Differential output growth rates were too insignificant to explain any substantial part of these enormous percentage differences in firm numbers. Relative crowding out of individual, small entrepreneurship from manufacturing was the apparent record of the U.S. economy in the quarter century after World War II.

Let me conclude with a brief reference to the significant fact of small business nonparticipation in the foreign commodity market. In the foreign market for manufactured commodities, historical data that could reveal the trend in small-enterprise direct participation are unavailable.[81] However, merely with respect to selling U.S.-produced goods, the long-run increase in the magnitude and complexity of foreign marketing operations (which with the rise of the multinationals in recent times have merged with foreign production operations) affords little reason to believe that the small-firm position could have improved with time.

It was hoped by some of the supporters of the 1918 Webb-Pomerene law that export associations free from antitrust strictures might open foreign marketing opportunities to small firms. But in a review of the Act's results by the Federal Trade Commission in 1967, the conclusion was that ''a half century of experience . . . reveals that associations have not proved effective instruments . . . for the expansion of exports by small firms. . . . In fact, associations play a significant role as bargaining agents for United States products only where domestic producers are few, membership coverage is high, and the United States position in world trade is large.''[82]

In other words, foreign marketing is the province of the large and medium-sized manufacturer. The situation in the early 1970s probably portrayed the whole twentieth-century experience well. At that time, a Senate

Committee estimated that of 253,500 manufacturing firms in the United States, only 18,850 did any exporting at all (in their own name), that the proportion of companies exporting increased with size of firm, and that of 235,000 "small" firms with less than 100 employees, only 5 percent did any exporting.[83] According to one foreign-trade specialist, of an estimated 300,000 manufacturing concerns in the early 1970s, 299,800 shared 48 percent of all the export business.[84] The Small Business Administration modestly concluded that "there appears to be no stampede of U.S. small and medium-size business firms into the international marketplace."[85]

In summary, it should be emphasized that in a sector whose output rather more than kept pace with the secular growth of real GNP, the number of plants and firms lagged far behind the increase in the total concerns in non-farm business. Hence, the small entrepreneur was pushed into nonmanufacturing activities. A comparison of the ratio of the number of operating firms to output, for all industries and for manufacturing, shows that—using 1929 as a base year—in 1963 the ratio stood at .600 for the former, but only .364 for manufacturing—even though manufacturing had grown faster between these two dates than had gross private product.[86]

Small-firm entry proved to be moderately easy in the short run, which meant that discontinuance was almost as high, turnover was accordingly high, and average life-span all too short. In the famous Poughkeepsie study many years ago, it was found that, over 70 years, only 53 percent of its manufacturing establishments lived more than three years.[87] But long-run survival of smaller units in certain subsectors of manufacturing remains a fact of business life in the mid-1970s, even as there is evidence of generally constricted market importance. Small manufacturing, highly sensitive cyclically, thrives on rapid economic expansion, withers under contraction.

Notes

1. Regional dispersion and structural differences will also have to be bypassed.

2. Later on this strict, imprecise assumption will have to be dropped, and one-plant firms will have to become merely a proxy for all small firms, despite the fact that some small firms will have more than one plant.

3. These adjusted totals are from Everett S. Lee, Ann Ratner Miller, Carol P. Brainard, and Richard A. Esterlin, *Population Redistribution and Economic Growth, United States, 1870–1950,* vol. 1 (Philadelphia: American Philosophical Society, 1957), p. 636, Table 3-1.

4. The census permitted the reporting of two or more plants as a simple establishment if they were under the same ownership *and* located in the same urban place.

5. In addition to the temporal delineation imposed by census data, I shall employ three analytical time periods: the cyclical short run, the intermediate period of about a decade (also partly census dictated), and the secular or long run.

6. The number of plants, recorded by the census at the very beginning of the cyclical recovery, reflected the depression past rather than the already strong upsurge in manufacturing output shown immediately below. Plant numbers apparently lag both upper and lower cyclical turning points.

7. Output estimates are from Robert E. Gallman, "Commodity Output, 1838–1899," in National Bureau of Economic Research, *Trends in the American Economy in the Nineteenth Century*, Studies in Income and Wealth, vol. 24 (Princeton: Princeton University Press, 1960), p. 43, Table A-1.

8. Calculated from the real NNP index in Lance E. Davis et al, *American Economic Growth* (New York: Harper and Row, 1972), p. 34, Table 2.9.

9. T. R. Saving and others have argued persuasively that the larger the "optimum" plant size, the greater the barrier to new entry. ("Estimation of Optimum Size of Plant by the Survivor Technique," *Quarterly Journal of Economics* (Nov. 1961), 75(4):585, 593. Saving uses value added by manufacture as his size criterion.

10. Table 6.1 presumes that for 1869–1919 there were no more manufacturing firms than there were establishments. The inclusion of 1904 is due to certain incomparabilities with 1899. The panel containing the nonfarm firm figures, from U.S. Bureau of the Census, *Historical Statistics of the United States, Colonial Times to 1970*, part 2, p. 911 (hereafter cited as *Historical Statistics*), excludes from that series not only farms but also self-employed without any employees, and professional services. The bottom panel encompasses a period of continued long-run relative decline in the share of value added accounted for by nonincorporated manufacturing firms (based upon establishment data). See *Historical Statistics*, Part 2, p. 688, Series P. 212–15.

The general conclusion regarding relative firm size trends as between manufacturing and nonmanufacturing may be illustrated schematically:

Time Period	Total Gross Product	Mfg. Gross Product	No. Mfg. Firms	Output per Mfg. Firm	Nonmfg. Gross Product	No. Nonmfg. Firms	Output per Non-mfg. Firm	Aver. Mfg. Firm/Aver. Nonmfg.
t_0	100	25	20	1.25	75	65	1.15	1.09
t_1	200	50	30	1.67	150	104	1.44	1.16

These numbers meet all the conditions of the generalization and are empirically satisfying.

11. Of course, there are entry constraints on the demand side, such as the price elasticity of the "market" demand curves for the small-firm group and the large-firm group separately conceived, which operate to restrict the small entrants *taken as a group* as those curves shift over time. The average individual firm is initially too small to be prohibited by such a constraint; but as the number of new small entrants increases, the *group* effects of demand constraint will become increasingly restrictive. (Note the implied duality of market opportunity.)

12. See Daniel Creamer, Sergei Dobrovolsky and Israel Borenstein, *Capital in Manufacturing and Mining* (Princeton: Princeton University Press, 1960), esp. p. 65. Also, Daniel Creamer, *Capital and Output Trends in Manufacturing Industries, 1880–1948,* Occasional Paper 41 (New York: National Bureau of Economic Research, 1954), pp. 42–45 passim. See also calculations based upon Kuznets in Paul J. Uselding, "Factor Substitution and Labor Productivity Growth in American Manufacturing, 1838, 1899," *Journal of Economic History,* (Sept. 1972), 32(3): p. 677.

13. Daryl N. Winn, *Industrial Market Structure and Performance, 1960–1968* (Ann Arbor: University of Michigan, 1975), pp. 20–21.

14. Edwin Mansfield, "Entry, Gibrat's Law, Innovation, and the Growth of Firms," *American Economic Review* (Dec. 1962), 52(5):1043.

15. Ibid. Creamer et al, pp. 61–63; and Winn, *Industrial Market Structure,* p. 21, n. 23. Capital/labor ratios as well as capital/output ratios have historically been lower for small firms than for large. For example, data for the years 1964–71 show that, using the census industry definitions as I shall have to do throughout, the "small business" industries, such as textiles, apparel, furniture, leather, fabricated metals, and miscellaneous manufacturing showed capital per worker ratios well below the average for all manufacturing. (See *Statistical Abstract,* 1975, p. 735, No. 1258).

16. For example, in 1904 the 113,946 establishments owned by individuals averaged $1/14$ the average size of establishments (measured by value of product) owned by corporations. These small establishments accounted for 13.8 of all wage earners but only 11.5 percent of manufacturing value of product. See Willard L. Thorp, *The Integration of Industrial Operations,* Census Monograph 3 (Washington, D.C.: GPO, 1924), p. 92, Table 38.

17. See *Historical Statistics,* Part 2, p. 688, Series P 212-215, cols. 213/215, relating to production workers in corporate and noncorporate establishments.

18. E. A. Heilman, *Mortality of Business Firms in Minneapolis, St. Paul and Duluth, 1926–1930* (Minneapolis: University of Minnesota Press, 1933). Cited in U.S., Temporary National Economic Committee, *Problems of Small Business,* Monograph No. 17 (Washington, D.C.: GPO, 1941), p. 59. See also the discussion and Table 77 on the same page.

19. See Victor S. Clark, *History of Manufactures in the United States,* vol. 3, 1893–1928 (New York: Peter Smith, 1949), p. 7.

20. See, e.g., Thorp, *Integration of Industrial Operations,* p. 89, and the insightful discussion by Alfred D. Chandler, Jr., on the nonconcentrated industries, especially his classification based on the relative importance of oligopoly, in "The Structure of American Industry in the Twentieth Century: A Historical Overview," *Business History Review* (Autumn 1969), 43(3):258–59, 270–71, 279–280. Chandler draws heavily upon the research of Harold C. Livesay and P. Glenn Porter.

21. The small manufacturer of standardized items, and particularly consumer products, could not usually market his output. He typically relied, except for certain producer's goods and perishables, upon commercial middlemen. See Glenn Porter and Harold C. Livesay, *Merchants and Manufacturers* (Baltimore, Md.: Johns Hopkins Press, 1971).

22. Calculated from Thorp, *Integration of Industrial Operations,* for 1904, p. 92. Of course, some multi-plant firms no doubt had "small" plants, and a small proportion of small firms had

"large" plants. We do not know exactly. Thorp's total establishments for 1904, 216,180, is a bit high; *Historical Statistics,* Part 2, (p. 666), estimates 213,444. But the difference appears too small to affect our large-small ratios.

23. *Historical Statistics,* Part 2, p. 652.

24. Thorp, *Integration of Industrial Operations,* p. 92. It will be observed that the "banker's panic" of 1907 failed to restrain a very substantial establishment growth in the quinquennium 1904–9, a period in which GNP increased at a substantial annual rate of 4.6 percent. The year 1904 was moderately poor for business activity, 1909 a good year.

25. But note that the minimum criterion was subsequently increased, destroying comfortable comparability over secular time.

26. There may be some inflation in the numbers of plants due solely to the rising prices of manufactured commodities over these years, for rising prices bring about an increase in census coverage where the criterion is product value. See Solomon Fabricant, *The Output of Manufacturing Industries, 1899–1937* (New York: National Bureau of Economic Research, 1940), pp. 328–30. It should be noted, however, that the price rise for industrial products was very moderate from 1900 to 1909, the decade of greatest plant growth, and substantial from 1909 to 1919, the decade of retardation of growth in the number of establishments.

27. *Statistical Abstract, 1975,* p. 733, No. 1253. Some 233,000 were organized under the corporate form.

28. The output estimates are calculated by applying Kendrick output indexes to Commerce Department BEA gross manufacturing product estimates in 1958 dollars. See U.S., Dept. of Commerce, *Long Term Economic Growth, 1860–1970.* (Washington: G.P.O., June, 1973), pp. 184–85.

29. Thorp, *Integration of Industrial Operations,* p. 92.

30. The equation I have been implying is clearly laden with heavy interaction effects:

$$E^1 = f\left[Q_m^1, \frac{1}{(Q_m/E)^1}, \left(\frac{Q_m}{Q}\right)^1\right]$$

where E^1 = rate of growth of plant numbers, $Q^1{}_m$ = rate of growth of manufacturing output, (Q_m/E^1) = rate of growth of average plant size, and $(Q_m/Q)^1$ = the relative growth rates of manufacturing output and GNP. The postulate underlying the inclusion of the last term on the right-hand side is that, e.g., when manufacturing output is growing comparatively slowly as compared with GNP, entrepreneurs will be repelled from entering manufacturing and will find their way into other sectors of the economy.

31. See, in this connection, Richard B. DuBoff, "Electrification and Capital Productivity," *Review of Economics and Statistics* (Nov. 1966), 48(4):426–31.

32. For 1900–19, see Daniel Creamer, *Capital and Output Trends,* p. 71, Table 15. For 1880–1900, see Uselding, "Factor Substitution," p. 677. Ratios are from Simon Kuznets.

33. See the discussion in Simon Kuznets, *Capital in the American Economy* (Princeton: Princeton University Press, 1961), pp. 199–219. Unfortunately, of the noncommodity producing industries, only the regulated industries are treated.

34. The series on the number of manufacturing *firms* in operation in 1929, p. 911, Series V-15,

records 257,000. To the census a "company consists of the one or more establishments of a given industry classification under a single control. A diversified firm . . . therefore is statistically several companies, since it has establishments in a number of industry classifications."—Ralph L. Nelson, *Concentration in the Manufacturing Industries of the United States* (New Haven: Yale University Press, 1963), p. 61. Still, the latter should have been reported as separate establishments, and the number of companies can never exceed the number of plants in existence. Therefore, the excess in the number of firms over the numbers of census plants was due to the census omission of thousands of very small plants with product value under $5,000.

35. See note 1.

36. The method of calculating output is the same as used previously. This 62 percent increase in plant size for ten years was almost as great as that for the twenty years 1899–1919.

37. Note that in both 1879–99 and 1899–1919, the percentage output increase was very much greater than the percentage plant-size increase. Not so in the 1920s.

38. Calculated from *Historical Statistics,* Part 2, p. 911, Series V-16 and 17; and Part 1, p. 239, Series F-230 and 231. Total firms for 1970 calculated from *Statistical Abstract,* 1973, p. 471, No. 755.

39. *Historical Statistics,* Part 2, p. 914, Series V-45.

40. Ibid., Series V-23.

41. U.S., Temporary National Economic Committee, *Problems of Small Business.* p. 48.

42. *Historical Statistics,* p. 915, Series V-63.

43. By profitability I mean rate of return on some asset base. See, for example, Edward D. Hollander et al, *The Future of Small Businesss* (New York: Praeger, 1967), p. 266, Table 11-A, "Manufacturing," column A. The literature is vast. See also TNEC, *Problems of Small Business,* p. 185 for inconclusive data for 1924–28.

44. See, e.g., Joseph W. McGuire, *Factors Affecting the Growth of Manufacturing Firms* (Seattle: University of Washington, Bureau of Business Research, March 1963), p. 91.

45. Daryl N. Winn, *Industrial Market Structure,* pp. 46–47, 111.

46. Organization for Economic Cooperation and Development, *Problems and Policies Relating to Small and Medium-Sized Businesses* (Paris: OECD, 1971), p. 57, Table IX. However, the very smallest class, assets under $1 million, showed no trend. It was the $1–$10 million class that brought down the small-firm share. It is noteworthy that the $10–$50 million category also experienced a steadily falling share.

47. Wholesale prices of industrial commodities rose 15 percent over the period (*Historical Statistics,* Part 1, p. 199, Series E-24). Of course, asset adjustments could be expected to lag behind this price rise.

48. Calculated from *Historical Statistics,* Part 1, p. 10 and Part 2, p. 914.

49. *Historical Statistics,* Part 2, p. 666.

50. Ibid., p. 911.

51. Ibid., p. 914 and *Economic Almanac* (i.e., *Statistical Abstract*), 1967–68, p. 142.

52. The number of manufacturing corporations had fully recovered by 1936.

53. Walter F. Crowder, "The Integration of Manufacturing Operations," in U.S., Temporary National Economic Committee, *The Structure of Industry*, Monograph No. 27 (Washington: G.P.O., 1941), p. 107.

54. The sum of firms thus calculated, 146,720, is, as usual, far different from the firm numbers in *Historical Statistics* (p. 911): 214,000. But then, product value must be $5,000 or more per annum. So we are neglecting over 67,000 tiny operations.

55. Crowder, *Structure of Industry*, p. 111.

56. Ralph L. Nelson, *Concentration in the Manufacturing Industries*, p. 35 and chap. 4. This chapter also discusses multi-plant operation and plant-company divergence in 1954.

57. A. M. Woodruff and T. G. Alexander, *Success and Failure in Small Manufacturing* (Pittsburgh, Pa.: University of Pittsburgh Press, 1958), pp. 16–20, 48, 55.

58. In U.S., Smaller War Plants Corporation, *Economic Concentration and World War II*. Report of the Smaller War Plants Corporation to the Senate Special Committee to Study the Problems of American Small Business. Senate Document No. 206, 79th Cong., 2d sess. Senate Committee Print No. 6 (Washington, D.C.: G.P.O., 1946).

59. Ibid., p. 311, Table B-1.

60. Ibid., p. 312, Table B-1.

61. Ibid., p. 316.

62. Ibid., pp. 314, Table B-3 and 318, Table B-4.

63. *Historical Statistics*, Part 2, p. 911, Series V-15.

64. *Statistical Abstract*, 1976, p. 760, No. 1301.

65. 1953 was a cycle peak, 1954 a recession year. I assume the 1954 census data reflect the peak-year influence rather than recession. To explain the census data using 1947 and 1954 as initial and terminal years, it is proper to refer to 1953 output, not 1954.

66. Edward D. Hollander et al., *Future of Small Business*, p. 225, Table 3-B.

67. See *Historical Statistics*, Part 2, p. 671, n. 6 and *Statistical Abstract*, 1960, p. 782, No. 1068.

68. *Historical Statistics*, Part 2, pp. 669–80. The sum of the increases shown here is 21,391, or 65 percent of our 33,000 increase (excluding the lumber and wood products industry) mentioned above.

69. See Harold G. Vatter, *Small Enterprise and Oligopoly* (Corvallis: Oregon State College Press, 1955), especially chap. 5; Thomas C. Cochran, *200 Years of American Business* (New York: Basic Books, 1977), pp. 71, 73, 186; Edward D. Hollander, *Future of Small Business*, p. xx; and Joseph D. Phillips, *Little Business in the American Economy* (Urbana: University of Illinois Press, 1958), pp. 62–63, and chap. 4.

70. The crude plant data in some of the "small business industries" suggest certain noteworthy exceptions to this generalization, i.e., in printing and publishing; stone, clay, and glass products; fabricated metals; machinery except electrical; and electrical equipment and supplies. Two very large industries in the small enterprise category experiencing significant declines in plant numbers were food and kindred products, and apparel.

71. From 11.2 percent of all plants to 22.4 percent, 1954–72. Regarding the use of these establishments to represent large firms, output per establishment in multi-plant-firm establishments averaged almost 16 times that for single-plant firm establishments. (Calculated by applying value-added shares to gross manufacturing product in 1958 dollars).

72. From 89 to 80 percent, a 10 percent drop. Like the use of an arbitrary fixed poverty line in the determination of the proportion of the population that is defined as poor, if such a trend continued for very long, the definition of small manufacturing would have to be changed to include some multi-plant firms. In any case, I am here using the single-plant firm as a proxy, and only for the period 1947–72.

73. Using a most liberal definition of "small," one writer estimated that "between 1954 and 1961, the percentage of Defense Department prime contract awards . . . received by small business dropped from 25.3 percent to 15.9 percent." Thereafter, there was some rise to 1967, followed by another "steady decline" through fiscal 1971. The writer pointed out that "in recent years the increase in the technological complexity of material procured by the Defense Department, and the procurement policy of acquiring systems from a single contractor responsible for a total package, have combined to place many proposed acquisitions beyond the capabilities of small business." See Clyde Bothmer, "The Small Business Administration Government Procurement Program," in Deane Carson, ed., *The Vital Majority* (Washington, D.C.: G.P.O., no date), pp. 356, 359, 351. These essays mark the twentieth anniversary of the Small Business Administration, set up in 1953. Hollander, *Future of Small Business,* pp. 155–161, finds no trend but is similarly pessimistic about the prospects for subcontracting in military procurement.

74. George J. Stigler, *The Organization of Industry* (Homewood, Ill.: Irwin, 1968), p. 73. Efficiency could be defined in various ways, e.g., unit costs, rate of return, life-span.

75. Wholesale prices of industrial commodities rose two-thirds between 1947 and 1972.

76. Using 1954 data, Victor R. Fuchs found that "the percent of an industry's value added accounted for by multi-unit plants provides a better basis for predicting rates of return than does concentration of ownership. The higher the multi-unit percentage, *ceteris paribus,* the higher the rate of return." "Integration, Concentration, and Profits in Manufacturing Industries," *Quarterly Journal of Economics,* (May, 1961), 75(2):291.

77. Joe S. Bain, *Barriers to New Competition* (Cambridge, Mass.: Harvard University Press, 1956), p. 189.

78. Weiss has also noted that "substantial markets exist in which suboptimal plants predominate, particularly in the unconcentrated sectors of the economy." Leonard W. Weiss, "The Survivor Technique and the Extent of Suboptimal Capacity," *Journal of Political Economy* (June 1964), 72(3):261.

79. *Historical Statistics,* Part 2, p. 94, Series V-13–19.

80. Calculated from ibid., p. 914, Series V-45 to V-52.

81. See U.S., House Select Committee on Small Business, "Participation of Small Business in Foreign Trade and Foreign Aid," *Hearings,* July 14 and 15, 1959, 86th Cong., 1st Sess. (Washington: GPO, 1959), esp. pp. 175–76.

82. U.S., Federal Trade Commission, *Webb-Pomerene Associations: A 50-Year Review* (Washington: GPO, June 1967), pp. 61, 64.

83. Twenty-second Annual Report of the Select Committee on Small Business, U.S. Senate, 92d Cong., Report No. 92-1280 (Washington: GPO, 1972), p. 113. Cited in Deane Carson, ed., *The Vital Majority*, p. 371.

84. Henry Kearns, in EXIM Bank Release, May 17, 1973. Cited in ibid., p. 367.

85. Ibid., p. 367.

86. Manufacturing output calculated from U.S. Dept. of Commerce, *Long Term Economic Growth*, pp. 184–85, Cols. A19, A20. Gross private product from *Economic Report of the President*, 1975, p. 251. Number of firms from *Historical Statistics*, Part 2, p. 91] Series V-13, V-15. The period selected for this statement is restrained by the enterprise data series in *Historical Statistics*.

87. TNEC, *Problems of Small Business*, p. 45.

7

MASTER PRINTERS ORGANIZE: THE TYPOTHETAE OF THE CITY OF NEW YORK, 1865–1906

Irene Tichenor

SMALL enterprise is at last receiving its due as a part of business history. Ten years ago, Ralph W. Hidy noted a subject needing historical inquiry: the little businessmen who have "carried out basic functions in American society" and the trade associations they formed.[1] This essay, which examines the Typothetae of the City of New York during its first four decades (1865–1906), offers a case study in this still-fertile area of investigation.

The Typothetae, an organization of printing firms, included most of the larger book and job houses in New York. In the context of the American printing industry, their proprietors were substantial businessmen; judged beside the railroad magnates, Wall Street financiers, and other business personalities who have dominated the historian's attention, the Typothetae printers were small businessmen indeed. Furthermore, in the way they operated (participation of the owner in management, dependence on local markets, absence of stockmarket financing, and personal relationships between proprietor and customer), they fit the accepted small-business pattern, despite considerable business volume in some cases.

Proprietors throughout American history have united, as have workmen, to promote and defend common interests. As industrialization advanced, proprietors formed purposeful, enduring organizations, frequently called employer associations. The proliferation of these societies in the late nineteenth century showed that the small businessman had begun to appreciate the influence on his success of many forces outside his own shop. He saw that he and his rivals had numerous common problems; he was becoming industry-oriented.

No definitive study of these organizations has appeared. Labor union proceedings have been the principal source for historical accounts of employer associations.[2] Consequently, most writers treat them as management's answer to organized labor.* Many employer associations were indeed antagonistic to organized labor, but this fact needs to be balanced by study of the host of other business problems that drew proprietors together.

In the New York City printing industry, labor relations provided neither the motive nor the sustaining force for the first employer association, the Typothetae. The problem of competition and an array of other business considerations preceded labor worries and were not submerged by them until the twentieth century. By then, discord over whether and how to deal with unions was so great that printers on local and national levels split into closed-shop, open-shop, and nonunion groups. A Typothetae cleavage in 1906 created the Printers' League, a group of closed-shop firms committed to cooperation and arbitration with unions. When they realized the folly of their disunity ten years later, the two groups reaffiliated as the New York Employing Printers' Association; henceforth, they cooperated on other business matters but retained individual labor policies.

This article deals with the pre-1906 Typothetae, its leaders, and the ways in which they tried to cope with the problems of being printing proprietors.

STATE OF THE PRINTING TRADE

Printing, like other industries, underwent considerable specialization in the nineteenth century. Since the invention of movable type in the fifteenth century, the printing process had consisted of two fundamental units: composi-

* The term "employer association" probably also helps account for this view; it invites contrast with "employee." But the contrast in terms need not connote antagonism. In the skilled trades, employer was traditionally the stage to which apprentices and journeymen aspired, not the label for a closed group hostile toward employees. "Employing printer" was synonymous with "master printer"—one who had been through the ranks and was now in business for himself, employing other journeymen. Until he became firmly established he might be employing printer on one project and journeyman on the next.

tion (typesetting) and operation of the press. While it was not impossible for the same man to be competent at the type case and at the press, this was less and less the case as machinery became complex, and as printing houses grew larger. By mid-century, compositor and pressman were distinct occupations in New York City except, perhaps, in the smallest shops, where the proprietor did much of the manual labor himself.

Specialization was characteristic of the master printers as well.* Far from being a publisher, bookseller, editor, and journalist as his earlier counterpart was, the mid-nineteenth-century New York City printer was a printer exclusively. He specialized in the manufacture of printed material; choice of content, editing, distribution, and price to the general public were in other hands. Although a few publishing houses had their own printing plants or composing rooms, and although some firms that considered themselves printers occasionally undertook to publish a volume, by the time the Typothetae was founded, in 1865, printing and publishing were two different functions, even when they took place in the same establishment. The vast majority of master printers were independent businessmen, who either fulfilled contracts with book and periodical publishers or undertook job work for a variety of customers.†

No New York City firm in the latter half of the nineteenth century attempted to produce all three types of printed products: newspapers, books, and job work, each of which required its own kind of machinery. Neither did these three form distinct branches, however. Only daily newspapers can be singled out from the otherwise overlapping industry. Because their credibility with readers and advertisers depended upon prompt, regular delivery, newspaper publishers preferred to have all production units under their control and usually within one plant. The printery, then, became a subdivision of the daily newspaper publishing firm, rather than an independent concern. With daily newspapers a special case, the balance of the industry was known as book and job printing. That phrase came to include magazines and non-daily newspapers—a meaningful alignment, since most printers of these periodicals also did job and sometimes book work. It was possible for work-

---

* Herein the terms "printer," "master printer," and "employing printer" denote proprietors of printing establishments, large or small. Workmen are referred to as "journeymen printers" or, more specifically, "compositors," "pressmen," and so on.

† Job printing in the late nineteenth century was understood to include everything except newspapers, large pamphlets, and books (i.e., posters, tickets, bill heads, and the like).

men, especially compositors, to cross the line between the dailies and book-and-job work; and labor organizations, after a temporary rift, encompassed both branches. Employers' organizations, however, did not.

The book and job printing industry, with which the Typothetae concerned itself almost exclusively, was complex indeed. Some firms specialized by product. Some performed only one step of production, such as stereotyping or presswork; others had comprehensive plants. There were many variations in between. Master printer Theodore Low De Vinne gave an accounting of New York City's printing industry in his 1872 *State of the Trade*. Some publishers, he said, had their own printing plants: all 24 daily newspapers, 3 or 4 other periodicals, and 6 book publishers. Independent printing firms vied for the remaining 370 periodicals and the books of 150 publishing houses. The 350 job offices were "more unequal in their appointments" than any other category of printers. At least half had no power presses and did "but an inconsiderable amount of business."[3] Although De Vinne did not say how many master printers were in business, the total had clearly mushroomed since the beginning of the century, when New York City numbered its master printers at about 15, and its journeymen at 80 or 90.

Several further peculiarities of the printing trade bear mentioning. First, it was a custom business. The customer decided content and sometimes format, and promptness of delivery was often crucial. Second, it was primarily a local trade, though competition from neighboring areas was always a problem for New York City printers. Publishers had a national market; printers did not. Third, it took little capital to enter the printing business. With a hand press, a few fonts of type, and a couple of boys, a journeyman could become a proprietor, albeit a marginal one. Underbidding by these novices was a constant annoyance to established printers.* Fourth, proprietors and workers alike had a sense of the history of the craft. They made

---

* Throughout the period covered by this essay, the book and job printing industry was characterized by its large number of single proprietorships, most of them doing a small volume of business. According to the 1905 census, New York City had only 1,283 proprietors for its 1,229 shops, meaning that more than 95 percent of the shops had single owners. While some of these may have done well, partnership or incorporation usually accompanied expansion. The census report did not summarize by city, but data for New York State are revealing. Of the 1,693 establishments (73 percent of which were in New York City), 64.2 percent were individual proprietorships and did only 25.7 percent of the business; partnerships, 19.3 percent of the shops, did 16.8 percent; and incorporated companies, 16.5 percent of the establishments, produced 57.5 percent of the industry's output. U.S., Bureau of the Census, *Bulletin 59; Census of Manufactures: 1905– New York* (Washington, D.C.: GPO, 1906), pp. 35, 78.

frequent references to great printers of the past and called printing the "art preservative of all arts." They seemed to feel, whether it was true or not, that printing by its very nature appealed to the more literate craftsman. In sum, there was considerable occupational pride in the industry.

THE TYPOTHETAE OF
THE CITY OF NEW YORK

Shortly after the outbreak of the Civil War, the leading book and job printers in New York City realized that they could more easily solve certain business problems if they had better contacts with each other. Wartime inflation, combined with a decrease in trade volume and loss of workmen, caused these businessmen financial hardship. Several substantial printers, who had been meeting for lunch to discuss business, proposed in late 1862 to create a formal organization for the purpose of exchanging trade information and promoting the prosperity of the printing business. Their efforts finally bore fruit in March 1865 with the election of officers and the selection of the name Typothetae.* In a series of conferences, the association developed price scales that reflected the economic consequences of the war. Some four-dozen firms paid dues to the society, but attendance at monthly meetings was disappointing from the outset. After holding annual dinners for a few years, the Typothetae of the City of New York (TCNY) ceased to exist as a formal entity. Leading printers continued to feel a common interest, however. On a number of occasions, notably to discuss wages with journeymen, they met informally as the Employing Printers of New York.

The Typothetae's revival in November 1883 reflected the printers' maturing awareness of the benefits of association. The 31 printers who signed the call for an organizational meeting hoped "to improve the trade and cultivate a just and friendly spirit among the craft." They planned "a permanent social and protective organization."[4] The social aspect was important; through monthly meetings, frequent dinners, and eventually national conventions, master printers better understood their common problems and developed a sense of unity. "Protection" referred to various threats to the sta-

* "Typothetae" comes from Greek words meaning "typesetting." The term seems to have been applied first by Frederick III to the printers of Germany, when he bestowed honors on them shortly after the invention of movable type.

bility of the trade; among them were cutthroat competition, inadequate accounting methods, unfavorable legislation of many varieties, and growing attempts by labor unions at shop control.

Membership was confined to New York City master printers, defined as "proprietors of book or job printing establishments, or publishers of books or newspapers . . . who employ their own [printing] workmen."[5] A few newspaper publishers belonged until the American Newspaper Publishers' Association, formed in 1887, suited their needs better; but from the outset, proprietors of book and job printeries dominated Typothetae policies and the membership roll. A year and a half after its reincarnation, one member made this lofty assessment of the TCNY: "Seeking no antagonisms, and further-ing no selfish aims, it is fast becoming a body of sufficient power to grapple with any subject affecting the business which it represents, while the bond of union that it forms cannot fail to greatly elevate and improve the trade."[6]

In 1886, the TCNY urged the formation of organizations similar to itself in all cities of more than 100,000 population. It appropriated funds toward organizational efforts, set up correspondence with leading printers in other cities, and sent speakers around the country. In March 1887, a TCNY Com-mittee on Organization in Other Cities reported the formation of Typothetae societies in Chicago and St. Louis. Within the next few years more than fifty such bodies came into existence. Like that of New York, other Typo-thetaes attracted the larger book and job printers.

Correspondence and personal contacts were important in spreading the Typothetae idea around the country. The successful campaign also owed much to the *American Bookmaker,* a trade journal which TCNY member Howard Lockwood had begun publishing in 1885. This monthly and its slightly older Chicago counterpart, the *Inland Printer,* were important com-munication vehicles in the U.S. printing industry. The *American Book-maker* * was never precisely a Typothetae house organ, but the opinions of Lockwood and his successors more often than not reflected those of the TCNY majority. It made Typothetae activities known throughout the coun-try. Numerous TCNY members contributed articles and columns.

With so much interest in founding local Typothetaes, it was only a matter of time until someone would call a national convention. The International Typographical Union provided the impetus by demanding a reduction of

* Subsequently called the *Printer and Bookmaker* and the *American Printer.*

hours in the printing industry from ten to nine per day without a reduction in wages. Meeting in Chicago in October 1887, master printers from across the country formed the United Typothetae of America (UTA). It was in part a defensive move, and in part a following of the "fashion of the day by which nearly all professions and trades and occupations of every description were organizing for mutual conference, sympathy, strength, and support."[7] Howard Lockwood, chairman of the New York delegation, became chairman of the executive committee and drafted the constitution. The UTA elected Theodore De Vinne of New York as its first president.

Postponement of the Union's campaign for reduced hours was probably due to vigorous local resistance, but the United Typothetae took credit. At its second annual convention, confident that its mere formation had been a setback to "immoderate" labor elements, it postponed any discussion of unions until the following year and concerned itself with trade practices, federal legislation affecting the printing industry, and organization of further Typothetae societies. This convention, held in New York City, was notable for its conciliatory tone. Even before the meeting opened, Lockwood proposed that if labor questions arose they be handled "with deliberation and after careful consideration." In his welcoming speech, TCNY member J. J. Little reminded his fellow proprietors that their individual rights were "no greater now than they were when . . . we were at the case or at the press." President De Vinne's address summarized the noncoercive nature of the Typothetae that would be for many years both its appeal and its weakness:

Our society is unlike any in the trade. It is voluntary and not coercive. We are here as free men, not pledged to blind obedience in support of any leader or any policy. . . . We do not propose to make arbitrary prices, rates or rules; to make combinations against our customers or the public; to fix or regulate the wages of workmen; to organize a crusade against any society. . . . Our society is based on the right of the individual as opposed to the arrogated rights of societies.[8]

By 1887, when the TCNY made a determined stand against the closed union shop, the society of master printers had assumed the role of speaking for its members on labor matters. In the ensuing years, one-shop disturbances and occasional citywide strikes engaged the Typothetae's attention. Yet whenever labor troubles subsided, the TCNY returned to its primary ongoing concern: unhealthy competition that kept prices too low. These two principal threats to business prosperity and stability (discussed in greater detail below) took much energy. The Typothetae, nevertheless, also found the resources for other undertakings.

In the early 1890s, the TCNY began circulating to its members a list of delinquent debtors. This "Wrong Font List," updated quarterly, allowed printers to avoid certain customers. Later the Typothetae expanded this service into a Law and Collection Department, which took over the actual collection of overdue debts owed to members and threatened lawsuits when appropriate.

Several TCNY members, notably De Vinne, W. W. Pasko, and Peter C. Baker, took a personal interest in the history of printing. Lockwood frequently ran historical articles in the *American Bookmaker*. As the two hundredth anniversary of the introduction of printing in New York approached, the Typothetae made plans for elaborate festivities at Delmonico's on April 12, 1893. The several days of commemorative events, involving historical societies and the trades allied to printing, celebrated not only William Bradford but all printing advances in the city since he set up his press in New York Colony.

By the early 1890s, though not all master printers belonged to the TCNY, no one in the printing industry of New York City could remain oblivious to its existence. As was the case with other Typothetaes, it exerted influence out of proportion to its numbers. Its activities were widely reported in the trade press and in the general newspapers. The formation of a national body and local societies in other cities had helped make "typothetae" a generic term; some contemporaries used the word without capitalization.

The depression of the mid-1890s destroyed many business enterprises, including a few Typothetae firms. So that the organization itself might survive, the TCNY drastically reduced the initiation fee from ten to two dollars and annual dues from twenty-four dollars to one. To compensate, it conducted subscriptions among the more prosperous members. Though the treasury dipped to forty-two cents in July 1895, the leading members were determined to keep the Typothetae afloat, even if the burden could not be shared equally.

Education of less experienced and less prosperous printers had long been a Typothetae mission. In a series of twelve lectures in the fall of 1899, Typothetae leaders shared their expertise on technical, labor, and business aspects of the printing trade. The lectures were such a success (and were given an even wider audience through the *American Printer*) that a second series was planned for March of the following year.

The Typothetae never approached its potential numerically. Unimpressive membership totals, however, are a poor index to Typothetae influence. According to contemporary accounts, virtually all the largest book and job printers of New York belonged. In their 1888 survey, TCNY printers learned that while they represented only 72 of the 511 book and job houses of the city (14 percent), they employed 41 percent of New York's printing workers, and owned 73 percent of its Adams power presses. Besides controlling a sizable portion of the printing trade directly, these prosperous printers also received some deference from others in the industry. They saw themselves as the "representative heads of the printing fraternity," as if, by a system of virtual representation, they would promote the interests of the entire trade. Though its dues and lavish social activities no doubt intimidated many lesser printers, and though its numerous membership drives failed to overcome this barrier, the society's influence was nevertheless far greater than mere numbers suggest.

PRIMARY ISSUE:
COMPETITION AND PRICES

Anything that would "elevate" the printing business came within the purview of the Typothetae, but protection of profitability was always a paramount objective. In the early years, the Typothetae saw most threats to profitability as a function of competition—competition from outside the "legitimate" printing industry, and the more insidious "unfair" competition from within.

Outside competition came from a variety of sources. Charitable organizations sometimes overstepped the bounds of their charters and printed material other than their own. The U.S. Postal Department's practice of selling stamped envelopes for the price of stamps undermined both the stationery trade and printers who stocked envelopes. The government even experimented with printing return addresses on stamped envelopes. The New York legislature proposed to use prison labor for state printing in place of contracts with established firms. Type founders, press manufacturers, and other suppliers of printing equipment occasionally did some printing to supplement their principal business, a practice that seemed grossly unfair to men trained in the printing art. The TCNY fought these sources of competition with resolutions, remonstrances, trade journal articles, and lobbies.

Competition from within the legitimate printing industry was a more complex matter. No one disputed that competition was healthy; certainly none of the Typothetae members would have condoned government regulation, or ownership, of the printing trade. Indeed, the Typothetae insisted that it did not itself "assume, in any way, to interfere with or regulate prices."[9] What it wanted was a gentlemanly, voluntary adherence to mutually determined prices, a tradition that—in theory, at least—dated as far back as 1795 in New York.

All the TCNY's efforts at uniform prices seemed doomed in the 1880s. As the major printers perceived it, their business was being threatened by beginners whose zeal was "not always accompanied with proper knowledge" and by experienced but unscrupulous printers who knowingly violated the informal code of ethics. A beginner could easily set up his own business; but in an already oversupplied trade, he could gain a foothold only by printing at rates lower than those of established houses. Many beginners failed to meet expenses and reverted to the ranks of journeymen; meanwhile they had depressed prices. Dealers in printing equipment exacerbated the problem by supplying beginners on easy terms, reclaiming the machinery when one hapless proprietor failed, and outfitting another novice with it. This policy, protested the Typothetae, "enables those who have no capital or reputation at stake, and no carefully acquired experience to guide them, for force themselves into business by underbidding, at ruinous rates, the better informed and regular members of the trade."[10] Though the magnitude of this problem is difficult to assess, the leading printers clearly felt threatened by it.

Competitive bidding among established houses was an even more delicate problem. The Typothetae seemed to want each printer to have his own clientele, to be known by the quality of his work, and to solicit business only through discreet trade-journal advertisements. Instead, the printing business was characterized by hired "drummers," and by proprietors who took others' business at any price to keep their own presses running. In the early 1890s the TCNY prepared an essay on "The Evils Which Result from Competitive Bidding and Their Prevention;" the United Typothetae appointed a committee to study these evils and "prepare such a code of ethics as will tend to elevate the dignity of the trade."[11] But the problem was not solved that easily. In fact, it worsened as a result of the general business slump that began in 1893.

Eventually, the Typothetae concluded that underbidding was a problem of education. If printers knew the actual cost of work, they would be more inclined to support higher prices. De Vinne, one of the proponents of this plan, had long preached that simply adding a profit percentage to the cost of labor and materials on a given job was incorrect. As he had argued two decades earlier in his *Printers' Price List,* wear of type, time lost for repairs, supervisory salaries, power, and other costs of maintaining the plant should be apportioned among all jobs. Since cost accounting was in its infancy in the late nineteenth century, this was a startling idea to men who had only a vague notion of their net earnings until the end of each year.[12]

The New York Typothetae members began to educate themselves, and then other printers, on the newly developed cost-accounting techniques. They made estimate blanks available to anyone in the trade. Isaac Blanchard gave lantern-slide lectures and blackboard talks to the TCNY on the methods he had developed; De Vinne offered to underwrite further dissemination of those methods to other interested printers. Recognizing that differences in equipment, plant size, and labor force meant differences in operating costs, the TCNY Committee on Improvement of the Printing Business surveyed printers of New York City in an effort to understand cost variations. Two books by TCNY printers, Isaac Blanchard's *Actual Cost in Printing* and Paul Nathan's *How to Make Money in the Printing Business,* were read and discussed across the country. The *Printer and Bookmaker* and the United Typothetae took up the cost-accounting cause and gave it national prominence among printers.

Thus far, the Typothetae had fought against depression of prices by development of more sophisticated cost-finding techniques, education of inexperienced proprietors, and pleas to the entire trade to eschew underbidding. A fourth approach, "combination," developed a considerable following among Typothetae members at the turn of the century. It is not always clear what the term meant to the printers who used it, though proponents generally desired some formal, binding agreement not to bid against one another, while each participant retained management of his own firm.

Some TCNY members were caught up in the general "trust" enthusiasm of the late nineteenth century. "On every side," said Charles Cochrane, "combinations and trusts are forming and ruinous competition is being replaced by establishing conditions to restrict price-cutting, and to permit proprietors to earn sure returns on their capital." Combinations were "the order of the day in all progressive lines of trade;'' they were inevitable and "essential to economy in business." The allied trades had begun to combine. "We have type trusts, ink trusts, paper trusts, envelope trusts, etc.," Charles Francis pointed out. Why not a printing trust? [13]

Printers in several cities had already formed combinations. The *Printer and Bookmaker* wasted no time in reporting trusts and rumors of trusts among printers in Duluth, Columbus, St. Paul, Chicago, Des Moines, Kansas City, Indianapolis, and Baltimore. The journal also explored the possibility of a New York City printing combination by soliciting the opinions of prominent printers. Some felt that combinations were feasible only in smaller cities, where printing firms were not so diverse. Others were determined to try partial combinations in New York. Eleven periodical printers, styling themselves the Inner Circle, agreed not to estimate on work until they had determined that no other participant had bid on it. The pact was sealed with a $1,000 promissory note from each of the eleven. Little is known of this group, later apparently called the Ben Franklin Club, with counterparts in other cities. [14] Their legal questionability under the 1890 Sherman Act and state antitrust laws probably encouraged such groups to keep their activities quiet.

Another partial combination involved medium-sized print shops. Charles Cochrane finally put his fervor to work in 1901 by forming, with the TCNY's blessing, the New York Master Printers' Association. In one sense, it was an alternative to the Typothetae for lesser printers, who had never felt comfortable among the industry leaders. But its scope was narrower; its main purpose was to eliminate underbidding among members. They simply agreed to confer with each other when asked to estimate on the same job. Sixteen months after the association's formation its president claimed that it included "almost half of the printers in New York." [15]

These efforts apparently eased the competition problem somewhat, though there was still considerable variation among prices charged by printing houses of different sizes. The largest firms tended to charge 5 to 10 percent more for any given job than the smallest. Some customers were willing to pay the higher figure for extra expertise and efficiency; some were not. This state of affairs apportioned the business among the city's printeries. By Cochrane's estimate, half the printing New York required could only be done by the fancier equipment of large houses. But if the substantial printers raised their prices unilaterally, they risked loss of less sophisticated printing to their smaller colleagues. Partial combinations, then, provided only a partial solution.

Some businessmen feared combinations and trusts as violations of self-regulating economic order; printers were among those who saw business combination as a natural outgrowth of increasing business efficiency. Even those who opposed a printing combination in New York did so not on philosophical grounds, but because they thought the New York City printing trade was too diverse to make it succeed.

That prices were kept too low by competition was the perennial Typothetae theme. Proposed solutions to the problem varied over time: uniform price scales, education of small printers, better cost accounting, and combination. Implicit in all Typothetae efforts to raise prices was the assumption that proprietors should band together to promote their joint cause and that those printers who failed to do so were degrading the entire trade.

SECONDARY ISSUE: LABOR

Though its stated goals were sufficiently broad to cover almost any contingency, the Typothetae began without a specific labor policy. The founders hoped from the beginning that closer association among printers would curtail ruinous underbidding, the primary evil of the trade; not until 1886 did they even seek a consensus on labor relations.

Labor conflicts had existed in the New York City printing industry for a century. Periodic questions of wages and working conditions had been dealt with traditionally by joint conference between representative master printers and journeymen. Though it is impossible to know how well these jointly determined scales were observed, the custom of settling labor disputes by negotiation was well established by the time of the Typothetae's inception. Since voluntary negotiation was an imperfect instrument, strikes occasionally punctuated the otherwise orderly book and job printing industry.

When the Typothetae began anew in 1883, labor was in the news; Congress was holding hearings on the relationship between labor and capital and would soon create the Bureau of Labor. Typothetae members could not have been innocent of the debate over status of the working man. Yet their decision to begin meeting again does not seem to have sprung from great anxiety over organized labor. Before the end of the year, the Union declared a new scale without Typothetae opposition or comment. Indeed, it was not until February 1885 that labor was even mentioned in the TCNY minutes, which discredits Charlotte Morgan's assertion that the Typothetae reorganized "primarily to meet the demands of the union."[16] At this meeting, the Typothetae authorized a committee of three "to take into consideration the prices paid for labor of every kind in connection with the printing business in this and other cities and countries."[17] To discharge its fact-finding task, the committee sent four hundred questionnaires to master printers across the nation. The *American Bookmaker* published the rather inconclusive results from a disappointing seventy-three replies in January 1886.

At the May 1886 meeting, with the new Typothetae in its third year, a discussion finally arose "as to the necessity of concerted action on the part of the Employers in the matter of the different labor demands being made from time to time." The committee appointed to formulate a plan of action suggested the organization of an "Employing Printers' Association with power to adjust and regulate matters relating to Employer and Employee," indicating once again that the TCNY did not consider labor negotiations one of its functions. The TCNY debated the proposal, held it over to the next monthly meeting, and ultimately dropped it because "many do not desire to enter into any combination having for its object mutual protection and safety."[18] Nevertheless, more and more members were feeling that the Typothetae should take positions on labor issues.

During the fall of 1887, the TCNY's burgeoning labor policy was put to a test. In September, the Typographical Union called for the customary joint meeting between representative employing printers and book and job compositors to discuss the wage scale. A TCNY committee headed by De Vinne took up "the whole subject of conferring with workmen," concluding that it was inappropriate for the Typothetae to make any agreement with the union but that it was "entirely . . . proper for this Committee as representatives of the employing printers of this city to hear any proposition which might be made by the workmen, or to undertake any office which would tend to please." Besides, said De Vinne, "the simplest rules of good breeding . . . would compel us to give a respectful hearing and answer."[19] On this genteel note began the relationship between the Typothetae and New York City's strongest printing labor organization, International Typographical Union No. 6. Since the Typothetae felt it could take no official action on the union's demands, its frequent meetings in September and October were "immediately followed by a meeting of employing printers," apparently the committee headed by De Vinne.

The wage issue was no stumbling block. Several other points certainly were, however, including a reduction of hours with no reduction in pay. Most egregious of all was a clause that would forbid proprietors to employ anyone without a union card. The union refused to remove the "card-office clause"; the Typothetae unanimously rejected it on October 6 and 10; and the union called a strike by some 700 compositors in 30 shops. Pressmen, feeders, stereotypers, and electrotypers briefly joined in a sympathy strike, bringing the total to a peak of about 1,200.[20]

The Typothetae, now holding daily meetings, no longer went through the motions of having separate employing printer meetings; it had accepted the role of employer spokesman on labor issues. Thirty TCNY members signed a resolution to display notices in their windows saying, "This is not a card office," and to advertise in neighboring cities for 1,000 compositors to be paid the rate demanded by the union.

Even with the assistance of a state arbitrator, the two sides could not arrive at a settlement. By the end of October, the union tacitly allowed its men to return to work; the TCNY's show of strength had been impressive. In its first big stand on a labor issue—one of shop control—the Typothetae had been dramatically victorious.

The nine-hour day, for which the ITU made this abortive bid in 1887, continued to concern the Typothetae of the City of New York for a decade. After rebuffs by the TCNY and the UTA in 1887, the journeymen printers de-emphasized the issue for a few years. Nevertheless, the master printers knew a struggle was inevitable, and many hoped to forestall it as long as possible. In March 1892, partly in reaction to a strike the ITU was waging in Pittsburgh, the New York Typothetae found enough unanimity to pass a resolution on the subject. Though Lockwood had shifted the *American Bookmaker*'s support to the nine-hour day, the TCNY "utterly opposed" the nine-hour movement and resolved to avoid any "premature discussion" of the subject because it would give "the appearance of doubt and vacillation" and hence would encourage the union.[21]

The business depression that began later that year postponed a confrontation for a time. The TCNY annual reports of April 1894 and 1895 noted that business had been poor, and there had been no labor difficulties. With so many men out of work, employees could not hope to make any gains. When prosperity began to return in 1895 and 1896, journeymen felt more secure, and a series of one-shop strikes ensued over a variety of issues.

In October 1896, the ITU proposed to its locals that they make the nine-hour day a priority. It was more than a year before the issue reached a climax in New York City. In December 1897, No. 6 notified the TCNY that the nine-hour day would go into effect in the city's book and job offices the following month. Though some TCNY members still opposed any reduction, a return of prosperity apparently softened some hearts. Enough favored compromise so that the union and the Typothetae reached an agreement for 56½ hours a week to be in force until the ITU announced that the nine-hour day would go into effect in the competitive district (east of the Alleghenies and north of Richmond), at which time the TCNY would concede the 54-hour week. Since shorter hours were inevitable, the best the Typothetae could hope for was to educate their fellow printers on the need for increased prices, which they set about to accomplish through circulars and trade-journal articles.

The diehards in the Typothetae, who refused to deal with unions at all, were sufficiently strong in the fall of 1899 to defeat a resolution at the annual UTA convention that a permanent board of conference be set up between that organization and the unions. While the United Typothetae could vote down a permanent arbitration mechanism, it could not ignore the unions altogether. The International Typographical Union had grown from 19,000 in 189 locals in 1887, when the UTA was founded, to 32,000 members in 411 locals in 1900.[22] The ITU, which predated the United Typothetae of America by nearly four decades, had suffered fragmentation as pressmen, bookbinders, and other craft groups split off to form their own unions, leaving the Typographers' Union—still the largest and strongest—to the compositors. However, now the journeymen were overcoming old jurisdictional jealousies. Already, in New York City, the various unions had formed an allied printing trades council and the same would soon happen on the national level.

To prevent ''undue interference from the unions,'' the UTA leadership proposed the establishment of a defense fund in 1900, collected and administered by the local societies. Contributions to the fund were half hearted for the next few years, though such issues as the eight-hour day, unionized foremen, and the union label kept proprietors uneasy.

Despite these disturbing matters, many Typothetae firms were still willing to bargain with unions on the best terms they could get. In December 1901, the New York Typothetae and the ITU local agreed upon a wage increase; all disputes were to be referred to a mutually chosen arbitrator. Yet both the Typothetae and the union were preparing for the fight that lay ahead. At its 1903 convention, the ITU set a goal of January 1, 1905, for the eight-hour day and took its strongest stand ever on the closed shop. The United Typothetae declared its opposition to any reduction of hours and modified its customary open-shop statement to one of anti-unionism.

There was much interest at this time throughout the country in the open- and closed-shop issue. The National Association of Manufacturers, which had turned its attention from developing overseas markets to opposing labor organizations at home, inspired the formation of the Citizens Industrial Association in 1903, expressly to oppose the closed shop and the union label.* At least two other employer organizations, the National Metal Trades Association and the National Founders' Association, adopted anti-union stances.

The Typographical Union had done much to overcome the localism that had weakened it from the beginning. It was time for the Typothetae to do the same. A UTA questionnaire to its members revealed a striking unanimity, particularly on the question of reduced hours. With many master printers placing their hopes on the national organization, the UTA finally established permanent headquarters in New York City and hired a salaried president. In 1904, with membership at its highest, the UTA decided to stand firm on the questions of hours and the closed shop. It would cost money, work, and maybe lives, the master printers intoned, "but what are money and work and life if we have not liberty."[23]

In New York, the Typothetae's contract with ITU No. 6 was about to expire. The union was eager for the eight-hour day. However, the International Typographical Union had extended its deadline one year to January 1, 1906; and, since the TCNY absolutely refused to discuss the shorter work day, No. 6 agreed to a one-year wage increase with no change in hours. Probably both the union and the Typothetae were grateful for one more year in which to build up their defense funds.

During that year, the TCNY made elaborate plans to resist the union's onslaught. It sought financial and moral support from publishers and suppliers.

---

* The TCNY sent delegates to the 1904 convention of the Citizens Industrial Association. That Association and the National Association of Manufacturers sent speakers to a January 1906 TCNY meeting.

Its members patronized the only "open" electrotyping establishment in the city to keep it running, since workers in union electrotype shops would refuse to handle their work during a strike. It arbitrated with the press-feeders' union to a satisfactory conclusion in early summer and secured the existing agreement with pressmen, hoping that these two unions would not complicate the anticipated struggle with the compositors. It enlarged the executive committee's powers. It solicited support and membership from every printer in New York City who employed 5 men or more, increasing its membership from 46 to 92. It participated in the establishment in New York of a UTA Linotype and Monotype school to provide Typothetae firms with nonunion operators and machinists. It employed ten field men to canvass towns in New York and neighboring states for compositors who would take the places of strikers. It obtained reduced rates from the railroads to transport these "free men" to the city. It made plans to house and feed those new compositors whose employers could not accommodate them. It increased the defense-fund assessment from .5 percent to 2 percent of members' mechanical payrolls, a move that caused some resignations; this left 86 members, only 69 of whom were paid up as of November 14, 1905.

On November 15, a month and a half before the contract was to expire, the TCNY made one last bid for a renewal. No. 6 responded that it would work eight hours a day at the present rate or else. On December 28, 1905, the New York Typothetae pledged itself to nine hours and the open shop.

When the strike began on January 2, 1906, the TCNY could claim only 44 printing houses committed to its policy, and 4 of them capitulated within the first two weeks. The proprietors of the remaining 40 offices dreaded eight-hours' work for nine-hours' pay less than they feared the closed-shop conditions that would surely result from capitulation; it was at heart not merely a question of hours and profits but of shop control, the same principle that had been at stake since 1887.

The strike was almost immediately successful in non-Typothetae shops. Helped by the American Federation of Labor, the Typographical Union was well funded for the conflict. The strikers were for the most part quite peaceful; the guards the TCNY had hired to protect their "free men" were unnecessary. Thanks to their elaborate preparations, the Typothetae diehards were able to stay in operation. Recording Secretary H. V. Boyer said in his April 1906 annual report, "It is hard, gentlemen, for us to write a history of our Typothetae year and not appear vainglorious." [24]

Measured industry-wide, Typothetae resistance to the 1906 strike, both national and local, was a failure. Nevertheless, the individual proprietors to whom the open shop was so important could take some pleasure in having preserved their shops from union control. Eventually even the TCNY printers granted the eight-hour day to their unorganized journeymen, while clinging religiously to the open-shop concept.

By one estimate, the 1906 strike cost the industry, as a whole, $20 to $25 million.[25] It not only severed Typothetae relations with the unions. It also brought the growing cleavage among employers to a climax. In the first few years of the twentieth century, the Typothetae abandoned its position that members were free to set their own policies. The 1904 constitution, redefining the loosely knit United Typothetae as a group of open-shop printers, caused serious defection. In three years, membership dropped from 1,348 to 803.[26] In August 1904, only 13 TCNY printers had paid UTA dues under the new constitution.

The local societies, too, lost members. Some printers feared the cost and business disruption that accompanied strikes; they began to feel that stability was more important than proprietor independence. Others became convinced of the justice of the shorter workday. Charles Francis noted, for instance, that pipefitters on the ground floor of his building were working eight hours a day "and getting more money than our men, who in reality are a better and more intelligent class."[27] Some master printers decided that labor unions were both inevitable and efficient as a vehicle for employee relations.

Charles Francis provided an alternative to the Typothetae for printers who, for philosophical or business reasons, could not accept the TCNY's unyielding anti-union policy. His Printers' League endorsed the closed-union shop and a system of arbitration that had found success in his native New Zealand. In 1909, three years after its founding, the league claimed 55 members, compared with the Typothetae's 31. It had wooed and won a number of longtime Typothetae members.

With the 1906 strike, the TCNY had finally arrived at a cohesive labor policy. However, it had cost the organization size and influence that it would never recover. In 1916, seeing how the split over labor policy had hampered their other activities, the Typothetae and the League formed an alliance, the New York Employing Printers' Association, Inc. On labor matters they retained their former policies, the Typothetae constituting the "open shop branch" and the League the "closed shop branch." In 1920, the society of medium-sized and small printing shops, the New York Master Printers' Association, joined the new body.

Although the Typothetae had been superseded, some printers remained sentimental toward the pioneer master printers' organization. They continued to hold Typothetae annual meetings until 1951, when they decided not to reregister the TCNY's state charter. Instead, still determined that the name Typothetae not fade from printing annals, they turned remaining funds over to the New York Employing Printers' Association to be used for a "Typothetae" scholarship fund.

CONCLUSION

As has been said of the United Typothetae, the TCNY printers saw that "the worst menace to the industry was disorderly strife among the master-printers themselves."[28] They invested great hope and effort in two premises: that an association of proprietors could tackle any problem they had in common, and that mere association would "elevate" their calling.

The association took up the whole range of business problems that confronted the master printer. Chief among them were prices for printed products and the inordinate level of competition that kept prices low. Labor relations was a secondary issue for a number of years. The Typothetae was able to resist the closed shop; with slightly less success, it tempered the movement for shorter hours. At the turn of the century, however, the secondary issue became primary. Fighting not only for profits but also for the principle of proprietor control, the Typothetae had little time, money, or energy for the range of activities that had characterized it earlier. The 1906 strike pared the New York Typothetae down to a small band of determined men, who in order to defend the labor policy they believed in, lost the breadth of participation for which the TCNY had always striven. Though the industry did not solve the cleavage over the closed shop, master printers eventually reaffiliated so that they could continue other activities of which the Typothetae had been the pioneer.

Biographical data on the 25 most active TCNY leaders of the 1880s and 1890s reveal striking similarities. Most of the men were born shortly before mid-century of British ancestry in modest surroundings in small northeastern towns. They typically received some public education and then served four-year printing apprenticeships before leaving for New York City. There they worked as journeymen and saved money to open their own businesses. From small beginnings, they added to their equipment and clientele until they had built up successful businesses that earned them comfortable livelihoods. They were proud of their chosen vocation and optimistic about the Typothetae's potential.

The men who composed the nineteenth-century New York Typothetae had many adjustments to make during their business careers. This generation's working lives spanned the most dramatic mechanical and human changes in the history of the printing industry. Of the principal challenges—constant development of new machinery and techniques, emergence of new business methods, growing competition, and a revolution in employer-employee relations—printers most easily took technological change in stride. This is not surprising, since it was practical printing, not business administration or personnel relations, in which they had been trained. Whenever Typothetae printers gathered, informal conversations turned to the merits of one press over another. The men eagerly adapted new machinery to their needs; some helped develop it.

In business methods, too, these printers showed adaptability and leadership. They developed cost-accounting techniques, which they taught to themselves and to anyone else who was receptive. Several Typothetae members wrote books on how to be a successful printing proprietor.

Price-depressing competition was the principal business challenge to the master-printers' resourcefulness. Oversupply of printing shops, inexperience of new proprietors, encroachment from out-of-town firms, and distrust among established printers all contributed toward the inordinate competition that kept prices low. In attempting to solve this problem, the printing proprietors modified the strict individualism that had served them well in a simpler day. TCNY speeches echoed the Social Darwinism of the times. Yet in practice the "fittest" (by whom these businessmen meant themselves) were being thwarted by marginal printers and by jealousy within their own ranks. Seizing upon "combination," some printing proprietors replaced individualism with joint action and collectivism. Printers were able to justify combinations that would advance their economic interests; their philosophies were not so flexible when it came to combinations of workers.

The most difficult adjustment for the printers involved employer-employee relations. Few of the proprietors were prepared, until it was forced upon them, to relinquish any shop control to workers, or to modify the paternalistic framework they had always taken for granted. Nevertheless, since nearly all of the Typothetae printers had come up through the ranks and some of them had belonged to the typographers' union, they were not totally out of sympathy with workers' concerns. In fact, they rather prided themselves on their benevolence as employers. They were dismayed, therefore, that the growing unions seemed intent on dictating wages rather than negotiating them. Dismay turned to recoil and alarm as the unions became more belligerent. These master printers valued harmony "between the workroom and the counting-room" above everything else except one thing: proprietor independence.

Notes

1. "Business History: Present Status and Future Needs," *Business History Review* (1970), 44:494.

2. Clarence E. Bonnett, *History of Employers' Associations in the United States* (New York: Vantage Press, 1956); A. K. Steigerwalt, *The National Association of Manufacturers, 1895–1914: A Study of Business Leadership* (Grand Rapids, Mich.: University of Michigan, 1964), pp. 107–8, 121–28; John B. Andrews, "Nationalisation," in John R. Commons et al., *History of Labour in the United States* (New York: Macmillan, 1918), 2:26–33 et passim.

3. *The State of the Trade* (New York: Francis Hart & Co. 1872), p. 18.

4. Typothetae Collection, 3, p. 1, Columbia University Libraries, Manuscript Division.

5. 1884 Constitution, ibid., XIV.

6. Howard Lockwood, *American Bookmaker* (1885), 1:10.

7. *Printer and Bookmaker* (1897), 25:73.

8. *American Bookmaker* (1888), 7:69, 99, 100.

9. Leaflet dated November 25, 1884, Typothetae Collection, 14.

10. De Vinne, *The State of the Trade*, p. 21; Typothetae Collection, III, p. 46.

11. *American Bookmaker* (1891), 13:154.

12. Theodore Low De Vinne, *Printer's Price List* (New York: Francis Hart & Co., 1869 and 1871); Typothetae Collection, 4:153; S. Paul Garner, *Evolution of Cost Accounting to 1925* (University, Ala.: University of Alabama Press, 1954), pp. 27–90.

13. *Printer and Bookmaker* (1899), 28:158, 214.

14. Charlotte Morgan, *The Origin and History of the Employing Printers' Association* (New York: Columbia University Press, 1930), pp. 89–93.

15. *American Printer* (1902), 34:508; Charles H. Cochrane in *The New York Master Printers' Association, The Makings and Doings of the Association* (New York: The New York Master Printers' Association, 1919), p. 112.

16. Morgan, *Employing Printers' Association*, p. 74.

17. Typothetae Collection, 3:18.

18. Ibid., pp. 36, 38–40.

19. Ibid., p. 58.

20. George Abbott Stevens, *New York Typographical Union No. 6: Study of a Modern Trade Union and Its Predecessors* (Albany: J. B. Lyon, 1913), p. 317.

21. Typothetae Collection, 3:179, 190.

22. George Ernest Barnett, *The Printers: A Study in American Trade Unionism* (Cambridge, Mass., American Economic Association, 1909), p. 376.

23. UTA Proceedings quoted by Elizabeth Faulkner Baker, *Printers and Technology: A History of the International Printing Pressmen and Assistants' Union* (New York: Columbia University Press, 1957), p. 283.

24. Typothetae Collection, 8:72.

25. Charles M. Francis, *Printing for Profit* (New York: Charles Francis Press, 1917), p. 315.

26. Leona M. Powell, *The History of the United Typothetae of America* (Chicago: University of Chicago Press, 1926), p. 193.

27. Letter to TCNY president William Green dated October 16, 1905. Typothetae Collection, 9:179.

28. Powell, *United Typothetae*, p. 13.

8

ORIGINS OF SMALL BUSINESS AND THE RELATIONSHIPS BETWEEN LARGE AND SMALL FIRMS: METAL FABRICATING AND MACHINERY MAKING IN NEW ENGLAND, 1890–1957

James H. Soltow

1

E VER since the appearance of the large corporation on the American scene in the late nineteenth century, the small firm has appeared to many observers as an anachronism. The logic of industrial structure held that "large-scale production, especially when conducted in large-size firms and plants, tends to result in maximum efficiency."[1] Thus, the small business was destined to disappear with the eventual rationalization of the economy.

Yet, small business has persisted in large numbers in America, as in other industrial nations, in the face of a major transformation of economic, social, and political environment. The rate of growth of the business population outside of agriculture has more than kept pace with the increase in human population since 1900.[2] In the same economic setting that encouraged the growth of large corporations, small firms continued to multiply in number. Furthermore, small business continued to occupy an important position in the American system of values as a symbol of opportunity and enterprise.[3]

Whether or not predictions about the disappearance of the small firm are realized at some point in the future, we must view small enterprises not only as "survivals of the past," but, more importantly, as economic units performing specific functions, and as part of the structure through which economic decisions are made in modern industrial societies. The most useful approach is to consider the individual firm as an element of the business system, defined by the late Arthur H. Cole as a network of diverse functional units linked together in mutually advantageous ties.[4] Recognizing that the business system as conceptualized by Cole embraces the totality of the business world or economy, we may conveniently focus on one industry to provide a setting within which to examine the operations of individual firms. One of the most striking features to be observed in an advanced economy like that of the United States is the performance of a set of industrial activities by a collection of firms in a wide range of sizes, making many different specific products, using varied technical processes, and experiencing diverse market conditions.

The existence of different kinds of firms implies different kinds of people who make economic decisions through these firms. Specifically, it is postulated that entrepreneurs in small business form a special group in society, with a set of motivations and behavior patterns not randomly distributed among the population as a whole, or even among men and women in business generally. These individuals seek to play a special entrepreneurial role, one that is different from that performed by executives in corporate bureaucracies. In contrast to the cooperation and teamwork expected of the "organization man" in the large corporation, the small business entrepreneur believes that he has greater scope to act according to a pattern of behavior reflecting traits of "individualism." Such an entrepreneur likes to be able "to make decisions instantly and to carry them out." He closely identifies himself with his enterprise and often derives a "sense of completeness" in seeing the total process by which his ideas are transformed into finished products. The small business entrepreneur takes satisfaction from the very multiplicity of tasks to be performed in the management of his firm.[5]

It is obvious that the type of entrepreneurial role envisaged by such individuals could be satisfactorily performed only within the framework of a small organization, in which the major decisions could be made and carried out by one executive, or, at most, two or three managers working together on the basis of informal, personal association, as opposed to a formal, bureaucratic relationship. If the size of the firm became too large for the owner-manager to make and carry out decisions by himself, the entrepreneur would be faced with a dilemma! He would be operating inefficiently with a pattern of direct management, or he would have to devise a bureaucratic structure of management.

In short, if an entrepreneur wished to play a role within the framework of a small organization congenial to his personal attitudes and goals in life, he would have to adopt a set of objectives that a small firm could achieve. Thus, we would expect to find in the behavior of the small firm and its entrepreneur a different relationship between strategy and structure from that characteristic of the large corporation. As Alfred Chandler has analyzed the experience of the giant enterprise, the strategy of growth, based on awareness by entrepreneurs of opportunities through expansion, required a new structure of administration to carry out operations in an efficient manner. In Chandler's words, "Structure follows strategy."[6] But this formulation may be turned around in developing a hypothesis appropriate to the analysis of the small firm: Among most members of the small-business population, structure, or the organizational form, is an important determinant of strategy, or the kind of activities carried out by the firm.

However, it was not easy for the aspiring small entrepreneur to develop an appropriate strategy which would bring true satisfaction. Traditionally, large numbers of small businessmen have entered what turned out to be for them blind alleys—relatively routine kinds of operations in which low entry requirements in terms of capital, skills, and imagination resulted in extremely limited opportunity even for those who survived the high degree of competition.[7] Some small firms have attempted to operate on the fringes of an industry dominated by an oligopolistic "leading core."[8] Other enterprises have functioned as "satellites," serving as a distributor of the products of one large corporation or as a supplier to a single large customer in a modern version of the putting-out system.[9] At best, owner-managers found little sense of independent entrepreneurship in these situations because of low incomes, instability of operations, and/or sharing with a large firm some of the decision-making functions with respect to pricing and even investment.

There was a type of strategy which entrepreneurs could employ in order to attain some measure of success for a small firm—success defined roughly as ability to stay in business, to earn over a period of time a return on capital beyond a wage for management, and to exercise a degree of independence in decision making. The successful small firm acquired a strong market position as a small firm by adapting to a niche in the market which afforded some degree of isolation from complete and direct competition with other firms, both large and small.[10] On the one hand, it exercised a strategy of size, turning small size into a positive advantage by operating in a segment of industry where the competitive tides ran in favor of smallness of the firm.[11] (We shall see later some of the specific tactics to carry out this strategy.) On the other hand, to provide protection against the direct competition of many other small firms, this type of enterprise developed a basis of product differentiation by providing unique services for customers, and by acquiring a reputation for dependability and reliability. To avoid establishing a dependent relationship, the small company normally sought to spread its sales among as many different customers as possible, preferably to those in different industries. The small firm, however strongly entrenched in its niche, had to be flexible enough to adjust to changes in technology, markets, and industrial structure.[12]

In any economy, only a relatively small number of firms successfully carried out this kind of strategy. At any given time, there existed an objective structure of opportunity, deriving from such forces as the state of technology and science, income levels, population distribution, and the current structure of the industry. Specifically, the opportunity for the small enterprise lay in occupying the interstices, or niches, which developed in the process of industrial growth. But the overall economic situation could be regarded as creating only incentives for entreprenuerial activity. As Glade has suggested, we can distinguish "a structure of differential advantage in the capacity of the system's participants to perceive and act upon such opportunities."[13] What is important then, from the point of view of the individual entrepreneur, is the ability to perceive the nature of the potential opportunity through interpretation of the environment, and to take appropriate action to capitalize on it. As Edith Penrose has observed, "The 'subjective' opportunity is a question of what it [the firm] thinks it can accomplish" in terms of developing a strategy or set of objectives.[14] But the opportunity is also limited by the resources at the entrepreneur's command—not only financial resources but, even more importantly, technical and managerial abilities. As Arthur Cole has stressed, entrepreneurship requires a solid operational base to be effective. Decisions have to be made and carried out along several channels in addition to determining the objectives of the enterprise:

developing an organization, securing adequate financial resources, acquiring efficient equipment, and developing markets.[15]

While analysis of statistical data may indicate some of the general characteristics of a business population, only a study of the histories of individual enterprises can reveal the patterns of strategy and the bases of decisions made by entrepreneurs. How did individuals holding certain generalized goals perceive opportunities, discern problems, and take what they believed to be appropriate action, using the resources at their command? A convenient way to study the development of strategy in the small firm is to focus on a particular set of industrial activities. In the next section, we shall direct attention to the historical experience of small firms producing various types of metal fabrication and machinery.

2

The generalizations that follow are based upon a study of the histories of 80 small companies, fabricators of metals or makers of machinery, located in eastern Massachusetts, and founded at various times during the period from the 1890s to the 1950s. Since few records were available by which to gain an understanding of the nature of entrepreneurship within the small firm, it was necessary to seek data from each company about its origins, policies, and activities. The historical accounts of the individual companies were intended to furnish more than case studies of "small-business problems." Rather, they were compiled to provide empirical data needed to understand the history of small business as an economic and social institution, stressing the role of individual decision making.

Metal working includes all types of industries which use metals as raw materials. Some establishments have specialized on the intermediate stages of processing metals, such as foundry work or stamping, the product of which would be used by other firms making a variety of items. Other establishments have concentrated on the manufacture of specific products, either consumer goods or producer goods. Within these broad categories many sorts of market and product differences have existed, as well as a variety of techniques and processes, thereby providing an abundance of opportunities for different kinds of enterprises. Many metal working firms in New England in the middle of the twentieth century employed the new technology based upon advanced scientific concepts, while others continued to empha-size the older tradition of mechanical skills. But there was considerable in-teraction between these two kinds of technology, as the growth of science-based industries created a need for the application of mechanical skills to produce new types of equipment and components.[16]

SUPPLY OF ENTREPRENEURS

Most of the founders of the companies studied entered independent business in the same, or closely related, field to that in which they had previous expe-rience as employees. Their backgrounds showed a strong technical orienta-tion, particularly among those who were skilled benchworkers or college-trained engineers. Even office employees usually had closely observed the production side of the business in which they worked. Similarly, many of the engineers and skilled workers who became entrepreneurs had gained some knowledge of the office side as the result of managerial or supervisory experience.

In the highly specialized lines of metal working, the technical and busi-ness knowledge required could normally be gained only from the inside of the industry. On the basis of their experience prior to entering independent business, potential entrepreneurs could learn not only what could be pro-duced, from the technical point of view, but also what could be marketed. On the basis of his knowledge of the industry, the entrepreneur could recog-nize the niches in the business world which the small firm could profitably occupy. For example, the general observer might have recognized a trend toward increased use of metal stampings in the 1920s, but the individual with experience in the industry, determined to start his own enterprise, knew what specific kinds of stampings a small firm could produce at a profit, and for what types of customers.

With the increasing complexity of technology and business, formal aca-demic training and managerial experience have become increasingly impor-tant. Although skilled workers continued to enter business for themselves in the mid-twentieth century, as they had in the period prior to World War I, limited education and bench skills were usually no longer adequate. But the higher level of education and more extensive experience which appeared to have become prerequisites for successful operation of a small business did not impose as great a limitation upon freedom of entry as might be expected at first glance. Rising educational levels of the population as a whole, and multiplication of management positions in large corporations, provided a growing proportion of working people with skills and experience.[17] Indeed, it would not be an exaggeration to regard Big Business as an increasingly important training school for potential small entrepreneurs.

Some entrepreneurs looked to the operation of their own enterprises primarily as a path to economic advancement. For men with limited educational backgrounds, like the shop workers, there usually existed little chance to advance beyond the level of foreman in the shop.[18] The only apparent method for the highly skilled individual to maximize his income was to set up his own shop based on his technical abilities. In contrast, college-trained engineers entering independent business from the 1920s on usually made this choice as an alternative to seeking advancement through a career in a large corporation. These enterprisers found the role of business bureaucrat, at whatever level they might have worked in the bureaucracy, an unsatisfactory one for them to play, even when they held reasonably remunerative positions. They often expressed a dislike for what they regarded as the tactics necessary to advance within a business bureaucracy (''office politics''), a sense of violation of one's own moral and technical code contained in certain corporate policies, or lack of interest on the part of superiors in ''doing new things in new ways.'' Many had careers marked by a considerable amount of job mobility, as they searched for opportunities that they believed to be suitable to their training and temperament. In short, they were men who would not accept the limitations imposed upon their individualism by employment.

While ambition to become an independent businessman provided strong motivation, the new entrepreneur had to carry out his enterprise within the context of the overall economic situation existing at a given time. Hopes and desires alone would not create a firm. Most entrepreneurs launched their firms with some objectives, typically attempting to fill a need in the business world before that need had become widely recognized. On the basis of their experience in industry, some founders had developed definite ideas about new products or substantial improvements in existing ones, ranging from a machine to sharpen saw blades (invented in 1904) to novel types of microwave equipment (conceived in 1955). One entrepreneur introduced a unique metal-finishing process into New England in the 1920s, when he obtained exclusive regional rights from the patent holder. Other founders envisaged novel types of service which they might offer, such as designing a system of specialized equipment for industrial users; or they sought opportunities in industries where problems involving application of new techniques remained to be solved.

FINANCING NEW ENTERPRISE

Perhaps no question has been so thoroughly debated with less conclusive and generally accepted answers than the "adequacy" of capital for small business.[19] Yet one point is clear: small firms have not obtained investment funds in the same way as large, well-known corporations. Special considerations, both economic and noneconomic, shaped the financial policies of small businessmen. In the first place, the cost of making a public offering of a small issue of stock through organized security markets was prohibitive. Furthermore, owners of small enterprises have usually been reluctant to share ownership, and possibly control, with outside investors. It might be true, as some writers have suggested, that the entrepreneurs in small business should more actively seek equity financing and that he "should take courage in the knowledge that risk capital is being bet on him."[20] However, the originator of a small business typically put into his enterprise not only all of his financial resources, but much personal effort as well, in his determination to become an independent businessman. He regarded as unfair the ability of outsiders to reap some of the fruits of his labor when they offered to back him financially only after his ideas had begun to show promise, for few investors would make commitments of capital on untried ideas of newborn enterprises.[21] At best, it would be difficult to reconcile the divergent goals of managers, seeking independence in a business of their own, and outside financiers, aiming for a high return on investment.

Personal savings of the original entrepreneur, sometimes supplemented with funds from relatives and friends, provided most of the initial capital of new enterprises. On the basis of the data about the New England metal working firms, it would be difficult to draw meaningful conclusions about trends in minimum amounts of capital required to enter independent business. Throughout the period since 1890, the amount of investment at the start appeared to depend less upon conceptions of minimum capital requirements than upon the amount of funds possessed by the founder at the time of entry.

In view of the emphasis placed upon "independence," it is not surprising that the keystone to financial policy was reinvestment of company earnings.

Even firms begun with relatively small amounts of original capital, if they proved to be unusually successful, could rely to a considerable extent upon corporate savings to finance growth. Reputation in the business community, gained through previous experience as a salaried manager, was a key factor in obtaining bank financing and in establishing credit with suppliers. Dollars secured through bank loans and materials acquired on credit released funds already held by entrepreneurs to be invested in fixed assets. In furnishing working capital, it could be said that "outsiders" made significant investments in small manufacturing firms. Resourcefulness of entrepreneurs could be considered as a capital asset. Need for funds could be minimized, particularly in the crucial early stages, by adapting machinery, converting to their purposes low-cost plant facilities, using unpaid or underpaid family labor, and keeping cash withdrawals for personal expenses at a minimum.

Penrose has drawn attention to the relationship between the financial resources that a firm can attract and the "very particular and possibly very rare sort of entrepreneurial ability [that] is required to launch successfully a new firm on a shoestring." She maintains that "difficulties attributed to lack of capital may often be just as well attributed to a lack of appropriate entrepreneurial services."[22] There is much in the financial histories of the Massachusetts metal-working firms to support these observations. Thus, the question of the "adequacy of small business financing" may well turn on the adequacy of individual small businessmen in tapping sources of funds and then making the best use of those available to them.

OWNERSHIP AND MANAGEMENT

The corporation was the characteristic form of legal organization among our group of New England metal-working companies. Most firms incorporated at the time of origin or in the early years of operation. But these corporations did not resemble the "modern corporation" analyzed by Berle and Means. Rather, small manufacturing enterprises preserved a close identity of ownership and management. In actual operation, they were similar to proprietorships, or partnerships, in spite of their use of the corporate form. Indeed, lenders often required the principal owners of small corporations to pledge personal property as collateral for short-term loans, regardless of the condition of the corporate balance sheet.

Direct management was typical in these companies, in contrast to the hierarchy of managers found in the large corporation. Yet owners of small enterprises met the problems of administration in a number of specific ways. In firms started by men who assumed all managerial responsibilities, at least in the initial stages, versatility was a basic requirement. Some companies followed the traditional pattern of the family as the unit in business, with brothers, brothers-in-law, cousins, or even husband and wife, dividing the responsibilities of administration. Managerial groupings dependent upon family relationships usually relied on chance to assemble individuals with complementary talents. Thus, some entrepreneurs whose ability lay on one side of the business consciously selected a partner or partners whose experience and skills would complement their own. Such an arrangement might intentionally include men with different temperaments as well as different talents, so that neither excessive optimism nor overcaution would unduly influence the firm's decision making. But experience sometimes illustrated the old adage that "there is no way for two people to be equal partners in any business" when basic disagreements on policy developed between partners.

Personal considerations played a major role in decisions by entrepreneurs about the location of their new enterprises. Because all of the founders were residents of New England and desired to remain in the area, there was little chance that any would have begun operations outside the region. The original entrepreneur appeared sometimes to make his decision about where to plant his firm on the basis of "preference for 'consumer location,' that is, where he would like to live." But he did not ignore "the question of 'producer location,' that is, the best place to earn a living." [23] On the basis of previous experience in the industry in which he entered independent business, the potential entrepreneur had a fairly clear idea of what kind of business might succeed in the New England economic environment. In contrast to most theory, which assumes that the entrepreneur decides first what to produce and then the most economical location, the sequence of decision making in practice could be stated in this way: (1) Locate in New England, or more specifically a community in eastern Massachusetts ("consumer location preference") and (2) then determine what products could be manufactured in the area with the capital (human and money) at his command.

In recruiting and dealing with production workers, small manufacturers employed a paternalistic approach, stressing the importance of personal relationships and fostering what they sometimes called "a family atmosphere" in their plants. To diminish the potential advantage that workers might derive from unions, employers provided wages and other economic benefits comparable to those received by labor in unionized plants. For these reasons, as well as the expense to unions of organizing small plants, few of the metal-fabricating companies had to engage in collective bargaining with representatives of organized labor. In seeking to discourage unionization of their work forces, owners were primarily concerned about potential union interference with their managerial prerogatives in directing their work forces, which they believed would limit their flexibility of operations. In labor relations, as in financial policy and other areas of decision making, entrepreneurs emphasized ''independence.''

In organizing productive facilities, entrepreneurs normally preferred to lease or purchase an available existing building, which might require renovation, rather than construct a new special-purpose structure. Similarly, they usually started business with used machinery or equipment which they improvised. Technical knowledge enabled them to adapt low-cost plant space and equipment to their specialized needs so as to minimize capital outlays. Cost data are lacking, but owners of companies housed in older buildings and using machinery purchased on the secondhand market might argue that any increase in operating and maintenance costs resulting from such practices would have been offset by lower fixed costs.[24]

THE SMALL FIRM AND THE MARKET

Regardless of the ingenuity which small manufacturers might apply to their financial and production problems, their efforts would come to little unless they considered carefully their product and marketing policies. Defining product lines, securing customers, establishing channels of distribution, and determining prices were all crucial matters for the new enterprise. For a small manufacturing enterprise to succeed, the entrepreneur had to make the key decisions about the kinds of goods and services to be offered, and the clientele to be served, within the framework outlined earlier—the adoption of a strategy of size to avoid direct competition with large corporations and the establishment of product differentiation to minimize potential competition of other small firms.

One tactic to carry out the strategy of size in the metal-working industries was to specialize in the manufacture of products with a limited total demand. The large corporation, oriented to mass production and mass distribution, was not likely to enter such fields; but a small enterprise could produce and market such items profitably. Among metal-working firms, the following illustrate producers of specialty items, each of which was among only a few sellers in its specific national market: (1) metal-core plugs for uses in the tar-paper, floor-covering, and newsprint industries, produced in a stamping plant employing 40 workers; (2) a special type of screen plate for paper mills, made by a company with 30 employees; (3) miners'-cap lamps, turned out in a plant with about 40 workers; (4) a specialized air valve produced by a firm with 15 employees. A complete list would be a long one, ranging from electronic clips to ships' clocks.[25]

Other companies, in employing a strategy of size, specialized on a specific process. These included such varied operations as machine shops, sheet-metal fabrication, screw-machine products, metal stamping, structural-steel fabrication, electroplating, heat treating, and metal finishing. These establishments normally served local or regional markets, primarily because of the need for maintenance of close relations between producer and customer during the fabricating process. Much of the custom work, done to the order of individual customers, involved nonstandardized design for special applications and special attributes of quality. Again, this was not a fruitful field of operations for the large corporation, with its mass-production and mass-distribution facilities.

By utilizing a strategy of size, small manufacturers in metal working were able to protect one flank by entering fields where they did not engage in "head-to-head" competition with big business. Successful adaptation to a niche which afforded a strong market position required, in addition, that the firm "do something different" from what could be done by other hopeful entrants into business with a small amounts of capital. If owners of small companies wanted to advance beyond merely routine operations, which might be pushed to the wall at any time in the competitive jungle characterizing many industries composed of small firms, they had to adopt a policy that encouraged product differentiation. For the small metal-working firm selling to well-informed and price-conscious industrial buyers, differentiation had to be based on special services to customers, reputation for dependability and reliability, and personal sales representation.

In providing service, the small manufacturer applied his detailed knowledge of sources of materials and parts and of production, designing, and scheduling to meet the unique needs of particular customers, often taking on the kind of work regarded by the run-of-the-mill producer as "too difficult.'' Sometimes, just being a person that people liked to do business with was a significant, if intangible, competitive factor. The seller's way of doing business, his reputation for fair dealing, courtesy, efficiency, and all the personal links attaching his customers to himself, were taken into account by buyers.[26]

On the basis of their previous experience, new entrepreneurs usually determined the segment of metal working in which they could gain a foothold, given the resources which they had at their command at the time of entry. With their background in industry, owners of new enterprises had a fairly clear idea of potential markets, customers, and often even the individuals in charge of purchasing the products they had to sell. A reputation in the industry, derived from experience as a salaried manager, also helped the new entrepreneur to obtain initial orders from customers who were as concerned about quality and ability to deliver as about a quoted price. Most companies, even when they had passed beyond the initial stage, continued to rely upon the efforts of owners to handle sales. In an enterprise which emphasized service and attention to the special needs of customers, the decision about the profitability of a particular order was a crucial one that could not be delegated to a salesman. The chief executive in a small firm, as the only man with knowledge of all aspects of company operations, had to determine the ability of his plant to produce what was required by the potential customer. Although many manufacturers necessarily relied upon one or two customers when they started operations, they moved to spread their sales among more clients as they enlarged production, because of the risks of such dependence. Most obvious was the danger of a change in the customer's policy, such as to ''pull in'' to its own plant work previously contracted out, but there was also the problem of economic pressure applied by a large firm which dominated a small company's sales.

No enterprise could afford to rest entirely upon its past achievements to maintain its market position. Even the firm strongly entrenched in its niche, based upon specialization in products or services, could find its position threatened by external circumstances such as changes in technology, markets, or industrial structure. The entrepreneur alert to the trend of developments began to develop a new set of objectives while his firm still possessed the ability to make a transition. He usually built upon the base of specialization in which his enterprise had acquired a special competence through experience. For most metal-working companies, the technological base—or the possession of a special competence involving machines, processes, skills, and raw materials—was the significant factor determining the direction in which the firm would grow.

3

A British economist has observed that "paradoxical as it may seem, though America is thought of as the home of 'big business,' it is also in a sense the home of 'small business.' "[27] The experience of metal fabricating in New England suggests some of the factors accounting for the persistence of a numerous small-firm sector and indeed the vigor of a segment of it.

Although many aspects of modern economic life have encouraged a trend toward bigness and "rationalization," an increase in the diversification of intermediate and final products associated with economic growth has favored industrial differentiation.[28] Within the intricate nexus of economic activities reflecting a complex division of labor among firms of varying size, entrepreneurs sought to adapt to niches in which small enterprises could carry on efficient and profitable operations.

Yet, the structure of division of labor by firm cannot be taken as given, since it may vary considerably even among advanced economies, the structure influenced in different ways by varying economic and sociocultural factors. As long ago as the 1890s, observers pointed out that the division of labor by firm was considerably more extended in American than in European industry.[29] This "lag" in specialization in Europe, as compared to the United States, appears to have persisted beyond the middle of the twentieth century. For example, a study of metal fabricating in Belgium, carried out in the 1960s, showed that small firms were more vertically integrated than similar companies in the United States. Small enterprises specializing in particular final products normally produced most of the components which they required, in contrast to American product specialists of this size, which concentrated on final assembly and contracted the manufacture of parts to process specialists, many of which were themselves small firms. Maintenance by product specialists of their own facilities to make components discouraged the organization of firms specializing in specific processes, which might have achieved some measure of success, as in the United States, by applying their functional skills to the solution of problems common to the manufacturers—both large and small—of a wide range of finished products.[30]

If the extent of the market is the principal economic force determining the division of labor,[31] the large size of the American economy is the most obvious explanation of the more extensive specialization found in the United States. But social and cultural factors also contributed to differences. Since the nineteenth century, American industrialists have assigned a higher value to efficiency than have their European counterparts, who have continued to emphasize "prowess," or pride in the process of manufacturing an article from start to finish.[32]

Regardless of the weight which one may attach to any specific set of factors in accounting for the extent of division of labor by firm in U.S. industry, the existence of a network of process specialists made it possible for product specialists to concentrate their resources on developing facilities for final assembly and on marketing, at the same time having access to the services of experts in the machining, stamping, cutting, and shaping of metals. Similarly, the existence of such a body of product specialists constituted an encouragement for process specialists in many narrowly defined lines in an industry like metal working.

As we indicated earlier, the objective structure of opportunity at any given time only created incentives for entrepreneurial action. Ability to perceive and to act upon opportunities in the economic environment was not evenly distributed in the population. Entry into independent business involved the investment not only of money capital, but even more importantly, of human capital—technical skills and business capability to determine objectives and to perform the many other tasks of entrepreneurship. Ingenuity was also a necessary characteristic, as the new entrepreneur had to be resourceful to devise expedients to meet problems that had no textbook solution. Finally, an essential ingredient in establishing a new firm was persistence in what some have called "getting through the knothole," the first few years of long hours, low monetary returns, and often discouraging circumstances. These were the "qualified" individuals who took advantage of the opportunities for small enterprise in the framework of the metal-fabricating industry of twentieth-century America.

Notes

1. P. Sargant Florence, *The Logic of British and American Industry: A Realistic Analysis of Economic Structure and Government* (Chapel Hill: University of North Carolina Press, 1953), p. 48.

2. Figures on numbers of firms are notoriously inexact, but the trends are clear. See the series on "total business enterprises," number of firms in operation," and "total concerns in business" in U.S., Bureau of the Census, *Historical Statistics of the United States, Colonial Times to 1970* (Washington, D.C.: G.P.O., 1975), pp. 911–13, and the explanation of coverage, pp. 908–9.

3. See Kurt Mayer, "Small Business as a Social Institution."

4. Arthur H. Cole, "Meso-Economics: A Contribution from Entrepreneurial History"; "Aggregative Business History," *Business History Review* (Autumn 1965), 39:287–300.

5. James H. Soltow, *Origins of Small Business: Metal Fabricators and Machinery Makers in New England, 1890–1957* and Orvis F. Collins and David G. Moore, *The Enterprising Man.*

6. Alfred D. Chandler, Jr., *Strategy and Structure: Chapters in the History of the Industrial Enterprise* (Cambridge, Mass.: M.I.T. Press, 1962), p. 14.

7. See Kurt B. Mayer and Sidney Goldstein, *The First Two Years: Problems of Small Firm Growth and Survival;* Mabel Newcomer, "The Little Businessman: A Study of Business Proprietors in Poughkeepsie, New York"; and Joseph D. Phillips, *Little Business in the American Economy.*

8. Harold G. Vatter, *Small Enterprise and Oligopoly: A Study of the Butter, Flour, Automobile, and Glass Container Industries,* observes that in these kinds of industries "small enterprise is often dependent enterprise, i.e., it surrenders part of its power to make independent decisions to large concerns, some of which may be its competitors" (pp. 110–11). For example, leading manufacturers of glass containers controlled entry by means of patents on equipment and containers but allowed a number of small concerns to exist as long as the latter followed price and output policies determined by the leaders. As one executive stated in the 1920s, "There is . . . the question as to what is to be done with the outsiders when dominated. How many shall be allowed to survive and at what price?" (p. 88).

9. A spokesman for Sears, Roebuck & Company summarized policy toward small suppliers in 1947: "Our concern is not with 'How much does a manufacturer make on his production for us?' but 'What does he do with those profits?' We feel that adequate sums should be plowed back into the business. . . . As a matter of fact, in all our important lines we require such a research program, with an agreed sum of money appropriated, the character of the research problems agreed upon, and the problem paid out of a definite apportionment of the unit price." Boris Emmet and J. E. Jeuck, *Catalogues and Counters: A History of Sears, Roebuck and Company* (Chicago: University of Chicago Press, 1950), p. 402.

10. See Richard B. Heflebower, "Toward a Theory of Industrial Markets and Prices," for a valuable theoretical analysis of niches in markets.

11. W. Arnold Hosmer, "Small Manufacturing Enterprises," elaborates a concept of strategy of size.

12. Howard F. Bennett, *Precision Power: The First Half Century of Bodine Electric Company,* shows the ways by which a small company retained over a long period of time a strong market position by consistently adapting to changing technology and industrial structure. By contrast, Theodore F. Marburg, *Small Business in Brass Fabricating: The Smith & Griggs Manufacturing Company of Waterbury,* illustrates how failure to adapt resulted in deterioration of market position and ultimate demise of the firm.

13. William P. Glade, "Approaches to a Theory of Entrepreneurial Formation," suggests the use of a type of bi-level situational analysis to formulate hypotheses about entrepreneurship.

14. Edith T. Penrose, *The Theory of the Growth of the Firm,* pp. 41–42.

15. Arthur H. Cole, "An Approach to the Study of Entrepreneurship: A Tribute to Edwin F. Gay."

16. Various aspects of the history of New England industry, especially metal working and machinery making, are discussed in the following: National Planning Association, Committee of New England, *The Economic State of New England* (New Haven: Yale University Press, 1954); Arthur D. Little, Inc., *Report on a Survey of Industrial Opportunities in New England* (Cambridge, Mass.: Arthur D. Little, Inc., 1952); Seymour Harris, *The Economics of New England: Case Study of an Older Area* (Cambridge: Harvard University Press, 1952); Charles E. Artman, *Industrial Structure of New England* (Part I of the Commercial Survey of New England; Domestic Commerce Series, No. 28) (Washington, D.C.: G.P.O., 1930); Martha V. Taber, *A History of the Cutlery Industry in the Connecticut Valley* (Smith College Studies in History, vol. 41) (Northampton, Mass.: Department of History, Smith College, 1955); George S. Gibb, *The Saco-Lowell Shops: Textile Machinery Building in New England, 1813–1949* (Cambridge: Harvard University Press, 1950); Thomas R. Navin, *The Whitin Machine Works Since 1831: A Textile Machinery Company in an Industrial Village* (Cambridge: Harvard University Press, 1950); Charles W. Moore, *Timing a Century: A History of the Waltham Watch Company* (Cambridge: Harvard University Press, 1945).

17. In 1890, only 1.3 percent of the population in the appropriate age group graduated from college, compared to 18.7 percent in 1950. These percentages were developed by dividing the number of college graduates into one-fifth of the total population, age 20–24. Based on data in U.S., Bureau of the Census, *Historical Statistics of the United States, Colonial Times to 1957,* p. 10, and *Statistical Abstract of the United States: 1955,* p. 123.

18. See John S. Ellsworth, Jr., *Factory Folkways: A Study of Institutional Structure and Change* (New Haven: Yale University Press, 1952). In his study of a New England factory, Ellsworth points out: "On paper the organization charts look like a simple promotional ladder, with workers at the bottom, foremen on the next step, assistants to managers on the next, and so on up. In practice this works only in exceptional cases. . . . The worker who could start at the bottom and work up would be a remarkable exception. He might go as far as foreman but probably no further, and there are intimations that even this modest rise is coming to require more than mere plant training and experience" (pp. 151–52).

19. Two studies made by specialists in the late 1950s reaċhed these respective conclusions: (1) "A review of financing facilities available to small business leads to the conclusion that they are inadequate"; (2) "Financing appears to have been adequate for the sector as a whole [i.e., small business] in the postwar period"—Federal Reserve System, *Financing Small Business.*

20. Paul Donham and Clifford L. Fitzgerald, Jr., "More Reason in Small Business Financing," *Harvard Business Review* (July–Aug. 1959), 37:96.

21. A Boston investment banker with an interest in small business pointed out to this writer that he and other investors like himself followed a policy of supplying only "second money" to small enterprises, in effect forcing the original entrepreneur to use his own resources to finance the discovery of any mistakes.

22. Penrose, *Growth of the Firm*, pp. 38–39.

23. Edgar M. Hoover, *The Location of Economic Activity* (New York: McGraw-Hill, 1948), p. 4.

24. The owner of a metal-fabricating firm argued that a company could "tax itself out of business by erecting fancy buildings" because of increased real-estate-tax assessments.

25. Patrick G. Porter and Harold C. Livesay, "Oligopoly in Small Manufacturing Industries," argue that concentration in small industries (those with total product value of less than $100 million annually) typically occurs in "survivors from the nineteenth century," activities "closely related to the older, agrarian-based economy of the nineteenth century." Their observation that "very few of the small oligopolies in this century are in new industries" may be correct in terms of their use of the census definition of "industry." However, the product lines for segmented markets, to which we have referred here, do not coincide with the concept of industry as applied by the census and used by Porter and Livesay. Heflebower comments that "markets for most products (broadly conceived) tend to settle into segments among which there are varying degrees of elasticity of substitution and of intersegment mobility"—"Industrial Markets and Prices," p. 123. Whether particular articles are the products of "old" or "new" industries may not be entirely relevant, as we stressed earlier the importance of interaction between the older set of activities based on mechanical skills and the newer science-based sector in New England metal fabricating and machinery making.

26. Hosmer, "Small Manufacturing Enterprises," p. 121. A survey of purchasing practices of large corporations, made in 1959, concluded with this rule for sellers in industrial markets: "Make the buyer feel important. Assure him that you appreciate his business. Don't take him for granted. He expects *personal attention*"—"How to Use Emotional Factors That Trigger Industrial Sales," *Steel: The Metalworking Weekly*, April 6, 1959. But such practices are as old as American manufacuring industry. Theodore F. Marburg points to the importance of personal sales representation in establishing product differentiation in the brass industry in the 1830s. "Historical Aspects of Imperfect Competition: In Brass Manufacturing During the 1830s," *Tasks of Economic History*, Supplemental Issue of the *Journal of Economic History* (Dec. 1943), 3:36.

27. S. J. Prais, *The Evolution of Giant Firms in Britain: A Study of the Growth of Concentration in Manufacturing Industry in Britain, 1909–1970* (Cambridge: Cambridge University Press, 1976), pp. 143–44. Prais, in contrasting the organization of manufacturing in the U.K. and the U.S., has made these observations: (1) that "America has relatively more large and more small enterprises, but fewer middle-sized enterprises than Britain"; and (2) that enterprises with under 100 employees accounted for a larger proportion of total manufacturing employment in the U.S. than in the U.K.

28. Allyn A. Young, "Increasing Returns and Economic Progress"; Edward Ames and Nathan Rosenberg, "The Progressive Division and Specialization of Industries."

29. See Joseph A. Litterer, "Systematic Management: The Search for Order and Integration," *Business History Review* (Winter 1961) 35:461–76, who cites contemporary observers, especially H. F. L. Orcutt, "Machine Shop Management in Europe and America. I. Specialization

vs. Generalization of Equipment and Product," *Engineering Magazine* (January 1899), vol. 16.

30. James H. Soltow, "Entrepreneurial Strategy in Small Industry: Belgian Metal Fabricators."

31. George J. Stigler, "The Division of Labor Is Limited by the Extent of the Market," pp. 185–93.

32. See Jesse R. Pitts, "Continuity and Change in Bourgeois France," *In Search of France,* Stanley Hoffman, ed. (Cambridge: Harvard University Press, 1963), pp. 235–304. Pitts argues that "specialization implies the necessity of focusing on a limited area of problem-solving," which is perceived to be contrary to the "belief in a man's capacity for top performance in any area he may choose" (p. 43).

Selected Bibliography

Ames, Edward and Nathan Rosenberg. "The Progressive Division and Specialization of Industries." Lance Davis and J. R. T. Hughes, eds., *Purdue Faculty Papers in Economic History, 1956–1966.* Homewood, Ill.: Irwin, 1967.

Bennett, Howard F. *Precision Power: The First Half Century of Bodine Electric Company.* New York: Appleton-Century-Crofts, 1959.

Cole, Arthur H. "An Approach to the Study of Entrepreneurship: A Tribute to Edwin F. Gay," *Journal of Economic History,* Supplement 6 (1946), pp. 1–15.

——. "Meso-Economics: A Contribution from Entrepreneurial History." *Explorations in Entrepreneurial History,* 2d ser. (Fall 1968) 6:3–33.

Collins, Orvis F. and David G. Moore. *The Enterprising Man.* East Lansing: Bureau of Business and Economic Research, Graduate School of Business Administration, Michigan State University, 1964.

Federal Reserve System. *Financing Small Business.* Report to the Committees on Banking and Currency and the Select Committees on Small Business, U.S. Congress, 85th Cong., 2d Sess., 1958.

Glade, William P. "Approaches to a Theory of Entrepreneurial Formation." *Explorations in Entrepreneurial History,* 2d ser. (Spring/Summer 1967), 4:245–59.

Heflebower, Richard B. "Toward a Theory of Industrial Markets and Prices." *American Economic Review: Papers and Proceedings* (1954), 44:121–39.

Hosmer, W. Arnold. "Small Manufacturing Enterprises." *Harvard Business Review,* (Nov.–Dec., 1957), 35:111–22.

Marburg, Theodore F. *Small Business in Brass Fabricating: The Smith & Griggs Manufacturing Company of Waterbury.* New York: New York University Press, 1956.

Mayer, Kurt. "Small Business as a Social Institution." *Social Research* (1947), 14:332–49.

Mayer, Kurt and Sidney Goldstein. *The First Two Years: Problems of Small Firm Growth and Survival.* Washington, D.C.: Small Business Administration, 1961.

Newcomer, Mabel. "The Little Businessman: A Study of Business Proprietors in Poughkeepsie, New York." *Business History Review,* (Winter 1961), 35:477–531.

Penrose, Edith T. *The Theory of the Growth of the Firm.* New York: Wiley, 1959.

Phillips, Joseph D. *Little Business in the American Economy*. Urbana: University of Illinois Press, 1958.

Porter, Patrick G. and Harold C. Livesay. "Oligopoly in Small Manufacturing Industries." *Explorations in Economic History* (Spring 1970), 7:371–79.

Soltow, James H. *Origins of Small Business: Metal Fabricators and Machinery Makers in New England, 1890–1957*. (Philadelphia: American Philosophical Society, 1965).

——. "Entrepreneurial Strategy in Small Industry: Belgian Metal Fabricators." *Proceedings of the American Philosophical Society*, (1971), 115:32–64.

Stigler, George J. "The Division of Labor is Limited by the Extent of the Market." *Journal of Political Economy* (1951), 59:185–93.

Vatter, Harold G. *Small Enterprise and Oligopoly: A Study of the Butter, Flour, Automobile, and Glass Container Industries*. Corvallis: Oregon State University Press, 1955.

Young, Allyn A. "Increasing Returns and Economic Progress." *Economic Journal* (1928), 38:527–42.

9

THE EFFECTS OF INDUSTRIALIZATION ON SMALL RETAILING IN THE UNITED STATES IN THE TWENTIETH CENTURY

Stanley C. Hollander

APPROXIMATELY three-quarters of the way through the twentieth century, the retail trade remains a haven for small business in the United States. The U.S. Census of Retail Trade, unfortunately for our purposes, tells us more about retail *establishments*—that is, individual stores and selling units—than about *firms*. But according to the latest available census, about 620,000 establishments, or more than one-third of the 1.7 million that operated for the full year 1972, reported having no paid employees on the enumeration date. (550,000 of these reported no payroll for the entire year.) Another 660,000 had only from one to five paid employees.[1] An indeterminate number of these low-employment establishments were actually components of larger organizations, as will be discussed later. Moreover, 62,000 of the zero-employment group and 125,000 of the one-to-five-employee establishments were eating and drinking places, which are included in the U.S. retail census but are counted outside that trade in many other countries. Nevertheless, even after adjusting for both of these factors, the remaining number of fragmentary, small retail businesses must be quite impressive. Or, looking at the sector in another way, the fifty largest retailing *firms* accounted for slightly less than nineteen percent of all U.S. retail trade in 1972.[2] Yet the large enterprises increased their market share at least up to 1972, and probably also since then.

BIG AND SMALL RETAILING

At any one moment, small retailers may see their problems as clustering around weaknesses in consumer demand; difficulties in obtaining goods, financing, or labor; or the irritations of government regulation (something they very much dislike in the abstract and *in toto,* but which they often favor on specific issues). In a sense, the ultimate limitation on small retailing arises from the facts of consumer demand, since that determines the total amount of business available to both large and small traders.[3] In another sense, the major problem of small retailing is the market share accruing to nonsmall firms. (Of course, individual small retailers often gain by acting as satellites to large ones.)

The history of big retailing in the United States needs little rehearsal. The three major forms of large-scale enterprise—that is, the mail-order houses, the department stores, and the chain stores—emerged in the second half of the nineteenth century. Both the mail houses and the department stores seemed to have adopted some chain-store characteristics between World Wars I and II in order to grow or to maintain position.

The two major general-merchandise mail-order companies began retail-store operations in the mid-1920s. By 1931, Sears, Roebuck and Company, the larger of the two, received more than half of its total sales volume from its stores.[4] The store-to-catalog-sales volume ratios continued on an upward trend for both firms until a very recent resurgence of catalog business.[5] The recent growth of catalog sales has been attributed to an increase in the number of working wives, with concomitant reduced shopping time, to desires to reduce automobile travel, and to the fact that in an inflationary period, catalog price increases often lag behind price changes in the stores.

The traditional downtown department stores began to lose market position in the 1920s because of centrifugal development of cities and the rise of chain-store competition.[6] Part of the department-store response was the merger of individual stores into what were called "ownership groups"—that is, highly decentralized chains, such as Federated Department Stores, Associated Dry Goods Company. The individual stores typically retained their traditional names, sometimes continued under the founding family's supervision, and enjoyed considerable autonomy in daily operations. The parent or corporate headquarters, however, provided increasing amounts of central direction and budgetary control, improved access to financing, encouraged some joint merchandising, and provided some common services. The merger movement, which continued after World War II, has by now left few major department stores outside of the ownership groups. Moreover, during the last thirty years, the individual store managements, whether independent or part of groups, have opened numerous suburban branches. Today, traditional department stores obtain about three-fourths of their sales from the branches, rather than from the downtown so-called flagship stores. Some branches are now located far from the store's original trading area.

Since the 1940s, the major changes in large-scale retailing have been extensions of chain-store principles. These have included the absorption of supermarket techniques by the food chains; the spectacular rise of self-service discount-department-store chains; attempts (with only mixed results so far) to apply mass-merchandising techniques to the sale of household goods through such institutions as furniture warehouses and catalog-appliance showrooms; and the rise of "retail conglomerates." The conglomerates, a phenomenon not yet adequately studied, maintain traditional lines of demarcation at the establishment level, but combine chains of different types at the firm level. For example, the Dayton-Hudson Corporation operates chains of traditional department stores, self-service discount department stores, bookstores, and specialty jewelry stores. Probably at least one-third of the largest retail firms are now engaged in two or more "types" of business.[7] Two researchers have very tentatively concluded that, after balancing the successes against the failures, the retail conglomerates have enjoyed above-average profits in recent years.[8] But little information has been gathered so far on either the internal operating aspects of retail-conglomerate management or on the movement's implications for the broader economy.

Two other important retailing developments, the growth of voluntary and cooperative chains, and the growth of franchising, have been favorable to small (or medium-sized) retailing and will be discussed later in this essay. However, any attempt to appraise the impact of industrialization on these, or on more atomistic, forms of small retailing will encounter some of the problems outlined in the next section. These problems are: (1) deficiencies in the data; (2) definitional difficulties; and (3) the indirect nature of the relationships between industrialization and retailing.

THREE PROBLEMS

DATA DEFICIENCIES

As the other essays in this volume will undoubtedly point out, collecting information about small firms is difficult in any case, regardless of industry or country. But a small retail enterprise is easier to overlook than, say, a small bank or a small railroad. And the retail trades do contain many truly tiny entities.

The first U.S. Census of Retail Trade was not conducted until 1929. It has since been repeated, expanded, and presumably refined at (generally) five-year intervals. Yet serious doubts exist as to whether the censuses, at least pre-1972, really captured the total number of small retail firms. Contrary to informed opinions and commercial sample surveys, the 1972 census showed an increase of about 150,000 retail establishments over 1967 instead of an expected decline. The unexpected extra numbers have been attributed to two factors: (1) failure to raise the dollar threshold (sales at a rate of $2,500 per annum) for inclusion in the census count, in spite of declines in the value of the dollar; and (2) new enumeration methods. The first factor admitted more marginal and part-time firms to the count; the second factor located many previously missed small businesses.[9] Pre-1972 comparisons of census counts with local tax and land-use records also suggested gaps in the enumerations.[10] Obviously, the omissions and the enumeration problems have clustered at the small-enterprise end of the spectrum.

DEFINITIONAL PROBLEMS

We have already noted one of the difficulties of defining retailing—that is, whether to include eating and drinking places. Similarly, farm supply, farm machinery, and plumbing–air-conditioning outlets, which had previously been counted as part of the retail trade were logically reclassified into the wholesale sector in 1972.

The concept of an "establishment" works quite well in the normal case of a store that has obvious, discrete physical boundaries, and in which all departments are operated by the same proprietor, partnership, or corporation. It fits some other common retailing situations less comfortably. For example, about one percent of all retail dollar sales are made by personal solicitation at the customer's residence, place of work, or similar location. Many house-to-house canvassing, party plan, wagon route, and other such direct selling companies, establish their solicitors as independent agents, rather than as employees, for legal, taxation, and insurance purposes. The census then defines each such "independent" agent as a separate establishment, even though many of them may be directed from a common central office. The distinction is not trivial for our purposes, since it may add between 50,000 to 100,000 small "establishments" to the retail roster. The decision as to whether a separate establishment is counted when a concessionaire operates a specific retail department, or unit, within a larger retail, or nonretail, enterprise varies with both the facts of the situation and the source of the Census Bureau's information about the concession.[11]

Defining "small" and "large" is even more puzzling. The zero and few-employee businesses (those that operate only a single small establishment of the sort mentioned in the introduction to this essay) clearly fall into the category that Phillips calls "little business."[12] The owners wait on customers and otherwise perform, rather than supervise, the work of the store; they normally lack substantial power in either buying or selling markets except perhaps for a very circumscribed locational monopoly; they are unlikely to join any trade or business organization; and their main goal must be survival rather than expansion. The bigger, yet nongiant, firms are more difficult to classify. Their owners often maintain a very comfortable life-style, and, particularly in the smaller cities, may well become leaders in civic, social, philanthropic, religious, or cultural groups. They can have considerable local influence even though they may fall short of the pinnacle of the power elite. Although actual or potential direct-communication lines may exist between the owners or top executives and practically every employee, the businesses may become bureaucratized and systematized miniatures of the giant corporations.

Yet those same middle-sized retailers may be individually quite powerless in their supply markets. To cite an extreme example, each of the fifty largest automobile dealers in the United States had sales in excess of $25 million in 1972. Yet, collectively, they only accounted for about four percent of all new-car dealer sales that year.[13] Automobile manufacturers obtain revenues from many sources besides domestic new-car dealers. It is apparent, therefore, that no one of these dealers, no matter how influential in his own community, could significantly influence the fortunes of a large automobile manufacturer.

LIMITED INDUSTRIALIZATION OF RETAILING

We must agree with McNair and May's comment that technology has had only minor direct influence on retail structure.[14] In comparison to mining, agriculture, and many forms of manufacturing, retailing has undergone little industrialization, in the sense of mechanization, during the twentieth century. Reductions in labor-intensity came primarily through transfer of functions to consumers (self-service). Increases in capital investment came largely from the use of larger and more elaborate buildings (supermarkets, enclosed shopping malls), concomitant larger merchandise inventories, and perhaps from locational competition.[15]

Elevator transportation, which made multi-floor department stores practicable and thus had a differential impact on large and small retailers, was popularized in the nineteenth century. Cash registers gained acceptance at about the turn of the century, subsequent to John H. Patterson's 1884 acquisition of the faltering predecessor to the National Cash Register Company.[16] But although cash registers probably proved even more useful to large retailers than to small ones, the machines were inexpensive enough to be used by establishments of modest size.

Many other twentieth-century technical innovations, such as neon lighting, store air conditioning, improved office machinery, frozen-food cabinets, and vending devices, were either not absolutely critical to retail success or, more commonly, could be obtained in small enough units to suit smaller retailers. Delivery vehicles changed, but more and more retailers either eliminated delivery service or contracted it out to specialist services. Although big retailing undoubtedly gained from mechanization during the first fifty years of the century, it did not obtain an overpowering advantage.

During the last twenty-five years, many grocery chains have greatly improved their methods of handling incoming merchandise, but these same improvements have also appeared in a number of wholesaler–independent-retailer systems.

The growing use of computers, likely to be combined with highly sophisticated electronic point-of-sale register systems that will maintain accurate real-time inventory records, will facilitate centralized decision making and thus promises to be especially advantageous to the chains. They may also induce excessive centralization and ultimately put some of their users at a disadvantage. On balance, though, the current technology will favor medium-sized and large retailing organizations.

The development and commercialization of some highly technologically laden products has also not necessarily promoted big, rather than small, retailing. New-car dealers will not retain their franchises if they become very small outlets, but as suggested earlier, they are not able to become giants. Gasoline retailing is a field of small businesses, with a low concentration ratio (the fifty largest firms do about 10 percent of the business) and with sales per station averaging about $100,000 in 1972. The fifty-firm concentration ratio is also relatively low (about 19.4 percent or close to the average for all retail trade) among radio, television, and electric-appliance dealers, but that figure is somewhat misleading because those dealers handle only a portion of all radio and television sales.[17]

Industrialization's main effects upon retailing in the United States so far have come through its impact upon factor markets, consumer markets, and upon retail operating and organizational methods. Many forecasters predict the ultimate development of highly sophisticated, computer-based two-way in-home cable-television ordering systems. Whether such systems will themselves become large-scale retailers or whether they will be used as communications vehicles by other firms is still an open question, as is the basic riddle of whether they will actually eventuate. But if they do appear, they are likely to alter the small-large retailer balance in favor of the large.

INDUSTRIALIZATION AND SMALL RETAILING'S FACTOR MARKETS

Instead of the traditional trilogy of land, labor, and capital, we shall divide the factor or supply markets for small retailing into locations, human resources, merchandise, and capital.

LOCATIONS

The primary geographic effect of industrialization has been upon the customer rather than upon the supply aspects of retailing. It has created the large metropolitan clusters of people, who are almost totally dependent upon the stores for all of their consumption goods. In the process of creating attractive markets for retailers, industrialization has also made suitable retail locations more expensive. On the whole, large retail organizations, with their greater economies of scale, have probably had some advantage in competing for and utilizing expensive locations, although some studies indicate that small retailing may obtain a relatively high market share in very densely populated areas.

Since World War II, an increasing portion of U.S. retail trade has been taking place in suburban planned shopping centers and malls. These malls provide few, if any, opportunities except perhaps an odd kiosk or two, for very small merchants. Even somewhat larger retailers often complain that the center developers, and the banks and insurance companies that finance the developments, prefer to deal with well-known national and regional chains. In any event, the dominant customer-attracting stores, often called "the anchor stores," pay a much lower rent per square foot of floor space than do the smaller, satellite stores. The anchor stores are almost invariably branches of well-known department stores in the large malls and supermarket-chain branches in the small "local" centers.

HUMAN RESOURCES

Some of the secular effects of industrialization upon the supply of retail workers and proprietors are fairly clear. The Clark-Fisher hypothesis holds that industrialization (or more precisely, economic development) transfers increasing portions of the working population to tertiary employments, a sector that includes retail trade. Preston found a Clark-Fisher effect in retail employment itself.[18] The industrialization of the extractive and processing industries has undoubtedly supplied many of the people who, through necessity or desire, have become small retail proprietors.

The cyclical impacts of industrialization upon entry into retail trade are less certain. Hall, Knapp, and Winsten have created a (cross-sectional rather than a longitudinal) model in which the supply price of independent shopkeepers is in good part a function of the availability of alternative employments.[19] Although they did not empirically test this portion of their model, it seems plausible and is reinforced by anecdotes of people who opened shops during the 1930s Depression for lack of anything better to do, or in hopes of obtaining their own supplies at wholesale. But census data (which, as noted, have their own limitations) do not depict a great rush into shopkeeping between 1929 and 1935. The reported number of active working proprietors increased less than .5 percent, while the number of establishments increased about 7 percent, thereby suggesting an increase in corporate retailing.[20]

Another cross-sectional study of American states sheds light on the cost of retail workers. Bucklin found a positive association between chain-store market share and high retail wage rates, both apparently flowing from the level of economic development. He commented that large retail organizations "reward their employees well."[21] Some of the rank-and-file chain-store employees might not agree with that statement, but in practice the larger retailers seem able to outbid small stores for desirable workers. At the same time, through work specialization, they probably are better able to use marginal employees.

At the turn of the century, social workers first criticized department stores as exploiters of women and then changed to praising them for having more generous personnel policies than the smaller shops.[22] The Federal Fair Labor Standards Act (minimum wage and maximum hour law), first adopted in 1938, contained an exemption of retail workers, which since 1961 has steadily been confined to smaller and smaller firms (currently firm volume of $250,000 or less).[23] However, a recent provision that allows lower wages to teen-age workers under certain conditions is known as the McDonald Clause, after the giant fast-food chain which espoused it.

MERCHANDISE

Industrialization created an enormous supply of goods to be moved through the marketing channel. As already noted, some of the new products, such as automobiles and gasoline, have been distributed primarily through small and medium-sized retailers.

Factory production of consumer goods, however, has also had adverse effects on small retailing. Artisan-retailers, such as the small bakeshops and confectioners who produced their own merchandise, custom tailors,[24] and custom dressmakers have become rare species. Standardized, packaged, advertised, and labeled products require far less technical knowledge on the part of the retailer and reduce the retailer's role as a consumer advisor. Nineteenth and early-twentieth-century retail-grocery trade magazines contained many articles on such subjects as how to recognize and blend different varieties of tea leaves, or the botanical and culinary aspects of various spices. Such articles are missing from the current publications. While the reduction in the technical knowledge needed makes entry easier for small (and other) retailers, it removes a traditional advantage of small retailers. It obviously facilitates large-scale mass merchandising.

The large distributors also enjoy many advantages in merchandise procurement. They deploy skilled, specialized buyers; they can go directly to domestic and foreign producers whenever it seems advantageous; they can exert considerable buying pressure; they can obtain quantity discounts and in-bound transportation economies through large purchases; and they may have goods made under their own specifications for resale under their private labels. Many of these advantages would not have arisen, or would have been at least partially vitiated, if the suppliers had not industrialized sufficiently to enjoy their own economies of scale. Conceivably, if the concentration were high enough to give a few retailers monopsony or oligopsony power, they could exert buying pressure against even rudimentary handicraft workers. But, in practice, much of the chain advantage comes in dealing with producers who want or need large orders. The major chain disadvantage, an inherent tendency toward standardization that may not suit all local markets, provides the smaller retailers' prime procurement advantage.

CAPITAL

The dollar capital requirements of small retailing depend on monetary inflation and deflation, store location, the type of merchandise handled, and the planned scale and style of operations. Some 1975–76 figures will, however, show that opening even a single store may require a substantial sum. The Bank of America prepared estimated ranges of initial investments for "hypothetical typical stores" occupying about 1,500 to 3,000 square feet and selling about $150,000 to $300,000 worth of apparel or hard goods. The estimated needed capital for gift, shoe, apparel, sporting-goods, toy, hobby-and-craft, automotive-supply, and camera shops ranged from $30,000 to $130,000 and seemed to center around $65,000 to $75,000. Smaller-volume shops selling horticultural plants and those selling bicycles were judged to need less.[25] The Department of Commerce reported the median 1975 investment for *franchised* food stores at $50,000 to $55,000, for franchised non-food retailers at $40,000, and for franchised fast-food establishments at $80,000. Median "start-up" cash requirements were about $20,000 except for convenience-food stores which needed only half that amount.[26]

Small retailers can obtain capital from numerous sources, including personal savings, friends, supplier credits, and bank loans, and from some governmental programs. But larger firms do have greater access to the capital market.

CONSUMER MARKETS

Twentieth-century industrialization affected consumers in at least two ways favorable to large retailers and disadvantageous to small ones. It changed consumer accessibility and buying patterns.

ACCESSIBILITY

Industrialization first concentrated population in cities and then, particularly after World War II, dispersed much of it to the new middle-class suburbs. Industrialization directly, or indirectly, provided much of the employment that drew people to the metropolitan areas. It also provided the transport media and other facilities that permitted the concentration of trade in those areas.

The downtown department store has often been described as a result of urban public mass transit, while the suburban shopping center is certainly the product of an automotive culture. The general-merchandise-catalog mail-order firms, one of the earliest types of nonsmall retailing, did draw their original strength from rural and small-town markets but, as noted, became more cosmopolitan in the 1920s and thereafter.

The chain-store picture is more complicated. Some chains, such as J. C. Penney & Company, began as, and for a long time continued as, small-town merchants. In general, though, chains have tended to grow and gain market share in proportion to urbanization and population density, at least up to a certain point. Their penetration seems to have been relatively lower, though, in the most densely populated areas, for reasons discussed under shopping behavior, and those areas may have favored the growth of strong, independent stores.[27] Recently many chain-store companies have become very much interested again in so-called secondary—that is, small-town-locations as a result of the high earnings of some of the companies currently cultivating those locations.[28] The ensuing chain-store rush to such towns will draw patrons to the selected communities and will help local merchants with compatible rather than competitive stocks; it will be a problem for others.

BUYING PATTERNS

In a broad perspective, the amount of time and effort that consumers are willing to devote to shopping appears to be inversely correlated with their wealth, or, in other words, with the level of economic development. Lifestyles that involve regularly spending a great deal of time in the marketplace haggling over, and savoring, the purchase of a limited assortment of goods appears associated with a very modest state of economic well-being.[29] The members of industrialized societies, with their greater command over goods and services, apparently want to spend as much of their leisure time as possible in the use, rather than in the acquisition, of their belongings. They constitute the markets for self-service and mass-merchandising operations, the style of retailing in which the large firms have the advantage.

Within this broad framework, however, economic development, industrialization, and population clusters do create at least two types of opportunities for small retailers. The large metropolitan areas, particularly, provide sufficient numbers of prosperous consumers who want, and will pay for, distinctive goods and services. This market is often considered as consisting of very high income, very fashion-conscious individuals but, with regard to specific goods or services, may also include many medium-income individuals. Gourmets, members of the counter-culture and others who want to differentiate themselves from the masses, hobbyists, and just plain lonely people who want some personal attention, may support quite a variety of small shops. According to at least one firm, moderately prosperous "blue-collar" factory and craft workers constitute the best audience for small "convenience" food stores, where the prices are substantially higher than in supermarkets. High-income and high-education-level neighborhoods, in contrast, do not provide adequate patronage for such stores.[30]

The larger cities also contain small communities of ethnic groups, and senior citizens and other disadvantaged citizens, who may utilize small shops for much of their staple purchasing. The predominance of small retailing in such neighborhoods may be due to the need to offer distinctive assortments tailored to ethnic tastes, the use of the storekeepers as intermediaries in dealings with the majority culture, a concomitant customer desire for ethnic identification with the proprietors, or the fact that the larger organizations have not found satisfactory ways of operating in those localities.[31]

OPERATING METHODS OF LARGE RETAILERS

Measuring scale economies in retailing is difficult and perhaps even impossible.[32] The margins, or differences between costs and selling prices, that retailers require will be affected by many factors besides the size of their operations. These factors include merchandise's susceptibility to loss of value (perishables, high-fashion goods), the relationship of handling costs to merchandise value, the supplementary services offered to customers, the portion of the total original-source-to-consumer marketing task performed by the retailer, the rate of utilization of establishment capacity, and the costs imposed by the particular environment in which the firm operates. Variations in these and other factors inhibit *ceteris paribus* efficiency comparisons between different-sized retail firms.

Conventional department stores that may be considered large firms in their selling markets, although individually less significant in their merchandise-supply markets, have become relatively high-cost operations. Their costs, however, include the provision of many supplementary services and amenities, the assembly of highly diverse collections of goods under one roof, and increasing emphasis on volatile fashion merchandise.

Within broad limits and subject to some exceptions, chain-store companies (and to a degree, independent merchants who have merged into chain-like systems) benefited from scale economies in running retail stores as consumer-supply institutions. The large chains can be quite efficient in assembling and dispersing large bundles of standardized goods, although they are often at a disadvantage in providing individualized service and close adaptation to local markets. They must be considered highly industrialized in terms of managerial technique, division of labor, utilization of skilled specialists, and rationalization of operations.

The smaller retailers have used three approaches to meeting the sets of large-firm advantages outlined above. They have sought to impose political handicaps on the larger organizations, they have adopted some chain-store organizational and operating techniques, and they have, consciously or otherwise, sought market niches that are sheltered from large-retailer competition.

SMALL RETAILER RESPONSE TO
LARGE RETAILING

HANDICAP LEGISLATION

Efforts to impose handicaps on large retailing, which first appeared in the nineteenth century, continued throughout the twentieth century and were particularly intense during the Great Depression of the 1930s. It is not completely clear how much of the initiative in seeking such legislation is attributable to wholesalers who saw their own interests tied up with those of small retailers, to organizations that decided to use a small-retailer image to camouflage other objectives, and to the actual grass-roots endeavors of the small merchants themselves. But the small storekeepers did support many attempts to curtail department-store, chain-store, and mail-order-house growth.

The Industrial Commission (1898–1902), an ad hoc group of Representatives, Senators and public officials appointed to investigate "the relations of capital and labor employed in manufacturing and general business" with special reference to combinations and monopoly, listened to small retailers' complaints about harmful competition from department stores.[33] The commission concluded that the department stores were crowding out the smaller dealers, but that this was due to inherent economies of scale and changed market conditions, and was beneficial to consumers.[34] (Actually, the conventional, nondiscount department stores, the type studied by the Industrial Commission, probably never accounted for more than 10 percent of total U.S. retail trade and eventually became rather high-cost, high-priced institutions.)

Attempts to impose restraints on the large retailers after 1900 took many forms, but the main efforts centered around chain-store taxation, control of resale prices, and control of merchandise-acquisition costs.[35]

CHAIN-STORE TAXATION

Between 1922 and 1929, the state legislatures considered numerous proposals for the imposition of burdensome taxes and other restraints on chain-store companies. Very few of these proposals were enacted into law and those few were quickly invalidated by the courts. The courts generally held that the taxes involved excessive use of the state's police powers or unconstitutional discrimination against the chains. But, in 1929, Indiana required all stores to pay a small annual fee, with the exact amount of the fee *per store* increasing progressively with the number of stores under common ownership. Although the actual dollar amounts set in the initial law were fairly trivial, the concept was obviously dangerous to the chains, since the legislature could gradually increase the taxes and the rate of progression without at any one moment appearing to be confiscating the chains. The U.S. Supreme Court upheld the Indiana law as a reasonable revenue enactment,[36] and shortly thereafter also sanctioned a Georgia law that placed a tax on all stores in chains of two or more outlets.

Between 1931 and 1940, 20 states besides Indiana and Georgia, out of the then-48, adopted anti-chain-store tax laws that survived court and public-referendum tests. Congressman Wright Patman, a long-time opponent of the chain-store movement, introduced a national chain-store tax measure in Congress in 1938 and followed it with other proposals that seemed to have reasonable chances of adoption.

The chain-store company managements, who at least up to 1931 had relied on the courts for protection against adverse taxation, gradually mobilized a political, as well as legal, counterattack. They began an intensive public-relations campaign and, particularly in fighting the possible national legislation, obtained the support of more politically potent groups such as consumer and farm organizations.[37] The grocery chains, which had the most outlets and thus the most to lose under the progressive taxation system, conducted intensive campaigns to sell the farm products that were in greatest oversupply and thus won many agrarian friends. The fact that the chain-store share of the total retail market peaked about 1933, then declined slightly in 1935 and 1939, and subsequently remained fairly constant through the 1954 retail-trade census, undoubtedly relieved some of the antichain tension. Rising prosperity and employment at the end of the 1930s also helped blunt the taxation movement. Some of the state laws were repealed, others lapsed, and there were few or no rate increases among the remaining ones. The national tax was never enacted.

RESALE PRICE CONTROLS

Under the federal antitrust-law prohibition against combinations in restraint of trade, manufacturers of consumer goods that moved in interstate trade generally could not control the prices at which dealers resold those items. (One licit exception was, and is, consignment selling, in which the manufacturer retains ownership until final sale and the dealers merely act as agents. But this involves so many other legal and marketing difficulties that it is often impractical. Manufacturers may also "suggest" resale prices, and in practice such suggestions range from legal recommendations to illegal coercion.)

Assuming any elasticity of demand, most manufacturers probably favor dealer price cutting, but a minority dislike it. They fear it will damage the brand image, make full-price retailers reluctant to handle the products involved, or lead the price-cutting retailers to mishandle the reduced items. Consequently, a small group of manufacturers unsuccessfully lobbied for a resale-price-control exemption to the antitrust laws during the 1920s and 1930s.

The situation changed drastically when the National Association of Retail Druggists (NARD) took up the cudgels for resale price maintenance ("fair trade") on behalf of its members, the owners of independent drugstores. The druggists, who mainly handled branded, nationally advertised, packaged cosmetics, patent medicines, and other such health, personal care, and beauty products, easily susceptible to price cutting, came to see controlled prices as the answer to the threat posed by price-cutting chain drugstores. Organized into very effective lobbying teams, they obtained a number of state laws during the early and mid-1930s. However, resale price maintenance did not become meaningful until the passage of the federal Miller-Tydings Act in 1937.

The Miller-Tydings Act was cleverly drafted to overcome congressional opposition to price maintenance and to take advantage of congressional sentiment for "states' rights," a reaction to the centralizing tendencies of Franklin D. Roosevelt's 1933 New Deal. (In spite of this draftsmanship, another parliamentary maneuver—attaching the legislation as a rider to a crucial appropriation bill—was necessary to avert a threatened presidential veto, which probably would have been sustained in Congress.) The law did not directly approve price maintenance, but instead waived the antitrust prohibition for goods moving into any state that authorized such resale price control. Since 45 states quickly passed such measures, the advocates felt that they had achieved about as much control as a direct federal law would have provided, but subsequent events proved this impression erroneous.

In 1951, the U.S. Supreme Court held that the "nonsigners' clause" in the Louisiana law, and inferentially the similar clauses in the other state laws, went beyond the congressional intent. These clauses, which were very useful in applying price maintenance to goods that were distributed extensively through indirect channels, required the supplier to sign a price-maintenance agreement with only one retailer in the state and then simply give notice to the rest of the trade that they were bound by that agreement.[38] The federal McGuire Act of 1952 provided the authorization previously lacking in the national enabling act, but the Supreme Court decision proved to be the first crack in a crumbling price-maintenance wall. An adverse decision from the highest court seemingly made the state courts more willing to question the retail-price-maintenance (r.p.m.) laws in their own jurisdictions. Their actions created at least temporary pockets of free trade, which then added to the three nonmaintenance states and the District of Columbia (Congress never passed a price-maintenance law for its own fiefdom) and thus created problems for the retailers in neighboring control states. The conflicting state-court interpretations and procedural requirements also created enforcement problems for manufacturers who wanted to use r.p.m. All of these factors, plus more basic economic forces, including in many instances manufacturer support, encouraged discount selling, and the increasing publicity given to discount selling made judges increasingly aware of the unrealities and un-equal enforcement of the price-maintenance agreements. In 1976, acting under the banners of consumerism and control of price inflation, Congress repealed the Miller-Tydings and McGuire acts so that r.p.m. was officially ended.

Resale price maintenance probably applied to less than ten percent of all goods sold in the United States even in its heyday. It had little effect, or none, on the small-merchant bankruptcy rate. It probably raised prices somewhat, although the exact effects are in doubt. It had fallen into such disuse by 1976 that its repeal was little noticed outside the trade press and had little impact.

While the druggists pursued r.p.m. during the 1930s, the grocers simulta-neously sought a different type of law, often called the Unfair Practices Act, or the Minimum Markup Law. The grocers sold many unbranded items that would not be susceptible to manufacturers' resale price controls, and they also had to preserve pricing flexibility because of the great perishability of their merchandise. So they sought laws that made it an offense to sell at less than acquisition cost (or acquisition cost plus some minimum markup) with intent to harm competition. These laws are mandatory rather than having the optional nature of resale price maintenance, and they rely upon the public authorities, rather than private lawsuits, for enforcement. District attorneys are very reluctant to prosecute under these laws, because intent to harm competition is difficult to prove and evidence of violation often rests upon complicated accounting data. Moreover, suing grocers for selling food to consumers too cheaply is not politically popular, so the authorities prefer to concentrate their limited law-enforcement budgets and staffs on more serious or more easily proven crimes. The unfair practices acts are sometimes used as potential threats in informal compliance efforts when a retailing firm severely disrupts competition in a small community, but, as with resale price maintenance, they have had little effect on chain-store growth.

CONTROL OF MERCHANDISE ACQUISITION COSTS

The most important piece of anti-large-retailer legislation is the Robinson-Patman Act (1936).[39] This law, which was originally drafted by attorneys for the U.S. Wholesale Grocers Association, was sometimes referred to in the press as "The Anti A & P Law" since it followed a Federal Trade Commission investigation into the price concessions that A & P and other large chains received from their suppliers. However, its provisions went beyond the FTC's recommendations, and the law has affected pricing practices for many basic industrial products. The Robinson-Patman Act thus deals with size, or at least the power that flows from relative size, in supply markets. The resale price maintenance and minimum markup laws, in contrast, were directed at behavior supposedly associated with size in the selling market, although in fact, some aggressive small retailers and local chains have been among the most ardent price cutters. The antichain taxes simply dealt with size per se.

Essentially, the Robinson-Patman Act prohibits differences in the prices charged different customers for goods of "like grade and quality when such differences tend to harm competition or to create a monopoly unless such differences are justified by differences in the costs of doing business with the different customers or are offered in good faith to meet the legally low prices of competitive suppliers." Other provisions that require suppliers to grant services and allowances to their customers on "proportionately equal" terms or that ban efforts to induce or receive discriminatory low prices are designed to prevent evasion of the law's prime requirement. The law only covers sales of goods in [interstate] commerce. Consequently, it has not been applied to sales of services and has been interpreted to exclude final retailer-to-consumer sales. Sellers have not been penalized for selling to wholesalers at lower prices than they charge retailers who buy similar quantities. Toleration of such sales is consistent with the sponsorship and purpose of the act, although it may strain the language of the law.

The legislation was very badly drafted and further damaged by extensive amendments during congressional debate. Variations in wording between clauses that should have had parallel construction are particularly troublesome. Enforcement is very uneven, and many large suppliers are probably in at least technical violation.

Yet the law has on occasion been invoked against chains, mail-order houses, and department-store companies and their suppliers. It has undoubtedly modified some buying behavior. One unanticipated effect, outside the grocery field, may have been to encourage large retailers to engage in specification buying, that is, to have goods made especially for them under their own private labels. Another paradoxical effect was detrimental to cooperative chains, a commercial mechanism for small retailers discussed in a subsequent section. On the whole, the Robinson-Patman Act has probably somewhat reduced or modified the large retailers' buying advantage, but it certainly has not eliminated that advantage.

OTHER LEGISLATION

A vast collection of other federal, state, and local laws has also been designed to help small retailers or to hamper large ones. A federal law that requires the posting of the manufacturer's list price on each new car (the so-called window-sticker) was enacted at the behest of independent automobile dealers who wanted to curb the pricing practices of some aggressive, volume-oriented competitors. In contrast, independent gasoline dealers, small pharmacists, and others in the retail and service industries have often sought state or local regulation to curb price advertising. (The U.S. Supreme Court has now held, at least in the case of pharmacies, that such regulations are unconstitutional violations of the right of free speech.) Local licensing laws have sometimes been intended to enforce compliance with health and sanitation regulations, and sometimes intended to restrict competition. Thus local ordinances for the licensing of florists may discourage some supermarket chains from attempting seasonal sales of plants and flowers at Christmas, Easter, and Mother's Day. Mandatory Sunday closing laws, now generally unenforced, spring from many motives, but in part represent the diverse interest of, on the one hand, most small retailers whose working hours must equal or exceed store hours and, on the other, large retailers who can employ shift labor. The list of all such laws is almost infinite.[40]

But much of this miscellaneous legislation has been so specific, so local, so ineffective, or so poorly enforced that it has had little effect on the national pattern of retail distribution. A few highly regulated trades, such as pharmacies and the retailing of alcoholic beverages, are exceptions to that statement.[41] But for most large retailers, handicap legislation has been a nuisance rather than a major disability.

Small retailers have also received some financial assistance, counseling, and information services from the U.S. Small Business Administration, and from other federal and local agencies. Some of this activity has been quite helpful to individual merchants, but, again, the total impact on the economy has probably been very limited.

ADOPTION OF CHAIN TECHNIQUES

Either upon their own initiative or that of their suppliers, some small retailers have tried to combine the advantages of independent store ownership with the benefits of large-scale retailing. The three major organizational structures used for this purpose, cooperative chains, voluntary chains, and franchising, differ somewhat in concept. But all involve the surrender of some autonomy in return for the rewards of group action.

Cooperative chains are formed by retailers who decide to engage in some joint purchasing and wholesaling. Voluntary chains are formed by wholesalers who agree to provide services to retailers who join their systems. Both of these types of affiliated retailing have found their greatest expression in grocery and supermarket retailing, but there are also examples in hardware, pharmacy, general-merchandise, and auto-supply retailing.

Generally the members of one of these chains use a common storefront design and insignia, and engage in joint advertising and other activities. The cooperative-chain central-purchasing and wholesaling units have historically worked on lower margins than those of the voluntary chains, but have provided the stores with fewer services. In recent years, the two types have become more alike. Membership is no longer confined to the owners of one or two small shops, and some participants have large multi-store operations. The central headquarters may also, for one reason or another, own quite a number of stores. Consequently, the distinction between the cooperatives and voluntaries, on one hand, and the corporate chains on the other, has also sometimes become slightly blurred.

Franchising is a popular, but vague, term that refers to many types of systems in which independent outlets sell goods or services under some form of central control. The U.S. Department of Commerce and some writers now use the term "traditional franchising" for the relatively long-standing plans used in the retailing of automobiles, trucks, and gasoline, and the wholesaling and bottling of carbonated nonalcoholic beverages. The number of these "traditional franchise" outlets is now declining, but they still provide about four-fifths of all franchise-industry sales volume.[42] Among the newer lines of franchise businesses, the word sometimes connotes membership in a voluntary chain, as in the case of small or "convenience" grocery stores. In other cases, it refers to the right to use a common name and operating style in return for the payment of license fees. In general, it implies some, often a very high, degree of central control and the imposition of considerable uniformity upon the outlets. The franchising firm may itself own and operate some of the establishments and some franchisees may have small or substantial chains of franchised outlets within the system.

The three types of affiliated retailing, and especially franchising, have sometimes made small retailers puppets within large organizations. But at their best (from the retailers' point of view) they have given small and medium-sized merchants collective power in some of their factor markets and they have implanted modern operating methods in businesses that would otherwise operate less effectively.

The proponents of the Robinson-Patman Act thought that cooperative chains could qualify for special discounts from suppliers that would pay central-headquarters' operating costs, but this has been ruled illegal. Some cooperative and voluntary chains have been racked by dissension or have been poorly managed. Franchising has often proved disadvantageous to its small business recruits. Overzealous and unscrupulous promoters have charged exorbitant fees for worthless franchises; franchisees have been induced to invest in facilities that never did, and probably never could have, become profitable; some franchise contracts impose unduly onerous and exploitative conditions upon the franchisees; and some franchisors have unfairly terminated or failed to renew some of their contracts in order to recapture ownership of the most profitable units for themselves.

In spite of these many difficulties and disadvantages, the three types of affiliated retailing discussed above have greatly benefited many small and medium-sized retailers. Fifty-seven percent of U.S. supermarkets were operated by members of cooperatives and voluntary chains in 1974.[43] The newer, "nontraditional" lines of franchising in the retail, restaurant, and service trades have been growing markedly with the most important sectors being fast-food restaurants, convenience grocery stores, and auto parts and service establishments.[44] While many have suffered disappointments, literally hundreds of thousands of retailers, mostly small but some not so small, have found these various types of affiliated business a viable method of operation.

Some small retailers survive, and prosper, by finding niches in the marketing system that can provide adequate business and yet are too small to be tempting to larger firms. These retailers may locate in small towns and villages; they may serve distinct population clusters in larger communities (ethnic neighborhoods, the residents of a single high-rise apartment house, or an academic group with special supply needs); they may feature considerable personal service and advice (sports professionals; shops at golf and ski clubs; interior design services combined with furniture retailing); or they may offer unique lines of merchandise (gourmet and specialty foods, arts and crafts shops). Some may survive by being willing to work harder, longer and/or more cheaply than paid employees would require.

Research on these and other conditions of small retailer survival and growth would be very difficult. Assigning the success of any one establishment to any one of these conditions would be just about as subjective as the usual statement of causes for business failure. But we are obviously limited in predicting future opportunities, and potential small merchants are obviously limited in selecting strategies, until we know more about how many small retailers have located themselves at what interstices of the marketing system.[45]

PROGNOSIS

The outlook for small retailing may be described as somewhat discouraging but not totally unnerving. Large enterprise, almost regardless of definition, gained less market share more slowly in retailing than in many other sectors, at least up to the 1972 census. While some major and medium-sized firms have grown strikingly since then, others (W. T. Grant, A & P) have had serious difficulties. Extrapolating past growth rates would indicate considerable room for small retailing for a considerable period of time.

Some factors, however, may accelerate large-firm growth. Technological advances in the form of electronic sales terminals and computer systems promise to improve merchandise management and decision making in the large firms. The same technology (which will be expensive) may also be available to moderate-sized merchants on a time-sharing basis but probably will fit better into some voluntary and cooperative chains. The large retailers will have the discipline to enforce such systems but will have to avoid over-centralization.

In the more remote event of technology advancing to commercially viable closed-circuit cable TV in-home ordering systems the small merchants will be further disadvantaged. Some discussions have treated these systems as likely to be relatively open-access communications media, available to all retailers in much the same way as the postal service, but that seems doubt-ful. Unless prohibited by licensing authorities, the system proprietors may become merchants on their own account; otherwise, they will probably sell costly privileges to a few large dealers.

As noted previously, many large chains are now intensively investigating and cultivating small-town markets. This trend will be beneficial to some small retailers who will play satellite roles in those communities where the most popular large retailers locate, but it should lower the total share ob-tained by small merchants in general.

The opportunities in selling distinctive merchandise and in offering exten-sive service will probably depend upon the business cycle, consumer demo-graphics, and consumer life-styles. Each generation of consumers wants to believe that it is freer and more individualistic in its tastes than its predeces-sor (although it may display considerable nostalgia for a more distant and misperceived earlier age), but the great mass of consumer purchasing is focused on a carrier wave of uniformity. Moreover, American department-store companies and some chain-store firms are now trying to preempt much of the high-style and distinctive-products markets; supermarket chains are opening delicatessen and gourmet departments. Nevertheless, if consumer real purchasing power remains relatively high, and particularly if the per-centage of working wives increases or remains constant, the economy will provide numerous opportunities for high-service and unique retail stores.

Some forecasters predict a plague of merchandise shortages in the fore-seeable future. If so, small retailers will enjoy more flexibility than large ones in handling the odd lots and small assortments that may come onto the market. The large retailers, however, with better resources, skilled special-ized buying staffs, access to primary producers, and the potential for signifi-

cant future purchases, should be the more attractive and successful customers in the supply markets.

The political battle between large and small retailers may well be over.
Large-scale retailing may have reached the critical mass at which further opposition becomes futile. Yet, if the economy should worsen and if the old
legislative fight should erupt again, the big retailers may be strangely vulnerable. Although some consumer polls give supermarket chains and other
large retailers fairly good marks, the popular support seems very shallow.
The supermarkets have been prime targets for consumer boycotts over rising
food prices and more recently were forced to abandon plans to eliminate
item price marking because of consumer (and retail labor) protests. The
farmers, who once cited the meat packers as their enemies, now single out
the food chains. The impersonality of the mass-merchandising stores and
high-style (and high price) images that many department-store and other
general-merchandise firms have adopted are not likely to win consumer support. The old liberal, industrial-organization-economist view, represented by
such names as Thurman Arnold and J. K. Galbraith, that big retailing was
good for the economy even if big manufacturing was not, has disappeared.

Thus, it might be that either great affluence or severe depression could
alter the small- and large-retailer market shares. But it would not be unusual
if unanticipated variables became the most influential factors in shaping the
retail population.

Notes

1. U.S., Bureau of the Census, *Census of Retail Trade 1972*, Volume 1: *Summary Subject Statistics* (Washington, D.C.: G.P.O., 1976), p. 1-37.

2. *Ibid.*, p. 1-114.

3. One to two decades ago, there was considerable interest, much of it sparked by John Kenneth Galbraith and Walt Whitman Rostow, in the idea of changing retail systems as a method of
fostering economic development or, in other words, in the retail trade as a cause rather than as a
result of the level of economic activity. That subject seems to receive much less mention today,
although the way in which an anachronistic distribution system can retard growth is still recognized.

4. Godfrey M. Lebhar, *Chain Stores in America: 1859-1962*, pp. 47–50, 409.

5. Measurement problems arise because many catalog sales are received at order desks located
in the stores.

6. James B. Madison, "Changing Patterns of Urban Retailing in the 1920's," in Paul Useld-ing, ed., *Business and Economic History*, 2d series (Urbana: Bureau of Business and Economic Research, University of Illinois, 1976), pp. 102–11.

7. For details, see *Fairchild's Financial Manual of Retail Stores*. New York: Fairchild Publishing Co., annual.

8. Robert F. Lusch and James M. Kenderding, "The Operating Dynamics of Chain Store Retailing in Recession and Recovery," paper delivered at the Midwest Business Administration Association annual meeting, St. Louis, Mo., March 30–April 2, 1977.

9. Conversation with official, Bureau of the Census.

10. The problem is not confined to the United States. A recent British article comments on a serious discrepancy between census reports of the retail pharmacy trade and figures derived from the mandatory register of the Pharmaceutical Society. "The Decline of the Independent Pharmacy," *Retail and Distribution Management* [London] (Sept.–Oct. 1977), 5:26.

11. For explanations of census definitions and procedures, see *Census of Retail Trade 1972*, Appendix A.

12. Joseph D. Phillips, *Little Business in the American Economy*.

13. *Census of Retail Trade 1972*, p. 1-2, p. 1-4.

14. Malcolm P. McNair and Eleanor G. May, *The Evolution of Retail Institutions in the United States*, p. 71.

15. Retailers, of course, complain about rising real-estate costs. But, a priori, one would expect locational costs (as a percentage of sales or on a deflated dollar basis) to be lower today when the consumer is more mobile than in the nineteenth century when so much trade was confined to a circumscribed downtown district. In other words, locational monopoly and hence monopoly rents *should* be lower today than one hundred years ago. Research is needed to determine whether this is the case. A somewhat similar question arises about department-store buildings, since modern department-store operators avoid the marble palaces that delighted nineteenth-century merchant princes.

16. Harry A. Toulmin, "John H. Patterson," *Dictionary of American Biography*, 2:304.

17. Gasoline service station and radio-appliance-television dealer sales and concentration figures from *Census of Retail Trade 1972*, pp. A-2, 74, 1-114.

18. Lee E. Preston, "The Commercial Sector and Economic Development," in Reed Moyer and Stanley C. Hollander, eds., *Markets and Marketing in Developing Economies* (Homewood, Ill.: Irwin, 1968), pp. 9–23.

19. Margaret Hall, John Knapp, and Christopher Winsten, *Distribution in Great Britain and North America*, pp. 134–35.

20. U.S., Bureau of the Census, *Census of Business 1939*, "Vol. 1 Retail Trade," (Washington, D.C.: G.P.O., 1946), p. 60.

21. L. P. Bucklin, *Competition and Evolution in the Distributive Trades*, p. 112.

22. See the series of articles, "Department Stores in the East" and "Department Stores in the West" that appeared in *Arena*, vol. 22 (1899).

23. 1976 amendments raise the exception in two steps to $300,000 by 1980 as partial adjustments for changes in the value of the dollar.

24. Custom tailors, who handcraft clothes to individually cut patterns, should not be confused with made-to-measure tailors who simply combine measurements and fabric choice into an order for factory cutting to standard patterns.

25. Bank of America (San Francisco) *Small Business Reporter*, Vols. 12, 13, various numbers.

26. U.S. Department of Commerce, *Franchising in the Economy 1975–1977* (Washington, D.C.: G.P.O., 1976), p. 43.

27. Hall, Knapp, and Winsten, *Distribution*, especially passim, pp. 98–137; Bucklin, *Competition and Evolution*, p. 112; Hirotaka Takeuchi and Louis P. Bucklin, "Productivity in Retailing: Retail Structure and Public Policy," *Journal of Retailing* (Spring 1977), 53(1):35–46. These analyses are based upon 1948 and 1967 data.

28. Lusch and Kenderding, "Operating Dynamics of Chain Store Retailing."

29. Although marketing writers generally accept this principle, it is the subject of considerable debate among economic anthropologists. See Luis Mott, Robert H. Silin and Sidney W. Mintz, *A Supplementary Bibliography on Marketing and Marketplaces*, Exchange Bibliography No. 792 (Monticello, Ill.: Council of Planning Librarians, 1975), pp. 4–5.

30. Y. Lee and K. Koutsopoulos, "A Locational Analysis of Convenience Food Stores in Metropolitan Denver," *Annals of Regional Geography* (March 1976), 10(1):104–117.

31. The best known report on this subject is D. Caplowitz, *The Poor Pay More* (New York: Free Press, 1967). Also see Frederick Sturdivant, ed., *The Ghetto Marketplace* (New York: Free Press, 1969).

32. K. A. Tucker, *Economies of Scale in Retailing*.

33. U.S., Industrial Commission, *Report*, 7:17–27, 14:xii–xiv.

34. Industrial Commission, *Report*, 19:548–49.

35. The standard discussion of these activities is J. C. Palamountain, Jr., *The Politics of Distribution*. Also see Lebhar, *Chain Stores in America*.

36. *State Board v. Jackson* (283 U.S. 527).

37. The material in this and the preceding two paragraphs has been drawn from Lebhar, *Chain Stores in America*, passim.

38. *Schwegmann Bros. v. Calvert Distillers* (341 U.S. 384).

39. Technically an amendment to the Clayton Act.

40. The Limited Price Variety Stores Association, now the Association of General Merchandising Chains, used to issue a comprehensive *Retailer's Manual of Laws and Regulations* at several year intervals. This highly useful service was discontinued about ten years ago, although a possible revival of the publication has been mentioned from time to time. For other moderately comprehensive surveys, see: S. C. Hollander, *Restraints Upon Retail Competition* (East Lansing: Bureau of Business and Economic Research, Michigan State University, 1965); Henry Assael, ed., *The Politics of Distributive Trade Associations* (Hempstead, N.Y.: Hofstra University, 1967); and S. C. Hollander, "United States of America," in J. J. Boddewyn and S. C.

Hollander, eds., *Public Policy Toward Retailing* (Lexington, Mass.: Heath-Lexington Books, 1972), pp. 367–404.

41. On the retail pharmacy trade, see: F. Marion Fletcher, *Market Restraints in the Retail Drug Industry* (Philadelphia: University of Pennsylvania Press, 1967) and J. F. Cady, *Drugs on the Market* (Lexington, Mass.: Lexington Books, 1975).

42. Department of Commerce, *Franchising in the Economy,* p. 2.

43. "Cooperatives and Voluntaries," *Progressive Grocer,* July 1975, p. 57.

44. Department of Commerce, *Franchising in the Economy,* p. 5.

45. Joseph D. Phillips, *Some Industrial and Community Conditions for Small Retailer Survival,* provides an interesting although probably outdated analysis of the effects of city size and community characteristics.

Selected Bibliography

Barger, Harold. *Distribution's Place in the American Economy Since 1869.* Princeton: Princeton University Press, 1955.

Berry, Leonard L., ed. "Special Issue on the Future of Retailing." *Journal of Retailing* (Fall 1977), 53(3).

Boddewyn, J. J. and Stanley C. Hollander, eds. *Public Policy Toward Retailing: An International Symposium.* Lexington, Mass.: Heath-Lexington Books, 1972.

Bucklin, Louis P. *Competition and Evolution in the Distributive Trades.* Englewood Cliffs, N.J.: Prentice-Hall, 1955.

Cady, John F. *Drugs on the Market.* Lexington, Mass.: Lexington Books, 1975.

Cox, Reavis, Charles S. Goodman, and T. Fichandler. *Distribution in a High Level Economy.* Englewood Cliffs, N.J.: Prentice-Hall, 1955.

Duncan, Delbert J. and Stanley C. Hollander. *Modern Retailing Management,* 9th ed. Homewood, Ill.: Irwin, 1977. Esp. ch. 1.

Edwards, Corwin. *The Price Discrimination Law.* Washington, D.C.: Brookings Institution, 1959.

Hall, Margaret, John Knapp, and Christopher Winsten. *Distribution in Great Britain and North America.* London: Oxford University Press, 1961.

Lebhar, Godfrey M. *Chain Stores in America: 1859–1962.* New York: Chain Store Publishing Corporation, 1963.

Mack, Ruth P. *Controlling Retailers.* New York: Columbia University Press, 1936.

McNair, Malcolm P., and Eleanor G. May. *The Evolution of Retail Institutions in the United States.* Cambridge, Mass.: Marketing Science Institute, 1976.

Palamountain, Joseph C., Jr. *The Politics of Distribution.* Cambridge: Harvard University Press, 1955.

Phillips, Joseph D. *Little Business in the American Economy.* Urbana: University of Illinois Press, 1958.

—— *Some Industrial and Community Conditions for Small Retailer Survival.* Champaign: Bureau of Economic and Business Research, University of Illinois, 1964.

Tucker, K. A. *Economies of Scale in Retailing*. Lexington, Mass.: Lexington Books, 1975.
U.S. Department of Commerce. *Service Industries: Trends and Prospects*. Washington, D.C.:
G.P.O., 1975.
U.S. Industrial Commission, *Report*. Vols. 7, 14, 19. Washington, D.C.: G.P.O., 1901, 1902.

10

SMALL-BUSINESS BANKING IN THE UNITED STATES, 1780–1920

Richard Sylla

THE role of small business in the history of American banking is perhaps greater than what obtains in any other nation. Small-business
banking reached the peak of its development and influence in the early part
of this century. In 1920, more than 30,000 independent commercial banks—
the great majority of which operated out of a single office staffed by a handful of employees in a small town—were present within the borders of the
United States. Since that time, the numbers of independent and small banks
have been greatly reduced through disappearances, mergers, and the expansion of branch banking. The small-business influence nonetheless remains
important in American banking, for there are today, over half a century
since the peak was reached, still more than 10,000 independent banks
operating in the country.

Among the industrializing nations of the nineteenth century, the United
States was unique in terms of the vast numbers of small, independent banks
that occupied central places in its monetary and financial system. The trend
of American banking development over time was also rather exceptional. In
other advanced economies of the nineteenth century, not only were the
numbers of independent banks smaller than in the United States, but also in
many cases those numbers were decreasing or increasing at much slower
rates. Banking development in England illustrates the more usual pattern of
banking consolidation from which the United States so markedly departed.
In the English case, the number of independent banks reached its peak of

some 700 units during the first quarter of the century. Joint-stock banks with branches then began to develop, and by the end of the century, approximately a dozen large banks dominated the English banking scene. In less extreme forms than in the English case, other industrializing economies exhibited this same pattern of increasing dominance by large, consolidated banking organizations.

Why did the United States differ? Why did small, independent banks continue to play a large and perhaps increasing role in the American financial system all the way into the 1920s? The answer—as we shall see—depends in large measure on the laws and regulations, or lack thereof, under which American banks were organized and operated. These external influences on banking development in America were reflections of the diffusion of political power among levels of government in a federal republic that was ever-growing in size. The diffusion of political power itself was part of an ethos that individual opportunity and enterprise were to be favored over the grand designs of the few whose wealth or political influence—at other times or under more centralized governmental arrangements—might have produced a less democratic, more elitist outcome. A small-business ideology has been present throughout American history. Although this ideology did not much affect banking until the 1830s, from that time forward it accounted for a number of the unique and—many would hold—peculiar characteristics of American banking development.

But politics and governments, laws and regulations, and the ideology of small business are not the entire story. The economic historian pays attention to such forces, but he is normally more sensitive to the economic rationale behind the march of events. If small, independent banks had been clearly and uniformly less efficient than large banks with branches, it is unlikely that Americans, always proud of their pragmatism in economic matters, would have maintained them for so long. The ideology of small business did not much hinder the growth of large manufacturing corporations operating across state, and even national, boundaries when technological and organizational developments made big business the efficient solution. Yet small business continued to flourish in banking. To understand why, one probably must consider the personal nature of many banking services, the costs of gathering information in an economy of continental dimensions with millions of small producers who were bank clients, and the well-documented reluctance of capital to migrate from surplus to deficit saving sectors during the great expansion of the American economy in the last century. These real economic forces operated along with ideology and legal arrangements to promote small-business banking.

This essay traces the progress and problems of small-business banking in America from the time the bankless thirteen colonies achieved independence from Great Britain to the early twentieth century, when over 30,000 independent commercial banks were operating in what by then had become the world's largest and most productive national economy. A brief discussion of summary data will first set out some dimensions of small-business banking over the period. The next two sections deal respectively with the era of state banking before the Civil War (when small business had to overcome numerous political and legal obstacles in order to gain a foothold in American banking) and the era of national banking after the Civil War (when, despite continuing legal obstacles, it ultimately reached full flower). The penultimate section considers the manner in which America's thousands of small and large banks were tied together into a nationwide banking system that promoted economic efficiency, and the ways in which the numerous bankers sought to associate in order to discover and give expression to their common interests in banking, politics, and legislation. The conclusion offers an interpretation of the contributions and drawbacks of small-business banking in the American experience.

LONG-TERM TRENDS

Banking as a specialized business activity did not develop in the British North American colonies during the seventeenth and eighteenth centuries. An interesting question—one which cannot be pursued here—is why banking did not develop in colonial America. It is evident that one of the chief functions of modern banks, namely furnishing an important part of the media of exchange, was widely demanded in the colonies. This function was not, however, discharged by banks but rather by a variety of other methods. Foreign coins circulated and a variety of commodities, at various times and places, were given full or limited legal tender as money. Book credits and bills of exchange were often used in commercial transactions. But by far the most noteworthy development of colonial monetary experience, and the one that very likely limited the need for banks of deposit and issue, was the circulation of paper money printed by virtually every colonial government. Commonly called "bills of credit," these monies entered circulation either by being paid out for public expenses or as loans to citizens secured by land, the common asset of colonial Americans. Directly or indirectly, the colonial paper issues were public debt. Colonial governments quickly discovered, however, that the demand for money in their rapidly growing economies was great enough so that there was little call for redemption of their paper-money debt. In some of the colonies, this rather pleasant discovery led to overissues of fiat paper and price inflation resulted, but in others the issues were managed in a relatively noninflationary manner.[1]

What caused Americans to have serious doubts about fiat money issues as a means of public finance—and what thus provided an impetus for the development of modern banking institutions in America—was not the experience of colonial governments but rather the experience with Continental paper money during the War of Independence. With limited taxing and borrowing abilities, the Revolutionary Continental Congress had no real alternative to financing the war with paper-money issues, and it had much colonial precedent in favor of such a course. So much of the Continental paper was issued, however, that by the end of the war in 1781, it had become essentially worthless. In that year Robert Morris, a Philadelphia merchant, was appointed by Congress to the post of Superintendent of Finance. One of his first measures was a proposal for a Bank of North America, a corporation owned by stockholders. It would have a capital of $400,000 paid in gold and silver; issue notes convertible to specie and accepted by the government in payment of amounts owed to it; hold funds of and lend money to the government and to private individuals. Congress chartered this corporation on December 31, 1781, but as the war was then over, the corporation turned from its intended public services to private business.[2] This was the first American bank.

From this small and late beginning—Europeans had first settled in America 175 years earlier, and modern banking operations had been carried out in Britain for over a century—the specialized business of banking emerged and grew up in the United States. Table 10.1 presents in summary form two dimensions of American banking's development from 1782 to 1920, namely the dimensions of the number of commercial banking institutions and the average capital stock of these institutions. The latter dimension, one of average bank size, is selected for its bearing on the questions

Table 10.1 Commercial Banks in the United States, 1782–1920: Their Numbers and
Capital Stock

(1)	(2)	(3)	(4)	(5)
		Average Authorized Capital Stock	Average Paid-In Capital Stock	Percent of Banks in Column (2) Covered in
Date	Number of Banks	($000)	($000)	Column (4)
1782	1	400	–[b]	
1790	3	1,033	–	
1800	28	622	–	
1803	53	470	318	13
1810	102	551	273	29
1820	327	488	278	44
1830	381	447	308	72
1835	584	528	358	91
1850	830 (1,228)[a]	–[b]	258 (186)[a]	100
1860	1,579 (2,687)[a]	–	268 (169)[a]	100
1870	3,776	–	157	100
1880	5,445	–	122	100
1890	10,679	–	101	100
1900	12,247	–	92	100
1910	24,514	–	81	100
1920	30,291	–	92	100

Sources: 1782–1810, from J. Van Fenstermaker, *A Statistical Summary of Commercial Banks
Incorporated in the United States Prior to 1819* (Kent, Ohio: Kent State University Press,
1965). 1820–35, from J. Van Fenstermaker, *The Development of American Commercial Banking: 1782–1837* (Kent, Ohio: Kent State University Press, 1965). 1850–1910, from Richard
Sylla, *The American Capital Market, 1846–1914* (New York: Arno, 1975). 1920, from Board
of Governors of the Federal Reserve System, *All Bank Statistics, United States, 1896–1955*
(Washington, D.C.: Board of Governors, 1959).

[a] Including private, *i.e.*, unincorporated, banks.

[b] Not available.

related to the extent of small-business participation in banking.[3] Perhaps
more pertinent, still, would be information on the distribution of banks by
the size of their capital stocks at the various dates, but such information
would be difficult to gather, given the paucity of information during the earlier years and the magnitude of the effort, given the large number of institutions, in the later years. Used in conjunction with the numbers of banks,
trends in average capital stock of banks can indicate when small business
was making its most rapid inroads in banking.

The march of banking was steadily upward over the entire period in terms of the number of independent institutions in operation. Before 1850, the data in column 2 of table 10.1 are not complete, in that they only show the number of banks operating under state charters of incorporation. It is known that private, or unincorporated, banks operated before 1850, but their numbers are not known, since they were neither sanctioned by, nor reported to, governments. Some idea of their relative importance in terms of numbers may be gained by estimates for 1850 and 1860, which have been added to the state-bank numbers for those years in order to produce the alternative totals in parentheses in table 10.1. The private banks tended to be small businesses in the antebellum years, as can be inferred from the way in which including them in the totals reduces the estimated average paid-in capital of all banks in the alternative totals for 1850 and 1860 in column 4 of table 10.1. For 1860, the average capital of all 2,687 banks is made up of 1,579 state-chartered banks averaging $268,000 of capital per bank and 1,108 private banks with an estimated average capital of only $30,000 per bank.

For, roughly speaking, its first half century, American banking was a business with banking enterprises of large average size, whether in comparison with other contemporary enterprises or when compared to later years. In these years, we may judge from column 3 of table 10.1, the charters of state banks authorized them on average to gather capitals of approximately half a million dollars. It was customary in these years for subscribers to the stock of banks to pay in only a part of their subscriptions and to owe, and be callable for, the remainder. Thanks to the painstaking research of J. Van Fenstermaker, for the years from 1803 to 1837 we have data on the paid-in capital for a progressively growing proportion of all banks; these averages, shown in column 4 of table 10.1 may be compared with the authorized capitals of 3. It appears from these data that state banks, on the average, operated with from one-half to two-thirds of their authorized capital. Nonetheless, with average ownership interests of $250 to $350 thousand, these banks were among the major private institutions of the early United States. Typically they were not small businesses.

Around the middle of the nineteenth century, a trend toward smaller average bank sizes—measured by capital stock—emerged. From then until the early twentieth century, banks increased by the thousands and then average capital stock fell to less than a third of what it had been in the early decades of the nineteenth century. Banking was quite remarkable in this respect, for in these decades, the average size of enterprises in most industrial and commercial sectors was very likely increasing. During the course of American economic development in the nineteenth century small-business banking waxed rather than waned. The reasons for this reversal of the more usual trend toward larger average producing units in other sectors will become clearer as we proceed.

THE ERA OF STATE BANKING, 1782–1863

The conditions that eventually allowed small-business banking to flourish in the United States were not present in the early decades. Small enterprise in any line of business is most likely to flourish when there is a minimal amount of political and legal interference, and when firms are free to enter or leave the business on the basis of individual estimates of the prospects for profitable operating. Because of the perceived public nature of—and therefore public interest in—at least some banking functions, such conditions have never been present in the business of banking in America. But there was progress toward these conditions from the early years, when public hostility toward banking was widespread, and political and legal interferences in banking were commonplace.

Much of the force behind these early hostilities and interferences derived from the fact that, from the beginning, the dominant organizational form of American banking enterprises was the corporation. Two centuries ago, the corporation embodied a fundamentally different concept from the form of competitive private-enterprise organization that later was to emerge and dominate much of the industrial and commercial world. The concept of the corporation then was one of monopoly privilege granted through a charter from crown or government in return for an assumption of obligations of a public or quasi-public nature. The public-service nature and public utility of banks was emphasized over and over by early bank promoters seeking charters for their projects. The arguments employed were most forceful in cases such as those of the Bank of North America and the Bank of the United States, where leaders like Robert Morris and Alexander Hamilton could point to specific services that the banks would perform for the national government. Even with these institutions, however, the more general public benefits of stimulating trade, furnishing a reliable and inexpensive medium of exchange, and attracting foreign investment in the shares of corporations with limited liability were also stressed. Arguments such as these appealed to state government leaders as well. Soon they were chartering banks and often taking part (in a few cases, all) of the stock in the hope that dividend income would reduce the need for taxation. Other bank promoters secured charters by tying their banking plans to perceived "public" works or needs of various kinds. Thus, the Bank of the Manhattan Company (1799) in New York was an adjunct of a project to improve the city's water supply; the Kentucky Insurance Company (1802) banked through a corporation ostensibly founded to insure riverboats and their cargoes; and the Miami Exporting Company (1803) banked after being organized and chartered to transport farm products from Ohio to New Orleans.[4]

The *quid pro quo* for the early banks' assumption of public duties or obligations was of course the privilege of monopoly. Such a privilege was wholly in keeping with the eighteenth-century concept of the corporation. Some months before the charter of the Bank of North America in 1781, Alexander Hamilton—in a letter to Robert Morris—had proposed a national bank to be chartered for thirty years with "'no other bank, public or private, to be permitted during that period.'"[5] The states of Massachusetts and New York actually conferred their own charters on the Bank of North America, granting it a monopoly of banking in those states for the duration of the War of Independence.[6] When the war ended and several more banks—including the Bank of the United States—were founded, the idea remained active of combining them into one national institution. But this course presented obvious difficulties once banks were going concerns, so their founders attempted instead to promote the idea of local or regional monopolies.[7] When these attempts failed, other tactics to restrict competition followed. The political parties in power in the states would give charters only to backers of, or those friendly to, the party. Banks themselves attempted to differentiate their product from those of their rivals by styling and calling themselves, for example, merchants' banks, mechanics' banks, farmers' banks, and planters' banks. And the corporate banks, though rivals, were as one in attempting to restrict or eliminate through legal processes the activities of private bankers who operated without the sanction of charters from state legislatures.[8]

The idea that banking promoted public purposes that deserved the status, privileges, and protection of corporate charters clashed in the early years of the United States with the common law tradition that anyone had the right to

engage in the banking business. Attempts by early chartered banks to promote and preserve monopolistic privileges served to stimulate private banking and therefore tended to undermine their position. Although the extent of
private banking operations in the early decades is unknown, it is evident that
private bankers posed a threat to the chartered banks. Between 1799 and
1818, a dozen state legislatures passed, at the behest of chartered banks,
some eighteen laws that either restricted the functions private banks could
perform or made private banks illegal. At the time these acts were passed, a
disproportionate number of new chartered banks were formed, which
suggests that private bankers sought relief from the so-called restraining acts
by switching to corporate status.[9] Some private bankers of uncommon abilities and resources—Stephen Girard, for example—managed to survive the
political and legislative onslaught but only after protracted struggles with
their chartered rivals and public authorities.[10]

By the fourth decade of the nineteenth century, the war to maintain monopolistic privileges and to restrict competition in banking had been lost in a
number of states including, most importantly, New York. The emergence of
new politico-economic principles, reinforced by rising economic interests,
was responsible for the defeat, and in the process a new concept of the corporation evolved. Roger B. Taney, as Andrew Jackson's Secretary of the
Treasury in 1833–34, announced the triumph of the new order in an oft-
quoted passage: "There is perhaps no business which yields a profit so certain and liberal as the business of banking and exchange; and it is proper that
it should be open, as far as practicable, to the most free competition and its
advantages shared by all classes of society."[11] At the time Taney penned
these words, the Jacksonians were busily engaged in preparing the demise of
the Second Bank of the United States as the national bank. Whether rightly
or wrongly—historians still debate the question—the Second Bank was
widely perceived as an elite institution with anticompetitive advantages and
goals. The bank became a symbol of the privileged positions that many
chartered banks had sought and often obtained.

In terms of progressive banking legislation, the landmark of the 1830s
was New York's free banking law of 1838. The law had two major objectives. One was to remove from the state legislature the exclusive power to
charter banks. This power—it had been demonstrated time and again—led to
political favoritism and corruption in the granting of charters, and to an-

ticompetitive restrictions in favor of existing banking corporations. The solution of New York in 1838 was to make the conferral of bank charters an administrative rather than legislative function of government, and to confer charters on any person or association complying with the general and specific conditions of the law. The second objective was to give circulating banknotes a solid backing by requiring that free banks deposit with the state comptroller acceptable securities, usually state or federal bonds, equal in value to the circulating notes. The New York law thus spoke to the two major concerns Americans had about their banking arrangements, namely, monopolistic privileges and insecurity regarding the values of the heterogeneous notes circulated by hundreds of banks.[12]

Free banking became the entering wedge for legally sanctioned small-business banking in the United States. Private banking continued as a non-sanctioned alternative; but without note-issue privileges, private banks were at a disadvantage compared to small free banks. Many private banks took out free-bank charters when they became available. And during the 1850s, free banking became widely available. By 1861, well over half of the states had adopted free banking with the New York law of 1838 usually serving as a model. As we saw in the previous section, it was during these early years of free banking that the average capitalization of American banks began a long decline that lasted until the twentieth century.

THE NATIONAL BANKING ERA, 1863–1920

During the Civil War, in 1863 and 1864, the federal government moved to implement what was generally regarded as free banking on a national scale. That, however, was not the main objective of the legislation, which perhaps explains why the objective was reached more in form than in substance. The principal objectives were to assist federal war finance by predicating national-bank-note issues on purchases of federal bonds, and to create a national currency to replace the existing and multifarious issues of the state banks. It was thought at the time that these objectives would be achieved rather simply and quickly by the conversion of state banks to national banks. When this did not occur, Congress in 1864 decided to force the issue by taxing state bank-note issues out of existence. Most state-chartered banks then joined the national system; in 1870, only 261 remained, whereas in 1860 there had been nearly 1,600.

Although the federal banking laws of 1863–64 were modeled after the 1838 New York statute, in several respects they departed significantly from the letter and spirit of free banking.[13] In the first place, a ceiling was placed on the total amount of national bank-note circulation; this, of course, was antithetical to the spirit of free banking. Secondly, capital requirements were set at what later turned out to be relatively high minimum levels that were graduated upward, in three steps, as the population of cities and towns in which banks were to be located increased. Finally, the 1864 law precluded loans secured by real-estate collateral.

These statutory provisions were not especially inappropriate at the time they went into effect. The nation did not, for example, suffer from a shortage of paper-currency during the Civil War. But soon after Appomattox, most of the allowable national bank-note circulation had been taken up by banks in the northwestern quarter of the country, so that little was left for the southern and western states. Similarly, the minimum capital requirements set out in 1864 were not out of line with the capitals of most state banks in 1860, but as small-town America expanded by leaps and bounds in subsequent decades, the minimum capital requirements of the 1864 act became a drag on the development of national banking in the South and the West. These developing areas were much more agricultural in their economic orientation than was the Northeast, which meant that the prohibition of lending on real estate also detracted from the extension of national banking. During the late nineteenth century, the National Banking System created during the Civil War was obviously ill-suited to the character of banking needs generated by the nation's westward movement. It was decidedly not a system that encouraged small-business banking.

More than anything else, these drawbacks of the National System account for its failure to become *the* banking system of the United States, as its makers had intended. The state-chartered banks were put down by the federal statutes of the 1860s, particularly by the 1865 law that taxed their notes out of existence, but they were not put out. Their recovery was for two reasons rather protracted. The loss of note-issue privileges impeded the recovery of state banking because in the newer, developing regions of the South and West note issue remained an important function and condition of profitable banking, as it earlier had been in the Northeast.[14] In addition, the state free-banking laws of the antebellum era, in the words of John James, "were in effect nullified by the National Banking Act, because they had been originally written to cover the chartering of banks of issue."[15] In some of the former free-banking states, the old laws were repealed, and banks were covered under general incorporation laws. In others, the old practice of incorporation through special legislature acts, with its attendant problems, reappeared. Perhaps under the mistaken impression that truly free banking was in effect under the federal laws, the states were slow to create new general-banking incorporation laws of their own. After the mid-1880s many states did enact such laws.[16]

The states did not only enact or reenact general banking laws. They also made the provisions of their laws much less restrictive to small business than were the National Banking laws. Minimum capital requirements typically ranged from $10,000 to $25,000, whereas the federal minimum until 1900 was $50,000.[17] Almost all of the states permitted their chartered banks to make loans on real-estate security. And other loan, as well as reserve, provisions of the state laws were similarly less restrictive than their federal counterparts.[18]

A remarkable revival of state banking, much of it of the small-business variety, occurred as these liberalizations became effective. By 1900, nonnational banks, a category that includes a large but declining number of private banks as well as state-chartered units, outnumbered national banks by 8,700 to 3,700, or more than two to one. Moreover, in every geographic region except New England, nonnational bank deposits exceeded those of the national banks.[19] By 1900, then, the "dual" banking structure of federally and state-incorporated banks, which has persisted in the United States down to the present day, was firmly established.

Between 1900 and 1920, American banks under the dual system enjoyed their greatest era of institutional expansion. The number of independent banks increased from twelve to thirty thousand. The geographical and institutional structure of the banking system in 1920 is summarized in table 10.2. Small-business banking was largely a phenomenon of the nonnational sector, and it flourished most in regions other than New England and the Middle Atlantic States, where American banking originated nearly a century and a half earlier.

Table 10.2 The American Banking Structure in 1920 (All Monetary Figures in $ Millions)

Regions	National Banks			Nonnational Banks			All Commercial Banks		
	Number	Capital	Deposits	Number	Capital	Deposits	Number	Capital	Deposits
New England	409	105.7	1,030.3	399	77.3	1,242.3	808	183.0	2,272.6
Middle Atlantic	1,680	372.6	5,564.5	1,479	463.3	6,029.1	3,159	835.9	11,593.6
South	1,990	229.6	2,154.9	6,137	287.1	2,402.5	8,127	516.7	4,557.4
East N. Central	1,367	228.9	2,449.6	4,617	329.5	4,300.3	5,984	558.4	6,749.9
West N. Central	1,579	154.7	1,481.7	7,655	240.1	2,630.8	9,234	394.8	4,112.5
Mountain-Pacific	999	131.7	1,480.1	1,980	156.0	1,926.8	2,979	287.7	3,406.9
United States	8,024	1,223	14,161	22,267	1,553	18,532	30,291	2,777	32,693

Source: Calculated from data in Board of Governors of the Federal Reserve System, *All Bank Statistics*, United States 1896–1955 (Washington, D.C.: Board of Governors, 1959). The regional groupings of states are as defined in Richard Sylla, *The American Capital Market, 1846–1914*. (New York: Arno, 1975), p. 22n.

COORDINATION OF BANKING
OPERATIONS AND INTERESTS

By the end of the nineteenth century, the American banking system was recognized as being unique in terms of the scope it had afforded, and would continue to afford, for the development of small-business banking. As the Indianapolis Monetary Commission, an independent reform group, described this development in 1898: "Nowhere save in the United States is there such a multitude of small and unconnected institutions. There is, perhaps no more striking characteristic of the banking system of the United States than the immense number of banks of low capitalization, and the absence of institutions of large capital with branches."[20] The great majority of American commercial banks at this time had nearly all of the characteristics of small business. Bank managements were independent and the managers often were, or were among, the owners of the enterprises. Banks typically were owned by individuals or small groups who had put up the initial capital. The area of bank operations was primarily local, and the owners, managers, and employees generally resided in the same community. Finally, compared to the largest city banks, the thousands—even tens of thousands— of country bankers were small in their scales of operation, whether measured by capital, assets, liabilities, or employees.

The proliferation of small banks in nineteenth-century America presented a host of problems that would not have been nearly as pressing for small enterprise in other lines of business activity. The nature of banking operations is such as to create direct interdependencies between banks. When, for example, one bank expands or contracts its lending, its demand liabilities in the form of notes and deposit balances change, and the changes have an almost immediate effect on the balance-sheet position and operations of other banks. Banks, in short, exist in a system, and when the number of banks increases, the channels of potential interaction between the units of such a system, as is well known, increase even more rapidly. One would therefore expect banks in a system to develop arrangements for recognizing and dealing with interdependencies that arise in the discharge of their day-to-day banking functions, and one would also expect that the difficulties of developing such arrangements would become great as the units of the system proliferate.

An economical way of simplifying the problem of coping with systemic interdependencies—particularly in systems with large numbers of units—is to have governments enact laws covering the manner of organization of units, operating rules and regulations to be followed by these units, and methods of supervising the system. In America, governmental solutions to some systemic banking problems were present from the beginning but, as one would expect, they tended to become even more important as the size of the system grew. Since governmental solutions to systemic problems were not especially necessary when the system was small in its early decades, their presence needs to be explained on other grounds. The first banks sought corporate charters from governments as a means of gaining both capital and public sanction for what was a relatively new business activity in America. In addition, American governments, from their long experiences with paper money, were among the first to recognize—as early as the eighteenth century—public concern for, and interest in, the nature of the medium of exchange.

So American banking, by offering great opportunities for small businesses, developed in a way that created growing problems of systemic coordination, and it developed from the beginning under strong governmental influences that could be helpful in solving banking problems, but could also create political and regulatory problems for individual banks and for the system. How did the banks cope with these problems? In general, and with varying degrees of success, the banks worked out arrangements among themselves to coordinate operating functions of the system, they cooperated with public authorities in developing legal and supervisory arrangements, and they sought to create a bankers' "voice" to promote their interests in politics and legislation.

Since the first American banks at the end of the eighteenth century were devised as regional monopolies, they found it in their individual interest to cooperate with one another in exchanging notes, settling balances, suppressing counterfeiting, and speaking out on public issues.[21] But when the banks, either individually or cooperatively, attempted to preserve their privileges by preventing or suppressing competition, they were less than successful. By the 1830s, as described earlier, the idea that in banking, as in other activities, free competition rather than privileged monopoly best served the economic needs of an expanding America was firmly established, and by the 1850s, it was widely implemented.

With the triumph of free competition under a variety of state and federal laws, the numbers of unit banks began to increase by leaps and bounds. The problem of coordination in such a large system then became one of how the individual banks could best cooperate with one another to their own and the economy's advantage. The solution was found in the development of an elaborate network of correspondent banks. The groundwork for correspondent banking was laid in the antebellum years, when small country banks, either voluntarily or at the behest of large city banks (the so-called Suffolk System of New England being a prime example of the latter pattern), began to maintain balances in city banks for purposes of note redemption and selling city funds or "exchange" to their local customers. New York City, the rising center of the nation's commercial activity, became the focal point of the emerging correspondent network, and New York banks began to compete with one another for the balances of outside banks by paying interest on them. In addition to being the leading commercial center, New York had the advantage of possessing the nation's most active securities markets. This advantage proved instrumental in making New York the focal point of the correspondent banking network, because it gave the New York banks an attractive outlet for lending the funds outside banks held with them, namely the short-term or call-loan market, where stock and bond traders used bank loans to carry securities.[22]

While New York banks profited by relending the balances of outside banks at rates above those they paid, the smaller country banks, whose local loan markets were much more seasonal in nature, benefited by being able to earn a return on funds that might otherwise have been idle. These mutual advantages were widely understood and appreciated; by 1850 roughly six of every seven chartered banks in the United States maintained balances in New York, and because these balances were very liquid—they could be recalled at any time—the banks and some state regulatory authorities began to count them as bank reserves.[23] The federal banking laws of 1863 and 1864 recognized these existing practices by making New York the central reserve city of the National Banking System, where country and city banks could hold legal reserve balances and by allowing national banks also to hold reserve balances in other designated reserve cities.

With these legal sanctions, the correspondent-banking network rapidly extended itself after the Civil War. Whereas in antebellum times it had been more regional than national in scope and had concerned itself mostly with note redemption and exchange functions, the correspondent network during the late nineteenth century developed into a system performing a wide range of functions for banks throughout the United States. These included, besides exchange, the collection of items such as checks, bills, drafts, and amounts due on security investments; the gathering and sharing of credit information; the purchase of commercial paper and securities for correspondent banks and their customers; interbank lending and rediscounting; and the offering of interest-paying interbank deposit accounts that provided banks with legal reserves, liquidity, and asset diversification.[24] It was the informal correspondent network rather than banking laws and regulations that created an integrated system for the thousands of small and independent banks of America. Through the correspondent network, private banks, state-chartered banks operating under a variety of laws, and the banks of the federal National Banking System were tied together into one system that functioned without much regard for political and jurisdictional boundaries within the country. This system fostered capital mobility among regions and thereby made its own important contribution to the development of a nationwide market in the United States. At the same time, it created conditions under which small-business banking could thrive.[25]

Although the operational requirements interests of individual banks thus led them to build an integrated system based upon correspondent relationships, the interest of bankers in politics and legislation, both of which impinged heavily on their enterprises, presented greater difficulties. The great virtue of the correspondent network, as far as the small bank was concerned, was that the bank could enjoy its many advantages merely by developing a correspondent relationship with one or a few larger banks in regional or national centers. But when a small bank wished to speak out on political and legislative issues, it could not have much influence merely by acting on its own. For that influence, the banks needed an organizational equivalent of the correspondent network that served them well in their ordinary business pursuits.

The first developments of a permanent nature in such a direction occurred, as an organizational theorist would expect, in local and regional coalitions. Perhaps because of the intensely individual and competitive nature of American banking after the first years, even on these levels, where relatively small numbers of banks could perceive common interests and organize at relatively low cost, coalitions were slow in developing. According to Fritz Redlich, the first such coalition emerged in 1853, when banks in and around

Philadelphia established the Philadelphia Board of Presidents and agreed that meeting periodically "for purposes of conference and interchange of views on such topics pertaining to the banking interests of this locality as will be considered proper subjects of discussion and action will promote stability and regularity in the business of banking."[26] Developments along similar lines soon followed at state, regional, and national levels but generally foundered by attempting to be exclusive (for example, to be for National Banks rather than all banks).[27] In 1875, a convention open to all bankers took place in Saratoga Springs, New York, and this led to the organization of the American Bankers Association (ABA) in the following year. The association had as vice presidents one banker from every state, and one of its organizational goals—eventually achieved—was to build state associations as subsidiary units. Through its work on the national and state levels, the ABA was instrumental in consolidating the views of thousands of bankers and giving them a powerful voice in legislative and regulatory proceedings where bankers' interests were at stake. Like the correspondent-banking network, the ABA represented a solution to bankers' problems that was consistent with, and even favorable to, the development of small-business banking.

CONCLUSION: THE RATIONALE OF SMALL-BUSINESS BANKING

Small-business banking in the United States had to overcome many obstacles before it flourished in the late-nineteenth and early-twentieth centuries. Some of these obstacles—the attempts of early American banks to preserve their privileged positions, and the heavy hands of laws and governmental regulations—have already been encountered in the foregoing discussion. There were others. In public opinion, from the agrarians of Pennsylvania—who in the mid-1780s were successful, albeit briefly, in repealing that state's charter of the Bank of North America—to the populists and progressives more than a century later, there was an uninterrupted train of thought that was suspicious of, and hostile toward, banks. This part of public opinion did not much distinguish between large and small banks, but because it was stronger in agricultural than in commercial and industrial areas, it tended negatively and differentially to affect the prospects for, and progress of, small-business banking. Such a body of opinion, operating through popular government, helped to retard the emergence of small-business banking at many times and places during the nineteenth century.

Antibanking ideas in public opinion were reinforced by many writers and scholars who studied banking. Early in the century, writers such as John Taylor of Caroline and William Gouge railed against banks in highly moralistic condemnations; while after the Civil War, scholars like William Graham Sumner and Francis Amasa Walker continued the attack, although in less emotionally charged terms.[28] Often these attacks contained a bias against small-business banking because of the lack of order, standards, and accountability that was alleged to have arisen as small banks proliferated. These contemporary views colored the interpretations of twentieth-century American banking historians—Bray Hammond's *Banks and Politics* and Fritz Redlich's *Molding of American Banking* are the leading examples—to such an extent that the defects of ninteenth-century banking arrangements became a staple of historiography.

One of the commonly cited defects of American banking was precisely the scope it gave to the development of small, independent banking enterprises. In the view of a large number of serious students of banking, far fewer and many times larger banks with extensive branch systems—which had long been the pattern in Scotland and was in the late nineteenth century rapidly becoming the case in England—would have been greatly preferable to the multiplication of small-business banks that was occurring in America. James summarizes the views of these contemporary students in the following passage:

> Branch banks were argued to make more efficient use of reserves, furnish a much larger volume of loanable funds from the same amount of resources, to offer superior management, and also to be safer because of the opportunity for diversification of risk over wide areas. The greatest advantages of branch banking, however, were seen to be its implications for the interregional transfer of credit or short-term capital. Credit could be extended to remote areas. Branch banking would allow the establishment of branch offices where the population was so small or sparse that an ordinary bank could not be supported, so that there would be no banking facilities at all available otherwise.[29]

Branch banking before the twentieth century had never really flourished in the United States. During the post-Civil War era, the overwhelming emphasis on independent unit banks as opposed to banks with branches was traced to the National Bank Act of 1864, which appeared to preclude branching for national banks. Since the national law influenced state banking laws, it seemed obvious to observers that branch banking along Scottish and English lines was being prevented in America by legislation.

These are reasons for doubting this widely held opinion. At the end of the century, nine states, including New York, allowed their state-chartered banks and trust companies to branch; three more states allowed branching for trust companies only. Yet in 1901, despite the openings created for branch banking in these jurisdictions, there were only 47 banks with a total of 85 branches.[30] If branch banking possessed so many advantages over unit banking, one wonders why it was so little adopted in states where it was legal. Small independent banks were increasing their numbers by the thousands between 1890 and 1920, when the entry barriers erected by earlier legislation were being eroded, yet branch banking lagged. Could it be that small-business banks possessed advantages over branches? The facts would seem to make such a suggestion.

If small-business banks had an advantage before the 1920s—when the automobile and other forces began to dismantle it—that advantage probably had to do with their superior information about local conditions and the quickness with which they could act in a fluid and rapidly developing economy. Visualize, if you will, a newly settled area on the frontier of nineteenth-century America. The railroad allows settlers to farm the virgin land and to market their products. A small town is created *de novo* to serve the surrounding countryside and to develop its own commercial activities as well. The farmers and the businessmen of the area are alike in their need for bank credit. They have an intimate knowledge of their own needs and resources and those of their own community. Would they be more likely to obtain, and obtain soon, the banking facilities they need and desire by being able freely to form their own small banking enterprises, or by requesting that a branch bank be opened by a larger institution some distance away and with less knowledge of, and interest in, the new community? Pending further information and hypothesis testing, one cannot, of course, be sure of the answer. But when the question is framed in such a way an answer is suggested, and this answer provides a rationale for the type of small-business banking that was so widely utilized in America up to a half-century ago. If the suggested answer is indeed correct, then the great influences of geo-

graphical expansion on the nature of American institutions during the nineteenth century—an influence found in so many other areas of American
life—would be seen to have operated on the business of banking as well.

Notes

1. The most thorough survey of colonial currency issues is by Leslie V. Brock, *The Currency of the American Colonies, 1700–1764*. Other useful works dealing with a variety of experiences and representing different and sometimes opposed interpretations are Richard A. Lester, *Monetary Experiments, Early American and Recent Scandinavian* (Princeton: Princeton University Press, 1939); Curtis P. Nettels, *The Money Supply of the American Colonies before 1720* (Madison: University of Wisconsin Press, 1934); Roger Weiss, "The Issue of Paper Money in the American Colonies, 1720–1774," *Journal of Economic History* (Dec. 1970) 30:770–84; and Robert Craig West, "Money in the Colonial American Economy," *Economic Inquiry* (Jan. 1978), 16:1–15.

2. See Bray Hammond, *Banks and Politics in America, from the Revolution to the Civil War*, especially chap. 2.

3. The measure of bank size, average paid-in capital stock, is far from perfect, but it avoids some problems of other measures. Average capital accounts per bank, a measure that would include surplus earnings not paid out to stockholders, depends on both dividend policies and the average age of banks, which changed markedly over the course of the nineteenth century. Average assets or liabilities per bank, another often-used measure of bank size, is not very suitable for long-term analyses because as market loan and investment returns vary in the long run, banks tend to vary their assets or liabilities per unit of bank capital in the opposite direction in order to maintain their profitability. All measures in nominal terms, such as the average capital data presented in table 10.1 lead to some distortions when between-year comparisons involve different price levels; fortunately, these distortions are not large for the nineteenth century, which was a rare period of long-term price-level stability when compared to earlier or later experiences.

4. See Hammond, *Banks and Politics*, chaps. 2–6.

5. As quoted ibid., p. 47.

6. Ibid., p. 51.

7. See Fritz Redlich, *The Molding of American Banking*, part 1, p. 21.

8. Ibid., pp. 20–30.

9. See Richard Sylla, "Forgotten Men of Money: Private Bankers in Early U.S. History."

10. Girard's struggles are set out in detail in Donald R. Adams, Jr., *Finance and Enterprise in Early America: A Study of Stephen Girard's Bank*.

11. U.S., Treasury Department, Secretary, *Reports on Finances, 1789–1849* (Washington, D.C.: Blair and Rives 1837–1849), 3:457.

12. On the history of free banking, see Hammond, *Banks and Politics*, chap. 18, and Redlich, *Molding of American Banking*, part 1, chap. 7. For a reasoned analysis of its effects, see Hugh Rockoff, *The Free Banking Era: A Re-examination*.

13. For a more detailed discussion of these matters, see Richard Sylla, *The American Capital Market, 1846–1914*, chap. 2.

14. Ibid.

15. John A. James, *Money and Capital Markets in Postbellum America*, p. 233.

16. Ibid., p. 234.

17. Ibid., pp. 226–32.

18. Ibid., pp. 36–39.

19. Sylla, *American Capital Market*, p. 54.

20. *Report of the Indianapolis Monetary Commission* (Chicago, 1898), p. 376, as quoted by James, *Money and Capital Markets*, p. 94.

21. See Redlich, *Molding of American Banking*, part 2, chap. 20. This chapter, titled "Cooperation Among American Banks," provides a most detailed survey of the evolution of cooperative arrangements during the nineteenth century.

22. The emergence of New York City as a financial center is best described by Margaret G. Myers, *The New York Money Market: Origins and Development*.

23. James, *Money and Capital Markets*, p. 97.

24. Ibid., pp. 99–103.

25. The recent book by John James, *Money and Capital Markets*, contains, in chap. 4, an excellent account of the functioning and vast extent of the correspondent banking network in the United States around 1900.

26. Quoted by Redlich, *Molding of American Banking*, part 2, p. 274.

27. Ibid., pp. 276–81.

28. Antibank writers and their sentiments are discussed in Richard Sylla, "American Banking and Growth in the Nineteenth Century: A Partial View of the Terrain."

29. James, *Money and Capital Markets*, p. 91.

30. Ibid., pp. 90–91.

Selected Bibliography

Adams, Donald R., Jr. *Finance and Enterprise in Early America: A Study of Stephen Girard's Bank*. Philadelphia: University of Pennsylvania Press, 1978.
Board of Governors of the Federal Reserve System. *All Bank Statistics*, United States 1896–1955. Washington, D.C.: The Board, 1959.

Brock, Leslie V. *The Currency of the American Colonies, 1700–1764*. New York: Arno, 1975.

Cottrell, P. L. and B. L. Anderson. *Money and Banking in England: The Development of the Banking System, 1694–1914*. Newton Abbot: David & Charles, 1974.

Gouge, William M. *A Short History of Paper Money and Banking in the United States*. New York: B. & S. Collins, 1835.

Hammond, Bray. *Banks and Politics in America, from the Revolution to the Civil War*. Princeton: Princeton University Press, 1957.

James, John A. "The Development of the National Money Market, 1843–1911." *Journal of Economic History* (December 1976), 36:878–97.

—— *Money and Capital Markets in Postbellum America*. Princeton: Princeton University Press, 1978.

Keehn, Richard. "Federal Bank Policy, Bank Market Structure, and Bank Performance: Wisconsin, 1863–1914." *Business History Review* (Spring 1974), 48:1–27.

Myers, Margaret G. *The New York Money Market: Origins and Development*. New York: Columbia University Press, 1931.

Redlich, Fritz. *The Molding of American Banking: Men and Ideas*. New York and London: Johnson Reprint Corp., 1968.

Rockoff, Hugh. *The Free Banking Era: A Re-examination*. New York: Arno, 1975.

Sumner, William Graham. *A History of American Currency*. First published in 1874. New York: Augustus M. Kelley, 1968.

Sylla, Richard. *The American Capital Market, 1846–1914*. New York: Arno, 1975.

—— "American Banking and Growth in the Nineteenth Century: A Partial View of the Terrain." *Explorations in Economic History* (Winter 1971–72), 9:197–227.

——"Forgotten Men of Money: Private Bankers in Early U.S. History." *The Journal of Economic History* (March 1976), 36:173–88.

Taylor, John. *An Inquiry into the Principles and Policy of the Government of the United States*. First published in 1814. London: Routledge and Kegan Paul, 1950.

Walker, Francis Amasa. *Money*. First published in 1878. New York: Augustus M. Kelley, 1968.

11

LABOR AND SMALL-SCALE ENTERPRISE DURING INDUSTRIALIZATION

David Brody

THE historian of the future," wrote the economist David A. Wells in 1889, "will doubtless assign" to the era just ending a unique place in human annals. Sweeping advances in the methods of production had given man "such a greater control over the forces of Nature . . . that he has been able to do far more work in a given time, produce far more product, measured by quantity in a ratio to a given amount of labor, and reduce the effort necessary to ensure a comfortable subsistence in a far greater measure than [was ever before] possible." Central to this economic revolution was the tendency "rapidly and inevitably leading to the concentration of manufacturing in the largest establishments, and the gradual extinction of those which are small." This constituted an evident imperative of industrial progress. "The concentration of production by machinery in large establishments [is] . . . in a certain and large sense, not voluntary on the part of the possessors and controllers of capital, but necessary or even compulsory." [1]

David Wells's contemporary perception remains very much our own. An expanding scale of operations seems to have been a persistent feature of American industrial innovation. Interchangeable-parts technology lodged the production of guns and clocks in factories early in the nineteenth century. After the War of 1812, the power loom prompted Boston investors to erect America's first truly large-scale factories in the form of integrated textile mills. In the middle decades of the century, advances in iron production, machine tools, and steam power led to a proliferation of integrated metal-working factories. The invention of the refrigerator car in the 1870s enabled meat packers to concentrate the processing of fresh meat in giant plants in the Chicago stockyards, and hence to benefit from the economies of the division of labor and utilization of byproducts. In steel, the integration of the stages of production—blast furnaces, Bessemers, rolling mills—vastly increased the size of the basic plants. Assembly-line techniques transformed automobile manufacture inside of a decade: by 1914, fourteen plants employed nearly two-thirds of the nation's auto workers. The Census of Manufactures for 1914 revealed the cumulative effect of industrial change on the scale of production: nearly a third of all industrial workers were employed in plants of 500 or more, another third in plants of between 100 and 500. And, with the integration of business units in this period, an increasing number of workers—at least a third of those in manufacturing in 1923—were in the employ of firms operating more than one plant.[2]

To focus on labor in small-scale enterprise seems, therefore, almost by definition to fasten on the retrograde aspect of the subject. This is a compelling recipe for scholarly neglect, given the historian's natural attraction to the forces of innovation and change. Yet, on several counts, a price has been paid for our inattention to the labor experience of small business in the industrializing age.

Even at the close of that period, small-scale manufacturing remained very considerable. If two-thirds of American workers in 1914 labored in plants of 100 or more, that left another third in smaller operations. With the line drawn at plants of 250, 53.8 percent fell on the lower side. There were roughly 54,000 establishments in 1914 employing between six and twenty workers, and that number actually held steady over the next decade, although proportionately the number of workers in such shops was shrinking.[3] What is of perhaps greater consequence, large-scale enterprise was a relatively late phenomenon in the course of industrialization. In 1870, only a handful of plants—the textile mills of upper New England, few iron and steel plants, the Baldwin Locomotive works—employed many more than 1,000 workers. For the nation's sixteen leading industries, the number of workers per plant averaged only 52 in 1870. The number reached 127 by 1900. Plant size actually increased most rapidly during the three decades after 1900. So that, for most of the formative period, the common experience of manufacturers was with comparatively small numbers of workers. The labor history of small-scale enterprise does not merit attention only on grounds of equity, however. By understanding that history, we may also advance our grasp of the dynamics of industrialization, in particular, as this was affected by changes in the size of work forces.

The Small Business Administration currently defines a small business as one employing under 250 workers. Not ten factories of over that size probably existed in the entire state of New York in 1830.[4] Half a century later, a plant of 250 would still have been considered a very substantial enterprise. For our purpose, however, what counts are not the relative differences, but the absolute ones. Our concern is with the problems employers faced that were specifically attributable to the size of the work force. So the meaning of "big" and "small" becomes *functional,* and refers to those thresholds at which further increases in the scale of operations altered how workers would be recruited and managed.

My hypothesis is that, as against the benefits that flowed from innovations tending toward larger-scale production, the resulting increase in numbers was in itself a negative factor for employers, so perceived by them and, in very large measure, so in reality. In certain respects, moreover, the problems relating to large work forces were peculiarly intractable, only belatedly confronted in any coherent way and, unlike other problems of production and management, not wholly resolved even well into the twentieth century. Or, to put the point another way, if any advantage accrued to small-scale enterprise, it was precisely that it did not need to recruit and administer large numbers of workers.

In the United States, industrialization began under markedly adverse labor-market conditions. Unlike England, agrarian America lacked the pauper laborers and preindustrial workers (especially the spinners and hand-loom weavers) who were the natural recruits for a factory system. Eli Whitney voiced the essential problem in 1798 when he landed his first government contract to manufacture guns on the principle of interchangeable parts: "I expect it will be necessary to employ from 120 to 150 workmen. I have no idea that it will be possible for me to collect *one third* of this number who have ever been employed in making any part of a musket or gun. The fact is I have not only the arms but a large proportion of the armourers to make."[5] Whitney surmounted the problem (not without difficulties that delayed the timely completion of his contract), but the labor shortage he faced generally militated in favor of factories substantially smaller in scale than what Whitney had envisaged.

For the next half-century, the prevailing pattern was for the wide dispersion of manufacturing in the rural areas of the Middle Atlantic and New England states. This was, to be sure, partly dictated by the existing level of technology—above all, by the dependence on sites for water power, but also, as in the case of early iron industry, by the reliance on ample sources of charcoal, or, as in the case of paper manufacture, by the need for large quantities of pure water for processing the rag fiber. But this dispersion also gave access to the principal source of available hands. By locating in a rural village, a manufacturer could draw on the depressed segments of the local population—the subsistence farmers, the renters and agricultural laborers, the handymen, and their wives and children. Among the labor patterns that resulted was the hiring of entire families in the textile mills of southern New England, the use of local women to do the unskilled work in the Berkshire paper mills, and the putting-out of much of the work in boots and shoes and other light-goods industries.

Once an enterprise outran the local supply of hands, recruiting entered a new plane of complexity. If skilled artisans were wanted, it might be necessary to send off to Europe, always an expensive and chancy undertaking. And to attract people from beyond the immediate vicinity—that is, beyond walking distance—required at the least an investment in company housing and, very likely, an increase in wage rates. As they grew, textile mills in southern New England sometimes made family units responsible for recruiting additional workers.[6] Where the putting-out system prevailed, it was possible to widen the primitive system of distribution to reach a wider range of working households. The imperative of business growth, whether technical or arising from rising customer demand, outweighed the problems of finding additional hands, but clearly the expanding manufacturer of the early nineteenth century encountered recruitment problems that did not face his smaller rivals.

No one, however, confronted a problem comparable to that of the integrated textile mills of Waltham and Lowell. Unlike virtually every other industrial enterprise of this early period, these mills started out on a grand scale and had to locate, in one stroke, a very large supply of workers. (Even a firm like Baldwin Locomotive, which expanded very rapidly during the 1840s, started on a small scale and built up its work force gradually.) The answer, of course, lay in the thousands of young women on the farms of rural New England. This was a brilliant solution, to be sure, but it was also a unique one. It took an investment in model factories, in boardinghouses, and in town building that only the resources of the Boston Associates could have managed (not to speak of the prestige to counter the prejudice against factory labor as morally corrupting and socially degrading). The supply of farm girls, moreover, was limited, and could not have satisfied the demand of a broader range of employers. As it was, the area from which the Waltham-style mills drew their girls widened each year and was reaching a limit in the late 1830s. By then, too, the initial optimism had begun to fade amidst the inexorable realities of the factory system. The discontent of the mill girls expressed itself, among other ways, in strike activity and agitation for the ten-hour day. How the textile mills might have solved their mounting labor-supply problems remains altogether uncertain had it not been for the arrival of the Irish and then the French-Canadians to replace the departing Yankee girls.

The flood of immigrants that began in the 1830s, carrying English and German artisans and unskilled laborers from Ireland, and later from the southern and eastern reaches of the continent, put a permanent end to America's endemic labor shortage. After mid-century, the availability of workers no longer placed any restraint on the scale of industrial operations. In fact, the recruiting advantage shifted over to the larger employers, partly by virtue of their prominence in the labor market, partly by virtue of their tendency to locate at strategic points in the transportation network, and partly because of a downgrading of skill levels with advancing technology.

No marked burden was placed thereby on small firms. For one thing, they also participated in the industrial relocation to population centers in this later period. From the first, certain industries not requiring power-driven machinery, such as clothing manufacture, had taken root in the commercial cities where labor was available and access easy to suppliers and markets. Improvements in steam technology prompted others to follow suit. An industrial city such as Newark, New Jersey, with 73.5 percent of its labor force engaged in manufacturing, housed an army of small firms producing hats, leather goods, jewelry, and trunks. Most rented space in large factory buildings equipped with central steam engines providing power for the tenants. Newark firms, which employed an average of 28.3 in 1860, were able to draw on a large pool of workers in what had become the nation's eleventh largest city.[7]

The labor movement also helped meet the recruitment needs of small business. Most craft unions undertook to maintain skill levels, to standardize wage rates, and to regulate the national labor market of their craft (including directing workers to labor-short areas). It was, in fact, largely for these purposes that national organizations emerged as the dominant institution of the American labor movement. Among employers operating on a small scale and dependent on skilled labor, the craft unions played a key role in maintaining an orderly labor market. In the case of the building trades, the unions actually assumed the role of labor contractor, providing skilled workers to builders on a job-by-job basis.

There was the fact, too, that the very technological advances giving rise to large-scale production eased the recruitment problems of smaller, less innovative firms. As the demand for wrought iron declined in the face of competition from steel in the 1880s and after, for example, the surviving iron mills found little trouble recruiting the puddlers and heaters who had earlier been in scarce supply.

It should be added, finally, that large employers did little to capitalize on certain advantages they had by virtue of their size and resources. Hiring practices tended to be informal and chaotic, with men selected randomly from the crowds gathered at the factory gates, or through pull with the straw boss. Even the largest of firms ignored the problems of labor turnover and did little to develop training programs. Not until after 1900 did large employers begin to heed the advice of such experts as Frederick W. Taylor and begin to rationalize their recruitment practices.

On the whole, small-scale operation did not impose significant liabilities in the search for workers during the industrializing period. In the early years, the advantage probably lay with the manufacturer whose needs could be met from the small labor pool in the vicinity of his mill. By mid-century, the inherent advantage shifted to the larger employer, but with sufficient compensating factors to assure the small employer of adequate access to the labor market. On balance, the nineteenth-century competition for workers between large and small firms must be rated something of a standoff. Quite a different conclusion would apply when it came to the management of workers.

Strictly speaking, preindustrial America afforded very little in the way of managerial experience outside the coercive forms associated with military service, the merchant marine, and involuntary labor. (It is worth noting that the one colonial industry that operated on a large scale—the iron plantations—depended not on free labor, but primarily on slaves and indentured servants.) The early factories generally relied on customary relationships deriving from artisan production. The mechanic-manufacturer was the master of the skills and technology (which he may well have had a hand in designing) in his mill. He exercised close supervision over production, and, in fact, might have worked side by side with his employees at first.[8] His relations with his hands were direct and personal, extending especially in the rural village into a network of social and religious connections.

When a committee of workers at the Collins Company—manufacturers of axes—protested a wage cut in 1833, the proprietor Samuel Watkinson Collins replied at length.

I am particularly pleased with the *candid manly* course which you have pursued in this crisis. . . . Instead of such disorderly and disgraceful conduct as we hear of in manufacturing communities in other countries on similar occasions . . . we find them here assembling quietly by the hundreds. Not at a Tavern to heat their blood and warp their judgment with grog, but in the cool open air in front of a temperance store where pen and ink and paper can be procured and business conducted in a truly *Republican town-meeting style.* That this assembly was composed of *cool, dispassionate, reasonable* men I want no better proof than I have in the appearance and character of the men who waited on me this morning as your committee. They would do credit to any community and I am proud to claim them as my fellow citizens.

The decision to cut wages derived from the need to keep the firm operating, and hence was taken in the interest of the entire community, and not (as had been rumored) out of Collins's greed and selfishness.

I trust that many in this community know me better, but it is not strange that some who have not been here long and with whom I have not had much personal intercourse should entertain such ideas and suppose that I wish to oppress them, whereas nothing could be further from the thoughts and intent of heart.

Evidently impressed, the workers voted "to go on cheerfully in the discharge of their duties," thanked Collins for his "approbation," and vowed "as residents here and as American citizens . . . to do all in our power to promote our common welfare."[9]

The mill village provided the social basis for the management of early American industry, whether it was the republican spirit of Collinsville, the evangelicalism of the New England textile towns, or the grim tyranny that prevailed in the iron-producing villages of Pennsylvania. Industrial discipline was a reflection of community ideology, and also to some degree, of its social structure—as was true, for example, in textile villages in which the authority of the family provided the first-line discipline inside the mill. And all of this, in turn, was capped by the presence of the mill proprietor (or his agent) who maintained close-knit ties to the community and exerted immediate oversight of all the operations of the mill. In a treatise widely read in the United States, the British textile man James Montgomery urged mill agents, "while guarding against too much *lenity* on the one hand, to be careful to avoid too much *severity* on the other . . . not too distant and haughty, but affable and easy of access, yet not too familiar."[10]

With the growth of the work force, the personal basis for management began to erode. Even as Samuel Collins had been making his plea in 1833, conditions in Collinsville had been changing, as evidenced by his reference to the strangers entering his mill. And when Collins faced a similar protest against wage cuts in 1846, he responded with the colder logic of the marketplace: anyone who thought he could do better elsewhere was free to quit. Partly reflective of his maturation as an industrial capitalist, partly of the increased size and diversity of the work force, Collins's response signaled the entry of his company into the ranks of those no longer able to base their labor administration on the direct, personal relationships that had characterized the first generation of small factories. (In his *Reminiscences,* Collins conceded the greater efficacy of the "spread-eagle reply" of 1833; he lost much of his labor force in 1846) Similarly, as mill labor grew more diverse and numerous in the textile industry, the family system gave way to the impersonal rule of shop regulations, payment to the individual rather than the father, and the abandonment of long-term contracts.

Confronted on the one hand by the unraveling of the social cohesion buttressing his authority, and by an increasingly large and anonymous work force on the other, the manager lost his capacity to exert close, personal direction over production at some point in the growth of his factory. The attraction of the putting-out system may well have included its ability to evade this problem without sacrificing the economies of scale. A great New York clothing manufacturer such as Lewis and Harford employed only 72 people, mainly cutters, on its own premises in 1849, but another 3,688 worked on its material in outside shops.[11] Much the same system operated in the boot and shoe industry of Lynn. Only well after mid-century, with the invention of the sewing machine and the increasing pressure for uniform quality and predictable output, did the manufacture of footwear and men's clothing move into the factory. (Under the proper conditions, on the other hand, the reverse could occur: in women's clothing, a highly rationalized division of labor subcontracted among tenement shops resulted in a decline of 32 percent in the average employment of establishments in that industry between 1899 and 1919.)

Technology and power requirements precluded a system of outside contracting in most industries. Metal-fabricating firms, ranging from locomotive building to clock making, brought contracting inside the plant. When it began operations in 1855, the Winchester Repeating Arms Company employed only one or two contractors, but, with the increased demand sparked by the Civil War and advances in gun design and manufacturing techniques, the production of components was turned over entirely to contractors, leaving to the management only the responsibility for providing materials, for inspection, and for final assembly. The contractors hired and paid their own men, supervised the work, and received a piece rate for the output of their departments, plus a day rate as employees. The Winchester Company, as its historian observed, was "able to avoid the problem of organizing and disciplining a large part of what was called the 'productive' labor force, while the piece-rate method of paying the contractor functioned as a crude incentive system."[12] New England machine-tool firms, operating on an order basis rather than mass production, gave work to inside contractors through a bidding system, rather than by making them virtual department heads. In varying forms, inside contracting became a widespread practice in fabricating plants during the nineteenth century and even into the twentieth century.

In metal-producing industries, the productive process demanded team effort under the direction of a craft worker. Puddlers, rollers, and molders assumed the role of labor supervisor. The tonnage rate might be set through a union contract, rather than by the individual negotiation characteristic of contracting. But the craft worker, like the inside contractor, took full charge of the work and of the men under him. Very much the same was true of the coal miner, who received a tonnage rate and paid his helpers, although his duties involved more his own labor than the supervision of others. It was not unknown, however, for a more elaborate form of contracting to exist, in which individual miners took over several rooms in a pit and had (as an outraged union miner from the Kahawha Valley wrote in 1888) "two to ten colored men working for them and they pay these poor fellows but from 50 cents to 75 cents a day." The influence of the trade union was consistently directed at resisting the exploitative possibilities inherent in these kinds of work—for instance, by fixing the rates for helpers and regulating a fair day's output—but not to limit the control of the craft worker over the work process.[13]

The nineteenth-century foreman fulfilled the same function over gang work and repetitive processes. An employee on salary, he was nevertheless no less autonomous a supervisory figure than the contractor or craft worker. He hired the workers under him, assigned jobs, maintained discipline (including the absolute right to fire), and was in general responsible for getting the work out. Only this last concerned the firm. How the foreman got the job done, as one disgruntled manager noted, "of course is under your own immediate management . . . and I am helpless unless I go in and do your work."[14]

It was precisely the admission of helplessness that was telling. When his operations grew beyond his capacity to supervise directly, the nineteenth-century manufacturer tended to carve his work force up into units small enough so that the accustomed forms of labor control could be maintained through the agency of contractors, craftsmen, and foremen. Undeniably, other influences were pushing in the same direction—the complexity of metal-product fabrication, the state of metallurgical technology, the ethnic diversity and high turnover of common labor. But the unifying thread was the decentralization of labor supervision in the large-scale enterprise. The conclusion to be drawn seems clear: whatever the imperatives in the direction of large-scale production, on the specific matter of managing workers, the nineteenth-century manufacturer conceded the superiority of the close, personal supervision that characterized small-scale enterprise. No better evidence of this fact could be adduced than the extent to which he sought to replicate those conditions in the context of the large-scale factory.

Decentralized labor administration was symptomatic of the uneven progress of American industrialism. For all his virtuosity at technological innovation, the enterpreneur was slow to confront the problems of management that went with large-scale, complex operations. "It was at one time thought to be practically impossible to manage a great railroad effectively," remarked Marshall M. Kirkman in his *The Science of Railroads* (5th ed. 1896). On the early lines, "management was personal and autocratic; the superintendent, a man gifted with energy and clearness of perception, moulded the property to his will. . . . But as the properties grew, he found himself unable to give his personal attention to everything. . . . He sought to do everything and do it well. He ended by doing nothing.'' The remedy, of course, lay in ''a suitable division of authority and management,'' and, with the Pennsylvania Railroad in the van, the railroads after the Civil War became America's testing ground for the principles of systematic management (Kirkman's work on management technique was but one of many examples).[15]

The same kinds of pressures built up in American manufacturing at a somewhat later time. Beginning in the 1880s under the leadership of men trained in engineering, the systematic-management movement attacked the traditional methods of factory administration as ''increasingly chaotic, confused and wasteful.''

''The old school of manufacturers,'' wrote Frederick W. Taylor in 1895, ''believe[s] in men, not in methods in the management of their shops. . . . The modern manufacturer, however, seeks not only to secure the best superintendents and workmen; but to surround each department of his manufacture with the most carefully woven network of system and method. . . . It is the lack of this system and method which . . . constitutes the greatest risk in manufacturing.''[16]

By the early twentieth century, large-scale industry was undergoing a managerial revolution scarcely less consequential than the earlier transformation of production technology. Cost-accounting methods generated precise data on both prime and overhead costs. Centralized systems were devised for purchasing and distributing materials. The steps in manufacturing processes were closely monitored for purposes of scheduling and coordinating operations. These measures required a thorough restructuring of factory administration to incorporate staff people, a record-keeping system, and an effective line of command down from the central office.

Stemming from the incapacity of traditional methods to control large-scale operations, systematic management did more than solve the problems of the big plant. It rendered obsolete those methods within the small plant as well. Once systematic management was in place, the large plant had a rationalized capacity to plan and direct its operations clearly better than what the head of a small firm could achieve by traditional methods. Nor did the latter have the ready means—and, what was equally important, the obvious incentive— to adopt systematic management, with its demands for specialized personnel and support departments and its formal approach to the problems of administration. The breaking of the managerial bottleneck in large-scale operations may well account in part for the great surge in the average size of industrial plant that is recorded in the census statistics for the period 1900–29. Beyond the single plant, parallel developments remedied the managerial weaknesses of the early industrial combines of the trust era and made the integrated firm a permanent feature of twentieth-century industrialism.

And yet—for all its record of success—in the one area of labor, the achievement of systematic management was problematic; and, for all its inferiority as a modern business form, the strength of small-scale enterprise in this sphere was undiminished. Although managerial reformers had left labor administration until last, the line they would take was foreordained by the logic of systematic management. The objective, as one expert remarked in 1900, was "to readjust the balance of responsibilities disturbed by the expansion of industrial operations, and to enable central control to be restored in its essential operations."[17] The assault on the autonomy of the contractor and foreman aimed first at matters of inventory and scheduling, but inevitably moved on to encompass wage rates and uniform conditions of work, and finally to recruitment and discipline. Certain of the foreman's labor functions were taken entirely from his hands, others were eroded by making them subject to uniform policies emanating from the plant administration. With Frederick W. Taylor, the application of systematic management to labor went to its logical extreme: the concentration of decision making in planning departments left no discretion in the hands of supervisory personnel; record keeping grew in complexity and coverage; and specialization of function reached the point of totally replacing the foreman with "gang bosses," "speed bosses," "inspectors," even "disciplinarians." The truly novel aspect of scientific management was its attempt to push the systematic method down into the work process itself. Taylor wanted to rationalize the large sector of activity that remained unsubordinated to the machine. All the examples cited in his *Principles of Scientific Management* (1911)—pig-iron shovellers, lathe operators, ball-bearing inspectors, bricklayers—involved workers who controlled the mode and pace of their tasks. By subjecting such "rule-of-thumb" jobs to time-and-motion study, and by standardizing the determination of labor prices through a rate-fixing department, Taylor hoped to complete the managerial control over labor that had begun with the division of labor, the assembly line, and the automatic process.

That a systematic approach was necessary for the labor administration of the large-scale factory seems altogether clear. But it does not follow that, as contrasted to other aspects of systematic management, rationalized labor administration gave to the large-scale enterprise a comparable advantage over the traditional labor administration of the small firm. Labor proved much more intractable a subject for rationalization than any other phase of plant administration. For all the elegance of its theoretical statement, Taylorism was never put into effect in the comprehensive, undiluted form envisaged by its founder. And even the objectives of a more moderate kind were only partially accomplished. This was true, for example, of so fundamental a matter as the subordination of the foreman to administrative direction. And it was true even of so concrete a problem as the rationalization of the wage-rate structure of the large industrial plant, which was accomplished in such industries as steel, autos, and meat packing only with the coming of collective bargaining after the 1930s. The acid test, however, involved labor motivation.

This had been the first concern of the proponents of systematic management when they turned their attention to labor. Would it not be possible, as the industrialist Henry R. Towne put it, to devise "some better method of bringing out of the men the best that is in them in doing their work?" [18] The question was prompted, first of all, by the notion that workers were naturally inclined to "soldier" (a favorite phrase of F. W. Taylor's) and to restrict output, and, increasingly, by doubts about the traditional rough-and-ready techniques of the foreman. "The reason why coercive 'drive' methods have prevailed in the past," remarked the labor-relations expert Sumner H. Slichter, "has been that a central management has been indifferent to the methods pursued by foremen in handling men but has insisted rigidly upon a constantly increasing output and constantly decreasing costs." [19] Well before 1900, systematic management was experimenting with incentive and profit-sharing plans. Taylor then put incentives at the heart of his scheme, but on this "scientific" basis: a guaranteed premium rate to be paid if productivity exceeded the standard determined by time-and-motion study. The next generation of labor experts, influenced on the one hand by the industrial-welfare movement and on the other by the new discipline of industrial psychology, moved beyond Taylor's simplistic conception of the worker as economic man. The 1920s saw a proliferation of "humanizing" labor programs—stock ownership to give "a sense of proprietorship," pensions and insurance "to help our workers get worries out of their minds," company unions to promote ''a growth in morale and in sympathy and understanding between employees and officials,'' and, crowning the structure, personnel experts who understood that ''the worker has a psychology all his own.'' As Charles Schwab of Bethlehem Steel put it in 1928: ''Industry's most important task in this day of large-scale production is management of man on a human basis.''[20]

Small business could scarcely emulate the labor-relations practices of corporate industry. At the close of the 1920s, only 6.5 percent of firms with fewer than 500 employees had industrial-relations departments, compared to over 30 percent for firms employing between 500 and 2,000, and 50 percent of those employing over 2,000. And on the touchstone program of progressive labor relations—employee representation—only 3 percent of workers covered in 1926 were in establishments of less than 1,000, while 62 percent worked in firms employing over 15,000.[21] Yet the liability to small-scale enterprise seems least likely in this most ambitious application of systematic management to labor administration. In no other area did the performance of modern management fall so short of its goals. All the evidence at our disposal, both direct and circumstantial, suggests the failure of large-scale enterprise to perfect the means for manipulating the will of the workingman. And, what is perhaps even more telling, a prime objective of rationalized labor relations—often explicitly stated—was to recover for the large-scale enterprise human dimensions of work that were inherent in the small business.

Of the fragmentary empirical evidence bearing on this point, two small studies seem especially pertinent. One is by the Bureau of Business Research of the University of Pittsburgh on the causes of failure of ten small metal-fabricating firms (averaging 236 employees) that had filed for bankruptcy in one U.S. District Court between 1936 and 1954. Notable among their underlying weaknesses were poor or inappropriate record systems and inept internal administration without clear lines of authority and properly trained personnel. The failure to adopt the elements of systematic management that were the hallmark of large-scale enterprise caused problems in every significant facet of their business activity save one. ''Conspicuously lacking from the record of the companies studied was any case where failure was directly traceable to labor trouble.'' And, in a comparison with ten successful small firms, all of whom were characterized by a concern for systematic management, investigators did not find a decisively better record of labor relations of the successful companies over the failed firms.[22] At least in this one respect, small business was spared the disadvantage that accrued from its lesser inclination or ability to adopt the systematic management that has characterized American large-scale enterprise in the twentieth century.

The second study, by the Industrial Relations Section at Princeton University, investigated 82 manufacturing plants in the Trenton, New Jersey, area in 1951–53 with this question in mind: What influence did plant size have on industrial relations? The smaller plants (defined, with some flexibility, as those having under 500 employees) suffered from a number of liabilities. Wages, fringe benefits, advancement opportunities were lower. Fewer than one in five plants with under 200 employees maintained an industrial-relations manager, one in three of the plants of between 200 and 500, compared to nine in ten of those between 500 and 1,000, and every larger plant. By a number of measures, nevertheless, the investigators gave higher marks to the smaller plants. They had lower turnover rates, fewer recruitment problems (because of an ability to rely on employees to recommend friends and relatives) and less labor-management conflict. And while labor productivity was not measured, the management interviews did not indicate concern on that score. In the smaller plants, the investigators perceived "a sort of self-discipline by the work force. It is the type of work pace and discipline that allows the worker to set his own schedule, but in time of stress or emergency he will speed up, sometimes phenomenally, to meet the needs of the management." All this the investigators ascribed to what they called the "personal approach"—that is, the ability of managers to maintain informal face-to-face contact with workers in the smaller Trenton plants.[23] Nothing in the genius of systematic management seemed able to compensate for that direct contact.

An expanding scale of operations was the companion of industrial progress in America. On that score, David Wells had surely been correct. But his confidence in industrial progress had blinded him to the intractability of the labor problems that accompanied large-scale enterprise. In the workingman, the entrepreneur encountered the one factor of production that was resistant to the logic of rational calculation that was at the heart of industrialization. When his work force grew large, the nineteenth-century manufacturer could not do better than to rely on the experience of small-scale operation. And if the emergence of systematic management encouraged efforts to rationalize the handling of workers in the twentieth century, the success registered was never sufficient to erase this anomaly in the triumphant progress of large-scale enterprise.

Notes

1. *Recent Economic Changes* (New York: D. Appleton and Co., 1889), reprinted in Sigmund Diamond, ed., *The Nation Transformed* (New York: George Braziller, 1963), pp. 27, 35.

2. *Abstract of the Census of Manufactures* (1914), pp. 410–11; *Recent Social Trends,* 2 vols. (New York: McGraw-Hill Book Co., 1933), 1:239.

3. *Recent Economic Changes,* 2 vols. (New York: McGraw-Hill Book Co., 1929), 1:167–68.

4. Louis McLane, *Documents Relative to the Manufactures in the United States,* 4 vols. (Washington: 1833, reprinted 1969), 3:48–59, 3:115–22.

5. Whitney to Oliver Wolcott, in Edward H. White, "Development of Interchangeable Mass Manufacturing . . . 1795–1825" (Ph.D. dissertation, University of Maryland, 1973), p. 84.

6. Barbara Tucker, "The Force of Tradition in the Southern New England Textile Industry, 1790–1860," (unpublished ms.), pp. 61–63.

7. Susan Bloomberg, "Industrialization and Skilled Workers: Newark, 1826–1866" (Ph.D. dissertation, University of Michigan, 1974), pp. 52–53, 56, 62.

8. See, e.g., Theodore F. Marburg, "Aspects of Labor Administration in the Early 19th Century," *Bulletin of the Business Historical Society* (Feb. 1941), 15:1–10.

9. Henrietta M. Larson, ed., "An Early Industrial Capitalist's Labor Policy," *Bulletin of the Business Historical Society* (Nov. 1944), 18:135–37.

10. Montgomery (1832) quoted in Alfred D. Chandler, *The Visible Hand: The Managerial Revolution in American Business* (Cambridge, Mass.: Harvard University Press, 1977), p. 69.

11. Egal Feldman, "New York Men's Clothing Trade, 1800–1861" (Ph.D. dissertation, University of Pennsylvania, 1959), p. 199.

12. John Buttrick, "The Inside Contracting System," *Journal of Economic History* (Summer 1952), 12:210. For a bibliographic reference on inside contracting, see Chandler, *Visible Hand,* note 54, p. 599.

13. Stephen Brier, "Interracial Organizing in the West Virginia Coal Industry," in Gary M. Fink and Merl F. Reed, eds., *Essays in Southern Labor History* (Westport, Conn.: Greenwood Press, 1977), pp. 26–27; David Montgomery, "Workers' Control of Machine Production in the 19th Century," *Labor History* (Fall 1976), 17:485–509.

14. Daniel Nelson, *Workers and Managers* (Madison, Wis.: University of Wisconsin Press, 1975), p. 42.

15. Reprinted in Diamond, *Nation Transformed,* pp. 81–91.

16. "A Piece-Rate System," *Transactions of the American Society of Mechanical Engineers* (1895), 16:856–907.

17. Samuel Haber, *Efficiency and Uplift* (Chicago: University of Chicago Press, 1964), p. 19.

18. Nelson, *Workers and Managers*, p. 52.

19. Ibid., p. 34.

20. David Brody, "The Rise and Decline of Welfare Capitalism," in John Braeman, et al, eds., *Change and Continuity in 20th Century America: The 1920's*, (Columbus, Ohio: Ohio State University Press, 1968) pp. 152–57; Haber, *Efficiency and Uplift*, p. 165.

21. National Industrial Conference Board, *Effect of Depression on Industrial Relations* (New York: NICB, 1934), pp. 4–10; *Recent Social Trends*, 2:844.

22. A. M. Woodruff and T. G. Alexander, *Success and Failure in Small Manufacturing* (Pittsburgh: University of Pittsburgh Press, 1958), pp. 31, 109.

23. Sherrill Cleland, *The Influence of Plant Size on Industrial Relations* (Industrial Relations Section, Princeton University, Research Report Series No. 89, 1955), pp. 43, 45, and passim.

12

THE FINANCING OF
SMALL BUSINESS IN THE UNITED STATES

Roland I. Robinson

THE financing of very small businesses is much like the financing of
persons and families. A prospective entrepreneur, inspired by a vision
of success and profit, canvasses first his own means, then those of his immediate family, and finally more remote relatives. If he is a man well regarded
by friends and neighbors, he may be able to secure supporting financing
from them. His aspiration is to do well, repay family and friends with a generous garnish of profits, and then to live well. If the entrepreneur approaches
the more formal channels of finance—banks and the like—his application
for funds is likely to be treated in much the same terms as any personal loan.
Is the prospective entrepreneur a man of good reputation? Has he a record of
having repaid earlier debts? Finally, and possibly most important, what collateral or surety can he furnish?

If the scope of our account were to be limited to very small, small businesses it would be an informal and not very factual account. Surprising as it
may seem in this day of many regulatory reports and the vast processing of
these reports by giant computers, a kind of statistical haze lies over this area
of finance. The reason is not lack of effort, but the very ambiguity which
surrounds the process. How are the business affairs of a grading contractor,
who owns a bulldozer, a backhoe, and a pickup truck with a transport
trailer; who gets by on the labor of himself and his sons—a very typical
small, small businessman—to be separated from his personal affairs? Is his
small orchard and garden business or personal? How do you classify his

pickup truck in which he also goes hunting and fishing? What is more, the tax regulations, far from helping to clarify this situation, give the small businessman every incentive for as much ambiguity as possible. However, our account is not to be limited to very small businesses but will extend into small businesses that are sometimes not so small at all.

PROBLEMS OF
SMALL-BUSINESS FINANCE

Surveys of small-business problems have generally placed finance as one of its leading problems, if not the most important one. The source of the complaint—if not the problem—has sometimes been that the complainers were not very sophisticated about financial affairs and expected financial support from sources, such as commercial banks, that cannot afford much risk; and they were looking for debt capital when their need was for equity funds.[1] Indeed, it can be said that at the present time the facilities for small-business finance in the United States are remarkably good.[2] A small business with valid economic expectations probably can find the financial support it needs. But this expectation is not without qualifications. It will probably be most useful to start this essay with an examination of the precise nature of financial problems in small business. In the following pages we shall examine some of the most common sources of such problems.

LONG TIME NEEDED TO REACH THE STAGE
OF PROFITABLE OPERATIONS

Some types of business operations mature slowly. During the early years of maturation, such businesses may need not only initial financing but, at later stages, repeated additions to invested capital. An example:*

> A series of small lakes was almost completely surrounded by swampy land. Even hunters hesitated to penetrate the swamps. A perceptive developer, however, surveyed the property carefully and conceived the idea of draining the swamps and, with terrain modification, to make the lakesides habitable resorts.
>
> The developer used his own resources plus money borrowed from his wife's

---

* This and the later examples cited in this article are all based on actual cases. Identification signs have been obliterated, however, so that comment on the cases can be candid and critical if the circumstances require it.

family to get the project started. He was even able to borrow a surprisingly large amount from a local bank using the land as security. The engineering aspects of the project developed fairly well according to schedule but in the beginning the marketing of the resort sites was slower than anticipated, partly due to a period of recession, but much more due to the fact that early buyers were hesitant to buy into an unproven development. For a while, it was necessary to rent cottages rather than sell them. In time, however, the project caught on with buyers and ultimately was very successful. However, the original developer had to yield such a large part of the equity in the project to get the successive stages of financing that his final diminished share in the profits was quite disappointing.[3]

Not all of the long-developing projects are success stories. Some such ventures sink virtually without a trace. Some, however, leave fragments which can be reconstructed into instructive even if discouraging stories. Such is our second example:

An early automotive engineer found drum brakes quite unsatisfactory. He was a racing enthusiast and wanted to develop better brakes. Because of a high reputation within automotive circles, he was able to get financial support for the engineering development of a new type of brake. His idea turned out ultimately to be the disc brake. He was able to develop good working models of such a brake. Such brakes were produced on a custom basis for racing cars with considerable success. However, the cost of producing the disc brake and the relatively short life of the brake pad led the mass producers of automobiles to resist adoption of the new brake.

The engineer repeatedly had to seek additional financing in his effort to develop more durable pads and to solve the production engineering problems of the new brake. For a while he turned his attention to a different application of the brake: the airplane. In the period approaching World War II, the size and speed of planes was increased very considerably. As a result the landing speeds of the plane were also greater. The combination of higher landing speeds and heavier planes would have required very long runways unless more efficient brakes could be developed. The engineer tried to work on his new and different problem, but his financial backing dried up (the effort had been going on for more than a decade) and he died a disappointed and frustrated man. The brake and the pads were developed by others and have since become commonplace.

High technology seems to have made this problem even more critical. Developmental time seems to be elongated by high technology, and the requirements for more safety testing have added to the time problem. As a result, projects with only distant prospects of profitability—even those with prospects of very great profitability—are shunned by experienced capital investors.[4]

The number of small businesses that are based on competence in sophisticated technology is not large, but such small businesses have had a special appeal for private investors and, in some periods, even for the stock market. The peculiar relationship of high technology and small business may have its foundation in the personalities and temperaments of persons involved in experimental science.[5] The histories of such persons have often shown an impatience with the bureaucracy of large organizations, and an independence of mind and action that seemed to fit best into the atmosphere of a small enterprise. Such persons are often endowed with strong egos (sometimes justified by the facts) and possibly rather eccentric behavior that does not fit well into conventional corporate structures. University-connected scientists sometimes fall into this category. It is more than coincidence that the peripheries of several of our leading schools of science contain a large number of small enterprises started by scientists who were originally connected with, and sometimes stay connected with, these schools. Sometimes government scientists, impatient with bureaucracy, have burst out of their jobs and started small businesses. An example:

> Five scientists, all working on nuclear-fusion research, attempted to get a nuclear reaction by showering microwaves on hot gas. No nuclear reaction followed but, instead, they got ultraviolet light. Later they said that their start came when they realized that the experiment was an "ultraviolet success rather than a nuclear failure." All but one stayed with their jobs, but they pooled savings, and the bachelor in the group quit his job and started work. Ultimately, most of them quit their jobs but they had to raise more capital, first within the group and later from a private venture capital company, American Research and Development. (The nature of such groups will be discussed later in this essay.) For seven years, the venture barely survived. They faced two types of problems: the engineering development into operational form of a laboratory idea (not always the strongest point of research scientists) and, then, a commercial application of the ultraviolet lamp. Finally they reached an acceptable level of product development and found a successful application. Currently they seem to be headed for success.[6]

The success stories of small high-technology companies tend to be remembered; the failures forgotten. However, it is clear that the survival rate has been low, although some of the successes have been spectacular indeed. In an era of ebullient economic optimism, these high-risk, high-technology ventures can usually find financing, but in periods of economic gloom, the sources of financing often turn to less risky ventures.

RAPID GROWTH CAN MAKE WORKING CAPITAL
DEMANDS BEYOND THE RESOURCES OF A SMALL BUSINESS

A small business presumably should be delighted with an unexpected
surge of growth. But growth can bring with it problems that are not easily
solved. This is illustrated by another example:

> A chemical engineer developed a treatment for waste paper which made it
> highly fire resistant. It could then be cheaply processed into a quite effective
> insulating material. The chemical engineer found the type of plant he needed for
> rent, and he was able to lease the machinery he needed. His own savings were ad-
> equate to get operations started. His timing could not have been better. The energy
> crisis brought on widespread demand for insulating material and, almost without a
> sales effort, this new concern quickly had more business than it could handle.
> However, he quickly found himself constantly short of cash. The reason: the bulge
> of accounts receivable strained the concern's working capital. The chemical engi-
> neer was able to solve this problem by factoring his accounts receivable. (Later
> this solution will be explained.)[7]

Rapid growth is not without end. That can also cause its own special
kinds of problems. Still one more example will illustrate this type of problem.

> A textbook publishing company representative knew that books of readings gen-
> erally lost money. However, except for small classes, the reserve shelf of the
> library is inefficient and some professors like books of readings. He conceived of
> the idea of publishing books of reading by cut-and-paste of original copy and off-
> set printing, which could be considerably cheaper than use of regular typeset. He
> quit his job and, using only his home—and the services of his wife as a cut-and-
> paste artist as well as secretary—he established a tiny "press." All of the offset
> printing was let by contract, and he had the print shops carry inventory and handle
> the shipping of orders. He also got an accounting service firm to do his bookkeep-
> ing. The operation was quickly successful and grew so rapidly that it outran the
> rather makeshift facilities. The salesman, based on his early record of success, was
> able to get financing for a small plant, in which he could centralize all of the
> operation except offset printing, which was still contracted out. The new plant
> reduced costs. However, other publishers soon copied his methods; and without a
> field staff, the salesman found his volume falling. Ultimately, the business col-
> lapsed and the salesman had to declare personal bankruptcy. His rapid growth was
> rather brief.

THE HIGH COST OF CAPITAL FOR SMALL BUSINESS

Modern theory of business finance has developed, and fairly well supported with empirical research, the concept that cost of capital is a linear

function of risk—risk being defined as variability of the expected returns.[8] But this modern theory has one added and extremely important corollary: the market will reward investors only for the assumption of such risk as cannot be covered by diversification. A diversifiable risk will not be rewarded by the capital markets. A simple illustration will illuminate the point.

Location is vital for a retail establishment. In spite of many efforts by marketing research to forecast the success of a location, mistakes are still made. The risk for a small single-outlet retailer is great. A chain of retailers, however, has advantages. It probably can command better market research for initial locations. When mistakes are made, however, their rectification is not necessarily too costly. They very likely were able to bargain a short-term lease at a higher rent for the initial experiment with a location. If it pans out badly, they can buy their way out of their lease inexpensively, move the inventory to a new location, and probably transfer the trained personnel as well. But such a mistake for a single-location retailer could be fatal.

What this means is that with this added risk, the cost of capital for small and nondiversified business is higher than for similar larger businesses, but a small business cannot, by strict economic logic, expect to recapture this extra cost from the market. The result is that most capital-intensive lines of business confront small businesses with a serious obstacle. The lines in which small business is more likely to be successful is in labor-intensive types of business, in which the proprietor is boss and can often recruit his labor force from the margins of the labor market, making it more productive than would be possible in a larger business: one with more formal but less effective lines of supervisory authority.[9] The "boss" works hard himself, and he can drive his fellow workers (employees, yes, but still fellow workers) harder than the line boss of a large corporation, who feels himself an employee.

FINANCE IS NOT ALWAYS A SMALL BUSINESS PROBLEM

The foregoing recital may exaggerate the problems of finance for small business. Some small businesses almost never encounter financial problems. If the aspirations of the owners are limited, and if there are circumstances or arrangements that can skirt the financing problem, it just never arises. Two examples will illuminate this case.

A high school teacher of vocational arts used his summers to augment his income by setting up a shop in his garage for the repair of lawn mowers. He quickly established a reputation for skill and dependability, and he had all the work he could do; soon he was employing one or two of his more talented high-school students to "help out." The business grew beyond lawn mowers into other machines with single-cylinder gasoline engines: snow blowers, Rototillers, mulchers, and finally even snowmobiles. His work became year-round, and he soon quit his teaching post. At that time, he moved his shop from his garage to an abandoned alley shop, with more space and better bench facilities. Even though his location was out of the way, the manufacturers of these various small machines urged him to become a dealer for them, but he elected to sell only lawn mowers, Rototillers, and snow blowers. His suppliers shipped him machines on consignment, so he had no problem of inventory financing. He sold for cash and had no problem of accounts receivable. In spite of a bad location, his faithful customers followed him and his business prospered. He was able to buy a much better home, to own more expensive automobiles, and finally to travel during his slack seasons. This fulfilled his aspirations in life and he had never faced any real financing problems.

The second example is from the mid–East Side of New York City.

Angelo, a first generation American, got his first job at 15 as a kitchen assistant and apprentice chef in a large hotel kitchen. In time he worked his way up to chef de cuisine, in which capacity he not only made menus but also bought all of the perishables. But his goal was a restaurant of his own, and he saved diligently to that end. In time, he found a location where an ambitious restaurant had failed. The location—a half-basement on a side street but near Madison Avenue, where advertising agencies abounded—involved a fairly high rent, but the place was already so well equipped that very little added investment was needed. Angelo installed his best friend as chef, he recruited waiters and kitchen help from the circle of his acquaintances, and he made his wife cashier. He opened with no more notice to the world than a new sign out front. Angelo arose at unholy hours and went to the markets to buy only the best vegetables and fish. He bought meat weekly. He had no printed menu; the daily menu was chalked on a blackboard in the kitchen and was memorized by the waiters. Angelo was his own *maître*, and he learned to remember his customers. Within a month of opening, he had more luncheon business than he could handle; dinner business was still on the slow side. Within six months, dinner business was overflowing. He stopped accepting reservations by phone, but he was usually able to find a table for regular customers, who soon included well-known persons, not only in advertising but also in publishing and the arts. Prices went up but the place remained crowded to capacity. The restaurant was quickly found by the food editor and reviewer of the *New York Times* and came to be listed in almost all restaurant guides. Angelo achieved his aspirations beyond his wildest dreams. He not only knew and recognized the great names of the street, he was recognized by them. And he never truly faced a financial problem. He had no aspirations for expansion; he liked his location and he made more money than he could spend.

A SHORT ANALYTICAL NOTE ON THE NATURE
OF SMALL-BUSINESS FINANCIAL NEEDS

So far we have not looked closely at the exact nature of financial needs. When small-business proprietors declare that they "need" financing, they usually mean that they want to find someone who will lend them money. Small businessmen are notoriously reluctant to share proprietary, or equity, interests with outsiders; they do not wish to have to share the profits expected.[10] The hard fact, however, is that a large fraction of small-business financial "needs" are for equity capital: capital that shares the risk but also stands to share in the gain. The formal canons of corporate finance have a variety of standards limiting the amount of debt that can be assumed. These standards can be applied to small businesses that have been in operation for some time, but they do not fit well the case of new small businesses. For almost twenty years, there has been a running dispute among the theorists of business finance as to the influence of debt in the capital structure on the cost of capital. The debate continues unresolved but in many ways it is a pointless dispute: the institutions for the supply of capital are not well adapted to the assumption of any great amount of risk. Since small business so often involves risk, it follows that the real need of most small businesses—no matter how much proprietors may resist the fact—is for equity capital. Our survey of solutions, therefore, will be mainly of sources of equity capital for small business beyond the amount that the initial entrepreneurs can provide.

SOLUTIONS TO SMALL-BUSINESS CAPITAL
NEEDS WITHIN PRIVATE SPHERE

Since small business really has a longer history than big business, it is clear that many of the financing arrangements have had a very long history. However, some of the arrangements for formal small-business financing are of comparatively recent development. In this section, we shall start with the oldest of these sources but shall then turn to some newer types of arrangement.

COMMERCIAL BANKS AS SMALL-BUSINESS LENDERS

Later in this essay, we shall deal with governmental guarantee of commercial bank loans to small business. However, commercial banks without any such outside support have long been, and continue to be, major suppliers of credit to small business. Since so many of the commercial banks in the United States are themselves small-business enterprises, this affinity of interests is not surprising. However, in more recent times, large banks have made special efforts to lend to small business. These efforts have sometimes taken the form of special departments for dealing with small-business financing. Some indirect ways of financing small business by commercial banks will be covered in a later section of the essay.

The principal requirement by commercial banks for making credit available to a small business is a record of successful operation. This creates a problem for a new small business that is seeking to establish itself. In a way, this defines the so-called problem of small-business finance. Established small businesses with a track record of successful operation do not have a financing problem in the United States. The problem of small-business finance—if there is a problem at all—is that of new small businesses that seem to have bright prospects but do not have a record of successful past operations. That is where venture capital is needed.[11]

THE LOCAL PRIVATE CAPITALIST

In almost every moderately sized or larger community in the United States, there are men who are ready and willing to become involved in new business ventures. Very often these men have already made a success of their own businesses and, having accumulated more capital than can be profitably reinvested in their own business, are looking for other opportunities. They do not wish to become involved in day-to-day management, but they stand close at hand as partners in such small businesses. Their participation is often for a limited period: building a business up to a level of profitable operation and then "cashing in their chips."[12] An example will help.

The owner of an automobile dealership, by means of unusual managerial skills, built his agency into the leading outlet in his area. He liked his location and did not wish to expand into other areas. He added a foreign car dealership to that of his domestic line but that was about as far as he could go in the automotive business. After paying off all debts, he soon built up a surplus which could not be reinvested profitably in his own business. He therefore started looking for business opportunities of other sorts locally. He became the equity owner of a fairly large apartment house. He put up the capital for a shopping center. He also invested in a multiple-house movie theatre complex in that shopping center. He found managers for these operations from among his salesmen; many became well-to-do in their own right and, while he kept a paternal interest in these operations, he sometimes sold out to these managers in due course. Almost every venture in which he participated did well.

The local private capitalist may be almost any person with a similar background: local bankers sometimes fill this role; lawyers are often involved. Lawyers sometimes are organizers of small venture-capital groups or partnerships or syndicates with corporate ownership. These venture-capital groups sometimes have the characteristic of combining not just money but talent. Again, an example will help.

A lawyer with a number of wealthy clients formed a venture-capital group of persons, based not on their wealth, but on their varied backgrounds. The group included: an accountant, an architect, an engineer, and a professor of marketing. The money came mainly from wealthy clients; the group was an informal (or formal) board of directors for a series of ventures.

INVESTMENT BANKERS: THEIR SPECIAL SITUATION DEPARTMENTS

Investment bankers have traditionally been associated with big corporate business. However, they are often also investment managers for individuals and families with large wealth. Both the partners in these investment-banking firms and wealthy clients may be sources of financing for new and risky, but promising, business ventures. The ventures in which investment bankers interest themselves are usually not as small as those covered by local private capitalists, but they still fall within the classification of "small" business by most of its formal definitions. Such small business investment departments are often labeled "special situation" departments.[13]

Investment bankers often have another goal in view. When they arrange the financing of a small enterprise by groups formed from within their own partners and wealthy clients, they may hope to "cash in" their profits by a public sale of the securities of an enterprise which can now attract investors from the public market for equities. These new-issue sales by investment bankers not only give them an added and very profitable activity, they release funds for still more new investments. This "going public" by a new small business has one serious risk: the instability of the stock market. Historically, these "going public" sales have been most successful when the stock market is strong, and investors are looking for new growth opportunities. In such strong stock markets, the stocks of companies that have gone public sometimes become "hot" issues and soon sell well above the original offering price. So far, this is fine both for the new investors and for the proprietors of the now publicly held small business. But stock markets can go down as well as up—and the affairs of a small business can turn about as well. If the stock price of the new issue drops precipitously, either because of a general market decline or because of a turnabout in the earnings report of this business, the results can be disastrous. An established corporation can survive a drop in the price of its equity security; a smaller and newer one may be unable to do so. Unfortunately, the incentive of investment bankers is often for a rather early "going public" sale, one which may, at least in terms of retrospective wisdom, have been premature. A local private capitalist may exact a higher price for his financial participation in a small business but he is also less likely to abandon it in time of need or prematurely.

PRIVATE VENTURE-CAPITAL INSTITUTIONS

There are a few, but only a few, private venture-capital institutions on a formally organized basis. American Research and Development Corporation is both the largest and the best known. Its best-known success stories are High Energy and Polaroid. It has also had failures, but the interesting point is that its *average* rate of return on its venture-capital investment has not been larger than more conventional business investment than can be accounted for by the greater risks assumed. The hypotheses of standard business finance seem to be borne out. Two other well-known institutions that have made substantial venture-capital investments are: the Rockefeller Brothers Fund and the J. H. Whitney Foundation. Since they are private, the investment results of their activities are not known.

Other rather formally organized, but closely held, venture-capital groups exist but little is known of their operations; they tend to avoid publicity. Almost all of these institutions, however, share one element in common with the "special situation" activities of investment bankers: they depend on the public securities markets as the vehicle through which they can "cash in their chips" (realize cash from what might otherwise be a frozen investment) in a small business venture.

While the stock market and other public securities markets have only a marginal role in the direct financing of small business, they do have a material impact on such financing. When the stock market is vigorous, venture-capital investors are likely to be willing to take chances, particularly if such investors feel "priced out" of the stock market. (That is, the level of stock market prices leaves few bargains to be found.) A weak stock market is likely to have the opposite effect.

↗   SUBSTITUTES FOR DIRECT FINANCING

If a small business is unable to meet its financial needs directly, it may be able to tap indirect sources of capital in a variety of ways. We shall deal first with indirect financing of fixed capital and then with the indirect financing of working capital.*

The most important form of indirect financing of fixed capital is leasing. While the rental of fixed capital objects is a very old practice, it is mainly in rather recent years that leasing has been extended to such a wide variety of objects. Leases are now available on: aircraft; computers; machine tools; earth-moving equipment; automotive fleets, including both trucks and passenger cars; and almost all types of fixed capital. A small business has to have a background of successful operation to be accepted as a lessee, but the standards for such acceptance are generally lower than those for the securing of direct financing. Leasing has been given considerable stimulus by tax rules and regulations. Competition among lessors has become so great that the cost of capital via a lease is often not much higher than through direct access in the markets. Sometimes, due to special tax circumstances, it may even be lower.

The indirect financing of working capital takes a variety of forms, several of which involve the participation of commercial banks. In the example of the insulation-material manufacturer cited above, the problem was that of large accounts receivable. If these receivables are owed by customers with acceptable credit standing, they can be sold to ("factored"), or hypothecated, with a lender such as a commercial bank. The credit standing of the account-receivable debtor, not its owner's, is what is important.

* Fixed capital is defined as productive equipment with long useful lives. Working capital is assets, some financial such as cash and accounts receivable but also inventory, which have a short life within a business. Working capital *needs* may be permanent but the units of assets that constitute it have a rapid turnover. The same physical asset may be either fixed or working: a tractor is working capital for a farm equipment dealer; fixed capital for a farmer.

If inventory needs are the financial problem of a small business, they may be financed by loans secured by legal hypothecation or bailment of the objects in the inventory. For example, the stock of automobiles held for sale by many automobile dealers is often financed by banks or finance companies. The reserve stocks of fuel (usually coal but sometimes nuclear fuel) held by public utilities is often bank-financed. Raw material processors, such as coffee-roasting companies, often use various forms of warehousing to finance inventories.

One indirect form of financing practiced by many small businesses is the slow payment, or stretching out, of accounts payable.[14] Practices with respect to trade credit in the United States vary greatly from the nominal terms by which it is extended. Discounts are given to encourage the prompt payment of bills. Some vendors follow rather rigid practices to assure the prompt payment of trade credit. For example, petroleum-product wholesalers usually will not deliver gasoline to a filling station until the previous delivery has been paid for. But, in some lines, trade credit practices are more generous. Disregard of the formal trade credit terms is rather more expected than not. Manufacturers and wholesalers of high-mark-up goods often fall into this category. For example, shops selling fashionable clothing often depend on being allowed (informally) slow payment of their trade accounts. It should be recognized that slow payment of payables only shifts the financial burden to the vendor; and if the vendor is also a small business, then there has been no net gain in financing—only a shifting of the problem to another business unit or sector.

GOVERNMENTAL AID TO SMALL-BUSINESS FINANCING

Governmental aid to small-business finance has taken a variety of forms. The simplest one has been governmental loans to small business by some designated governmental agency. The most striking example of this is the Small Business Administration (SBA).[15]

The second form of aid has been loan insurance or guarantee. That is the dominant direct form of aid by more recent SBA policy. The third form of aid has been through a wide variety of tax incentives or tax benefits. Some of these have aided small business directly and therefore made it a more attractive investment; other tax features have stimulated small-business investment by private investors. This section will explore each of these devices and attempt an evaluation of their effectiveness.

➤ SMALL BUSINESS ADMINISTRATION

Most of the federal government's concern about small business has been expressed in its independent agency: the Small Business Administration. The SBA was created by legislation in 1953, but the original act has been amended many times—most importantly in 1958, 1964, 1966, and 1974.[16] Financing is not the sole activity of the agency. Since this evolution is covered in another essay in this volume, comment here will be limited to the financial aspects of its operations.

The largest fraction of SBA business loans are made jointly with private lenders.[17] Almost all of the loans involve a guarantee by the SBA of such a fraction of the loan as to protect the private lenders from serious loss. In some cases, the private lenders supply all of the loan funds, with the guarantee being the only participation by the SBA. Loans of this type have totaled between one and two billion dollars in each of the last several fiscal years. Commercial banks are the principal private lenders, although a few other private financial institutions also seek out and receive SBA guarantees.

In recent years, special emphasis has been placed on the availability of credit for minority-owned businesses. The SBA authority for such emphasis is contained in authorizing legislation that is separate from the legislation covering general business lending; as a result there is some presumption that the credit standards in such cases are somewhat more liberal. Loans to minority businesses may be made by private lenders with SBA guarantee, but this arrangement does not appear to have been as successful as the general business-loan program of the SBA. As a result, a larger fraction of minority-business loans are made wholly with SBA-provided funds.

As a matter of policy, the SBA has tried to minimize the proportion of loans in which it supplies all of the funds. So far, this policy has been reasonably successful, but the SBA continues to feel that private participation in such lending is not as enthusiastic as it should be. For example, rather than private lenders initiating a proposed loan program to a small business and then seeking out SBA participation and guarantee, the negotiations are likely to run in the other direction. A small business, failing to get the financing it seeks from private sources, may then go to the SBA with an application. The SBA, after review and decision that the application has merit, may take the initiative in approaching a private lender in the same locality as the applicant business and urging it to participate in such a credit extension. In other words, the SBA supplies more initiative in the making of such loans than private lenders.

A modest fraction of SBA-supported financing is through the channels of local or state development companies. These development companies get some capital from the SBA but try to raise as much in their localities as is possible. All too often the locally raised amounts are small. The SBA has not yet admitted that the development-company program is not working well but outside opinion takes that view. No new development companies have been formed for several years and some of the older ones have become inactive.

The SBA also has a disaster-loan program. What constitutes a validating disaster is determined by national proclamation, at which point the SBA is authorized to lend on somewhat more liberal terms to help in the restoration of normal business operations. The SBA has been quite effective in making the availability of such credit well known in disaster areas. In spite of such publicizing, however, the volume of credit has been rather small.

LOSS RECORD ON SBA LOANS

The SBA has found that although a fairly large proportion of its loans are not repaid according to the original terms, ultimately collections appear to be about 95 percent of the loans made. However, some unrecognized losses may exist. In its first 23 years, the SBA has recognized losses of between 3 and 4 percent of the total loans made. It estimates that ultimately the loss rate may be as high as 6 percent.[18]

This loss rate of 6 percent may be compared with a loss rate of less than 1 percent on commercial bank loans. Loss rates are not much higher than those on loans that finance the purchase of automobiles, household appliances, and similar consumer goods. Even the loss rates on unsecured personal loans are below the 6 percent level. Small-business finance confronts private lenders with one of the highest risk rates in the whole spectrum of private credit.

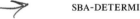 ### SBA-DETERMINED MAXIMUM INTEREST RATES

The SBA sets maximum allowable interest rates for loans it guarantees or itself extends. These allowable rates are changed according to money-market conditions but the margin above the prime loan rate has regularly been less than the loss rates reviewed above.[19] There is, thus, a clear element of subsidy in SBA operations. The reluctance of private lenders to make unguaranteed loans to small business thus becomes quite understandable.

SMALL-BUSINESS INVESTMENT COMPANIES (SBICS)

The first five years of operation of the SBA made it abundantly clear that simply providing a government agency for the supply of *credit* to small business was not enough; what small business needed even more was *equity* capital. Since it seemed inappropriate that government should get into this business directly, the compromise hit upon was to authorize the creation and organization of private investment companies that would specialize in supplying small-business equity capital.[20] Two kinds of governmental support for these "Small-Business Investment Companies" (SBICs) were provided: The SBA was authorized to provide so-called leverage financing (really a kind of equity capital for the investment companies themselves) and various tax benefits, which made the private investors in SBICs exempt from some of the tax burdens that fall on unsheltered private investors.

When the new SBIC system was initiated in 1958, a great many of these companies were set up, some of which were much attracted by the tax-sheltering advantages. About half of the new SBICs were sponsored by financial institutions, mainly commercial banks. A large number of the SBICs were organized by already-existing venture-capital groups of the type that has already been described. A few of these SBICs even became companies listed on the New York Stock Exchange, and for a while, these companies enjoyed an enthusiastic following in the market.

After less than a decade, some of the original enthusiasm wore off and the program lost both in zeal and reputation. About 500 licenses to organize SBICs were granted by the SBA but, after a period, the number of active SBICs dwindled to about 250. Since then, there has been a kind of stabilization of the remaining SBICs; a good fraction of the survivors have now been operating for ten to fifteen years.

The average size of SBICs tends to be fairly small; the median size still smaller. The present average size is from three to four million dollars each. The average SBIC has about 50 investments to about 30 or 40 small business enterprises on its books. The average investment is from $60,000 to $100,000. The surviving SBICs, in general, are now moderately profitable. It is not clear, however, that this would be true if we included those SBICs that failed or liquidated. A very rough judgment might lead to the conclusion that, in spite of the strong support by the SBA, and the great tax advantages, the system had not, in total, returned a profit to its investors. There may have been a net social contribution from the system, but if so, a part of it was at the expense of such investors.

Legislation in 1968 authorized the formation of Minority Enterprise SBICs (MESBICs) but this program did not develop much momentum until 1972. The present number of MESBICs is about 80 and it still seems to be growing, though less rapidly than at first. The average size of MESBICs is much smaller than that of SBICs, about one million dollars. The investments they make also average smaller in size: between $30,000 and $40,000 each. The record is still too short to judge just how well this system will develop.[21]

TAX BENEFITS FOR SMALL-BUSINESS ENTREPRENEURS

The formal tax aids the lawmakers have created for small business are mainly three in number:

1. Small-business owners of unincorporated enterprises are given a fairly generous interpretation of "personal service income," so that most of the income of prosperous small-business proprietors is subject to the 50 percent tax limit. This helps proprietors who have fairly large amounts of capital invested in their businesses.

2. Incorporated small businesses were given a generous graduation of tax rates by the Revenue Act of 1978:

Taxable income	Tax rate
$0 to $25,000	17
$25,000 to $50,000	20
$50,000 to $75,000	30
$75,000 to $100,000	40
Over $100,000	46

The small business corporations that benefit most from this graduation are those who can justify large retention of earnings and *do* retain them.

3. Investors in SBICs and MESBICs are given the potential of generous treatment of losses in such investments. (So-called Section 1244 tax cases.)

A possible fourth formal benefit of the way in which taxes are applied to small businesses exists in the Investment Tax Credit. The dollar limits on such credits can reduce the benefits for very large businesses; they would rarely touch a small business.

The *informal* tax aids, however, are substantial. The pickup truck of a small contractor can be charged as a business expense but, in fact, this pickup truck may pull his camper, take him hunting, and—if he is single— be his courting vehicle. The business life and personal life of a small businessman are so intertwined that even with zealous tax supervision, it is hard to separate expenses that apply possibly to one aspect of life, possibly to the other. An example will help:

> The operator and owner of a small radio station acted as his own time salesman. He sold air time for cash to some customers, but with many he worked out exchange or barter deals. The station owner eats many meals at expensive restaurants without being charged; he plays golf free, and enjoys free vacations at a nearby lake—all in exchange for free air time. The luxury car he drives is almost always a "loaner" from a car dealer. The clothes he wears are given to him free. The accounting records of the station show little profit but the owner lives a luxurious and rather conspicuous social life.

FRANCHISING OF SMALL BUSINESSES

The franchise is a very old business practice. Many types of business are inherently local and small in size. However, a central agency that aids in management, promotion, and financing often can increase the chances of success considerably. We have franchise chains for fast foods, motels, dry cleaning, offset printing, weight-reduction "studios," and many other activities. In many ways, the dealerships that national manufacturers establish for the marketing of their products might be thought to be brought within the category of franchising.

The extent to which the centralized grantor of franchise aids in financing varies greatly. Some franchisers actually supply capital to franchisees, but this is usually avoided if possible. Most franchisers establish minimum amounts of capital that must be provided by each franchisee. The commonest form of aid offered by the franchiser is to be an agent in the arrangement of financing. A fast-food franchiser, for example, will usually require that the prospective franchisee have enough means to supply all of the working capital required for the proposed operation, plus a respectable down payment on the required capital equipment. The franchiser will also require that the building follow the architectural design he specifies and also have the suitable signs and symbols. The franchiser will then take the initiative in seeking some local investor who will put up the capital for this building plus the installed equipment and the external signs. An investor would ordinarily be very hesitant about supplying capital for any such special-purpose operation: the risks of loss and bankruptcy are too great. However, the franchiser can supply some powerful arguments and guarantees. In the first place, the discipline of the franchisers enforced methods of promotion and management offer an above-average chance of success for the franchisee. Second, the franchiser can guarantee the investor in the property that if the franchisee fails to perform in a satisfactory method, or approaches financial difficulties in his operations, the franchiser will take over control of the operations and keep the franchise going until a replacement franchisee with new working capital and greater prospects of success can be found. Investors are sometimes offered an additional incentive: not only the fixed interest but also some percentage of the gross, or of the profits, so that—if the enterprise is highly profitable—the investor will share in the benefits.

Motel franchising has been one of the most distinctive of this field. Because motels involve an unusually large capital investment for a small business, they illustrate the problems, as well as the promises, of this system of small-business operation. Motels were very seriously overbuilt in the United States during the late 1960s and early 1970s. While many were independent operations, a large fraction came from the area of franchise. In the subsequent shake-out, some franchisers were remarkably successful in keeping the properties they had franchised in viable condition. But some simply were unable to fulfill the implied, if not contractual, promises of their earlier representations. Some investors lost rather heavily. The record of franchised motels, however, was clearly better than that of the independent operations. Franchise was not a panacea, but it certainly proved to have some real advantages.

THE MARKET FOR SMALL BUSINESSES

A small business may be very successful and produce an excellent income for the proprietor; yet, it can ultimately face him with a very great problem: how to sell it when he wishes to do so. Buyers can usually be found, but very often they are buyers with such limited resources that they cannot make a satisfactory equity investment. If the proprietor can find a buyer with assured competence to operate the business, such as a trusted employee or someone else with experience in the type of business represented, then the problem can be solved.[22] The retiring proprietor can form a partnership, with an understanding that a major share of profits will be used to gradually buy out his share in the business. An example will make this evident.

A chemical engineer, tired of city life, started a small plating business in a rural area. He deliberately kept the business small and had only one employee. When he reached retirement age, he "sold" the business to the employee but allowed for payment over a fifteen-year period. He remained as an inactive partner—working only at peak periods of demand. The former employee, now an employer, in due course found an apprentice employee. The fifteen-year payment period furnished a kind of annuity to the former proprietor.

When society was more stable, this problem was not as difficult as it is now. A small businessman might reasonably expect a son or sons to take over the business. Social mobility has reduced the frequency with which a family business can be kept within the family.

Moderate-sized businesses generally do not face a serious problem if the stock market is reasonably strong. Larger corporations are frequently anxious to acquire smaller businesses in order to sustain or accelerate growth. A small business acquisition can have advantages for both parties. The proprietor of a small or moderate-sized business, in selling out to a larger business, may get his payment not in cash but in the shares of the acquiring corporation. In this way, he can defer what might otherwise have been a large capital-gains-tax liability. The acquiring corporation can benefit from a growth in earnings per share if the following conditions are met: if the ratio of the market values of its shares (exchanged for the acquisition) to the earnings of the acquired firm is less than the market price–earnings ratio, growth in earnings per share automatically follows.

This exposition of advantages, however, also demonstrates one of the disadvantages which still attaches to small-business operations: even at best, such businesses seldom can command as good a price from the market as larger businesses. In the above illustration, the smaller price–earnings ratio for the small business implies a lower evaluation of its earnings capacity. However, this is entirely in keeping with modern business-finance theory.

Since a small business usually is not as diversified as a larger business, such added risk is not going to be compensated for by the market.

MINORITY SMALL-BUSINESS ENTREPRENEURS

Among the social programs initiated in the mid-1960s by the Johnson administration was one aimed at aiding small-business entrepreneurs from minority segments of the population. The SBA was the principal vehicle for this program, which had two aspects: managerial assistance and aid in financing. This essay will deal only with the second of these aspects.

In the early years, many obstacles were encountered in implementing the financial-assistance program. Probably the greatest obstacle was simply that relatively few members of minority groups had the initial financing and self-confidence needed to start a small business. The management-assistance part of the SBA program became a project for persuading minority groups that such efforts were feasible and might be rewarded with success. More recently, the volume of financing for minority businesses by the SBA has started to grow. In 1976, the first year for which figures are available, 21 percent of the SBA loans in number, and 13 percent in dollar volume, were such credits. These percentages are not far from the proportion of minority groups to the total population. While the largest share of these loans were to blacks, a fair number went to Chicanos, Puerto Ricans, American Indians, Asians, Eskimos, and Aleuts.

WOMEN AS SMALL-BUSINESS ENTREPRENEURS

Except for a few special lines of business (knit shops, typing services, and so on) women have seldom been business entrepreneurs, small or otherwise. Even in the manufacturing and marketing of women's clothing—an industry which has tended to be small in average-firm size—men have dominated the entrepreneurial function. It has been estimated that women own only 4 percent of all small businesses and that many of these have been inherited from deceased husbands.

One of the goals of the women's movement has been to change this situation. So far, there is no statistical evidence (or evidence of any other kind) suggesting that this movement has yet achieved much success. However, one gain has clearly been made. Commercial banks, and some other financial institutions, have been under strong pressure to review lending procedures to be sure that sex discrimination is not practiced. Though statistical evidence is lacking, the pressure has been widely enough felt so that some changes must have been made. SBA loans or loan guarantees to small businesses operated by women account for less than one-twentieth of their total.[23]

BIG BUSINESS AID TO SMALL BUSINESS

The relationship of big business to small business is often one of cooperation rather than competition. Manufacturing of automobiles may be big business but the marketing of them by dealers is small business. Two examples will help to clarify the situation.

In many areas of the United States, banks are either prohibited from establishing branches or are severely limited in such operations. Small banks, however, depend on larger banks for many services (for example, check collection and supply of foreign exchange) which are usually lumped together under the general term of "correspondent bank" services. The services go both ways: small banks may supply their larger city correspondents with desirable loans which are too large for the small country correspondent to handle unaided. Another interesting service is that of selling banks. Small family-controlled banks may come up for sale when the proprietor reaches retirement age or dies without a successor manager within his family. Correspondent banks almost always are not only happy and anxious to find a buyer for such banks but will often supply the buyer with financing on very generous terms.

The second example might be thought to be more in the area of management than finance, but it represents a historical development that is relevant to both.

At one time, the great integrated petroleum companies not only engaged in exploration, refining, and wholesale marketing but also attempted to own and operate the final retail outlet: the ubiquitous "filling station." The system did not work very well; but when these stations were leased or sold to individual proprietors, the results improved. Smallness was a positive advantage. The zeal of profit-seeking entrepreneurs was stronger than the skills and guidance of a large corporation! Most filling stations are now small independent businesses.

PRESENT STATE OF
SMALL-BUSINESS FINANCE

In spite of a quarter of a century of rather active federal government aid to small-business finance, the complaint is still heard that small business suffers from inadequate financing. How valid is this complaint?

The cost of external capital for small business is undoubtedly high; the more relevant question, however, is whether it is higher than the risk justifies. There are as many opinions as there are authorities, but the author of these words shall use this brief space to present his view: in the area of more conventional small businesses, the cost of capital is not higher than justified by the degrees of risk faced. The relatively high failure rates of small businesses, particularly in their early years of life, give the first kind of supporting evidence. The second level of evidence is harder to document, but it seems to be equally true: a rather large fraction of small businesses, even though they survive, provide their proprietors with only a skimpy living. High-profit small businesses exist, but they are a minority of the total. Investors from the outside are justified in demanding high potential returns for their risky investment in small businesses.

One exception to this judgment will be admitted immediately: the case of businesses involved in high technology, the finance of which was formerly stimulated by the hopes of high realized profits through ultimate sale to the public securities markets. The volatility of these public securities markets presents a real dilemma for public policy. Should high technology—or for that matter, other forms of very high risk but also high profitability—small business have to depend on the availability of capital which, in turn, is strongly influenced by the erratic swings of the stock market? That is probably the most important unsettled problem in small-business finance.

Notes

1. Neil Murphy, "Commercial Bank Lending to Small Business." Small Business Administration, *The Vital Margin* (Washington, D.C.: G.P.O. 1973), pp. 83–92. (Hereafter SBA.)

2. Roland I. Robinson, "Small Business in the Money and Capital Markets," SBA, pp. 39–58.

3. *Wall Street Journal*. The *Journal* carries frequent feature stories on small business, such as November 17, 21, and 24, 1977.

4. Roland I. Robinson, *Financing the Dynamic Small Firm* (Belmont, California: Wadsworth, 1966); Mark Rollinson, "Venture Capital," SBA, pp. 183–96; see also *Venture Capital,* a periodical published episodically by S. M. Rubel and Co.

5. *Small Business and Society,* Hearings before the Select Committee on Small Business of the U.S. Senate 94th Congress 1st Session, Dec. 2–4, 1975. (Not much on finance but indirectly suggests psychological traits of entrepreneurs that may explain financial difficulties.)

6. *Wall Street Journal.*

7. *Ibid.*

8. Robinson, *Financing the Dynamic Small Firm.*

9. *Small Business and Society,* Hearings; Report of the SBA Task Force on Venture and Equity Capital for Small Business. SBA, January 1977.

10. L. S. Ritter and Roland I. Robinson, "Availability and Cost of External Equity Capital for Small Business Ventures," *Financing Small Business,* Select Committee of Congress on Small Business (Washington, D.C.: G.P.O., 1958).

11. Neil Murphy, "Commercial Bank Lending to Small Business," SBA, pp. 83–92.

12. Ritter and Robinson. "Availability and Cost."

13. *Ibid.*

14. Robert W. Johnson, "Trade Credit as a Source of Funds" (for small business). SBA, pp. 123–40.

15. See *Annual Reports* of Small Business Administration. (Recently in two parts with narrative account in Part I and statistics in Part II.)

16. *Ibid.*

17. *Ibid.*

18. *Ibid.*

19. Neil Murphy, "Commercial Bank Lending," SBA, pp. 83–92.

20. Kermit L. Culver, "Small Business Investment Companies," SBA: *The Vital Margin,* pp. 59–82; R. C. Osborn, "Providing Risk Capital for Small Business; Experience of the SBICs," *Quarterly Review of Economics and Business* (Sept. 1975), 15(1):77–90; also see *Venture Capital.*

21. See *Annual Reports* of Small Business Administration.

22. Verne A. Bunn and C. D. Terflinger, *Buying and Selling a Small Business* (Wichita, Kans.: Wichita State University, 1963), for SBA (not outmoded by time); D. E. Kellogg, "How to Buy a Small Manufacturing Business," *Harvard Business Review* (Sept. 1975), 53(5): 92–102.

23. See *Annual Reports* of Small Business Administration.

Selected Bibliography

Allen, Louis L. *Starting and Succeeding in Your Own Small Business*. New York: Grosset and Dunlap, 1968. (Old, but still one of the best of the "How to" books; by the President of Chase Manhattan Capital Corporation.)

Belew, Richard C. *How to Negotiate a Business Loan*. New York: Van Nostrand Reinhold, 1973.

Entrepreneur Press of Santa Clara, Calif. Publishes nonacademic pamphlets and short books related to small business.

Forbes Magazine. Writer T. P. Murphy frequently contributes articles on current small business finance.

Greene, Gardiner G. *How to Start and Manage Your Own Business*. New York: McGraw-Hill, 1975. (A nonacademic "How to do it" book.)

Gross, Harry. *Financing for Small and Medium-Sized Businesses*. Englewood Cliffs, N.J.: Prentice-Hall, 1969.

Journal of Small Business Management. Quasi-academic but with only a few articles on finance.

Small Business Reporter. A Bank of America proprietary series on small business management, including an elementary booklet: "Financing Small Business." 1976.

Wartman, Leon A. *Successful Small Business Management*. New York: Amacom, 1976. (A current nonacademic "How to do it" text.)

13

LAW AND SMALL BUSINESS IN THE UNITED STATES: ONE HUNDRED YEARS OF STRUGGLE AND ACCOMMODATION

Lawrence M. Friedman

THIS article deals with how law favored or disfavored small business in United States history. But first, we come up against a problem: What do we mean by "small business"? There are government programs in the United States which are willing to call a business "small" so long as it has less than 500 employees.[1] This of course will not do for a historical essay. Industrial giants of the early nineteenth century might be "small businesses" today. For our own purposes, we shall use a rough, rather eclectic working definition: for us, a business is small when it is unincorporated, does not do business across state lines, and is under the control of a single family, or a group of associates who are in personal contact day by day.[2] Clearly, for much of the nineteenth century most business *was* small business. Logically, we could also include other small economic units, people who worked for themselves, rather than for a "boss"—farmers, artisans, craftsmen. This economic class was numerous and strong in the nineteenth century, and indeed well into the twentieth. In this article, we shall not generally deal with farmers and artisans. Our primary focus will be on small shopkeepers and tradesmen.

I wish to thank Anne Doolin for help in the research. A student term paper by Carey R. Ramos (1979) directed my attention to some points of trademark law.

SOME THEORETICAL CONSIDERATIONS

Compared to other societies, American society has a long tradition of economic mobility. This was from the beginning a country of self-made men. There was never a landed aristocracy; commerce and industry were never concentrated in the hands of a few families, as was true in many countries (and is still true today). Even in the 1970s, in the era of big business, the United States is very decentralized economically. There are only a few automobile companies or steel mills, but there are enormous numbers of shopkeepers, merchants, landlords, and small entrepreneurs.

A second key fact of American society is *federalism*. Throughout the nineteenth century and well into the twentieth century, federalism was taken very seriously. This was true of the economy, as well as the polity. The center of gravity was not in Washington, D.C.[3] It was always in the states and localities. The Constitution of 1787 set up what was, in effect, a national common market. Goods and people could, and did, freely cross state lines. Most business was small, under our definition; business stayed at home and did not cross the boundaries of its local community. Government was highly decentralized. Power was diffuse. The legal system followed the same pattern. There was no strong *national* legal profession; bench and bar were local, and quite parochial. A judge was simply a lawyer with enough politics or skill to win an election or get an appointment. He tended to come out of local politics; once on the bench, there he sat, in his own little realm.

The general theory of law and society asserts that a legal system responds to social forces; the preponderance of exerted power determines the outcome of legal struggle.[4] Very roughly, this means that what the system does reflects social forces within society, in rough proportion to their power and weight. But legal *structure* may also have an effect. It acts as a kind of prism, gathering, shaping, bending rays of force that enter the system at one end. Structure itself, to be sure, is in the long run the product of social forces. But in the short run, it affects thought and behavior, just as a bridge guides and controls traffic over a river.

Local small business has often had great political (and legal) power *because* of the way the legal system is constructed. Small business has most of its leverage locally; it dilutes the political strength of small business when power flows from the towns to state capitals, from state capitals to the federal government. The higher the levels of government, the less responsive to a small local merchant. A Chevrolet dealer in a small town in Kansas cuts a big figure in his town; he is a smaller (but still powerful) figure with his delegate to the Kansas legislature; a smaller (but still weighty) voice with his congressman, and not much of a whisper with any of the great federal departments. In strongly centralized countries, small business loses ground, legally and politically, on issues where big business has its own opposing interests. The development of "small business" programs in the last generation is belated recognition of the slow oozing of power away from this class.

Big business, in turn, is sometimes weak locally. The owners are absentees, with heavy sunk costs. Railroads, in the late nineteenth century, were an outstanding example. They were eagerly courted at first by local communities. Nothing was too good for the railroads. Towns struggled with each other to get the lines drawn near or through them. They raised money for the railroads, subscribed for their stock, floated bonds. A generation later, the railroads were bogeymen, the targets of heavy attack and regulation. Still, only at the national level were there tools of sovereignty which can control *big* business. The railroads, crossing state lines, were beyond the reach of small towns. Politically, too, small businessmen are rather conservative; they tend to be individualists, men and women who oppose government regulation on principle (except if it helps them directly). In fact, regulation and red tape are often more of a burden on small than on big business. In short, small businessmen are ambivalent about regulation, and their demands on government are inconsistent, pragmatic, shifting. They want freedom, but they want restraint on others. They stand between the giants and the masses. They must fight their larger competitors to stay alive; but they need help, too, with their customers.

SMALL BUSINESS AND THE LAW:
THE STRUGGLE TO CONTROL COMPETITION

Small businessmen, quite naturally, have always felt the need to protect their competitive position. Small business is local, and has a local market. It tries to build up for itself a little sphere of protection—made up of good will and personal familiarity. Such a business is threatened above all by "outsiders"—businesses which move in on small local markets. In American legal history, we find many signs of the struggle of the small merchant to protect his market. The local merchants felt almost as if they had a claim of right to their business enclave. There were two threats: from small, marginal outsiders (peddlers, for example); and from big businesses (the chain stores and mail-order houses).

In many communities, in the late nineteenth century, merchants were able to get their towns to impose heavy license fees on peddlers. Peddlers had no political power; they could resist these laws only feebly. Some towns charged fees so high that they were almost confiscatory. A Wisconsin law of 1905 allowed cities and villages to extract up to $25 a *day* in license fees from transient merchants.[5] A Connecticut law of 1897 required a state license, a city license, and bond of $300 from "itinerant vendors."[6] The heaviest burden fell on outsiders: an Oakland, California, ordinance of 1894 charged nonresident peddlers double the amount of the resident peddler's licenses.[7]

Big business "outsiders" were a tougher nut to crack. In the long run, small business fought a losing battle. The federal structure of the country, of course, vitally affected the course of this battle. Local, "populist" levels of government were likely to favor small business. Appeal courts were on the whole more "national" minded than local courts or legislatures. The federal level was the most difficult. The federal constitution, after all, set up a national free-trade area, as we mentioned. And the U.S. Supreme Court, at least occasionally, took a stance less parochial than the small-town druggists and local merchants would have wanted. These men spoke with a loud voice in legislatures and at city hall; in Washington, D.C., they carried less weight.

The battle raged roughly from 1870 on. The stakes were high; but this struggle has gotten little attention from historians. It lacked the blood and guts of the war between capital and labor. Besides, much of it was waged in technical, legal terms; ideology was hardly salient. We shall look at a few examples. One was the issue of resale price maintenance. Could a manufacturer fix a price for his product, and insist that the retailer *must* sell at that price? This was the question in the well-known case of *Dr. Miles Medical Company* v. *John D. Park & Sons Company*,[8] decided in 1911. Dr. Miles had set up an elaborate scheme to make sure retail dealers would not cut prices. He sold only through "contracts," or "agency agreements," under which druggists promised to hold the line. Park, a wholesale drug business, refused to enter into these "contracts," and actively sold Dr. Miles's products at "cut prices." The Supreme Court, speaking through Charles Evans Hughes, upheld the wholesale druggist. The arrangements made by Dr. Miles Medical Company were illegal restraints of trade.[9] On the surface, it looks like the retailer—the small business—won, and the manufacturer lost. But the real losers in the case were small druggists; the real winners, big drug companies and chain stores. *Dr. Miles* was a setback for the cause of the local merchants. The state courts, in the years before *Dr. Miles,* tended to uphold the price-maintenance schemes. So in *Grogan* v. *Chaffee,* a California case,[10] a manufacturer of olive oil plastered on every bottle a notice that the price was fixed ($1.35 per half gallon, $2.50 per gallon can). Defendant, a retail grocer in Pasadena, broke ranks and cut prices. The California Supreme Court upheld the contract. Here the *apparent* victory was that of the bigger business; but the real thrust was the opposite.

Dr. Miles laid down a national rule that resale price agreements were illegal; the Federal Trade Commission, on behalf of the government, took action against at least some firms that broke the rule of *Dr. Miles.*[11] Manufacturers tried various ways to get around the decision; sometimes these worked, sometimes not.[12] The legal confusion satisfied nobody. Small business, of course, remained bitterly opposed to *Dr. Miles.* Louis D. Brandeis, who considered "bigness" a "curse," branded the case a disaster. The "prohibition of price-maintenance imposes upon the small and independent producers a serious handicap"; it could drive them to "combination." This in turn would push ahead the "process of exterminating the small independent retailer" already "hard pressed by capitalistic combinations—the mail-order houses, existing chains of stores and the large department stores."[13]

No wonder then that a "strong movement" developed to revive "fair trade." Trade groups made up of small retailers in drugs and cosmetics led the way.[14] The state legislatures obliged, beginning with California in 1931. Under the California law, a contract for sale or resale of branded or trademarked goods was not illegal merely because it provided that the goods could not be resold "except at the price stipulated by the vendor."[15] This law, and others passed in other states, legalized resale price contracts. In 1937, against the background of the Great Depression, Congress passed the Miller-Tydings Act. This amended the Sherman Antitrust Act; "contracts or agreements prescribing minimum prices for the resale of a commodity" were no longer violations of federal monopoly, so long as they were legal under state law.[16]

Resale price maintenance was a weapon against the chain stores, a monster that threatened small retailers with ruin. The great chains, with their vast buying power and huge volume, could always undercut the corner grocery or drugstore. But if this advantage was leveled off, no one would need to buy from the chain stores. Hence the battle against chain stores was a major factor behind passage of the Robinson-Patman Act of 1936.[17] This act outlawed "discrimination in price between different purchasers of commodities of like grade and quality," if the discrimination had a tendency to "lessen competition."[18] Small business was also the heart of the antitrust movement: it was not the workman who most feared the giant corporations, but the small shippers, merchants, and farmers. The movement led to the federal Sherman Act (1890), which outlawed "monopoly" and contracts "in restraint of trade." Many state laws both before and after dealt with the same problem. The Clayton Act (1914) created the Federal Trade Commission to carry out antitrust policy. What lay behind the movement was not so much ideological dedication to the free market, as a fear of the immense power of big business; the "trusts" had it in their power to destroy or gobble up small, local units of business, and to extract toll from the farmers and merchants. The Sherman Act was a symbolic victory against "bigness"; and it remained largely symbolic—the government let it lie fallow for years, and the federal courts gutted it with ruthless "interpretation."[19]

The fate of the Sherman Act reminds us that small business "victories" did not necessarily stick, and did not necessarily end the war against bigness. In the end, bigness prevailed—whether because of inexorable economic laws, or their political strength, is a question one can leave open. That political strength, however, was vast, not only because of themselves, but also because of those who depended on them. Big labor has no interest, for example, in policies that favor small business over large. Hence, we are not surprised to find a whole *history* of symbolic victories. At the height of the agitation against chain stores, a number of states passed special tax laws discriminating against them. Indiana was the first to do so, in 1929. The chain stores fought back in the courts. The United States Supreme Court narrowly held the statute constitutional.[20] This was a victory—but what was it worth? The *highest* annual tax, under the Indiana law, was $25 per store, for stores in really large chains.[21] This kind of money was only a pinprick to the giant corporations. The tax law allowed the legislature to claim it had responded to the little man's wishes—at trifling cost.

In general, small business won *real* victories only when the opposition was weak and voiceless. To find these victories, we have to look past the big, famous movements in law. Generally speaking, the law did answer calls made on it; these came from big business and from small business, on big issues and small; each type of business posed its own demands. The response depended on the opposition. Let us take, for example, occupational licensing. A movement began, essentially in the late nineteenth century, to require licenses for many occupations. Following the pattern of doctors and lawyers, these occupations managed to get laws passed which closed the doors to amateurs, and gave the trained "professionals" a monopoly of the trade. All this was done in the name of public health or safety. Generally speaking, the courts upheld these laws. We do not usually think of this as a movement of "small business," but in fact many occupations protected by licensing laws *were* small businesses—pharmacists, plumbers, owners of barbershops.

Occupational licensing laws were passed rather easily, it seems. It was the classic case of diffuse and disorganized opposition. If barbershop owners managed to get their state to pass a law getting rid of unlicensed barbers, who would say no? Certainly not the "scab" barbers; and there was no *organized* group made up of people who went to barbers for haircuts.[22]

Similarly, the law easily responded to big business, when its opposition was weak or diffuse. Many changes in law were beneficial to big business, but were not seen in that light, or were simply accepted as just or natural. One example was the rise of trademark protection.

Big business, with respect to consumer goods, has to market its products in many places. Big business therefore has a special need for "brand names" and trademarks. The name "Shell" is worth a great deal to the oil company that uses that name. A trademark act was passed in 1870.[23] Since there was no organized opposition, the law of trademarks grew smoothly and rapidly. There were some zones of conflict, however. Suppose some small local businessman presumes to call his cheese, bread, or linens "Shell." Can the oil company protest? At first, courts refused to favor the owner of the trademark—cheese, bread, or linen is not oil; a trade name will only be protected for the immediate product line, or for very closely allied products. This reasoning tended, on the whole, to favor small businesses in these disputes. Yet gradually the courts extended more protection to holders of trademarks and trade names. Trademarks and brand names would be protected in related markets the holder of the trademark *might* enter, or where the public might be confused. One well-known case concerned the "Aunt Jemima" trademark. This was a picture of a laughing black woman; the product was flour. A small firm "borrowed" the trademark for syrup. The flour company won the case.[24] This extension of trademark protection clearly benefited large producers. The case law zigged and zagged, however; now it responded to the demands for more protection of brand names; now to fears of the "monopoly power" of big businesses (especially chain stores) which controlled the trademarks. It was, however, an issue with ethical overtones; a business that used someone else's trademark seemed to be "stealing" something that did not belong to it. Ultimately, trademarks and brand names gained the right to enormous protection; the "monopoly" argument faded over the years.

CREDIT AND COLLECTION PROBLEMS

Small business faced problems with customers, as well as with competitors. Again, generally speaking, the response of the legal system depended on who the "customers" were. If they were less likely or able than small businessmen to exert pressure on the legal system, the small business demand was likely to carry the day. A whole flock of doctrines and laws, which we ordinarily do not think of as connected with small business, may have been really enacted to help out small business generally, or to help some particular line of business. For example, an Illinois law of 1889 made it a crime to get "food, lodging, or other accommodation at any hotel, inn, boarding or eating house with intent to defraud the owner or keeper." A customer who left without paying his bill, or "surreptitiously" removed his luggage, was prima facie guilty of fraud.[25] Clearly, this was a law to help out hotelmen and restaurants vexed by customers who cheated on their bills.

The Illinois law dealt with a small example of a big problem. The problem was credit and collection. Merchants had to sell on credit; they liked easy credit. But they also needed quick and easy ways to collect on their debts. As cities grew and trade expanded, credit became a more and more serious problem, even for small local merchants. More and more goods were sold to people the merchant did not know personally, and whose credit was also unknown. Businessmen developed new tools for selling: conditional sales contracts and chattel mortgages, for example. These two devices had several traits in common. The seller reserved title; he continued to "own" the goods, until they were paid for completely. If the buyer skipped payment, the seller could repossess with a minimum of fuss. These devices spread rapidly through the business world, and generally speaking, the courts enforced them.

Conditional sales, chattel mortgages, and other devices of this general type were used for goods that had a resale value, and which were sold on the installment plan. That made them especially appropriate for such expensive items as pianos and sewing machines. These, of course, were manufactured by large-scale businesses. So, for example, the Singer Sewing Machine Company, at the end of the nineteenth century, "rented" its machines to "lessees," for $5 a month. Singer had the right to repossess if the "rent" went unpaid. At the end of the "rental" period, the "lessee" could keep the machine. This gave the company protection against defaulting buyers—and against third parties, often small businesses, to whom the "lessee" might sell, pledge, or mortgage the machine.[26] Also, some of the buyers were small businessmen—like the defendant in one Michigan case, who bought a "Puffer soda-water apparatus," from a Boston company, promising to pay $25 per month—seller keeping title meanwhile.[27]

The grocer or the doctor could not handle debts in this way. He had to deal in cash; if he extended credit, it was unsecured. Yet competition, if nothing else, forced merchants and professionals to give credit to customers. The clothing store, the grocer, the doctor had to collect through ordinary processes of law. It is no surprise to find that debt actions by merchants and professionals swelled the civil dockets of courts in the late nineteenth century. Robert A. Silverman studied civil litigation in Boston's trial courts, 1880–1900. The courts handled a huge volume of work for certain kinds of businessmen. In 1900, liquor dealers brought, on the average, 1.5 cases apiece; drug dealers, 1.49; grocers, .30; liquor stores, .11; clothing stores, .61. Furniture stores, on the other hand, rarely sued their customers; they could repossess the goods instead, when buyers skipped payments.[28]

In the lower trial courts, civil process was relatively easy and efficient. It became even more so when the states began to set up small claims courts. This was a movement that began in the second decade of the twentieth century; the court in Cleveland (1912) was probably the first. Court reformers, who argued for the new system, proclaimed these as courts for the people;

they would be a "mighty force" in making justice more real for the "humbler classes."[29] Actually, in the event, the courts often turned into collection mills, serving small tradesmen and professionals. They were places where such individuals could collect their debts with a minimum of expense or legal fuss.[30]

How are we to assess these developments? On the surface, it looks as if the law responded to the cold-blooded interests of merchants. The consumer was at a disadvantage—legally, socially, financially. In other words, in the struggle for law, small business tended to lose when facing big business; but to win advantages against the poor who bought their goods and needed their services. But before we condemn the system completely, we need to remember that credit did become available to great numbers of people. Millions had a chance to buy goods and services they could not have obtained otherwise. What resulted was a society which produced a great deal and consumed a great deal. Whether the process was "good" or "bad" depends on how one judges the society it helped to make.

SMALL BUSINESS AND LAW REFORM

After 1870 or so, the economy became more and more "national"; business more and more stretched its hands across state lines. This was also a period in which jurists began to work hard to "reform" the law, in the interest of clarity and order. A special goal was to make commercial law more uniform throughout the country. Between 1890 and 1910, a number of "uniform" laws were drafted and, by and large, enacted. Even more successful was the Uniform Commercial Code, put forward from about 1950.

Basically, jurists generated these reform laws themselves; they did not spring up from the merchants. The uniformity they achieved was largely formal. Insofar as they took mercantile opinion into account at all, it was not the voice of the small businessman they listened to. Since he tended to be strictly local, inconsistent state laws affected him much less than they affected, say, big mail-order houses, companies whose sales flowed across state lines. The changes, in any event, were largely cosmetic. Massive social and economic change in the twentieth century produced massive change in law and government—change in labor law, tax law, regulation of business, welfare law. These were far more decisive than the games of the jurists in transforming the world of small business.

Recently, the national government has set up programs explicitly for "small business." There is a Small Business Administration inside the federal government. The first stirrings came during the New Deal; but the important laws date from after the Second World War. The Defense Production Act of 1950 expressed the "sense of Congress" that "small-business enterprises" should be "encouraged" to play a role under the Act.[31] Small Business Acts were passed in 1953 and 1958, creating the Small Business Administration.[32] One hears a lot of rhetoric, in Congress and in government, about the virtues of small business—the independent, small-businessman, according to Senator Benton of Connecticut in 1950, "represents the leadership and initiative which have helped this country survive the cold winters of depression and war." Small business was "the core of . . . community life."[33] The government offers loans, disaster relief, technical assistance. "Small-business," like the family firm, or rare animals, needs (and gets) special help to stay alive.

On the other hand, what government does *in general* is not all benign. Small business has little power in Washington. Many government programs are quite destructive to small businesses. Urban renewal, for example, bulldozed hundreds of small businesses to death. Everybody praises small business in general; but small businesses contribute more than their share of legal pariahs—"slum landlords," loan companies, merchants who sell to the poor at retail, auto dealers, and others. There is a certain element of scapegoating in programs against "slum landlords," "loan sharks," and other small and marginal businesses. The modern welfare state tends to criminalize some small businesses, and to squeeze others out of the market. Small retail businesses, too, suffer greatly from modern urban diseases. They are victims of riot and crime. They find loans and insurance hard to get. Red tape can be more of a burden to small business than to big business. Despite the rhetoric, then, and the Small Business Administration, the place of small business in the legal system is indeed ambiguous—just as it is in the ladder of power, where they sit halfway up the scale. Small business survives by finding niches and crevices in the market; the protection of the law is, as it has been, less decisive than appears at first glance.

Notes

1. 13 Code Fed. Reg. § 121.3–8(b)(1), for example. Other regulations use criteria based on gross receipts; and here we find maximum figures from $1.5 million (any "concern bidding on a contract for cleaning and dyeing") to $42 million (stockpile purchases). 13 Code Fed. Reg. § 121.3–8(e) (8) (ii); § 121.39(a)(3).

2. On general problems of definition, see Joseph D. Phillips, *Little Business in the American Economy* (Urbana: University of Illinois Press, 1958), pp. 8–20; the federal Small Business Act defines a "small-business concern" as "one which is independently owned and operated and which is not dominant in its field of operation," 15 U.S.C.A. § 631.

3. See James S. Young, *The Washington Community, 1800–1828* (New York: Columbia University Press, 1966).

4. Lawrence M. Friedman, *The Legal System, A Social Science Perspective* (New York: Russell Sage, 1975).

5. Laws Wis. 1905, chap. 490; Lawrence M. Friedman, *Contract Law in America* (Madison: University of Wisconsin Press, 1965), pp. 165–66.

6. Laws Conn. 1897, c. 152.

7. *Gen. Municipal Ords., City of Oakland, Cal., in effect Jan. 1, 1895* (Oakland, Cal., 1895), p. 41, ordinance as amended Dec. 17, 1894. Resident peddlers of "candy, confectionery, flowers, ice cream, or hokey pokey" paid $5 a quarter; peddlers "from vehicles drawn by animal power," $15; from handcarts, $10; peddlers of food paid $15 a quarter.

8. 220 U.S. 373 (1911).

9. Oliver Wendell Holmes, Jr. dissented. Holmes felt the free market would ultimately decide at what price goods would be sold. If Dr. Miles charged too much, people would stop buying its products. "There may be necessaries that sooner or later must be dealt with, like short rations in a shipwreck, but they were not Dr. Miles's medicine" (at page 412). He saw no particular harm in the arrangements that the company made; hence no reason to strike them down as illegal.

10. 156 Cal. 611, 105 P. 745 (1909).

11. FTC v. Baker and Sons, 1 FTC 452 (1919).

12. A. D. Neale, *The Antitrust Laws of the United States of America* 2d ed., (Cambridge: The University Press, 1970), chap 10. In FTC v. Beechnut Packing Company, 257 U.S. 441 (1922), there was no written agreement between Beechnut and its jobbers, wholesalers, and retailers, but Beechnut let it be known that anyone who did not follow the "suggested" prices would never handle a Beechnut product again. The FTC order halting this practice was sustained by the Supreme Court.

13. Louis D. Brandeis, *Business—A Profession* (Boston: Hale, Cushman & Flint, 1914), pp. 259–60. Brandeis dissented in the *Beechnut* case (note 12).

14. Neale, *Antitrust Laws,* p. 283.

15. Cal. Stats. 1931, ch. 278; Laws N.Y. 1935, ch. 976.

16. 50 Stats. 693 (August 17, 1937). The commodity had to be one that bore the "trademark, brand, or name of the producer," and which was "in free and open competition with commodities of the same general class produced . . . by others."

17. 15 U.S.C.A. §13, 49 Stat. 1526 (June 19, 1936).

18. See, in general, Carl H. Fulda, *Food Distribution in the United States, the Struggle between Independents and Chains* (Association of American Law Schools, 1951).

19. On the background and interpretation of the Sherman Act, see William Letwin, *Law and Economic Policy in America, the Evolution of the Sherman Antitrust Act* (New York: Random House, 1965).

20. State Bd. of Tax Comm'rs of Indiana v. jackson, 283 U.S. 527 (1931). This was a 5–4 decision; the four most conservative justices dissented.
   In Singer Sewing Machine v. Brickell, 233 U.S. 304 (1914) an Alabama law of 1911 imposed a tax on every "person, firm, or corporation selling or delivering sewing machines either in person or through agents." The tax was $50 a year for each *county* in which the business was carried on. The Supreme Court upheld the law.

21. Laws Indiana 1929, ch. 207. The act licensed and taxed all stores; but fees for the first store were $3 a year; for the second store, $10; for the 21st and above, $25.

22. See Lawrence M. Friedman, "Freedom of Contract and Occupational Licensing, 1890–1910: A Legal and Social Study," *California Law Review* (1965), 53:487.

23. 16 Stat. 198, 210 (July 8, 1870); on the background of trademark law, see Frank I. Schechter, "The Rational Basis of Trademark Protection," *Harvard Law Review* (1927), 40:813.

24. Aunt Jemima Mills Co. v. Rigney & Co., 247 F. 497 (C.C.A. 2 1917).

25. Laws Ill. 1889, pp. 167–68.

26. See, for example, Singer Mfg. Co. v. Converse, 23 Colo. 246 (1896); William W. Morrill, *Conditional Sales and Bailments, with Forms* (Albany, N.Y.: M. Bender, 1901), pp. 15–16.

27. Tufts v. D'Arcambal, 85 Mich. 185 (45 N.W. 497 (1891)).

28. Robert A. Silverman, *Law and Urban Growth: Civil Litigation in the Boston Trial Courts, 1880–1900* (Ph.D. dissertation, Department of History, Harvard University, June 1977), Table III.1, page 69.

29. Reginald Heber Smith, *Justice and the Poor* (New York: Carnegie Foundation for the Advancement of Teaching, 1919), Bulletin no. 13, p. 53.

30. Smith recognized this facet, too, in his writings; he spoke of the needs of "small tradespeople," forced either to wipe small claims off their books, or sell them "at a ridiculous discount to professional collection agencies." Ibid., p. 42.
   The account above holds true mainly for the North and West of the United States. The situation in the South was, in some ways, quite different; this was a more primitive economy, and lien and collection laws were part of a sinister system designed not for consumer sales but to keep black farm workers tied to the land, and freeze in place a cheap, docile work force. If the northern worker sometimes "owed his soul" to the company store, the southern black worker often "owed his soul" to local landowners—or local merchants. The courts were zealous, to say the least, in insisting that workers pay the price.

For the system, see Daniel A. Novak, *The Wheel of Servitude, Black Forced Labor After Slavery* (Lexington: University of Kentucky Press, 1978); Pete Daniel, *The Shadow of Slavery: Peonage in the South 1901–1969* (Urbana: University of Illinois Press, 1972).

31. 50 U.S.C.A., App. §2151, 64 Stat. 815 (Sept. 8, 1950).

32. 15 U.S.C.A. §633, 72 Stat. 384 (July 18, 1958).

33. 96 Cong. Record A721 (Jan. 30, 1950) (address of the senator at a banquet of the Norwich, Connecticut Chamber of Commerce).

14

SMALL BUSINESS AND URBAN POWER: SOME NOTES ON THE HISTORY OF ECONOMIC POLICY IN NINETEENTH-CENTURY AMERICAN CITIES

David C. Hammack

S MALL businesses are the foundation of democracy." This slogan, in one or another of its many variations, has frequently been proclaimed by historians and social scientists, as well as by small businessmen seeking the aid and protection of government. In years since World War II, small business has often looked for support to the federal government, but in the nineteenth century its natural protector seemed to be the municipality—or so at least many historians have supposed. In turn, it has often been asserted that small business was particularly good for the local community. As late as 1946, C. Wright Mills and Melville J. Ulmer concluded a study of six middle-sized and small cities with the assertion that "in small-business cities the environment was favorable to the development and growth of civic spirit," while in "big-business cities, civic spirit was stunted or distorted" and local affairs were dominated by the selfish and indifferent "officials of the large absentee-owned firms."[1] In the course of some observations on the history of the economic policies of nineteenth-century American cities, this

In preparing this paper I benefited greatly from comments and suggestions by my colleagues David Abraham, Douglas Greenberg, and Theodore Koditschek, and from the work of two unusually able undergraduate research assistants, Michael Shill and Elaine Soffer, who helped track down several elusive bits of data.

essay will consider two closely intertwined questions: How did small businesses fare in the competition for power in American cities? How did the economic policies of American cities affect small businesses during the nineteenth century?

If we define "small business" in relative terms as referring to productive and commercial enterprises that were small for their time, so that in the years before 1870 small businesses include most artisanal shops, foundries, small retail units, and the like, but do not include the great wholesale enterprises, the more substantial banks, or the textile factories and railroads, it seems clear that small businessmen did not control the governments of the larger cities. Edward Pessen has shown that "an unbroken succession of eminent and wealthy merchants and attorneys" served as Mayor of New York down to 1850,[2] and that men of similar position consistently filled the offices of mayor and councilman during these years in Boston, Brooklyn, and Philadelphia.[3] An equally careful study of Chicago describes those who served as mayor during the first thirty years after that city's founding in 1837 as members of the "commercial elite,"[4] while Richard C. Wade concluded that the "mercantile community" dominated Pittsburgh, Cincinnati, Louisville, and St. Louis even in their first years, before 1830.[5] Nearly all of New Haven's mayors between 1784 and 1840 were lawyers, but they were also, in nearly every case, closely associated with their city's merchant elite.[6]

Local economic elites held the local offices in smaller cities as well—indeed, they held on to those offices to the end of the century and beyond, well after their counterparts in the big cities had given them up.[7] But in most small cities the local economic elite consisted of small businessmen, and their opponents for local office were more often local labor leaders than the owners of big businesses or professional politicians. "Middle-class entrepreneurs" held most leading positions in Kingston, New York, during the 1850s; an "entrepreneurial class" governed "economic, political, and associational life" in Hamilton, Canada, and merchants, tradesmen, small manufacturers, bankers, and lawyers supplied nearly 60 percent of the aldermen for Springfield, Massachusetts, during the 1850s, and over 90 percent during the 1870s.[8] Similar patterns have been detected in cities as diverse as Ypsilanti and Lansing, Michigan; Nashville, Tennessee; and Waltham, Massachusetts, during most of the nineteenth century.[9] Even in these smaller cities and towns, some small businessmen were more likely than others to hold office. With a few exceptions, manufacturers and builders appeared in the guise of alderman or mayor much less often than did wholesale and retail merchants, real-estate developers, and the lawyers, insurance agents, and others who provided services to local business.[10]

If we define power in Weberian terms as "the chance of a man or of a number of men to realize their own will in a communal action even against the resistance of others who are participating in the action," it follows that those who held office did not necessarily hold power.[11] The officeholders did not necessarily act in the interests of their small-business colleagues: those who gained office may have worked for other economic interests, or for political or office-holding interests of their own. They may also have found that local office gave them little authority over matters of concern to small business. National and state governments did establish basic economic policy in nineteenth-century America, but a good deal was left to the cities. Municipal economic policy had a history of its own, and that history had some significant implications for small businesses. This is still a largely unexplored field, but we know enough to distinguish three periods in the history of municipal economic policy, to suggest some connections between those periods and the history of business organization, and to identify some problems for future research.

The first period runs from late colonial times into the early nineteenth century; outside of New England, it was the era of the closed, corporate, commercial municipality: an era which afforded special protections and advantages to many small businesses. Or so at least the legal record seems to suggest. According to Jon C. Teaford, the latest student of this record, "The colonial municipality intervened . . . at every step in the transport, sale, and purchase of commodities."[12] According to law, many trades could be followed only within an incorporated municipality, and then only by those who had been admitted to the status of "freeman" of the town. By granting freeman status sparingly, and otherwise limiting entry into trades, colonial cities could limit competition and protect established tradesmen. The municipalities themselves assumed the large expenses entailed in providing wharves, docks, and ferry slips, as well as those involved in constructing and maintaining market-houses, abattoirs, and other commercial facilities.

To protect the reputations of shopkeepers and artisans—and hence the reputation of the entire community as a good place to shop—municipalities also had the power to inspect the goods offered for sale, imposing standard weights and measures and even, in some cases, insisting on specified qualities of craftsmanship. Local officials also had the power to impose some order on the labor market, and in particular to protect the interests of orphans, servants, and apprentices. To protect urban consumers, but also indirectly to support the interests of farmers and retail shopkeepers against those of middlemen who might hope to operate on a large scale, local authorities were empowered to prevent such activities as forestalling, engrossing, and selling by sample. Municipalities also set cartage, ferrying, and other transport rates. In return for these various aids and protections, and perhaps in deference to some sense of economic morality, some at least of the craftsmen accepted municipal regulation of the prices of such essentials as bread, beer, and wood.[13]

According to Teaford, efforts to restrict entry into trades, to control competition, and to ensure quality had all been given up by the middle of the eighteenth century, in New York, Pennsylvania, and Virginia as in old England itself.[14] So too, the apprenticeship system and other measures to ensure community control over the labor market were also in decline.[15] Yet municipal regulation of trade had not come to an end at the beginning of the nineteenth century. New York City was still regulating the price of bread as late as 1821, and both New York and Philadelphia closely controlled the operations of butchers down to that date—on paper if not in fact.[16] Indeed New York City was still acting "to regulate the admission of freemen" as late as 1815.[17] As late as 1831, it was still enforcing laws against forestalling and huckstering; regulating weights and measures; limiting the number of butchers in the Fulton Street Market, so that those who were already established would not lose income; and subsidizing the General Society of Mechanics and Tradesmen.[18] Teaford's own figures show that while the proportion of municipal ordinances dealing with trade and its regulation declined steadily during the eighteenth century, a third of the ordinances of New York and Philadelphia, and more than a quarter of those enacted in Albany and in Charleston, South Carolina, between 1805 and 1808 still concerned the traditional subjects of the closed commercial corporation.[19]

Richard B. Morris once observed that America was "a land where guilds failed to thrive and industrial labor monopolies faced ever-increasing laissez-faire opposition." [20] American municipalities did not resist laissez-faire with anything like the tenacity of the small German cities, in which it was almost impossible to distinguish between guild membership and citizenship. In the German cities, master craftsmen and shopkeepers used a wide variety of legislative and legal instruments to protect established small businesses and to discourage large-scale forms of production and distribution until the last quarter of the nineteenth century.[21] Municipal trade regulations had passed from the American scene by that time. But Sir John Clapham's remark that local regulation of wages in England "died harder than historians used to think—and the memory of it did not die," can also be applied to the municipal regulation of trade in the United States.[22]

Apart from Teaford's study of municipal charters and ordinances, we have no comprehensive study of the decline of the characteristic economic policies of the closed commercial municipal corporation. In particular, we lack an analysis of the impact of changing municipal economic policies on the fortunes of economic interest groups of all kinds, including small businesses in their diverse variety. Morton Horwitz recently remarked that for many years historians of economic policy in America were "more concerned with finding evidence of government regulation than they were in asking in whose interest these regulations were forged."[23] While we now know a good deal about the decline of municipal regulation, we do not know very much about who benefited from that decline.

In the small cities of Germany, it appears that master craftsmen and shopkeepers as a group benefited from the continuation of municipal regulation well into the nineteenth century. But in America it may well have been small businessmen of just this sort who happily helped to dismantle the structure of municipal control. According to Eric Foner, the majority of Philadelphia's artisans had become "thoroughly disillusioned" with price controls by 1780.[24] Fifty years later, artisans and small proprietors in New York City's Workingmen's Party were protesting against "all licensed monopolies," and calling for "the sale of all city-owned property in the markets, elimination of market taxes and reliance on property taxes for revenue, abolition of nonenforceable laws against forestalling, [and] permission for butchers and hucksters to sell anywhere in the city." In later years, New York's Locofocos restated and augmented these demands, insisting on "the abrogation of all inspectorships over articles of commerce" and "the repeal of all laws under which the Common Council . . . restrain or prohibit the freedom of trade."[25] In New York, at least, shopkeepers and artisan-proprietors played a prominent part in Jacksonian politics: and what they sought was the elimination of municipal control over their affairs.[26]

It is true that small businessmen opposed the continuation of municipal control, it may also be the case that it was the great merchants who favored the continuation of colonial policy in this regard. The historian's habit of viewing politics in terms of parties, and not in terms of classes, or what Carl Harris recently called "economic interests groups"[27] to ask, "Who were the Whigs?" but not to ask, "What did the great commission merchants want—and what did they get?"—makes it difficult to answer this question at present. In party terms, it is interesting that Pennsylvania's anti-Constitutionalists, Federalists, and Whigs, all—at one time or another—seem to have favored the continuation of municipal regulations over the activities of shopkeepers and artisans.[28] Yet several historians have found it difficult to correlate party voting patterns with the economic characteristics of voters during the Jacksonian period; for the years before 1837, according to others, it is difficult to distinguish between the economic policies of Jacksonians and non-Jacksonians in the state legislatures.[29] Here again the evidence from legal history is suggestive: according to Morton Horwitz, the period between 1790 and 1820 saw "the forging of an alliance between legal and commercial interests."[30] And, in Horwitz's view, legal decisions as well as legislation in these years shaped a pattern of subsidy to innovative economic enterprise that threw "a disproportionate share of the burdens of economic growth on the weakest and least organized groups in American society."[31] These legal changes had the effect of destroying traditional property rights where those rights interfered with economic development. Horwitz does not discuss municipal trade regulations, but those regulations—where they provided aid and protection to small businessmen—can be seen as a species of property, which was swept away by legislatures, and perhaps the courts, in the period when the lawyer-merchant alliance flourished.[32]

So far as we can now make it out, the era of municipal business regulation came to an end in three phases. First, many aspects of regulation which benefited small businesses were removed, often during the same years in the mid-eighteenth century when similar regulations were falling by the wayside in England. Then, during the period of the American revolution and the creation of state constitutions, municipalities lost what independent standing they had enjoyed, becoming the mere creatures of state governments which might change municipal charters at will, and which were not inclined to grant to any given municipality, or set of municipalities, the exclusive right to the practice of any trade.[33] Finally, small tradesmen found the remaining municipal regulations more restrictive than protective, and fought to have them removed. Whether from inertia or from self-interest, municipal councils, usually controlled by the great merchants, successfully resisted the final elimination of municipal regulation until the late 1830s or later. We do not know what small shopkeepers and artisans thought about the first of these phases; we have some indication that they welcomed the second on ideological or political grounds, and while they seem to have fought the remaining regulations after about 1790, we do not know that they did so in every municipality, or whether they were united and continuous in their fight. Much of the evidence, moreover, comes from New York, Pennsylvania, Maryland, and Virginia. New England had a weak tradition of municipal regulation, and the later phases of the story probably took a different course in southern cities, which shaped their institutions to accommodate slavery.[34]

The second period in the history of municipal economic policy during the nineteenth century was above all the period of what Robert Lively has called the "American System."[35] As municipalities moved away from the regulation of business in this period, they turned to its promotion through direct investment. A large number of studies have examined municipal investment in canals and railroads; also important, though less studied, were municipal investments in bridges, paved and lighted streets, wharves, market buildings, and other commercial facilities, and in water supply and sewer projects.[36] Municipal investments of this sort had eighteenth century antecedents, but they did not dominate economic policy until after the 1820s. In the major eastern cities, at least, local expenditures were very low to that point, but then rose in three stages—punctuated by the financial panics of 1837, 1857, and 1873—to a plateau that was maintained from the mid-1870s into the 1890s.[37] Increasingly strict legislation and increasingly narrow court rulings discouraged the cities from enlarging their budgets after the mid-1870s; in some respects, the second period came to an end at that point.[38]

It is not clear how the economic policies of the American System affected small businesses. From time to time, small businessmen protested against the privileges and loans made available to the corporations which built canals, railroads, and other facilities; or against the taxes required to pay for municipal investments.[39] But in many cases small businessmen endorsed a policy of "municipal mercantilism," designed to increase trade and raise property values for every enterprise in the locality.[40] Their endorsement was not necessarily ill-considered. Only when we know more about the impact of taxes on different segments of each city's population will we be able to say whether the burden of municipal investment was fairly distributed; Carl Harris has recently shown that it is possible to determine the impact of tax policies, at least for the later part of the century.[41] Against the costs to each economic group, we would want to set off the benefits. The growing network of local and regional improvements did, by the 1870s or 1880s, do much to create the national market in which large manufacturing corporations throve.[42] But it also contributed to local economic development in most places, and hence to the creation of many niches and interstices in the economy which could most profitably be occupied by small businesses.[43]

It does seem clear that the impact of the American System on small business was incidental, and that the second period of municipal economic policy was even more dominated by the bigger business interests, particularly those of the wholesale merchants, than the first had been. Merchants, after all, did hold most municipal offices in these years and seem to have exerted dominant influence over most state economic policies as well.[44] And while many merchants enthusiastically supported the American System, it eventually worked against their interests even more than against those of the small businessmen. By the 1870s, according to Glenn Porter and Harold C. Livesay, wholesale merchants were losing to large-scale manufacturers and to investment bankers the dominant economic position they had held from the time of the earliest settlements.[45] It is striking to note that as they lost their economic positions, they also began to withdraw from municipal officeholding in the major cities, and that the period of increasing municipal involvement in the American System came to an end. It was in the 1870s that judges Cooley and Dillon successfully urged that courts could go behind legislative acts to determine whether municipal expenditures were intended for a legitimate "public purpose," and it was in the 1870s that municipal budgets, which had grown in spurts between 1820 and 1860 and then had ballooned in the ten or twelve years from the beginning of the Civil War, reached the level they were to hold for fifteen or twenty years.[46]

American municipalities expanded many services in addition to those explicitly designed to aid business during the years between 1820 and 1890.

School systems, fire departments, police departments, and water and sewer services all took an enduring form in the 1840s and 1850s, and held that form for most of the rest of the century. Park systems, first discussed in the 1850s, began to be introduced on a large scale in the late 1860s. It is sometimes suggested that small businessmen were more likely than others to insist that these services be held to a minimum.[47] But we have very few studies of the question, as we have few studies of the benefits provided by such services to businesses of any size, or of the impact of the associated costs. It does appear to be the case that the great merchants and their professional allies urged the introduction of these services in the 1830s, 1840s, and 1850s,[48] but then failed to provide leadership for maintaining, improving, and expanding them in the 1870s and 1880s, when per capita expenditures on education, in particular, actually declined in many cities.[49] This lapse in the evolution of municipal policy may have been another casualty of the difficulties faced by the wholesale merchants and the general confusion of leadership associated with the rise of big business.

The impact of the delayed and disrupted development of these services on small businesses was probably incidental, and may in some cases have worked to their advantage. Unlike major investments in intercity transportation facilities, such facilities as schools, parks, police stations and firehouses, streets, water mains, or sewers can be added to in small increments. They can be located so as to help some interests sooner or more fully than others. Carl Harris has shown how these characteristics of the standard urban services enabled small and middling businesses in Birmingham, Alabama, to use municipal government for their own purposes after 1870. That city's very large mining and steel-processing firms were able to secure just the services they wanted, and to veto most of those they did not want, during the last thirty years of the century. But the much smaller commercial establishments located in Birmingham's central business district were also able to secure much of the fire and police protection, paving and street cleaning, and lighting services that *they* sought. Unable to shift the cost of these services—or even a fair share of the costs of municipal government as a whole—onto the very large mining and manufacturing firms, the firms of the central business district paid most of the cost themselves. The smallest businesses, such as grocery stores in working-class districts, paid more than their share of taxes and received less in the way of services.[50] In other cities, some small businessmen also benefited from local development policies.

Sam Bass Warner, Jr.'s *Streetcar Suburbs* shows that both the City of Boston and the region's Metropolitan District Commission provided the middle-class suburbs—their small businessmen as well as their residents—with the water and sewer facilities, streets, and trolley services they needed, to some extent at the expense of the central city's poorer residents.[51] A similar pattern characterized New York, where outlying middle-class districts received municipal services more rapidly than the almost equally fast-growing working-class districts downtown, and where a very large suburban territory was consolidated with the central city in 1898 largely to make it possible for the central city to subsidize suburban development.[52] And in Milwaukee, as Roger Simon has shown, late nineteenth-century development policy, which left the introduction—and assigned most of the cost—of local sanitary improvements up to each locality, residential areas and their associated business districts sought and received facilities in the exact precedence that their relative wealth would suggest.[53] It may also be that the building codes, fire regulations, and health-inspection standards that were largely developed for the first time in these years gave special advantages to particular groups of small businessmen—such as those whose products and services were to be controlled—but this is almost entirely an unexplored field.[54]

In a number of smaller industrial cities during these years, small businessmen allied themselves with workingmen during periods of industrial unrest, as Herbert Gutman and David Brody have shown.[55] These small business-labor alliances were quite successful during the 1870s and 1880s: the very years when wholesale merchants were on the decline, and the large industrial corporations were in formation. But such alliances did not appear everywhere, and even when they were most vigorous they did not succeed in preserving the artisanal form of production, or in instituting measures that encouraged the stability of small businesses and discouraged the growth of large ones.[56] If they had—if Swift, for example, had found that local regulations prevented him from establishing his chain of retail butcher's shops—the structure of occupations in American cities—and hence the history of occupational mobility—would have been very different.[57]

The last decade of the nineteenth century saw the start of a third period in municipal economic policy—the period of municipal progressivism. American historians have lavished on this period some of the attention they have denied to the earlier years of the nineteenth century, but we still do not have an adequate account of municipal economic policy in the progressive period. The studies that we do have suggest that professional, corporate, banking, and landowning elites emerged in the nineties to play once again the leadership role their counterparts had relinquished in the 1870s, but that local government by no means ignored the interests of small business.[58]

Municipal progressivism was accompanied by a great outburst of flamboyant rhetoric, but it involved substantial change as well. There is no doubt about the fact that municipalities (and to an apparently lesser but unknown extent other agencies of local government as well) took on a rapidly widening range of tasks after 1890. Taking the decline in price levels into account, municipal expenditures changed very little on a per capita basis between 1880 and 1890, then rose rapidly in the next ten years. In the United States as a whole, state and local expenditures combined rose from $9 to $15 per capita, or 66 percent, between 1890 and 1900.[59] The increase was not universal; there was a decline of 17.8 percent in Birmingham, Alabama, and the increases in established eastern cities, which started from a much larger base, were smaller than the national average: 21 percent in New York City, 24 percent in Boston, 59 percent in Providence.[60] These increases reflected the expansion of established services, especially public education and the police, as well as the addition of new services and facilities, particularly in fields related to public health: large new expenditures were devoted to the improvement of water and sewer systems, to the expansion of health departments and the modernization of municipal hospitals, and to the acquisition of parks, swimming pools, and public baths.[61]

None of these new and expanded municipal facilities and services directly helped small businesses, and it is increasingly clear that the effective demand for them came from those who owned and managed the larger businesses, from the leading professional groups, and from settlement-house workers and others involved in the social welfare and the social gospel movements.[62] In New York and some other large cities the increased expenditures were the product of policies designed to improve the lot of the poor sufficiently to promote social harmony and to add to the electoral appeal of patrician politicians.[63] But small businessmen could not be left out of account in the detailed development of these policies: they continued to have a significant influence over the allocation of police services, the location of schools, and the timing of sanitary improvements.[64] And their opposition to high taxes could not be ignored: as municipal budgets rose in the 1890s, reformers in one city after another sought to meet taxpayer criticism by shifting some of the additional burden onto the larger businesses, especially those, such as the utility companies and real-estate speculators, that had long escaped their fair share of taxation.[65] As Eugene Tobin and others have shown, the utilities and railroads were capable of considerable resistance through the legislatures and the courts, but in many localities the higher taxes of the progressive period were apparently imposed somewhat less disproportionately on small taxpayers, including small businesses.[66]

The progressive period was also an era of increased regulation of economic activity. There was no longer any attempt to protect the local monopolies of shopkeepers and artisans, but at the municipal level small businesses may have benefited from some of the new regulations. Though we have no satisfactory study of the point, it would appear that regulations designed to force utilities to treat all customers on the same basis protected some small businesses from exorbitant charges or difficulties in securing service, and that fee schedules that gave discounts to customers who purchased gas or electricity in bulk may have subsidized small-business consumers at the expense of residential consumers. On the other hand, many of the new regulations of the hours and conditions of labor, and of the labor of women and children, were designed to bear most heavily on fields dominated by small firms, such as baking and food processing, and the manufacture of novelties and especially of clothing. And in New York City, at least, civic and social reformers, who would later help develop the policies of "corporate liberalism," worked through the local government, as well as through the agencies of private charity, to mediate a series of major strikes in the garment manufacturing industry just at the turn of the century. The result, as Melvyn Dubovsky has shown, was the creation of effective labor unions, despite the opposition and resistance of the industry's small manufacturers.[67] Progressive economic regulation—like progressive policies for services, public facilities, and taxation—was not particularly directed at small businesses as such, and affected them in various ways, sometimes advancing and sometimes interfering with their interests. In this respect progressive policies were like those of the previous fifty years.

The history of municipal economic policy in the United States remains a largely unexplored field of study. Yet American municipalities have always had economic policies of some sort. This essay has stressed the features common to the policies of all cities, suggesting that these defined three periods of municipal economic policy, lasting from the colonial period through the nineteenth century and into the twentieth. The first period, in which municipalities outside New England served as closed commercial corporations, had its origins in English history and declined more slowly than has been supposed through the eighteenth and early nineteenth centuries. The second period, the era of the American System and of aggressive "municipal mercantilism," had its origins in the early years of the nineteenth century and continued into the 1870s or 1880s. The period of municipal progressivism—in which municipalities left the promotion and subsidy of long-distance transportation to other agencies and turned with new intensity to the improvement of their own physical, public-health, educational, and recreational facilities—began in the 1890s and continued into the 1920s. It would seem that the great wholesale merchants largely set the direction for municipal economic policy in the first two of these periods, and that large business interests, elite professionals, and social-welfare reformers had most to do with the third. Small-business interests seem to have had an independent but subordinate impact on municipal economic policy in all three periods, with that impact increasing, perhaps, at the end of the nineteenth century, as the economy became more fully differentiated, the economic elite fragmented, and the great wholesale merchants lost their dominant position in the organization of business. Small businesses in American cities, unlike their counterparts in German cities, were unable to use municipal regulation to retard the growth of large corporations, but by the end of the nineteenth century they were increasingly able to insist that at least some corporations pay their share of municipal taxes.

Reflecting the incompleteness of the literature on the subject, this summary remains unsatisfyingly broad and general. We do not yet know nearly enough about the lines of municipal policy regarding physical development, planning, and construction; we know little about the impact of most municipal economic policies, or the economic impact of municipal educational, policing, and social-welfare policies; and we know still less about the incidence, or the effects, of municipal taxation. Since most of the knowledge we do have is based on studies of one or, at most, just two or three cities, it is impossible even to begin to suggest how municipal economic policy, and its effects on various economic interests groups, may have varied according to a city's size, range of economic functions, geographic location, age, population composition, or other relevant variables. We do know that there were regional differences, just as there were changes over time. Whether differences between cities were large enough to obscure the broad outlines of the history of municipal economic policy sketched here remains to be seen.

Notes

1. C. Wright Mills and Melville J. Ulmer, "Small Business and Civic Welfare," *Report of the Smaller War Plants Corporation to the Special Committee to Study Problems of American Small Business*," Senate Document 135, Serial Number 11036, 79th Congress, 2nd Session (Washington, D.C.: G.P.O., 1946), conveniently reprinted in Michael Aiken and Paul E. Mott, *The Structure of Community Power* (New York: Random House, 1970).

2. Edward Pessen, "Who Has Power in the Democratic Capitalistic Community? Reflections on Antebellum New York City," *New York History* (Apr. 1977), 58:132.

3. Edward Pessen, "Who Governed the Nation's Cities in the 'Era of the Common Man'?" *Political Science Quarterly* (Dec. 1972), 87:591–614, reprinted in Pessen, *Riches, Class, and Power Before the Civil War* (Lexington, Mass.: Heath, 1973). See especially pp. 282–88.

4. Donald S. Bradley and Mayer N. Zald, "From Commercial Elite to Political Administrator: The Recruitment of the Mayors of Chicago," *American Journal of Sociology* (1965), 71:153–67.

5. Richard C. Wade, *The Urban Frontier: Pioneer Life in Early Pittsburgh, Cincinnati, Lexington, Louisville, and St. Louis* (Cambridge: Harvard University Press, 1959; reprint, University of Chicago Press, Phoenix edition), p. 112. According to Wade, the merchants held undisputed sway down to the War of 1812, but while they continued to sit "on local councils" they did not always agree with the expansive policies of many local governments during the 1820s (pp. 276–80). Unfortunately Wade does not develop this last point. According to Daniel Aaron, "Bankers, merchants, and lawyers" who "had tie-ups with every important financial and commercial firm in Cincinnati" controlled that city's council—Aaron, "Cincinnati, 1818–1838: A Study of Attitudes in the Urban West" (Ph.D. dissertation, Harvard University (Ph.D. dissertation, Harvard University, 1942), p. 112.

6. Robert A. Dahl, *Who Governs? Democracy and Power in an American City* (New Haven: Yale University Press, 1961), pp. 11–24. In the succeeding years of the nineteenth century, according to Dahl, enterpreneurs who led large and small banks, manufacturing companies, and mercantile enterprises consistently held the office—*Who Governs*, pp. 25–31.

7. Studies which show that professional politicians had taken over the top local offices in large cities in or shortly after the middle of the nineteenth century include Gabriel Almond, "Power and Plutocracy in New York City" (Ph.D. dissertation, University of Chicago, 1939); Sam Bass Warner, Jr., *The Private City: Philadelphia in Three Periods of its Growth* (Philadelphia: University of Pennsylvania Press, 1968), chap. 5; and Bradley and Zald, "From Commercial Elite to Professional Administrator." For discussion of the substantial sociological litera-

ture on the "bifurcation of power" between economic and political elites in twentieth-century American communities, see David C. Hammack, "Problems in the Historical Study of Power in the Cities and Towns of the United States, 1800–1960," *American Historical Review* (1978), 83:343.

8. Stuart M. Blumin, *The Urban Threshold: Growth and Change in a Nineteenth Century American Community* (Chicago: University of Chicago Press, 1976), pp. 41, 166–89; quotation from p. 181; Michael B. Katz, *The People of Hamilton, Canada West: Family and Class in a Mid-Nineteenth-Century City* (Cambridge: Harvard University Press, 1975), p. 177; Michael H. Frisch, *Town Into City: Springfield, Massachusetts and the Meaning of Community, 1840–1880* (Cambridge: Harvard University Press, 1972), pp. 241–45. According to Katz, 15 of 48 elected officials in Hamilton during 1851 and 1852 were among the town's 130 "business officials," and 75 percent were in the top decile of wealth-holders.

9. For Ypsilanti, 1823 and after, see Robert O. Schultze, "The Bifurcation of Power in a Satellite City," in Morris Janowitz, ed., *Community Power Systems* (Glencoe, Ill.: Free Press, 1961), pp. 19–80; for Lansing, Donald A. Clelland and William H. Form, "Economic Dominants and Community Power: A Comparative Analysis," *American Journal of Sociology* (1964), 69:511–21; Mayer N. Zald and Thomas A. Anderson, "Secular Trends and Historical Contingencies in the Recruitment of Mayors: Nashville as Compared to New Haven and Chicago," *Urban Affairs Quarterly* (1968) 3:53–68; Howard M. Gitelman, *Workingmen of Waltham: Mobility in American Urban Industrial Development* (Baltimore: Johns Hopkins University Press, 1974), p. 112. Small businessmen also held local office in Natchez, Mississippi, according to D. Clayton James' *Antebellum Natchez* (Baton Rouge: Louisiana State University Press, 1968), pp. 93–96; late nineteenth-century Syracuse, New York, according to John H. Lindquist, "An Occupational Analysis of Local Politics: Syracuse, New York, 1880–1959," *Sociology and Social Research* (1965), 49:343–54; and in nineteenth-century "Bay City, Massachusetts," according to Peter H. Rossi and Alice S. Rossi, "An Historical Perspective on the Functions of Local Politics," in Daniel N. Gordon, ed., *Social Change and Urban Politics; Readings* (Englewood Cliffs, N.J.: Prentice-Hall, 1973), pp. 49–64.

10. James H. Soltow's excellent study of the "Origins of Small Business Metal Fabricators and Machinery Makers in New England, 1890–1957," *Transactions* of the American Philosophical Society, New Series 55 Part 10 (1965), found that while some executives of such firms joined local voluntary or social associations, "none participated directly in local politics" (p. 50). In contrast to those who had to cultivate a local market or clientele, Soltow's small manufacturers felt they could spare no time from the management of their enterprises. For the temporary success of workingmen in small industrial cities, see Alan Dawley, *Class and Community: The Industrial Revolution in Lynn* (Cambridge, Mass.: Harvard University Press, 1976), chap. 8; Herbert G. Gutman, "The Worker's Search for Power: Labor in the Gilded Age," in H. Wayne Morgan, ed., *The Gilded Age: A Reappraisal* (Syracuse: Syracuse University Press, 1963), pp. 38–68; Gutman, "Class, Status, and Community Power in Nineteenth-Century American Industrial Cities: Paterson, New Jersey: A Case Study," in Frederic C. Jaher, ed., *The Age of Industrialism in America: Essays in Social Structure and Cultural Values* (New York: Free Press, 1968), pp. 263–87; David Brody, *Steelworkers in America: The Non-Union Era* (Cambridge: Harvard University Press, 1960), chap. 6.

11. Weber's definition appears in his classic essay, "Class, Status, Party," in *From Max Weber: Essays in Sociology,* edited and translated by H. H. Gerth and C. Wright Mills (New York: Oxford University Press, 1946). For a full discussion of the issues involved in the historical study of power, see Hammack, "Historical Study of Power."

12. Jon C. Teaford, *The Municipal Revolution in America: Origins of Modern Urban Government, 1650–1825* (Chicago: University of Chicago Press, 1975), p. 16.

13. Teaford, *Municipal Revolution*, pp. 16–34; Richard B. Morris, *Government and Labor in Early America* (New York: Columbia University Press, 1946; reprint, Harper & Row Torchbook edition, 1965), pp. 363–89.

14. Teaford, *Municipal Revolution*, pp. 47–63. In England, Justices of the Peace and other local officials continued to set artisans' wages under the Elizabethan Statute of Artificers down to the 1760s, though the practice had been dying out for at least thirty years by that date, as W. E. Minchinton concludes in his recent survey of historical writing and evidence, *Wage Regulation in Pre-Industrial England* (Newton Abbott, England: David & Charles, 1972), pp. 20–27.

15. In *Government and Labor in Early America*, Morris places little emphasis on the decline of apprenticeship, but he does note a progressive shortening in the length of terms, p. 371. According to Teaford, municipalities gave up their efforts to regulate apprenticeship in the 1730s—*Municipal Revolution*, p. 50. A good survey of the problem in one city is provided by Carl F. Kaestle in *The Evolution of an Urban School System: New York City, 1750–1850* (Cambridge: Harvard University Press, 1973), pp. 96–99.

16. Teaford, *Municipal Revolution*, pp. 95–100.

17. Morris, *Government and Labor*, p. 371.

18. *Minutes of the Common Council of the City of New York, 1784–1831*, vol. 19, May 3, 1830–May 9, 1831 (New York: M. B. Brown, 1917), pp. 110, 233–4, 672, and passim.

19. Teaford, *Municipal Revolution*, pp. 18, 52, and 109.

20. Morris, *Government and Labor*, pp. 363–64.

21. Mack Walker, *German Home Towns: Community, State, and General Estate, 1648–1871* (Ithaca, New York: Cornell University Press, 1971).

22. W. E. Minchinton quotes this remark of Sir John Clapham's in *Wage Regulation*, p. 27.

23. Morton J. Horwitz, *The Transformation of American Law, 1760–1860* (Cambridge: Harvard University Press, 1977), p. xiv.

24. Eric Foner, *Tom Paine and Revolutionary America* (New York: Oxford University Press, 1976), pp. 179–80.

25. Walter Hugins, *Jacksonian Democracy and the Working Class: A Study of the New York Workingmen's Movement, 1829–1837* (Stanford: Stanford University Press, 1960), p. 162.

26. Hugins, *Jacksonian Democracy*, p. 164.

27. Carl V. Harris, *Political Power in Birmingham, 1871–1921* (Knoxville: University of Tennessee Press, 1977), chap. 3.

28. Teaford, *Municipal Revolution*, pp. 82–85; Hugins, *Jacksonian Democracy*, pp. 158, 162–166 (though Hugins does not make the point, his evidence indicates that the Workingmen's Party in New York increased its emphasis on the municipal regulation issues during the years when Whigs controlled the city's council and mayoralty).

29. Lee Benson, *The Concept of Jacksonian Democracy: New York as a Test Case* (Princeton, N.J.: Princeton University Press, 1961); Ronald P. Formisano, *The Birth of Mass Political Par-*

ties: Michigan, 1827–1861 (Princeton: Princeton University Press, 1971); William G. Shade, *Banks or No Banks: The Money Issue in Western Politics, 1832–1865* (Detroit: Wayne State University Press, 1972); Herbert Ershkowitz and William G. Shade, "Consensus or Conflict? Political Behavior in the State Legislatures During the Jacksonian Era," *Journal of American History* (1971), 58:591–621. After 1837, according to Ershkowitz and Shade, Whig and Democratic policies toward banking did diverge.

30. Horwitz, *Transformation of American Law*, p. 140.

31. Ibid., p. 101.

32. Horwitz does discuss judicial innovation in one area of business regulation, that concerning the relations between masters and apprentices, employers and employees. This he describes as the "classic" example of the redefinition by the courts of "all economic relationships in terms of contract." *Transformation of American Law*, pp. 207–8.

33. Teaford, *Municipal Revolution*, chaps. 5 and 6.

34. Teaford, *Municipal Revolution*, chap. 3; Richard C. Wade, *Slavery in the Cities: The South, 1820–1860* (New York: Oxford University Press, 1964). Wade found evidence that cities in the Ohio Valley followed the lead of those in the mid-Atlantic states in the matter of business regulation, and that they were inclined to *increase* such regulations between 1815 and 1820. See *Urban Frontier*, pp. 79–83, 280–82; Wade, *Slavery in the Cities*.

35. For a review of the literature on this subject, see Robert A. Lively, "The American System: A Review Article," in *The Business History Review* (March, 1955), 29:81–96.

36. Good general accounts of municipal expenditures for these purposes can be found in Blake McKelvey, *The Urbanization of America, 1860–1915* (New Brunswick: Rutgers University Press, 1963), and Ernest S. Griffith, *A History of American City Government: The Conspicuous Failure, 1870–1900* (New York: Praeger, 1974). Seymour Mandelbaum's provocative analysis of the politics of public works development in *Boss Tweed's New York* (New York: Wiley, 1965) is challenged by Eugene P. Mohring's meticulous analysis of the city's public works in his 1976 City University of New York Ph.D. dissertation, "Public Works and the Pattern of Urban Real Estate Growth in Manhattan, 1835–1894."

37. For a comment on the poor quality of our data on the history of municipal finances, see Lance E. Davis and John Legler, "The Government in the American Economy, 1815–1902: A Quantitative Study," *Journal of Economic History*, (Dec. 1966), 26:514–52. For the outline suggested here, see Ernest S. Griffith, *The Modern Development of City Government in the United Kingdom and the United States* (London: Oxford University Press, 1927); Charles Adrian and Ernest S. Griffith, *A History of American City Government: The Formation of Traditions, 1775–1870* (New York: Praeger, 1976); and Griffith, *American City Government: The Conspicuous Failure*, pp. 13–22, 224–34.

38. On the judicial imposition of controls over municipal expenditures, see Clyde E. Jacobs, *Law Writers and the Courts* (New York: Da Capo Press, 1973 reprint of University of California Press 1954 edition).

39. Charles N. Glaab, *Kansas City and the Railroads* (Madison: State Historical Society of Wisconsin, 1962).

40. Robert R. Dykstra, *The Cattle Towns* (New York: Alfred A. Knopf, 1968); the phrase "municipal mercantilism" is that of Julius Rubin, *Canal or Railroad: Imitation and Innovation*

in Response to the Erie Canal in Philadelphia, Baltimore, and Boston (Philadelphia: The American Philosophical Society, 1961).

41. Carl V. Harris, *Political Power in Birmingham,* chaps. 5 and 6.

42. On the growth of the national market, see Alfred D. Chandler, Jr., *The Visible Hand: The Rise of Modern Business Enterprise in the United States* (Cambridge: Harvard University Press, 1978), especially part 2.

43. Soltow, "Origins of Small Business," pp. 10–11.

44. Suggestive accounts on this little-explored subject include Rubin, *Canal or Railroad;* Formisano, *Mass Political Parties;* and Michael F. Holt, *Forging a Majority: The Formation of the Republican Party in Pittsburgh, 1848–1860* (New Haven: Yale University Press, 1968).

45. Glenn Porter and Harold C. Livesay, *Merchants and Manufacturers* (Baltimore: Johns Hopkins University Press, 1971).

46. Jacobs describes the impact of Cooley and Dillon in *Law Writers and the Courts,* chap. 4.

47. Gitelman, *Workingmen of Waltham,* p. 112.

48. The largest number of studies on these points deal with education; see in particular Michael B. Katz, *The Irony of Early School Reform* (Cambridge: Harvard University Press, 1968); Kaestle, *Urban School System;* Stanley K. Schultz, *The Culture Factory: Boston Public Schools, 1789–1860* (New York: Oxford University Press, 1973); Selwyn K. Troen, *The Public and Schools: Shaping the St. Louis System, 1838–1920* (Columbia: University of Missouri Press, 1975); David B. Tyack, *The One Best System: A History of American Urban Education* (Cambridge: Harvard University Press, 1967); and James F. Richardson, *The New York Police: Colonial Times to 1901* (New York: Oxford University Press, 1970); on water and sewer improvements, see Nelson M. Blake, *Water for the Cities* (Syracuse: Syracuse University Press, 1956).

49. For changes in per capita expenditures on various municipal services, see Edward Dana Durand, *The Finances of New York City* (New York: Macmillan, 1898); Charles P. Huse, *The Financial History of Boston from May 1, 1822, to January 31, 1909* (New York: Russell & Russell reprint of Harvard University Press edition of 1916); J. H. Hollander, *The Financial History of Baltimore* (Baltimore: Johns Hopkins Press, 1899); and H. K. Stokes, *The Finances and Administration of Providence, 1636–1901* (Baltimore: Johns Hopkins Press, 1903).

50. Harris, *Political Power in Birmingham,* passim.

51. Sam Bass Warner, Jr., *Streetcar Suburbs: The Process of Growth in Boston, 1870–1900* (Cambridge: Harvard University Press, 1962), chap. 7.

52. David C. Hammack, "Participation in Major Decisions in New York City, 1890–1900: The Creation of Greater New York and the Centralization of the Public School System" (Ph.D. dissertation, Columbia University, 1973), chaps. 5 and 6.

53. Roger D. Simon, *The City-Building Process: Housing and Services in New Milwaukee Neighborhoods, 1880–1910* (Philadelphia: The American Philosophical Society, 1978).

54. Two preliminary surveys of the history of building relations in one city are John P. Comer, *New York City Building Control 1800–1941* (New York: Columbia University Press, 1942), chapter 2, and Joseph Daniel McGoldrick, Seymour Graubard, and Raymond J. Horowitz,

Building Regulation in New York City: A Study in Administrative Law and Procedure (New York: Commonwealth Fund, 1944), pp. 38–76.

55. Gutman, "Class, Status and Community Power;" Brody, *Steelworkers in America,* chap. 6.

56. John T. Cumbler, "Labor, Capital, and Community: The Struggle for Power," *Labor History* (1974), 16:395–415.

57. On the ease with which Swift set up his chain of retail butcher's shops, see Alfred D. Chandler, Jr., "The Beginnings of 'Big Business' in American Industry," *Business History Review* (Sept. 1959), 33:1–31.

58. Estelle Feinstein, *Stamford in the Gilded Age* (Stamford, Conn.: Stamford Historical Society, 1975); Hammack, "Participation in Major Decisions," chap. 7; Harris, *Political Power in Birmingham,* chap. 12.

59. Griffith, *American City Government: The Conspicuous Failure,* p. 160.

60. Calculated from Harris, *Political Power in Birmingham,* p. 291; Durand, *Finances of New York City;* Huse, *The Financial History of Boston;* and Stokes, *Administration of Providence.*

61. Griffith, *American City Government: The Conspicuous Failure,* pp. 155–77.

62. See, for example, Tyack, *One Best System;* and the general perspective suggested by Robert Wiebe in *The Search for Order, 1877–1920* (New York: Hill and Wang, 1967).

63. Hammack, "Participation in Major Decisions," chap. 7.

64. Harris, *Political Power in Birmingham;* David C. Hammack, "Participation in Major Decisions," chaps. 5 and 6.

65. Huse, *Financial History of Boston,* p. 302; Hollander, *Financial History of Baltimore,* p. 277; Durand, *Finances of New York City,* pp. 238–46. At the same time, however, the continued municipal reliance on the property tax and the failure to tax corporate shares, or other forms of personal property, was widely believed to shift the tax burden from the wealthy to small taxpayers, including small businessmen. See Durand, pp. 190–95; Stokes, *Administration of Providence,* pp. 265–77; Hollander, p. 261; Huse, pp. 208–9, 298.

66. Eugene M. Tobin, " 'Engines of Salvation' or 'Smoking Black Devils': Jersey City Reformers and the Railroads, 1902–1908," in Michael H. Ebner and Eugene M. Tobin, eds., *The Age of Urban Reform: New Perspectives on the Progressive Era* (Port Washington, N.Y.: Kennikat Press, 1977), pp. 142–55.

67. Melvyn Dubovsky, *When Workers Organize: New York City in the Progressive Era* (Amherst: University of Massachusetts Press, 1968).

15

LILLIPUTIANS IN BROBDINGNAG: SMALL BUSINESS IN LATE-NINETEENTH-CENTURY AMERICA

Harold C. Livesay

AMERICAN historians have viewed their country's past from a variety of perspectives—social, political, intellectual—but only in their assessments of the second half of the nineteenth century has economic history supplied the dominant theme. In that period, industrialization became such an overwhelming dynamic that historians of all persuasions find themselves grappling with its consequences—urbanization, as a result of the marshaling of an industrial labor force; political protest, as an outcry against the consequences of changes in the business system; pragmatism, Social Darwinism, and Christian Socialism, as the intellectual patterns explaining business's behavior and the public's adjustment to it.

Economic and business historians have themselves approached the period in varying ways, often dictated by their own political persuasions and their interpretations, logically enough, often reflect their personal reactions to the twentieth-century consequences of nineteenth-century developments. The great period of American industrialization has been interpreted (among other ways) as the era of bourgeois revolution, as a time when a great chance for socialism went a-glimmering, as a period in which the seeds of the twentieth-century Democratic-party coalition were planted, as the triumph of the machine over poverty, or as the logical outgrowth of entrepreneurial behavior within the American marketplace, with its particular spatial, climatic, political, and demographic dimensions.

All these interpretive lenses, however, tend to have a common focal point, the big business institution, whose emergence was the hallmark of the late nineteenth-century economy. Many have disputed the origins of "big business" and more yet have debated its consequences, but few have denied its primacy. Henry Adams, ruefully contemplating the values of a society that replaced the cathedral with the dynamo; Alan Nevins, celebrating the achievements of "industrial statesmen" such as John D. Rockefeller; Alfred D. Chandler, Jr., methodically and matter-of-factly analyzing and chronicling the evolution of the corporately owned, professionally managed, multiunit, diversified enterprise; Gabriel Kolko, seeing business's controlling mentality insinuating itself everywhere, even into the very agencies nominally created to curb corporate behavior—all these and others reflect the myriad fascinations of a single phenomenon. Under these ministrations, the second half of the nineteenth century has been indelibly marked as an era dominated by "the Rise of Big Business."[1]

That the late nineteenth century did see the emergence of business institutions of a size, complexity, and power greater than any mankind had ever known is a fact so obvious, so compelling that it has led to widespread acceptance of an apparently logical corallary assumption: as big business waxed mighty, small business faded away. A lot of evidence can be assembled to support this proposition. Visual evidence, for example: an American who lived from 1850 to 1900 lived to see the steeple-dominated skylines of his youth blotted out by the effusions of the corporate mills, smokestacks, and blast furnaces that towered over everything. Statistics for the period, coarse as they are, chart the steadily rising contribution of corporate enterprise to the national income. Institutionally, the change was equally graphic: by 1900, Andrew Carnegie's mills made more steel than all of England's combined and made it at a price that drove small operators permanently from the field. Carnegie and other "captains of industry" commanded capital resources, industrial populations, and business revenues that dwarfed those of many a small nation around the globe.

Often enough such growth was accomplished on a diet of small-business competitors, as John D. Rockefeller digested dozens of erstwhile independent rivals into the corporate anonymity of Standard Oil.

The rising public outcry against these developments lent credence to the notion of big business's omnipotence. Certainly, many small businessmen felt they were engaged in a fight for their lives and consequently turned up in the front ranks of those agitating for regulation of the railroads and control of monopolistic trusts. The American proclivity for nostalgia lent a poignancy to protests then and turns up in interpretations penned even now. Late-nineteenth-century Americans often felt that with the coming of big business, something was lost, something good, decent, precious, and traditionally American. Whether those happy days of yesteryear ever actually existed is irrelevant; many people thought they did, and their emotional appeal was voiced in slogans and demands of the time—in, for example, the battle cry of the Knights of Labor: "Every man his own boss." The fact that this painful loss of individuality, open competition, and economic self-reliance was a result of the unrestrained exercise of those very qualities made the experience all the more harsh, vexing, bewildering.[2]

Steeped in many of the same notions that prevailed among the nineteenth-century citizenry, and confronted with an even more awesome display of corporate power and its consequences, twentieth-century American analysts—historians salient among them—have therefore, while chronicling the rise of giant enterprise in the nineteenth century, simultaneously written the epitaph for small business. This obituary, however, like so many tossed off by social scientists (they have pronounced England "finished" several times in my lifetime) turns out, under close examination, to be premature.

Small business, despite the undeniable rise of its giant counterparts, continued to play several vital roles in the American economy throughout the nineteenth century, and in the twentieth as well. If small business can be defined as I define it here, as any enterprise in which three or fewer individuals hold controlling ownership and small enough to be operated with no more than one layer of supervision between owners and workers, then vast areas of the American economy remained its province as late as 1900.[3] In fact, as Glenn Porter has pointed out, big business, which to contemporary Americans means most business, was to nineteenth-century Americans a phenomenon largely restricted to transportation, manufacturing, and to a lesser extent, banking.[4] Significant as these were, they were by no means all-inclusive of economic activity.

Virtually all of American agriculture in 1900 was small business, and it is difficult now (though it has become easier recently) to appreciate just how important this sector was. Farm output contributed almost a quarter of Gross Domestic Product in 1900. The farmer, as customer, contributed additionally: one-sixth of all machinery sold in the United States in 1900 was farm machinery and it totaled twice the expenditure on electrical machinery in the same year. At the end of the century, as much money was invested in agricultural equipment and structures as in manufacturing and mining combined. As producer, consumer, and investor the farmer bulwarked the economy that supported the rural population, and that population in 1900 vastly exceeded (46 million vs. 30 million) the urban population despite decades of intense industrialization.[5]

For city dwellers and farmers alike, the distribution network that supplied them with consumer durables and perishables remained in 1900 as it had always been, a network of wholesale and retail houses that came under the rubric of small business. Sears, Roebuck & Co., together with a handful of imitators, were proving the viability of corporate mail-order concerns, but altogether they accounted for a minuscule fragment of retail sales. Chain stores were yet in their infancy. Only in the sale of producers' goods, technically complex consumers' goods such as sewing machines, or perishables like meat and bananas that required refrigerated facilities, had corporate distribution networks become a major factor, and even in these lines, the final sale was often made by an independent businessman—a commission merchant, a franchised dealer, or a neighborhood shopkeeper. Altogether small businesses still supplied employment for nearly two-thirds of the 27 million Americans working in 1900.[6]

Visible evidence thus can be misleading and any number of eyewitness accounts can add up to an incomplete description, as Voltaire pointed out long ago, remarking that the whole world once knew that the sun went around the earth because everyone could see that it did. Everyone was wrong, nevertheless. Big business might tower over the skyline, corporations like International Harvester might dramatize corporate power by riding roughshod over strikers, business moguls might claim the headlines by hosting dinners at Delmonico's that cost a dozen men's annual wage, and by cavorting on horseback amid the banquet tables, but the fact remained that even in 1900, the great majority of Americans went about their daily affairs dealing infrequently, if ever, with big business directly.

Indirectly, of course, big business's dominance in transportation and its rising importance in manufacturing and banking affected the quotidian life of most Americans and directly impacted upon a steadily increasing number. By 1900, nearly all Americans working in transportation industries were employees of big business, as were two-thirds of those with manufacturing jobs. That corporate dominance of manufacturing would increase and that big business would increasingly obtrude into wholesale and retail trade was a trend so obvious that it stirred increasing public unrest, manifested in waves of political protest that rolled higher as the nineteenth century waned, swelling to the flood tide of Progressivism that swept the land in the first decade of the twentieth century.

The pervasive *angst* generated by big business's swelling power is not hard to understand; by 1900, it seemed that if recent trends continued unchecked in the future, small business might be driven from the economy, taking with it the cherished American option of self-employment. By 1900, big business had already ousted hundreds of small competitors from manufacturing fields such as petroleum refining; tobacco manufacturing; primary metal smelting, refining, and processing; electrical machinery production; and rubber processing. Where all this might end no man could say, but it seemed that if J. P. Morgan and his trust-building ilk had their way, all of American manufacturing and distribution would join transportation as the exclusive preserve of big business.

By 1900, Americans had had fifteen years of watching as hundreds of once-proud family firms succumbed to the blandishments or assaults of the trust-makers and disappeared into corporate anonymity.[7] Even Cyrus McCormick and Andrew Carnegie, symbols of the American dream of the self-made man and of that most cherished of traditional American qualities, rugged individualism, ultimately sold out to International Harvester and United States Steel, respectively. Small wonder, then, that so many Americans saw their economy in the throes of an ineluctable process that increasingly rendered the small businessman an irrelevant, obsolete species and might soon make him extinct.

In fact, however, the process, while perhaps inevitable, was a complex one that left small business a significant, and in some ways an increasing, role to play. Certainly the evolution of a mature industrial society called forth business units of increasing size and complexity in the United States, as it has in every society, regardless of political system, that has undergone the same economic transformation. But the appearance of more and bigger businesses did not, in fact, eliminate the possibility for small businesses to survive and prosper. Some manufacturing fields—textiles, clothing, leather, lumber, and furniture, for example—proved strikingly unfertile ground for the nurturing of trusts and, in fact, as many late nineteenth-century mergers failed as succeeded.[8] Even successful corporate giants rarely monopolized all aspects of their particular industries. United States Steel and its corporate rivals dominated the manufacture of steel, but small specialized firms, such as the Lukens family's Coatesville, Pennsylvania, plate rolling mill, remained alive and well, pygmies prospering under the price umbrella erected by the giants.[9]

Trusts and other mergers, in fact, often left small businesses undisturbed, concentrating instead on rounding up major producers. However much the public might lament the passage of Carnegie Steel and McCormick Farm Machinery from the scene and see in their disappearance an omen for all family business, the fact was that both firms (and dozens like them), despite their family ownership, had, by the time of their inclusion in a trust, long since grown into big businesses in their own right.

Nor did the rise of big business eliminate the opportunity for individual entrepreneurs to start small businesses that survived and prospered. In fact, something like the reverse transpired. Between 1870 and 1900, the American population doubled, but the number of business establishments tripled. A proliferation of small enterprises accounted for all but a tiny fraction of this growth. For these new firms, as well as for already existing small businesses, the growth in size and potency of big business seems to have had little effect on the chances of survival, despite the gloomy presentiments of contemporary observers and the somber reflections of modern historians. The rate of business failures in 1900 (92 per 10,000 concerns) was little higher than in 1870 (83 per 10,000). In the intervening years, it fluctuated not according to the number and size of big businesses operating in the economy, but rather with the rise and fall of the economy as a whole, a functional relationship that continued unchanged in the twentieth century.

What the emergence of big business produced in the second half of the nineteenth century, then, was not the elimination of existing small businesses or the stifling of opportunity to create new ones, but instead a shift in small business's role in the U.S. economy. That economy was not, as many feared then and have suggested since, a zero-sum game in which every big business gain resulted in a small business loss, where the ping of corporate emergence produced a pong of proprietorship collapse. Despite small business's elimination from transportation, its diminuendo role in manufacturing and banking, its declining contribution to GNP and the job market, its fading influence at the seat of national political power, small business continued to supply a vital, albeit no longer the most prominent, strand in the American business fabric.

The viability of small enterprise in the corporate era stemmed from two sources: retention of some traditional roles that had originated in the pre-industrial era, and the discovery that big business created new opportunities for some of its smaller brethren even as it eliminated others. Through the last half of the nineteenth century and on into the twentieth, small business—in farms and fisheries and grocery stores, in needle trades and haberdasheries and dry-goods shops, in sawmills and furniture and construction firms—continued to feed, clothe, and house most Americans. Its distribution network, which since colonial times had carried manufactured goods to the most distant reaches of the far-flung American hinterland, adapted itself as readily to the stream of goods (with the technologically complex exceptions mentioned above) pouring from late-nineteenth-century American factories as it had in pre-Revolutionary times to the trickle of wares sailed across the Atlantic or hammered out in American artisanal shops.[10]

It was in the new world of big business, however, that small business paradoxically found its greatest opportunities and made its most dynamic contributions, bolstering the emerging industrial economy in ways that no statistical measures can properly evaluate. Small business became a crucial link in the supply line that kept giant, mass production industries moving; small business originated a multitude of innovations—in the technology of products and production methods, and in managerial techniques—that became part of giant enterprise's stock in trade; and, finally, small business, in doing all these things, often metamorphosed into big business, infusing new blood into the corporate stream and shouldering aside geriatric giants in the process.

Small businessmen often found corporate enterprise a source of custom, not competition. One corporate patron could provide as much business as hundreds of individuals, and at greatly decreased selling cost. In the 1890s, before the advent of the automobile industry, for example, Alfred P. Sloan's Hyatt Roller Bearing company led a marginal existence, skating along the ragged edge of bankruptcy as Sloan and his sales manager crisscrossed the country trying to persuade proprietors of small machine shops to adopt their new, low-friction bearings. With the arrival on the scene of the Ford Motor Company (1903), Buick (1904), General Motors (1908), and others, Sloan found a handful of customers so anxious to absorb his entire production and have him multiply output many times over that they taught him several tricks of survival in the new corporate competitive world. Cadillac's Henry Leland told him that automobile manufacturers would increasingly demand interchangeable parts and persuaded Sloan to install the precision-machining techniques required to produce them. Ford's Harold Wills showed him that doing business with Ford and GM eliminated advertising and other selling costs and that these savings could be translated into lower prices that assured competitive survival and higher profits.[11]

Sloan's was not an isolated experience, but one shared by Charles Stewart Mott, the Dodge brothers, the Fisher brothers, Charles Kettering, and many other small proprietors whose ability to produce components made them indispensable to the automobile industry. Nor was such an interdependency between large and small business limited to the automobile industry. It was, in fact, a widespread phenomenon, found all across the spectrum of the economy. Seen in terms of individual firms, the late-nineteenth-century world of small business thus discloses numerous individual tragedies in which a large firm throttled a small one, but viewed as a whole, the small-business economy was a Hydra, growing two heads for every one lopped off.

Small business's emergence as the source of technological and managerial innovations adopted by its larger brethren derived from small enterprise's powerful will to survive. The spirit (or delusion, as some would have it) of individualism was too deeply entwined in the American psyche to be unraveled. American businessmen for generations had seen their firms as an extension of themselves. Their self-respect was bound up in the fortunes of their business, and business success offered the shimmering prospect, not only of wealth and power, but also of public esteem and social mobility for themselves and their children. Confronted with the reality of big business's presence, many individualistic American entrepreneurs determined to salvage what they could of the old virtues, some by working with big business but not for it, others by equipping their family's firms for survival in the corporate era. The results often produced a galvanic effect on the American economy.

Thomas Edison belonged to the first category. In his youth, Edison worked in two industries that were among the first to succumb to corporate domination: railroads and telegraph companies. Edison, however, had no mind to spend his life at the beck and call of others. He wanted to be his own master, and as soon as the products of his fecund mind had established his reputation as a virtuoso inventor, he severed connections with Western Union and struck out on his own.

In his laboratory at Menlo Park, Edison functioned as traditional proprietors always had: his shop was his domain and his word the unquestioned law. He decided what projects to work on and who would undertake them. Working day and night, he kept his hand and mind on everything. The laboratory's existence, however, depended on the corporate economy, for Edison, for all his disdain of accounting and system in his own business, was a shrewd judge of the economic winds. Only big business, he knew, could afford to finance the research for, and manufacture of, the kind of products he best understood and was determined to create: technically advanced items for which a mass market existed. Consequently, he focused his efforts on two kinds of projects: ideas of his own that he could sell to big business, and jobs undertaken at the specific request (and with the financial support) of large corporations.

Menlo Park, under Edison's aegis, prospered as an "invention factory," the first of its kind; Edison himself existed as an inventor-soldier of fortune aligning himself temporarily with this or that corporate principality, but vowing permanent allegiance to none. Often he accepted subventions from more than one company to explore the same technical frontier, then sold his discoveries to the highest bidder. He was reviled as a man "with a vacuum where his conscience should be," damned as a "professor of duplicity and quadriplicity," badgered in court, fleeced by Jay Gould, and shunted to the sidelines by J. P. Morgan, who administered the ultimate insult by omitting Edison's name from the masthead of General Electric, the trust formed of companies that existed to exploit Edison's electrical patents.

Through it all, Edison survived, made and lost several fortunes, gave the world the electric light, the phonograph, motion pictures, the mimeograph, an improved telephone, discovered the phenomena that led to x-rays, the vacuum tube, wireless telegraphy, radio, and television, and made scores of other discoveries ultimately woven into the intricate web of modern industrial technology.[12] In his wake came many other individualists—Thomas Watson at IBM, Sol Linowitz at Xerox, Edwin Land at Polaroid—who proved that Edison's performance was a precedent, not a fluke. In the hands of these and similar men, small business has continued to be a source of technological pioneering. So much so, in fact, that some observers believe that small business has made a more dynamic contribution to research and development than its giant counterparts.[13]

In the realm of managerial innovation, small business has made an equally dynamic contribution. Amongst the Carnegies and McCormicks, forced by business conditions, age, or the lack of qualified successors, or seduced by the charms of instant wealth in the form of trust certificates, to surrender family control of their firms, there were some, like Pierre Dupont, who refused to yield. Raised in the Dupont company and family compound on the banks of the Brandywine River in Wilmington, Pierre breathed in the anachronistic atmosphere of two traditions. The first, European manorialism, his ancestors had brought from France and installed, complete with rights of inheritance and obligations of *noblesse oblige,* as the managerial policies of their American powder mill. The second was the American tradition of viewing one's business as an extension of one's self. Together these traditions penetrated to the core of his soul and remained there, unwavering, until the day he died.

To Pierre Dupont, as to generations of Duponts who preceded him, the family was the company and vice versa; the head of one was, de facto, the head of the other. Given the shape of the family tree, Pierre grew up aware that he was unlikely to reach the top, but confident that a place high up was his to claim in due time. Through a combination of industrial accidents, calculated decisions, and geriatric coincidences that need not be elaborated here, Pierre found himself in 1902 in a position to control the Dupont Company's affairs. In the years preceding, he had acquired a scientific education at MIT, and added to it a working knowledge of modern corporate finance and cost-based managerial techniques. The latter two, he realized, were swiftly becoming prerequisites of business survival, but the Dupont Company, as he had learned during a frustrating interlude working there in the mid 1890s, did not bother with either one.

Once in a position to control his company's destiny, Pierre followed a course that reflected his dedication to tradition and his pragmatic acceptance of contemporary business realities. He rapidly installed cost accounting, systematic organization, and the whole accompanying panoply of modern bureaucratic management.

Realizing that even the Dupont family, large as it was, could not supply an adequate pool of qualified managers to staff the rapidly expanding organization, and that the company could no longer afford to place family members, regardless of qualification and aptitude, in positions of responsibility, he forced nepotism to yield, at least partially, to meritocratic selection. None of his actions, however, signaled a change in his attitude toward the company as a family operation. Outsiders might be required to supplement family members' contributions, but Pierre thought that some Dupont should always head the company, that a qualified one would always be available, and that the succession must be assured.

Accepting the necessity of yielding some measure of managerial control, however, was an attitude dictated by his fierce, fundamental determination that ownership must always remain in the family. The company was his heritage, a legacy received by family right, not to dispose of at will, but to preserve and pass on to the next generation of Duponts. In order to carry out this duty in an economy where survival demanded efficiency, in an industry where efficiency demanded size, Pierre accepted the fact that his company must grow, bursting free of its century-old pattern of moderate size, modest ambitions, limited product line, and antiquated methods of production and management.

If expansion, growth, diversification, and modernization were to be accomplished without the loss of family control, Pierre knew that the transformation must be financed through a combination of retained profits and capital advanced by the family. That he could raise massive capital in Wall Street, or at banking houses such as Morgan's, Pierre well knew, but he knew equally well, having seen the process at work all around him in his apprentice years, that such finance demanded as its price a measure of control. This price Pierre would not—indeed, given his self-imposed imperatives, could not—pay. Since the Dupont Company was relatively small—its greatest pre-World War I net worth was less than Carnegie Steel's net profit in 1900—and the Dupont family wealthy, but not spectacularly so, Pierre knew that every investment dollar had to be put to good use. Neither the company nor the family could afford expensive mistakes.

Pierre consequently established as a guideline for all investment decisions the principle of return on investment. Every proposed project had to compete with every other on that basis. No longer was it adequate to show that an investment would make money; project sponsors had to convince the executive committee that their scheme would make more money than could be made elsewhere. Inevitably, this principle caused Pierre to demand that his subordinates perfect a new managerial art, market forecasting, and install it as an integral part of Dupont company management methods. This innovation, perhaps the last significant addition ever made to the "American System of Management," took time to perfect, but its success led, as always, to emulation and it was ultimately adopted across the spectrum of American industry, becoming a keystone of modern management practice. Ironically this technique, now regarded as indispensable for corporate survival, resulted from Pierre Dupont's obsession with preserving as much as possible his company's traditional, proprietary, preindustrial virtues against the encroachments of the modern, corporate, industrial era. As sometimes happened, his defensive strategy led to the creation of an awesomely powerful offensive structure, one that carried the Dupont Company from a sleepy, provincial powder firm to an aggressive, global, diversified enterprise.[14]

Pierre Dupont, Alfred Sloan, and others previously mentioned, were only a few of the entrepreneurs who turned their small firms into big businesses. Indeed, in the late nineteenth century and since, small business has proven a fertile spawning ground for giant enterprise. The list of America's five hundred largest industrials is dotted with examples: some—Ford, Dupont, Proctor and Gamble, Westinghouse, Eastman Kodak, Goodyear, Kraft, Goodrich—of nineteenth or turn-of-the-century vintage; others—IBM, Xerox, Polaroid, Boeing, Grumman—of more recent origins.[15]

The advent of big business thus did not herald the demise of small enterprise in the United States. In the last half of the nineteenth century, small business—while suffering individual casualties through competition, obsolescence, or the mortality of its owners—nevertheless, found ways to survive as an institution. Preserving some of its traditional roles and finding new opportunities in the new industrial age, small business not only performed vital services for the economy, but in addition injected dynamic growth factors into the big-business sector as well. Its vitality and contribution remain underestimated, its fate described in tones of lamentation by commentators swayed by nostalgic *tristesse,* bards playing sad songs on blue guitars. But then all historians, even I, labor with the problem described by Wallace Stevens:

I

The man bent over his guitar,
A shearsman of sorts. The day was green.

They said, "You have a blue guitar,
You do not play things as they are."

The man replied, "Things as they are
Are changed upon the blue guitar."

And they said then, "But play, you must,
A tune beyond us, yet ourselves."

A tune upon the blue guitar
Of things exactly as they are."

II

I cannot bring a world quite round,
Although I patch it as I can.

I sing a hero's head, large eye
And bearded bronze, but not a man,

Although I patch him as I can
And reach through him almost to man.

If to serenade almost to man
Is to miss, by that, things as they are,

Say that it is the serenade
Of a man that plays a blue guitar.[16]

Notes

1. The literature on all aspects of this period is enormous and beyond recounting here. Good summaries, with helpful bibliographic references can be found in John A. Garraty, *The New Commonwealth* (New York: Harper & Row, 1968); Glenn Porter, *The Rise of Big Business, 1860–1910* (New York: Crowell, 1973); Thomas B. Brewer, ed., *The Robber Barons: Saints or Sinners?* (New York: Krieger, 1970).

2. On this subject too there is an abundance of material. Among the more salient works are Richard Hofstadter, *Age of Reform* (New York: Vintage, 1955); Robert Wiebe, *Search for Order, 1877–1920* (New York: Hill and Wang, 1965).

3. All definitions of "small business" are to some extent arbitrary, and the line that separates it from big business is a difficult one to draw. From my own studies of business institutions, I have concluded that a structural distinction most closely approximates reality and is more useful than any based on value of assets, volume of business, or number of employees. Some small businesses were, of course, incorporated and some big firms were not, but for the sake of stylistic variety, "corporate" enterprise in this essay refers to big business as I define it here.

4. Porter, *Big Business,* chap. 1.

5. These data and all others used in this essay are drawn from relevant tables in U. S. Bureau of the Census, *Historical Statistics of the United States, Colonial Times to 1957* (Washington, D.C.: G.P.O., 1960).

6. A detailed account of the changing role of wholesale and retail merchants can be found in Glenn Porter and Harold C. Livesay, *Merchants and Manufacturers* (Baltimore: Johns Hopkins University Press, 1970).

7. The literature on the emergence of trusts essentially began with William Z. Ripley, ed., *Trusts, Pools, and Corporations* (Boston: Ginn, 1905) and has expanded ever since. Among the most useful on the long list are Willard Thorp, *The Integration of Industrial Operations* (Washington: G.P.O., 1924), and Ralph L. Nelson, *Merger Movements in American Industry* (Princeton: Princeton University Press, 1955).

8. Shaw Livermore, "The Success of Industrial Mergers," *Quarterly Journal of Economics* (Nov. 1935), 1:68–96. The causes and implications of Livermore's data have been explored by Alfred D. Chandler—briefly in "The Structure of American Industry in the Twentieth Century: A Historical Overview," *Business History Review* (Autumn 1969), 43:255–98, and at greater length in *The Visible Hand* (Cambridge: Harvard University Press, 1977).

9. I am indebted to Prof. Julian Skaggs of Widener College for information on Lukens.

10. Porter and Livesay, *Merchants and Manufacturers*.

11. Sloan tells his own story in *Adventures of a White Collar Man* (New York: Scribners, 1941) and *My Years at General Motors* (Garden City: Doubleday, 1963).

12. Edison's career was examined at length by Matthew Josephson, *Edison* (New York: McGraw-Hill, 1959) and more briefly and recently by Ronald W. Clark, *Edison: The Man Who Made the Future* (New York: Putnam, 1977).

13. For example, Robert T. Averitt, *The Dual Economy* (New York: Norton, 1971).

14. Pierre Dupont's career has been discussed in several perspectives by Alfred D. Chandler, Jr., particularly in *Pierre S. Dupont and the Making of the Modern Corporation* (New York: Harper and Row, 1971) (co-authored with Stephen Salsbury) and in *The Visible Hand*, which places Dupont's contribution in the overall context of the development of American managerial techniques.

15. See for example, *Fortune* magazine's most recent list of "The 500 Largest U. S. Industrial Corporations."

16. From *The Collected Poems of Wallace Stevens*. Copyright © 1936 by Wallace Stevens and renewed 1964 by Holly Stevens. Reprinted by permission of Alfred A. Knopf, Inc.

16

ECONOMICS AND CULTURE IN THE GILDED AGE HATTING INDUSTRY

David Bensman

THE men's fur felt hatting trade was clearly divided, into two branches in 1880. One was stiff hatting, centered in Danbury, South Norwalk, and Brooklyn; the other soft hatting, concentrated in Orange, Newark, and Philadelphia. Although there were important differences between them, fundamentally both resembled the garment trades, with which they were closely allied.[1]

Most important, the industry was oriented to changes in taste or fashion. In the stiff hat trade, the fashion leaders, D. D. Youmans, Robert Dunlap, and Edward Knox, in New York, and Joseph A. Miller in Philadelphia, unveiled new derby styles, in January, for the spring season,[2] and in June for the fall. While fashion changes were not radical, each season the hats would vary in the depth of their crown, the cut of their brim, the roll of their curl, and their color and trimming.

Upon receipt of the proposed styles, the manufacturers would set their most skillful journeymen at work producing a few dozen sample hats, in each of the price ranges, for derbies varied in price according to the quality of the fur mixture, and the ribbon, the exactitude of the pouncing, and the grace of the curl. After setting prices for the samples, wholesalers (jobbers) sent their commercial travelers out to the New York City, northeastern, southern, and western markets, drumming up orders from haberdashers wherever they went. Only after the first batch of orders had been placed did the jobbers telegraph their orders to the waiting hat factories, which would finally begin production in earnest.[3]

The soft hat trade was less fashion oriented; consumer demand came mainly from the South and West, and remained relatively consistent from year to year.[4] Consequently, factory owners in Orange, Newark, and Philadelphia could form their fur and size their bodies in advance of the orders, waiting only the distributors' telegram to put the finishing touches and trim on their goods.[5] But even soft hat sales were subject to fluctuations in weather, which might accelerate or retard orders, to changes in color preferences, and to periodic swings of taste. Since manufacturers made up their bodies in advance, such changes left them with unneeded stock on hand, eating up capital needed elsewhere, and generating costly interest charges.[6]

Both stiff and soft hat firms also resembled the garment trades in the small size of their shops. In 1880, Connecticut's 34 stiff hat factories averaged only 92 employees, with capitalization of $24,000, of which tools and machinery accounted for perhaps one-eighth. New Jersey's 79 soft hat shops were, on average, even smaller, employing 68 hands each, and $17,000 capital.[7]

But few factories resembled the median type. Far more common were the less substantial "commission shops," which could be established for as little as $300. An enterprising journeyman could rent an old hat shop, buy or rent a few tools, and commence business. A New York or Newark merchant house would furnish him formed hat bodies to make and finish, and the commission manufacturer would set his employees to work making and finishing hats. For weeks the entrepreneur would have to pay the men out of his own pocket; only when the merchant house received orders from wholesalers for finished goods would it begin to pay the shop owner for the hats he had produced.[8]

Because it cost so little to set up a commission shop, competition was intense, as a disillusioned hat manufacturer complained to the *Hatter and Furrier:*

A cut-throat system that is fatal to every honest man has come into operation in the [commission] shops. . . . A few men in Orange have been accustomed to keep up an incessant bidding for work. If work gets slack in their shops, they will go to New York, bid from one quarter of a cent to two cents less per hat, until business . . . is booming in their shops. Then the next-door and other commission men must follow that example. The result of this is that the coal men, the working men, and the dealers in the raw material must stand the cost when a crash comes. Now this business has taught the "commission" men such ultra economy that they are able to subsist on a crust.[9]

A commission manufacturer who kept his production costs very low might make a profit. But few were able to go into business on their own. Where could they get access to sufficient credit to pay for the fur, dyestuffs, and labor needed to produce hats for sale to the wholesalers? At the height of a busy season, an independent factory owner, whose firm was capitalized at $25,000, might have liabilities of $12,000 for stock on hand alone. Few commission shop owners could ever gain access to that kind of money.[10]

And even if a manufacturer did expand his credit basis and productive capacity, he still had to compete with all the little commission shops for the jobbers' orders. The wholesalers dominated the industry, driving hat prices inexorably downward. Hats that sold for $6.50 in 1860 brought only $3.50 twenty years later.

Each manufacturer went on, continually and fiercely contesting with each other, who shall cut fastest and deepest, as if the only object in life worthy of man was the gratification of an ambition to be the cheapest and meanest of . . . hat makers. From $18 [per dozen wholesale] to $16.50; from that to $15, then what were termed $15 hats were sold at $14.50 and $14. Then came $13.50, and then began the occupation of selling what are euphemistically termed second hats, which in days of honesty were used to heat up the boilers.[11]

Moreover, although the decline in quality standards in the face of fierce cost-cutting during the depression of the 1870s was a major problem; the higher standards that followed did not improve things, for retailers and jobbers passed on stricter standards without increasing commensurately the prices they paid manufacturers.[12]

Often manufacturers would grumble that they could make no profit on the jobbers' orders, but even if they could, they still faced serious difficulties. For example, the fur mixture used to produce the sample might become unavailable, go up in price, or unaccountably become more difficult to work with, in which case the journeymen would demand higher piece rates, nullifying the manufacturers' projected income.[13] Or consumer demand might change in mid season, causing jobbers to cancel orders for goods already in the works, but not yet shipped and paid for. To forestall the dreaded countermanding telegrams, manufacturers would strain to get out orders as quickly as possible, but, since stiff hats took four to five days to complete, factory owners were often left in the lurch.[14] Finally, defects in the hats could kill the manufacturers' hopes:

Each hat is taken separately [by the jobber], subjected to a critical inspection, the slightest evidence that the fur ever had a dag in it, a missing stitch, a speck of stiffening, the ordure of a fly, no matter how low the quality, back comes these single hats, and away goes the profit on the case; bad as this is it is not equal to the practice of the jobber in pretending he has no time to examine and ships hats without looking at them, and awaits the retailers' return of them to him (and then to the factory).[15]

When the jobber finally got around to paying, he did so on terms extremely advantageous to him. He did not pay for the goods he had received from the factories and sold to the hat retailers until six to eight months after placing his order; and when he was paid, he deducted a "cash" discount of 10 to 15 percent of the bill.[16] A factory owner's ability to obtain credit to buy raw materials in November, when he would not receive payment for his goods until the following August, proved a difficult stumbling block for all but the most ingenious of entrepreneurs.

Because manufacturers were so helpless in the face of the jobbers' price cutting, they constantly sought to reduce labor costs. As we shall see, there were numerous ways of doing so, and although results were mixed, the general trend for hatters' wages was clearly downward. Piece rates in 1880 were more than 10 percent below those of 1870.[17]

To summarize, hat manufacturers were vexed, in the years between the recovery from the depression of 1873 until the onset of the depression of 1893, by intense competition which exerted a strong downward pressure on prices. This competition was fostered by wholesalers, who encouraged veteran craftsmen to establish small commission shops for hat "making" and "finishing."

The manufacturers tried a variety of techniques to escape from the wholesale merchants' web, or otherwise to insure profitability. In 1878, leading factory owners organized a trade association to force jobbers to pay their bills promptly and to reduce the "cash discount." Association members pledged to do business only with wholesale houses that agreed to their terms. Within three years, it became clear that the divisive force of competition had broken the manufacturers' solidarity, and by 1883, the jobbers regained control and restored their former business practices.[18]

Another challenge to the jobbers' power did not require hat manufacturers to act in concert. In the midst of the depression of 1873, some factory owners tried to mechanize the processes of hat "making" and "finishing," thereby decreasing the unit cost of hat production to levels the commission shops could not match.

But mechanization was not altogether successful during the years 1878–93, particularly in the finishing shops. The available machinery turned out hats that were considered inferior to medium- and high-quality hand-made hats. And in the lower grades, machine-made fur-felt hats were more expensive than were comparable machine-made wool hats, or fur-felt hats made by low-skilled labor.

James H. Prentice, Brooklyn's leading hat manufacturer, gambled heavily on finished lathes and presses in 1877–78, as the depression of 1873 eased; he lost. Within a year, he had to sell off his machinery to satisfy creditors, and soon his firm disbanded altogether.[19]

The introduction of sizing machines in the "making" departments was more successful. There, the major problem proved to be the organized "makers' " opposition to the new machines. In most cases, the manufacturers' threat to revoke union recognition caused the journeymen to cease obstructing the machines.

Nevertheless, for the period 1873–93, as a whole, jobber-sponsored competition prevailed in the hatting industry. Manufacturers remained helpless in the face of the jobbers' cost cutting. In response, they tried assiduously to reduce labor costs.

There were many different ways to do so. They could pressure the unions to accept lower piece rates; they could hire low-skilled, non-union men; they could set prison inmates to hat making, and they could further divide the labor process. During the years 1876–85, manufacturers tried all these means of cutting labor costs, with varying degrees of success. But serious problems remained:

1) Jobbers decreased hat prices whenever manufacturers reduced labor costs.

2) Manufacturers could not dispense with union labor because they had to produce high-quality hats.

3) There was much labor strife as unions resisted wage cuts and work-rule changes. The South Norwalk strike of 1884–85 was but the most virulent of many.

In order to solve these problems, manufacturers took a different tack, inaugurating in 1885 a brief era of relative tranquility in labor relations. On the initiative of the Hat Finishers' National Trade Association, most hat manufacturers began to pursue a national trade agreement with the "makers' " and "finishers' " unions, offering journeymen stable employment, high wages, and peaceful resolution of disputes in return for the unions' aid in closing the hatting industry to entrepreneurs who might seek to produce hats cheaply by hiring low-skilled non-union labor.[20]

While the unions and the new manufacturers' association pursued a national agreement, the unions began issuing and promoting a union label. The hat manufacturers actually supported this effort, hoping the label would educate consumers to buy only hats made by "fair" employers. In addition, the industrialists and journeymen cooperated on efforts to raise the tariff on imported hats.

The manufacturers' various efforts to free themselves of accursed competition and low prices were partially successful during the years spanning the depressions of 1873–93. These years witnessed an increase in the scale of operations of typical firms. A few of the largest manufacturers succeeded in going into business for themselves, freeing themselves from the tyranny of commission merchants and jobbers.

U.S. Census figures indicate that the average New Jersey firm in 1890 embodied 150 percent of the capital of the average firm in 1880, employed 110 percent of the number of employees, and paid 130 percent of the wages.[21]

These aggregate figures masked significant changes in the Garden State's hatting industry. In Orange, the increase in the size of the average firm was much greater than for the state as a whole, while in Newark, nearly fifty shops, producing low-grade hats, competed for commission business, making Newark the capital of America's cheap fur felt hat manufacturing trade.[22]

During the boom times of 1887, Orange's large firms picked up the lion's share of the business, the *Hatter and Furrier* reported, and small firms fell behind. The trend seemed so clear that the Journal flatly predicted that "in ten years, there will be fifteen large factories in Orange."[23] By 1891, the journal reported that Orange firms were exploring the possibility of keeping their factories open year-round, because they had grown so large that overhead expenses were significant even in slow times.[24]

The process of growth is reflected in the pages of the *Hatter and Furrier* in 1887. The paper reported that:

1) Cummings and Matthers announced plans to expand in February.

2) F. Berg began erecting a new factory for $8,000 and McGall and Allen began putting up a three-story brick building in April.

3) McGall and Allen and E. V. Connett needed more space to meet booming demand in September.

4) Austin, Draw and Company was adding three forming machines in September.

By late March 1888, McGall and Allen announced plans to add a new forming machine, with a new boiler, two devils, and eight forming machines.[25]

Looking back on the Orange hatting industry's last decade, in September 1889, the *Hatter and Furrier* reported that the number of active firms had declined from 33 to 27. Only three of the original firms were still operating under the same name in the same location. Of the entrepreneurs holding an interest in the hat factories in 1879, at least three had died, twelve had returned to the bench to work as journeymen, and two were foremen.

While few firms enjoyed spectacular success, for most, the trend was toward expansion.[26]

THE CULTURE OF
HAT MANUFACTURERS

Up to this point, the hat manufacturers' behavior has been explained purely in economic terms. In pursuit of profits in a competitive market, they organized an association to improve the terms of their relations with wholesalers, introduced machinery, hired non-union men, and battled the unions for concessions on work rules and piece rates. Finally, in the years 1885–93, they acted in concert with the hatters' unions to maintain high prices and wages, and to freeze out "unfair" domestic and foreign competition.

A cultural perspective throws additional light on the hat manufacturers' behavior. Factory owners were not simply entrepreneurs in a competitive business environment; they were also people with particular backgrounds, habits of thought, and values.

Many manufacturers began their working lives as apprentice and journeymen hatters. In Orange, New Jersey, for instance, there were 52 hat manufacturers in 1880. Of the 37 who proved traceable in census schedules and union records, at least 17 had worked at the bench ten years before, and another had served his apprenticeship. Only 14 had been engaged in manufacturing for the entire decade, and it is likely that some of these had begun their careers as journeymen as well.

Frederick Berg was one of Orange's hat manufacturers who had started out as an artisan. He was born in Hesse-Darmstadt, the son of a poor farmer. His father uprooted the family and moved to Poland in search of better yields but when these failed to develop he returned home. Young Frederick attended district schools and helped his father out on the farm until he was 16, when he followed his brothers' footsteps to Vienna, capital of the Austro-Hungarian Empire. There he apprenticed himself to the hatting trade. When Berg completed his term, in 1854, he began traveling throughout Europe, taking his place at the bench in numerous cities on the Continent. After two years, he ended up in Danzig, where he received notice to report home to face military service. The obedient, young journeyman returned to draw a high number in the draft lottery. At this point, free of social obligation, Berg emigrated to the United States.

Through a friend he met aboard ship, Berg learned of the opportunities for European hatters offered by Orange's hatting industry, and went to that city straight from his disembarkment in New York. In Orange, which was growing rapidly because of the new soft hat craze, young Frederick secured a position as journeyman in the small hat shop run by Christopher Nickel, a Bavarian immigrant. Berg soon married his boss's daughter, Anna, and after serving in the New Jersey infantry for nine months in 1862, he began saving up to go into hat manufacturing. Berg opened a shop in 1864, with $2,000–$3,000 of his savings, and built his firm slowly on a commission basis; by 1880, he was the first Orange manufacturer to bypass the commission merchants and sell his own hats direct to retailers. His large brick factory provided work for 200 hands.

Berg's home was in the pleasant upland western section of Orange, on Hillside Avenue. There he lived with his wife, their six surviving children, a cousin, a boarder, and two caretakers. In 1889, when Berg's sons were old enough to take over the firm, he went into the coal business; by then, his personal worth approached half a million dollars. His interests extended to the Second National Bank of Orange, the Republican Party and the Lutheran Church; he discharged his civic responsibilities by serving on the Board of Assessors.[27]

Manufacturers like Frederick Berg absorbed during their apprenticeships and terms as journeymen a craft-specific subculture, among the features of which were:

- a belief that "the interests of the journeymen and their employers are one and inseparable."
- a belief that journeymen should control their work in their factories.
- a special language and group-specific customs that created a sense of group identity.
- a code of manly conduct, involving loyalty to one's fellows, honesty and impartiality, prudence, and independence in the face of authority.
- a preference for alternating bouts of hard work and leisure.
- enjoyment of beer-drinking, baseball and other outdoor recreational activities, practical jokes, and punning.
- belief in the value of tradition.
- a pragmatic, nonspeculative approach to social, economic, and political problems.

While it is evident that journeymen who became hat manufacturers could not retain all of their former values, evidence suggests that they did not abandon craft values altogether.

If we look at labor relations in the years 1885–93, for example, we find that under the terms of the trade agreements most hat manufacturers and shop crews observed, the journeymen were allowed, in large part, to retain control of the production process. Skilled workers were allowed to determine the pace of their labor, they could share out the work among themselves, and they could force employers to hire unionists in turn.[28]

When employers and journeymen disagreed about the proper application of a work rule, their dispute was settled by a method long practiced by the craftsmen; arbitration committees composed of men from shops not party to the dispute took testimony and rules. Under the trade agreements, most of these committees were made up of equal numbers of journeymen and employers, but for two years, Brooklyn manufacturers allowed committees composed exclusively of journeymen to resolve labor disputes; they explained this surprising decision by declaring journeymen "honorable men."[29]

This is not to say that the trade agreements gave the unionists *carte blanche*. Journeymen had to agree to honor "bills of prices" (piece rates) for six-month seasons, and limit the number of shop meetings. Nevertheless, under the trade agreements, manufacturers allowed craftsmen to maintain the bulwark of their craft culture—their control of the work process.[30]

The trade agreement was not the only policy pursued by hat manufacturers that enabled journeymen to maintain their traditional ways at work. The fight against prison hat production was the first of the joint efforts by employers and employees to maintain prices and labor standards. In the years 1878–83, manufacturers accompanied journeymen to state legislatures in New York, New Jersey, Connecticut, and Massachusetts to testify against businessmen who secured state contracts to put prison inmates to work making men's felt hats. Although prison labor was widespread at the time (convicts were employed in many industries) it was hatters and their employers who took the lead in opposing this popular scheme for cutting taxes.

Only two or three years after the prison labor fight ended successfully, hatters and their employers teamed up again in an effort to decrease the tariff on hat materials, and to increase the tariff on hat imports. Once again, employers had found a way to help themselves while enabling their men to preserve their culture at the same time.[31]

The most impressive evidence that manufacturers maintained close ties to their men was the way they cooperated in politics. In local electoral contests in the hatting towns, hatters and their employers quite commonly ran on the same slate, either as Republicans or Democrats. Moreover, when, in the mid-eighties, hatters responded to the growth of Knights of Labor politics and nominated Workingmen's slates for local offices, manufacturers could be found on those tickets.

Thus C. W. Murphy, a Danbury hat manufacturer, was the Workingmen's candidate for Borough Treasurer in 1886.[32] Similarly, Chris McCulloch, an Orange hat manufacturer, who also worked at times as a foreman and journeyman, was labor's candidate for Mayor in February 1886.[33]

More significant still is the career of Lawrence T. Fell of Orange. Fell was a hat manufacturer and real estate dealer who was appointed New Jersey Factory Inspector in 1883 by Governor Leon Abbett. In 1886, when John J. Craigie, a Newark hat finisher, campaigned for Fell's post, with the support of the Essex County Trades' Assembly, which Craigie had organized, Orange journeymen supported Fell, the local favorite, so vigorously they considered withdrawing from the Assembly and they succeeded in prolonging Fell's tenure. He held on to his post until 1895, when "a hostile state senate rejected his reappointment."[34]

In office, Fell justified the Orange hatters' support. According to Herbert Gutman, the leading historian of labor in New Jersey during the Gilded Age, Fell "became a vigorous proponent of enlarged and more effective labor legislation. He worked diligently under difficult circumstances to enforce the school and factory laws, and he cooperated openly with'' the New Jersey Federation of Trades and Labor Unions.[35] His work exposing the illiteracy and stunted growth of the state's child factory workers resulted in passage of a child labor law.[36]

Gutman interprets Fell's career as evidence that in Gilded Age America ''non-industrial capitalists—persons with power and prestige locally and persons committed to competitive private enterprise and the acquisitive spirit in their own dealings—responded equivocally or critically to'' the industrial revolution that threatened contemporary community norms and social relationships.[37] While this conclusion appears valid, and useful in explaining the case of Lawrence T. Fell, another factor can be added—Fell's direct experience with ''justice'' in labor relations in the hatting industry.

CONCLUSION

Hat manufacturers in late-nineteenth-century America were small businessmen caught up in a highly competitive economic environment. New York-based commission merchants dominated the market, forcing hatting firms to search continually for means to reduce production costs.

In the years 1876–85, such pressure induced employers to attempt to extract concessions from their organized employees to reduce labor costs. The manufacturers' efforts often provoked strikes, culminating in the prolonged South Norwalk strike of 1884–85.

The compromise settlement of the South Norwalk strike inaugurated a period of industrial peace in the hatting industry. At the unions' initiative, the unions and manufacturers' association reached joint agreements to maintain labor standards and limit competition in the industry. Firms refusing to participate in the agreements were denied the unions' label.

The trade agreement collapsed during the depression of 1893, because producers of low-grade, low-cost hats, some made by new machines, had begun to make inroads in the hat market. As the depression lifted, conflict rather than cooperation characterized the industry's labor relations.

Such an explanation of the hat manufacturers' labor relations policies is accurate but incomplete. The employers' cooperation with their men, and their tendency to allow the hatters to maintain a large degree of control over

their work, reflected the influence of culture as well as economic imperatives. Many manufacturers began their working lives as apprentices and
journeymen. As young men, they were socialized in the hatters' way of life,
a subculture of the larger culture of American skilled workers.

At the backbone of that tradition was an insistence that journeymen control the work process, hiring and firing, and even the pace and rhythm of
work.

Recognition of the fact that hat manufacturers in Gilded Age America
were not whole-hearted "entrepreneurs," with fully-formed conceptions of
economic rationality, helps explain why they allowed their men to maintain,
in part, their culture of work during the 1880s.

Notes

1. Until 1880, one of the two principal hatting journals was called the *Clothier and Hatter*
because it published information on both industries.

2. *Hatter and Furrier,* Jan., 1882, p. 17. The *Hatter and Furrier* commented that the Miller
derby had a decidedly flat set brim, and was the subject of very favorable comment for its clean
and shapely lines. The Youmans' derby was called boldly unconventional, for its brim was very
flat set, and so broad at the corners as at first glance to appear out of shape.

3. *Hatter and Furrier,* Oct. 1888, p. 13; Feb., 1889, p. 20; Nov. 1892, p. 33; *Hat, Cap and
Fur Trade Review,* March 1882, p. 149.

4. *Hatter and Furrier,* March 1890, p. 19.

5. *Hatter and Furrier,* Oct. 1889, p. 11.

6. *Ibid.,* Feb. 1889, p. 19.

7. U.S. Census Office, *Census of Manufactures,* 1880, p. 45. The hatting industry had the
lowest ratio of capital invested to value of production of any industry.

8. *Hatter and Furrier,* Oct. 1889, p. 15; *Hat, Cap, and Fur Trade Review,* May 1879,
p. 178.

9. *Hatter and Furrier,* March 1882, p. 27. In 1885, 22 of 27 hat shops in Orange made hats
on commission only. *Ibid.,* Oct. 1885, p. 35; Nov., 1892, p. 26; July, 1889, p. 27.

10. The case illustrated is L. H. Johnson and Co. of Danbury. See Dun and Bradstreet, "Field
Agent Reports, Connecticut," 12:184.

11. A disillusioned manufacturer, writing in *Hat, Cap, and Fur Trade Review,* March 1882,
p. 199.

12. New Jersey Bureau of Labor, *Annual Report* (1881); pp. 154–55. "The general prosperity
has created a demand for a better grade of goods." Also see *Hatter and Furrier,* Sept. 1885,
p. 18; Oct. 1885, p. 35; Aug. 1888, p. 47.

13. *Hatter and Furrier*, Aug. 1885, p. 13; Aug., 1880, p. 1.

14. *Ibid.*, March, 1886, p. 8.

15. *Hat, Cap and Fur Trade Review*, March 1882, p. 149. Also see *ibid.*, May 1879, pp. 177–79; April 1879, p. 157; June 1879, pp. 198–200.

16. *Hatter and Furrier*, Nov. 1882, pp. 15, 18. In 1893, manufacturers were still suffering disadvantageous terms of sale. Manufacturers' bills to jobbers were commonly dated March 1 to September 1, and jobbers had three months after those dates to pay. Consequently, goods sold to jobbers in September would not be paid for until nine months later. *Orange Chronicle*, Oct. 21, 1892.

17. U.S. Census Office, *Census of 1880*, vol. 3: 105.

18. The Association's activities are chronicled in two trade journals, the *Clothier and Hatter*, and the *Hat, Cap, and Fur Trade Review*, 1878–83, *passim*.

19. *Clothier and Hatter*, Dec. 1878, p. 33; Feb. 1879, p. 7; *Hatter and Furrier*, Dec. 1882, p. 13.

20. *Hatter and Furrier*, Dec. 1885, p. 7.

21. U.S. Census Office, *Census of Manufactures*, 1880, p. 45, U.S. Census Office, *Eleventh Census* (1890), v. 6, p. 850.

22. *Hatter and Furrier*, August 1891, p. 30.

23. *Hatter and Furrier*, Dec. 1887, p. 19; Sept. 1887, p. 11; Jan. 1888, p. 21; Feb. 1890, p. 19, March, 1890, p. 20; Oct. 1890, p. 21; May 1891, p. 19.

24. *Hatter and Furrier*, May, 1891.

25. *Hatter and Furrier*, Feb. 1887, p. 15; April 1887, p. 15; Sept. 1887, p. 15; Oct. 1887, p. 16a; March 1888, p. 15.

26. *Ibid.*, Sept. 1889, p. 15. In Jan. 1885, the journal noted similar changes were taking place in Brooklyn. *Ibid.*, Feb. 1885, p. 11.

27. William Pierson, *History of the Oranges*, pp. 98–99. *Hatter and Furrier*, Nov. 1888, p. 25.

28. See David Bensman, "Artisan Culture, Business Union," Ph.D. dissertation, Columbia University, 1977, chapter 3.

29. *Hatter and Furrier*, March 1889, p. 23; June 1889, p. 33.

30. In 1890 the Danbury Hat Manufacturers' Association commented on their trade agreement with the journeymen in the following terms: "These agreements . . . are calculated to do justice to both employer and employee, and the fact they have stood the test of nearly five years . . . is complete evidence of their justice and usefulness. We are not aware of another instance in this, or any other industry, where such harmonious relations have existed for so long a period between such a number of trade unions, including a large membership, and their employers. This has been a subject of general comment and commendation, for it had been thought impossible to maintain such pleasant relations between organized labor and its employers. The manufacturers' association admit the right of the employees to belong to their various unions, and approve of their doing so, as long as the unions will make just agreements, equally protective of the rights of employers and employed."

31. *Hatter and Furrier*, Feb. 1888, p. 12. In 1888, the Brooklyn hat finishers thanked three Congressmen for receiving courteously a manufacturer who had gone to Washington to campaign for the protective tariff.

32. *Ibid.*, March 1886, p. 46.

33. *Hatter and Furrier*, March 1886, p. 9.

34. Herbert Gutman, "A Brief Postscript," in *Work Culture and Society* (New York; Vintage Books, 1977), p. 280.

35. *Ibid.*, p. 281.

36. *Ibid.*, p. 295.

37. *Ibid.*, p. 255.

17

THE ROLE OF SMALL BUSINESS
IN THE PROCESS
OF SKILL ACQUISITION

Eli Ginzberg

1. INTRODUCTION

EVEN a summary presentation of the process of skill acquisition is possible only if the dimensions to be treated are severely restricted. An attempt to sketch all that transpired over more than two centuries during which the colonial settlements were transformed into a national and international economy—with more than 215 million persons and an annual output of approximately $2 trillion—would necessitate book-length treatment. Moreover, it could be carried out successfully only by an economic historian whose life's work has focused on the role of human resources in American economic development.

Limitations of space and of expertise force me to follow a different structure, more conceptual and schematic; a foreshortened time perspective—the eighteenth and nineteenth centuries prior to the coming of age of the mass-production economy—is employed only to bring out the special qualities of skill acquisition that characterize the American development.

2. WHAT IS SKILL?

Skills are differential competences that enable some men and women to perform critical economic tasks that most other members of the labor force lack the ability to undertake, or that they are unable to carry out competitively. Skills are acquired through a combination of general competences (the ability to learn), specific learning, and experience. To illustrate: in a premechanical society one will not find individuals who can undertake even simple repairs. This was the situation in Peking in 1945; the only automobile mechanics were Japanese prisoners of war. The importance of experience in skill acquisition can be illustrated by the misperceptions of the great statistician Harold Hotelling, who, buying a car in the early 1930s, turned down the offer of the dealer for driving lessons. He told the dealer that he could learn to drive from a book. A week later, he had to buy a second car!

As the title underscores, the acquisition of skill must be viewed as a process in which the individual acquires, over time, mastery of successive elements which are prerequisite for his later accomplishments. Initial learning takes place in the family. The child is exposed to cognitive learning and character training, both building blocks for successful adjustment to school. The process continues, in and out of school; the school is responsible for instructing the child in basic subjects, and the family and the larger community provide experiences and reinforcements that relate more to general personality, development, and value formation.

Sooner or later, depending on the stage of economic development, schooling comes to an end, and the young person (especially male) makes the transition into employment, in which the process of skill acquisition shifts from more general learning that occurred earlier to more specific knowledge and competences that the individual must acquire to perform his required tasks. The latter occurs for the most part through observing and imitating fellow workers, with some degree of assistance from the foreman.

Since skill must be acquired, it requires learning; since competence requires continuing efforts, the attitudes and behavior of the individual worker are critical in determining the outcome. Unless he is willing to make the investment required in terms of time, effort, wages foregone, the payment of tuition, the purchase of tools, and still other outlays, he is unlikely to become a skilled worker. Whether he is willing to make the required investments will depend on his personality, his opportunities, his prior training, and his assessment of whether such special efforts will pay off in the future in terms of a better job and a career, more income, or higher status.

These last considerations, although formulated in terms of the costs and benefits financed by the family as the young person prepares for adulthood, are deeply embedded in the structure and development of the society and economy, which establish the incentives and rewards that are obtainable by different individuals and groups. In many parts of the antebellum South slaves had a quasi monopoly on a wide range of skilled work. It was very difficult for a free white man to acquire these skills. But a generation—surely two generations—after the Civil War, segregation had become so firmly established in the slowly growing southern economy that black men were largely precluded from acquiring skill or, if they succeeded, from securing employment as skilled workers.

3. SOME NINETEENTH-CENTURY PERSPECTIVES

The fact that the developed nations look so much alike in the last quarter of the twentieth century should not blot out the unique characteristics of U.S. economic development in the nineteenth century. Some of the major dimensions are noted below, particularly as they bear on the question of skill and skill acquisition. As far as the special focus on "small business" is concerned, one broad generalization will go a long distance. If it is assumed that the date when modern industrialization, with the large corporation, came into its own is the end of the nineteenth century—the Sherman Anti-Trust Act was passed in 1890—then most of what is singled out here relates to the world of small business, with only a few exceptions, such as the recruitment of labor for the railroads.

Adam Smith, writing in 1776, makes the point not once but repeatedly that the American colonies were short of labor and that wages were correspondingly higher than in the more advanced, but more populated, countries of Western Europe. Moreover, he calls attention to the fact that with free land available, men had an option to strike out on their own and establish themselves as independent farmers.

Let us look more closely at what the scarcity of labor and free land implied for skill acquisition, not only in colonial America but well into the closing decade of the nineteenth century—which is usually taken to mark the end of the frontier.

Men who acquired skill demonstrated by that fact alone that they had certain differential strengths in terms of aptitude, education, application, and ambition. As such, they were not likely to remain content with whatever status in life they were able to achieve early in adulthood, even if it placed them one or two rungs above their companions and neighbors. They were likely, in a country of great opportunities based not only on free land but on rapid economic growth, to find multiple opportunities to transform themselves from hired hands to entrepreneurs—the clerk who opened a store; the sailor who became master of the vessel; the artisan who was taken into partnership by his employer and who later bought him out.

The American economy was in constant turmoil because it offered opportunities for the ambitious and the able to improve themselves by moving from one type of economic activity to another with an eye to the main chance. This chance was predicated more often than not on buying and selling rather than on craftsmanship and production. As Thorstein Veblen pointed out around the turn of the century, the basis for wealth accumulation by farmers was linked more to the appreciation of land values than to improvements in the output of agricultural products.

One must look more closely at the interplay among rapid economic growth, homesteading, the rising value of urban and agricultural land in settled areas, and skill acquisition. To note some of the more important linkages: the fact that a young man could always strike out on his own by moving west and settling on new land available for the taking created an environment in which the frontiersman had to develop diversified skills in order to survive and prosper. Distances between settlements reinforced this trend toward self-sufficiency. While one's neighbors could be relied upon to assist in major undertakings, such as helping to erect the framework of a barn or home, most of the time the farmer had only himself, his wife, and his children to get whatever tasks needed doing carried out satisfactorily.

With labor and skills in short supply, the American farmer became an avid customer for farm machinery at an early stage, especially in the large single-crop areas of the Middle West. This made each family farm a vocational school, where youngsters—especially young men but also young women—had an early exposure to coping with mechanical devices. When the flow away from the farms accelerated during the second half of the nineteenth century, this native labor force was well positioned to move into industry with little or no difficulty; this was quite unlike the pattern of most rural-urban movements, in which the newcomers required a considerable period of orientation before they could be fitted into the industrial structure and could perform effectively.

The openness of the American society and the absorptive capacity of the

American economy for all sorts of newcomers—skilled and unskilled, from urban and rural backgrounds, English-speaking and not, immigrants who could not return to their homeland, and those who planned to do so—created a backdrop of mobility, flexibility, and personal responsibility.

There was no one established way, such as formal apprenticeship, for American workers to acquire skill. Moreover, the likelihood of a person remaining in his chosen occupation throughout his entire working life was much less than in older, more structured societies. Some skilled workers grouped themselves into trade unions or other organizations to protect themselves against the "dilution of skills" which would jeopardize their job security and lower their earnings. Such defensive actions were relatively weak because of the loose attachment of many skilled workers to their current occupations. Even as late as the post-World War II era, Eli Chinoy (*Automobile Workers and the American Dream*) found that the aspiration of going into business for oneself remained a powerful fantasy, if not the goal, for many men on the assembly line.

Another important aspect of the dynamism of the nineteenth-century United States was the fluidity of class and all of its manifestations. Children of those at the lower strata of the social and economic hierarchy showed repeated evidence of the "demonstration effect" of moving out of their parents' status; they were "making it" in the sense of rising on the skill and income ladder. For many years, candidates for the presidency had an advantage if they could claim that they were born in a log cabin. The most important consequences of a more fluid class structure were the goal formation of young people and the behavior of employers. In a more structured society, only the exceptional person would set for himself career objectives that involved work and status far above his parents. But in the United States, the ethos was that any determined young man could aim as high as he wanted, and would be likely to achieve his goal through a combination of perseverance and luck. The correlative fact that employers were more interested in what a man could do than in the family from which he came made it easier for the young person without advantage to forge ahead.

Broad access to free public education, at least outside of the South, was a further important contribution to skill acquisition. Most men and women had the opportunity to acquire the basics needed for further self-development. The fact that young women, as well as young men, had access to schooling also facilitated broadening the competence of the labor force. By the middle of the 1800s, more and more women were employed in teaching positions, thereby releasing men for other work; and by the end of the century, when office work was beginning to expand rapidly, more and more young women filled secretarial, clerical, and related positions.

There are other aspects of public education that warrant attention because they have interfaced with skill development. The first may be defined as the strong vocational bias in American higher education, represented by the land-grant colleges (1862), which made public funds available to expand the corps of competent persons capable of contributing to the development of agricultural, engineering, and technical activities. Unlike European universities—which were still heavily humanistic in their basic orientation, elitist, and concerned only with the preparation for the classical professions of medicine, law, theology, and public service—the state-university movement in the United States was strongly vocational, open to children of the middle- and even low-income groups. The movement was much broader in its programming, taking in most fields of endeavor in which specialized knowledge could add to the productivity of the worker.

There are several additional characteristics of nineteenth-century economic development that can shed light on the skill-development process. The first relates to the role that immigration played in contributing both directly and indirectly to the pool of skilled workers. A considerable number of skilled workers were found among immigrant groups, who, for political or ideological reasons, decided to leave their homeland to seek a new life on the other side of the Atlantic. This was true for some of the British, German, Scandinavian, and other immigrants, who were drawn by the promise of freedom, opportunity, and democracy rather than forced out by economic necessity. On occasion, active recruitment by large firms (steel companies) and self-contained groups, such as the Mormons after they reached Utah, stimulated the inflow of skilled workers.

The large Jewish immigration from Eastern Europe that accelerated after 1880 was comprised of many persons with urban roots who possessed a range of skills, including the needle trades, shopkeeping, and bookkeeping.

But the large inflows of Irish, Slavic, and Italian immigrants consisted overwhelmingly of persons of rural background, with little or no formal education, and with few skills other than the ability to do simple laboring jobs. The successive waves of these immigrants, from the time of the Irish famine (1840s) up to World War I, had an important indirect influence on the process of skill acquisition. In the face of the substantial, if not steady, expansion of the American economy, which resulted in an increase in gainful workers between 1850 and 1910 from 7.7 million to 37.4 million, those already in the labor force were "sucked up" into better paying and more skilled work. This left room at the bottom for the newcomers, who were dubbed "greenhorns," which epitomized their lack of knowledge about American life and conditions.

Here was another powerful "demonstration effect." In time, an immigrant could look forward to advancing up the occupational and income ladder. And his children would definitely be in a better position to improve their lot, particularly after they had the advantages of attending local schools, mastering English, and feeling at home in their surroundings.

The heavy concentration of various ethnic minorities in different sections of the nation's larger and medium-sized cities—Boston, New York, Cincinnati, Chicago, Milwaukee, San Francisco, Buffalo, Pittsburgh—provided another environmental support for skill acquisition. The progression from peddler to pushcart owner to storekeeper was characteristic of many Jewish immigrants, who had made a living in the old country through the buying and selling of goods. The fact that so many of their fellow ethnics lived in the same neighborhood and continued to use their mother tongue made it easier for the newcomer to gain a toehold. The newcomer from Ireland might find his present job in a local saloon, or, if lucky, might be helped to get a job as a streetcar conductor. The padrone system—labor contractor—found work for many of the unskilled Italian workers in the expanding construction industry. The Slavs followed each other into the packing houses and other tough low-paying jobs that characterized much of Chicago at the turn of this century.

This would be a representation, then, of the principal trends affecting skill acquisition in the early transformation of the U.S. economy from an agricultural-commercial system to an advanced industrial system, roughly from the establishment of the country in 1789 to 1890 or 1900:

> The relatively open nature of the economy, with its opportunities for moneymaking, served as a spur and a goal for many native-born persons and immigrants, who would work very hard under the conviction that with only a little luck they could look forward to substantial advancement on the occupational and income ladder and that their children for certain would gain from their efforts.

The heterogeneity of the American population, the absence of hoary institutions, the relative fluidity of class structures, the development of ethnic enclaves, broad access to the public schools, and the legitimacy of moneymaking as a social goal, all contributed to the national ethos that the worth of a man was to be judged by what he earned, not by his education or his work.

The combination of rapid transformations in the economy with constantly expanding opportunities for moneymaking, from the California gold rush of 1848 to continuing speculation in land, worked against the establishment of a nationwide set of training institutions geared to skill acquisition—the graduates of which could form labor organizations and/or could secure licenses from the state which would assure them status and protect their work and income. Of course, there was some growth of craft unions and an increase in licensed technicians and professionals. But for the most part, the scale and dynamism of the American economy were such that the relative shortage of skill and the lack of attachment of skilled workers to their employers and their occupation were a major contribution to the uniquely American pattern of mass production, in which management sought to escape from dependence on skilled workers by breaking down the production process into smaller, simpler, and more routinized parts.

If one focuses on the linkages between business and skill acquisition, one simple conclusion would be that the processes described refer primarily to small or, at most, medium-size business, since there was relatively little large business during most of the nineteenth-century. A more sophisticated formulation would take note of the additional dimensions: the ease with which individuals with modest capital could start a business created a powerful magnet for workers, most of whom were at least quasi-skilled, to try to make the transition to entrepreneurship. From a narrow perspective, this continuing large outflow from the skilled occupations into entrepreneurship could be viewed as a loss from the pool of scarce skills. But when the carpenter, the plumber, the drayman, or the painter stopped working for his boss and set himself up as boss, it was certain that if he succeeded and prospered in his new role, he in turn would be generating training and employment opportunities for other workers; in the long run, his metamorphosis contributed to swelling the total pool of skill and competence.

4. A TWENTIETH-CENTURY RETROSPECTIVE

The prototypical institution of twentieth-century U.S. economy is the large corporation that dominates manufacturing and looms large in communications and retailing. But having noted the dominance of the large corporation in these important sectors, one must quickly add that in the modal type of small and medium-sized business enterprise, owners play the dominant if not exclusive role in management. When one adds together the shrinking but still substantial numbers of farm owners, self-employed professionals, the large number of families that own businesses in manufacturing and particularly in the service sectors, it would be a major error to view the American economy solely as a complex of large organizations. Moreover, there are new and important symbiotic relations being established between large organizations and small businesses through such devices as licensing, dealerships, franchises, and still other arrangements. But our critical concern here is less with the transformation of entrepreneurship than with the changing structures that are shaping and reshaping the process of skill acquisition in the twentieth century, particularly in the second half of this century.

In order to sharpen the contrast between the earlier and later stages of skill acquisition in the American economy, between early and mature industrialization, the following factors must be considered:

The elongation of formal education to a point at which the new entrant into the labor force has completed, on the average, between 12 and 13 years of schooling, with over 1 out of 4 having attended school for 16 or more years.

The associated growth of professional, technical, and managerial positions in the economy for which schooling is often the preferred or only method of qualifying.

The preference of large organizations for relying on high-school and college graduates with general knowledge and competence, and to rely also on their own internal training and promotion programs to assure their organizations of a work force with the specific skills required.

The rapid growth of the not-for-profit sector—government and nonprofit institutions—which has come to provide close to 1 out of every 3 jobs in the economy.

The substantial efforts to modify curricula of the high school and the first two years of college (junior college) to provide more occupational instruction as an educational alternative for those who are not capable of, or attracted to, pursuing humanistic or scientific learning.

The substantial role of the Armed Services, particularly since 1940, as an important training institution for both meeting its own skill requirements and, indirectly, adding to the national pool through the skills acquired by veterans.

The substantial expansion of the federal government since the early 1960s, which has provided skill training and retraining for various disadvantaged groups whose potential employability could be improved.

The large inflow of women (mostly married women) into the labor force since World War II, reflected in the fact that they have accounted for 3 out of every 5 new workers.

The accelerated growth of the service sector, which today is the source of 2 out of every 3 jobs in the American economy; agriculture, mining, manufacturing, and construction provide only 1 out of 3 jobs.

The tendency of employers to keep adjusting their hiring requirements to the rising standards of educational achievement, reflecting the increasing proportion of high-school and college graduates among new entrants.

The continuing discrimination in developmental and employment opportunities, particularly with respect to race and sex, despite public and private policies devised to reduce it.

While the foregoing elements do not exhaust the critical changes that have occurred in the social and economic frameworks during the present century, they do include the more important transformations that must be considered in assessing the existing structure for skill acquisition in the United States, particularly from the vantage point of small business.

The present skill-acquisition process has the following dominant characteristics:

The most important preparation for skilled work in an advanced service economy, which characterizes the United States at the beginning of the last quarter of the twentieth century, is the role of formal schooling. What employers seek most in new workers is an ability to learn; a competence with basics, that is in words and numbers; and a positive motivation toward a job and a career. To the extent that prospective workers have these qualities, large employers, in particular, face no difficulties in obtaining the skills they need.

A recent study by the Conference Board suggests that the large corporations spend in excess of $2 billion annually on training different groups of workers through on-the-job, classroom, extramural, and still other programs.

One consequence of this substantial training effort by large employers, including the Armed Services, is the enlargment of the pool of partially and fully trained workers which helps smaller employers to meet their skill requirements. My associates Yavitz and Stanback uncovered some years ago in their study, *Electronic Data Processing in New York City,* that many small service firms were able to get a start in this new industry or to expand their operations because they were able to hire specialists at night or on weekends to solve particular problems without having to add them to their regular payroll. The clustering of many small tool-and-die shops in the Detroit area can also be explained in part by the advantages that they derive by dipping into the pool of skilled workers who have full-time jobs with the automobile manufacturers, but who desire to pick up some extra work.

To a considerable degree, this same pattern exists at higher levels of the occupational ladder, in which one is dealing, for instance, with college graduates in the fields of marketing or advertising. Some of the large consumer-product firms, such as in the food or pharmaceutical industries, hire large numbers of executive trainees; the companies spend several years orienting and training these employees to find that many leave to join smaller firms that cannot afford such heavy training costs but are able to meet competitive salary levels once these specialists have had the benefit of several years of experience.

A comparable pattern exists in certain branches of the federal government. Young lawyers, accountants, and economists go to work for a limited number of years with the Internal Revenue Service, the Antitrust Division of the Department of Justice, or with one of the administrative agencies charged with regulating the behavior of the railroads, the airlines, the power industry or communications. After they have acquired a good understanding of how the government deals with the problems in these specialized areas, they often move out of federal employment to join a large, medium-sized or even small service firm or an operating company which hires them because of the specialized background they have acquired.

Another not well understood symbiotic relationship involving large and small business is reflected in franchising, agency, or licensing arrangements, whereby the large organization provides varying types of training for small enterprises, agents, or employees. In a national market such as the continental United States, there are substantial economic gains in brand identification of commodities or services that provide the consumer with some assurance as to quality. There is a further economic advantage in these arrangements: the national producer or distributor is able to standardize his system of instruction and thus reduce the unit costs of training.

Apprenticeship has continued to play a constricted but important role in skill preparation, particularly in the construction trades and to a lesser degree in the training of tool-and-die makers and other advanced industrial workers. A large number of workers, however, reach journeyman status even in these fields through informal routes, such as a combination of formal schooling, on-the-job training, self-instruction and multiple jobs.

There has been a vast proliferation of skilled and technical education in both the public and private sectors, as reflected in the enlarged flow of funds into vocational education in high schools, the development of occupational curricula in junior and community colleges and the large number of for-profit institutions that provide occupational preparation from the training of pilots to instruction in office skills.

Since 1962, the federal government has entered upon a vast expansion of manpower programs, some part of which has been focused on specific occupational training—both institutional and on-the-job. While the smaller part of what has been estimated to be a cumulative expenditure of $60 billion in the first fifteen years of this effort has been directed to training per se—most of the funds have been spent on income-transfer efforts in the form of job-experience and public-service jobs—the federal manpower training effort must be viewed as a new and important addition to the national training structure.

The post-World War II period witnessed a rapid expansion of the health-services industry to a point at which it represents the largest single employer in the country in 1977, larger than construction or agriculture, with close to 5 million workers out of an employed population of about 90 million. While there has been a major shift in the education of nurses and technicians from hospital settings to educational institutions, the former continue to be important trainers by running hospital schools of nursing and various in-house training programs for technicians and auxiliary workers.

5. APPRAISAL AND OUTLOOK

At the beginning of the last quarter of the twentieth century, the skill-acquisition process, with special reference to small business in the United States, has the following characteristics:

Professional, technical, and managerial personnel are drawn increasingly from the pool of college, professional, and graduate schools. Many owner-managers of small businesses, however, are people who have achieved their position with modest educational background supplemented by experience gained in the world of work.

At the level of foreman and skilled worker, apprenticeship systems continue to be important, particularly in the construction trades and in selected medical occupations. However, the largest source of such workers is made up of individuals who have succeeded in adding to their knowledge by progressing through formal training programs of large organizations; and/or through "picking up" skills by moving from job to job, often supplementing these experiences with selected formal course work.

A high proportion of technical, skilled, and quasi-skilled workers in white-collar occupations—particularly in sales, clerical, and services— usually acquire their specialized competences through work experiences and on-the-job training. In these large sectors of the economy, small and medium-sized firms continue to predominate.

A wide range of occupational groups, from funeral directors to beauticians, have sought to organize themselves into trade unions or other types of associations which seek to use their political influence to limit the conditions of entrance into their occupation by requiring newcomers to be certified or licensed, or both.

Discriminatory patterns of development and employment have placed major barriers in the way of minority-group members and women seeking to gain access to training and employment in skilled or technical positions. However, since the passage of the Civil Rights Act of 1964, these barriers have been lowered and there are grounds for believing that they will be less severe in the future than they have been in the past.

From the vantage point of my governmental positions (since 1962) as chairman of the National Manpower Advisory Committee and the National Commission for Manpower Policy, it is my considered judgment that the American economy did not suffer from any significant skill shortages throughout this fifteen-year period. At worst, there were spot shortages of workers in a few locations and in a few occupations, which were usually relieved within a short period by accelerated training.

The substantial expansion of educational and training opportunities for all sectors of American society since 1960 has largely eliminated the "financial" barriers to training that earlier had blocked many in the lower-income groups from acquiring skill. Currently and prospectively, the major difficulties that many individuals face in acquiring skill are weaknesses in their formal educational achievements. It is not possible to become a tool or die worker if one cannot read blueprints or do arithmetic.

From a policy perspective, the large investments that the United States has made in broadening and deepening its expenditures for education have provided a large pool of reasonably well-prepared young people who can move easily into the expanding white-collar sector of the economy. And a sufficient number of young people are willing to enter training for blue-collar skilled jobs except possibly in such occupations as coal mining, foundry work, and other strenuous and dangerous jobs. But until now, these fields have not lacked skilled workers.

The major challenges that the United States confronts in the area of skill acquisition are to improve the rate of job expansion so that all who are able and willing to work, the trained as well as the untrained, have an opportunity to do so; to improve the linkages between schools and training institutions, and the world of work; and to use more efficiently the large sums that it invests in education and training to assure that these investments are more responsive to the needs of the individuals and the economy. In meeting these three challenges, small and medium-sized businesses have a significant role to play in the future—as they have played in the past.

INDEX

LIST OF CONTRIBUTORS

ROWLAND BERTHOFF is Professor of History at Washington University

RICHARD WALSH is Professor of History at Georgetown University

SUSAN E. HIRSCH is Assistant Professor of History at Loyola University of Chicago

STUART M. BLUMIN is Associate Professor of American History at Cornell University

CLYDE GRIFFEN is Lucy Maynard Salmon Professor of History at Vassar College

SALLY GRIFFEN has taught at colleges of the State University of New York.

HAROLD G. VATTER is Professor of Economics at Portland State University

IRENE TICHENOR is a doctoral candidate in History at Columbia University

JAMES H. SOLTOW is Professor of History at Michigan State University

STANLEY C. HOLLANDER is Professor of Marketing in the Graduate School of Business Administration at Michigan State University

RICHARD SYLLA is Professor of Economics and Business at North Carolina State University

DAVID BRODY is Professor of History at the University of California, Davis

ROLAND I. ROBINSON is Professor of Finance, Emeritus, at Michigan State University

LAWRENCE M. FRIEDMAN is Marion Rice Kirkwood Professor of Law at Stanford University

DAVID C. HAMMACK is Assistant Professor of History at Princeton University

HAROLD C. LIVESAY is Professor of History at the State University of New York, Binghamton

DAVID BENSMAN is Assistant Professor of Labor Studies at Rutgers University Graduate School of Education

ELI GINZBERG is A. Barton Hepburn Professor of Economics, Graduate School of Business, and Director, Conservation of Human Resources, at Columbia University